Microsoft® Office 2003 for Healthcare

Ahmad Hashem, M.D., Ph.D.

Steve Johnson

Perspection, Inc.

Que Publishing
800 East 96th Street
Indianapolis, IN 46240 USA

Microsoft® Office 2003 for Healthcare

Copyright © 2005 by Perspection, Inc. and Que Publishing

International Standard Book Number: 0-7897-3211-4

Library of Congress Catalog Card Number: 2004107577

Printed in the United States of America

First Printing: October 2004

07   06   05   04   4   3   2   1

Trademarks

Warning and Disclaimer

Bulk Sales

Que Publishing offers excellent discounts on this book when ordered in quantity for bulk purchases or special sales. For more information, please contact

U.S. Corporate and Government Sales

1-800-382-3419

corpsales@pearsontechgroup.com

For sales outside the United States, please contact

International Sales

international@pearsoned.com

Publisher
Paul Boger

Associate Publisher
Greg Wiegand

Acquisitions Editor
Stephanie J. McComb

Authors
Ahmad Hashem
Steve Johnson

Contributors
Nicholas Chu
Jane Pedicini

Managing Editors
Steve Johnson
Charlotte Clapp

Project Editors
Elise Bishop
Tonya Simpson

Production Editor
Beth Teyler

Indexer
Ken Johnson

Proofreader
Holly Johnson

Technical Editors
Nicholas Chu
Melinda Lankford

Publishing Coordinator
Sharry Lee Gregory

Interior Designers
Marian Hartsough
Steve Johnson

Page Layout
Beth Teyler
Kate Lyerla
Joe Kalsbeek
Blaine Lyerla
Ryan Suzuki
Michelle Mitchell

Acknowledgements

Perspection, Inc.

Microsoft Office 2003 for Healthcare is based in part on work developed by the professional trainers and writers at Perspection, Inc. to the standards you've come to expect from Que publishing. Together with co-author Ahmad Hashem, M.D., Ph.D., we are pleased to present this training book.

Perspection, Inc. is a software training company committed to providing information and training to help people use software more effectively in order to communicate, make decisions, and solve problems. Perspection writes and produces software training books, and develops multimedia and Web-based training. Since 1991, we have written more than 60 computer books, with several bestsellers to our credit, and sold over 4.5 million books.

This book incorporates Perspection's training expertise to ensure that you'll receive the maximum return on your time. You'll focus on the tasks and skills that increase productivity while working at your own pace and convenience.

We invite you to visit the Perspection Web site at:

www.perspection.com

Acknowledgements

The task of creating any book requires the talents of many hard-working people pulling together to meet impossible deadlines and untold stresses. We'd like to thank the outstanding team responsible for making this book possible: the writers, Ahmad Hashem and Steve Johnson and contributors, Nicholas Chu and Jane Pedicini; the editors, Elise Bishop and Tonya Simpson; the technical editors, Nicholas Chu and Melinda Lankford; the production team, Beth Teyler, Kate Lyerla, Joe Kalsbeek, Blaine Lyerla, and Ryan Suzuki; the proofreader, Holly Johnson, and the indexer, Michael Brackney.

Annie Milner, director of training at DigitalCare, Inc., Robin Raiford, R.N., Ammar Halawa, M.D., and Oubai Bounie contributed to the healthcare examples used in this book, and we'd like to thank them for their important contributions.

At Que publishing, we'd like to thank Greg Wiegand and Stephanie McComb for the opportunity to undertake this project, Sharry Gregory for administrative support, and Sandra Schroeder for your production expertise and support.

Dedication

Ahmad would like to thank his wife, Serene, and his three children, Malak, Ameer, and Younos, for putting up with the long hours needed to finish this work. He also would like to thank his parents for their love and support.

Steve would like to thank his wife Holly and his three children, JP, Brett, and Hannah, for their support and encouragement during the project.

About the Authors

Dr. Ahmad Hashem is a global healthcare productivity manager for Microsoft's Healthcare and Life Sciences Industry Solutions Group. He is responsible for defining and guiding implementation of Microsoft's worldwide strategy for empowering information workers across the Healthcare and Life Sciences industries. Before joining Microsoft in 2000, Ahmad was CIO at a healthcare e-learning company in Santa Monica, California, director and acting COO at Medical Archival Systems in Pittsburgh, and a National Library of Medicine fellow in medical informatics at the University of Pittsburgh Medical Center. In addition to his doctorate in medicine from the University of Damascus, Ahmad holds a Bachelor of Science degree in computer science from the University of Massachusetts and a doctorate in medical informatics, Cognitive Program, from the University of Pittsburgh. Ahmad can be reached at ahmad@hashem.net.

Steve Johnson has written more than 20 books on a variety of computer software, including Microsoft Office XP, Microsoft Windows XP, Macromedia Director MX and Macromedia Fireworks, and Web publishing. In 1991, after working for Apple Computer and Microsoft, Steve founded Perspection, Inc., which writes and produces software training. When he is not staying up late writing, he enjoys playing golf, gardening, and spending time with his wife, Holly, and three children, JP, Brett, and Hannah. When time permits, he likes to travel to such places as New Hampshire in October, and Hawaii. Steve and his family live in Pleasanton, California, but can also be found visiting family all over the western United States.

We Want to Hear from You!

As the reader of this book, *you* are our most important critic and commentator. We value your opinion and want to know what we're doing right, what we could do better, what areas you'd like to see us publish in, and any other words of wisdom you're willing to pass our way.

As an associate publisher for Que Publishing, I welcome your comments. You can email or write me directly to let me know what you did or didn't like about this book—as well as what we can do to make our books better.

Please note that I cannot help you with technical problems related to the topic of this book. We do have a User Services group, however, where I will forward specific technical questions related to the book.

When you write, please be sure to include this book's title and author as well as your name, email address, and phone number. I will carefully review your comments and share them with the author and editors who worked on the book.

Email: feedback@quepublishing.com

Mail: Greg Wiegand
           Associate Publisher
           Que Publishing
           800 East 96th Street
           Indianapolis, IN 46240 USA

For more information about this book or another Que title, visit our Web site at www.quepublishing.com. Type the ISBN (excluding hyphens) or the title of a book in the Search field to find the page you're looking for.

Contents

C

Foreword

It's never been easy to be a healthcare professional, and the pressures are only getting worse. Helping fellow professionals in one way or another often figures into the motivations of those who have left the joys of a medical practice to pursue healthcare from a different vector. Some are called into research, giving up the rewards of helping individuals with the hope that they might contribute insights that can lead to the helping of many.

After medical school, my own path took me to the University of Pittsburgh and a doctorate in medical informatics, with visions of helping healthcare professionals help their patients through better management of data. Fortunately, I see that vision coming true, especially as I work with my colleagues at Microsoft to create tools that give healthcare professionals the information they need at any time, and at any place—including over a wireless device as they attend to a patient at bedside. We call this initiative to provide seamless, yet secure, access to data on an anytime, anywhere, basis Healthcare Without Boundaries.

Although we are proud of our work, the great wonders come from what we see after we release our products, as healthcare professionals do things with our software that we never envisioned. Healthcare professionals, by nature—or through selection and training—have a scientific mind and a driving curiosity. My colleagues and I are constantly dazzled by what healthcare professionals are creating by using Microsoft technology in unexpected ways. And often the work is done by private practitioners looking for ways to create their own solution because they either couldn't afford a prepackaged one or couldn't find a solution that answered their creative visions.

Medical Economics magazine recently ran a story about Robert Novich, a New Rochelle, NY internist who needed an electronic medical records system for his solo practice. Suffering from sticker shock and the inflexibility of the commercial EMRs he looked at, he decided to create his own—using Microsoft Word and a fax machine. Lab reports and other documents received by fax are directly imported into the computer for digital storage. Working with his son Jeff, who was a college student at the time, Dr. Novich created a system that uses Word templates to simplify creation of medical records and Explorer to provide instant file access; slashing time from pulling information out of file cabinets. The system also creates and manages electronic prescriptions. The results? Dr. Novich said, "I feel like a brand new doctor."

Microsoft recently sponsored a contest looking for innovative ways in which the Office suite of applications had been used by healthcare workers. The response was overwhelming—not because of the technology, but because of the innovative ways it was being deployed to solve real-world problems.

> *Cecil Lynch, an M.D. and medical informaticist who teaches at the University of California at Davis is using Microsoft Access to help the U.S. Centers for Disease Control (CDC) enhance the efficiency of its disease surveillance system.*

Dr. Duke Cameron of the Division of Cardiac Surgery, Johns Hopkins Hospital, came up with the idea of using the Outlook Calendar to schedule operating rooms, to help assure the OR is properly setup with specific implant devices and other special equipment or supplies before the surgical team arrives.

Nick Hoda, a psychologist-in-training at Mississippi State University, uses Microsoft Excel charts and graphs to show his elementary school clients coping with learning and behavioral problems...that their behavior really is getting better. He uses the same charts with teachers and administrators to win his young clients another chance at the classroom.

So, the pressures facing healthcare professionals are great, but so are their resources. Information technology is one resource, this book is another, but the greatest of all is the innate curiosity and drive to discover and create that seems to be so much a part of those who are drawn to this noble profession.

Ahmad Hashem, M.D., Ph.D.
Global Healthcare Productivity Manager
Healthcare and Life Sciences
Microsoft Corp.

Introduction

Welcome to *Microsoft Office 2003 for Healthcare*, a visual quick-reference book that shows you how to work efficiently with Microsoft Office 2003. This book provides complete coverage of basic and intermediate Office 2003 skills.

Find the Best Place to Start

You don't have to read this book in any particular order. We've designed the book so that you can jump in, get the information you need, and jump out. However, the book does follow a logical progression from simple tasks to more complex ones. Each task is no more than two pages long. To find the information you need, just look up the task in the table of contents, index, or troubleshooting guide, and turn to the page listed. Read the task introduction, follow the step-by-step instructions along with the illustration, and you're done.

How This Book Works

Each task is presented on no more than two facing pages, with step-by-step instructions in the left column and screen illustrations in the right column. This arrangement lets you focus on a single task without having to turn the page.

How You'll Learn

Find the Best Place to Start

How This Book Works

Step-by-Step Instructions

Real-World Examples

Troubleshooting Guide

Step-by-Step Instructions

This book provides concise step-by-step instructions that show you "how" to accomplish a task. Each set of instructions include illustrations that directly correspond to the easy-to-read steps. Also included in the text are timesavers, tables, and sidebars to help you work more efficiently or to teach you more in-depth information. A "Did You Know?" provides tips and techniques to help you work smarter, while a "See Also" leads you to other parts of the book containing related information about the task.

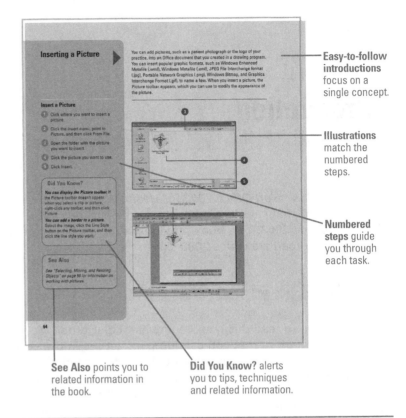

Easy-to-follow introductions focus on a single concept.

Illustrations match the numbered steps.

Numbered steps guide you through each task.

See Also points you to related information in the book.

Did You Know? alerts you to tips, techniques and related information.

Real-World Examples

This book uses real-world examples to help convey "why" you would want to perform a task. The examples give you a context in which to use the task. You'll observe how a healthcare organization could use Office 2003 to get jobs done.

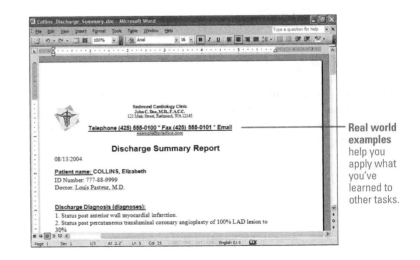

Real world examples help you apply what you've learned to other tasks.

Troubleshooting Guide

This book offers quick and easy ways to diagnose and solve common Office 2003 problems that you might encounter. The troubleshooting guide helps you determine and fix a problem using the task information you find. The problems are posed in question form and are grouped into categories that are presented alphabetically.

Troubleshooting points you to information in the book to help you fix your problems.

Getting Started with Office

Introduction

Dr. Octo Barnett once said that "the practice of healthcare is dominated by how well information is processed, reprocessed, retrieved, and communicated." Healthcare is fundamentally about information, and healthcare professionals are under increasing pressure to accomplish more, and do it better and faster. Microsoft Office 2003 provides the tools to do this and more. Each of its programs—Word, Excel, PowerPoint, Access, Outlook, Publisher, and OneNote—has a special function, yet they all work together.

Office **Word 2003** is a word processing program you can use to create documents, such as reports and referral letters. Office **Excel 2003** is a spreadsheet program to help you organize, analyze, and present data, such as monitoring staff development activities and preparing budget reports. Office **PowerPoint 2003** is a presentation program to help you create and deliver professional presentations. Office **Access 2003** is a database program you can use to store and manage large collections of related information, such as patient demographics and quality indicators. Office **Outlook 2003** is a communication and information management program to help you manage e-mail messages, appointments, contacts, and tasks. Office **Publisher 2003** is a publishing program to help you create newsletters or a practice Web site. Office **OneNote 2003** is a flexible note management program to help you take, organize, and find notes.

Every Office program uses the same structure of windows, menus, toolbars, and dialog boxes, so you can focus on creating the best document in the least amount of time. In addition, you can perform basic actions the same way in every program. For example, in each Office program, you open, save, and close documents with the same buttons or commands. When you have a question, the identical help feature is available throughout the Office programs.

What You'll Do

Start an Office Program

Use Task Panes

Choose Menu and Dialog Box Options

Work with Toolbars

Create a New File

Save a File

Save a File with Different Formats

Open an Existing File

Find a File or Text in a File

Arrange Windows

Get Help in an Office Program

Get Help from the Office Assistant

Close a File

Get Office Updates on the Web

Repair and Recover Office Programs

Quit an Office Program

Starting an Office Program

The two quickest ways to start any Office program are to select an Office program on the Start menu or double-click a shortcut icon on the desktop. By providing different ways to start a program, Office lets you work the way you like and start programs with a click of a button. When you start an Office program, a program window opens, displaying a blank document, where you can create a new document or open an existing one.

Start an Office Program from the Start Menu

1. Click the Start button on the taskbar.

2. Point to All Programs.

3. Point to Microsoft Office.

4. Click the Office 2003 program you want to open.

5. The first time you start Office, an Activation Wizard opens; follow the instructions to activate the product.

Did You Know?

You can create a program shortcut from the Start menu. Click the Start menu, point to All Programs, point to Microsoft Office, right-click a program, point to Send To, and then click Desktop (Create Shortcut).

You can start any Office program and open a document from Windows Explorer. Double-clicking any Office document icon in Windows Explorer opens that file and its associated program.

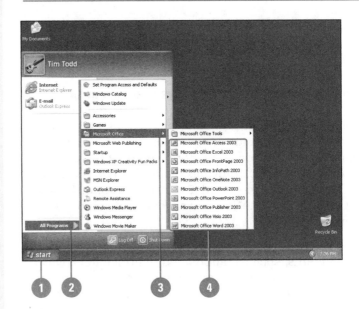

Using Task Panes

When you start an Office program, a task pane appears by default on the right or left side of the program window. The task pane displays various options that relate to the current task. There are several types of options available on the task pane. You can search for information including healthcare-specific information such as drug reference and medical journals available via subscription, select options, and click links, like the ones on a Web page, to perform commands. You can also display different task panes, move back and forth between task panes, and close a task pane to provide a larger work area.

Use the Task Pane

1. When you open any Office Program, the task pane appears on the right or left side of your screen.

2. Click an option on the task pane.

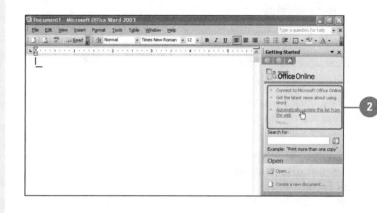

Open and Close Task Panes

1. Click the View menu, and then click Task Pane.

2. To open another task pane, click the list arrow on the task pane title bar, and then click the task pane you want.

3. To switch between task panes, click the Back and Forward task pane buttons.

4. Click the Close button on the task pane.

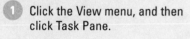

Choosing Menu and Dialog Box Options

A **menu** is a list of related commands or options, located at the top of the window. For example, the Edit menu contains commands for editing a document, such as Delete and Cut. You can right-click a word or object to open a **shortcut menu**, which contains menu commands related to the specific item. Clicking a menu command followed by an ellipsis (...) opens a **dialog box** (a specialized window), where you choose various options and provide information for completing the command. As you switch between programs, you'll find that all Office menus and dialog boxes look similar and work in the same way.

Choose Menu Commands

1. Click a menu name on the menu bar, or right-click an object (such as a toolbar, spreadsheet cell, picture, or selected text).

2. If necessary, click the expand arrow to expand the menu and display more commands.

3. Click a menu command you want, or point to the arrow to the right of the menu command to display a submenu of related commands, and then click the command you want.

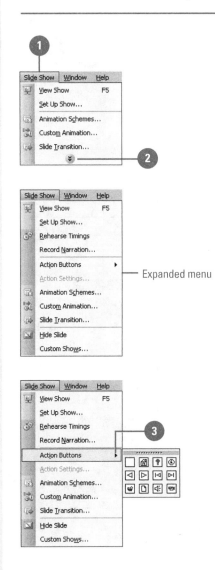

Expanded menu

Choose Dialog Box Options

All Office dialog boxes contain the same types of options, including:

- **Tabs.** Click a tab to display its options. Each tab groups a related set of options.

- **Option buttons.** Click an option button to select it. You can select only one.

- **Spin box.** Click the up or down arrow to increase or decrease the number, or type a number in the box.

- **Check box.** Click the box to turn on or off the option. A checked box means the option is selected; a cleared box means it's not.

- **List box.** Click the list arrow to display a list of options, and then click the option you want.

- **Text box.** Click in the box and then type the requested information.

- **Button.** Click a button to perform a specific action or command. A button name followed by an ellipsis (...) opens another dialog box.

- **Preview box.** Many dialog boxes show an image that reflects the options you select.

Tabs   Text box

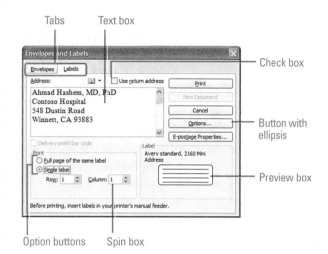

Check box

Button with ellipsis

Preview box

Option buttons   Spin box

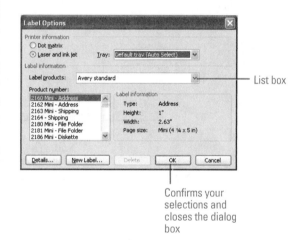

List box

Confirms your selections and closes the dialog box

Working with Toolbars

Each Office **toolbar** contains a collection of buttons you click to select frequently used menu commands. Most programs open with a Standard toolbar (with commands such as Save and Print) and a Formatting toolbar (with commands for selecting fonts and sizes) side by side. You can also display toolbars designed for specific tasks, such as drawing pictures, importing data, or creating charts. If you're not using a toolbar or want to position it in another place, you can hide or move it. When you move a toolbar, you can dock it to the edge of a window or allow it to float in a separate window. The toolbars are personalized as you work, showing only the buttons you use most often. Additional toolbar buttons are available by clicking the Toolbar Options list arrow at the end of the toolbar.

Display and Hide a Toolbar

① Right-click any visible toolbar.

② Click the name of the toolbar you want to display or hide.

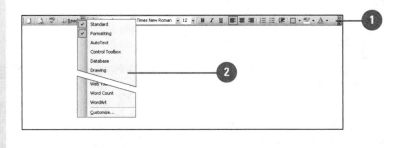

Move and Reshape a Toolbar

◆ To move a toolbar that is docked (attached to one edge of the window) or floating (unattached) over the window, click the gray dotted edge bar on the left edge of the toolbar, and then drag it to a new location.

◆ To return a floating toolbar to its previously docked location, double-click its title bar.

◆ To change the shape of a floating toolbar, drag any border until the toolbar is the shape you want.

Drag any toolbar using the gray bar.

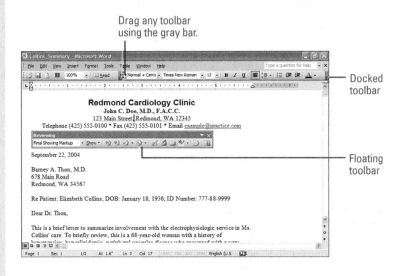

Docked toolbar

Floating toolbar

Display Toolbar Options on a Toolbar

◆ To display more buttons on a toolbar, click the Toolbar Options list arrow at the right end of that toolbar.

Click to display any hidden buttons.

Customize a Toolbar

1 Click the Toolbar Options list arrow on the toolbar you want to change.

2 Point to Add Or Remove Buttons.

3 Point to the toolbar name.

4 To add or remove a toolbar button, click the button name in the list. A check mark means the button appears on the toolbar; no check mark means it doesn't.

5 When you're done, click anywhere in the document window to update the toolbar.

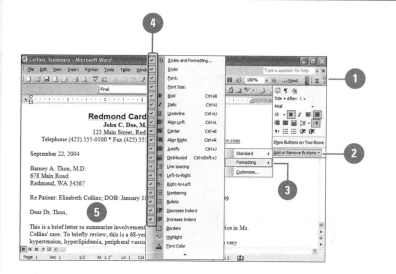

Did You Know?

You can display a toolbar button's name. To find out the name of a toolbar button, position the pointer over the button on the toolbar. The name of the button, or the ScreenTip, appears below the button.

Office personalizes toolbars. When you first open a toolbar, the buttons you used most recently are visible. Click the Toolbar Options list arrow to display any other toolbar buttons. To display the full toolbar, double-click the gray dotted edge bar on the left edge of the toolbar.

Creating a New File

Office makes it easy to create many common documents based on a template or by using a wizard. A **template** opens a document (such as a letter) with predefined formatting and placeholder text that specifies what information you should enter (such as a patient's address). When you start an Office program, a blank document opens based on a default template. The default template defines the page margins, default font, and other settings. A **wizard** walks you through the steps to create a finished document tailored to your preferences. First the wizard asks you for information, and then, when you click Finish, the wizard creates a completely formatted document based on the options and content you entered. If you can't find the template you want on your computer, you can check the Office Online Web site for more.

Create a File Using a Default Template

1. Click the File menu and then click New.

   TIMESAVER *Click the New button on the Standard toolbar to create a file with the current default template.*

2. Click a default template with the style you want.

3. If prompted, perform one of the following:

   ◆ Double-click an existing file as a template.

   ◆ Enter a file name, and then click Save.

   ◆ Follow the wizard's step-by-step instructions. Click Next to move to the next wizard dialog box.

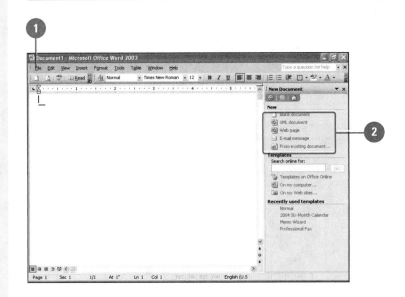

> ### Did You Know?
>
> **You can search for a template, including healthcare ones.** Click the File menu, click New, type a keyword, such as "healthcare" or "medical," in the Search Office Online box, and then click the Go button.

Create a File Using a Template or Wizard

1. Click the File menu, and then click New.

2. Click On My Computer.

3. Click the tab for the type of document you want to create.

4. Double-click the icon for the template or wizard you want to use.

5. If you choose a wizard, follow the step-by-step instructions. Click Next to move to the next wizard dialog box.

6. When you reach the last wizard dialog box, click Finish.

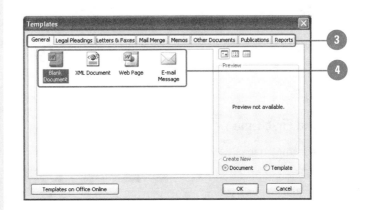

Get Templates on the Web

1. Click the File menu, and then click New.

2. Click Templates On Office Online to open the Microsoft Web site in your browser.

3. Click the link to the template you want.

4. Click Download Now, and then follow the online instructions.

Saving a File

Saving your files frequently ensures that you don't lose work during an unexpected power loss. The first time you save a file, specify a file name and folder in the Save As dialog box. The next time you save, Office saves the file with the same name in the same folder. If you want to change a file's name or location, you can use the Save As dialog box again to create a copy of the original file.

Save a File for the First Time

1 Click the Save button on the Standard toolbar.

2 Click an icon on the Places bar to open a frequently used folder.

3 If necessary, click the Save In list arrow, and then click the drive where you want to save the file.

4 Double-click the folder in which you want to save the file.

5 Type a name for the file, or use the suggested name.

6 Click Save.

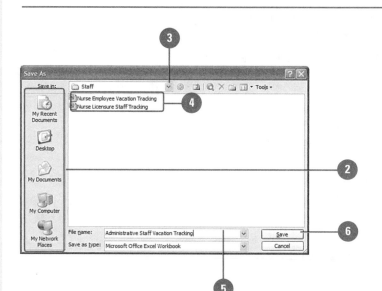

Did You Know?

You don't need to worry about file name extensions. When you name a file, you do not have to type the file name extension. The Office program adds the correct file name extension to the name you give your file. However, if you clear the Hide Extensions For Known File Types check box on the View tab in the Folders Options dialog box (in My Documents, click the Tools menu, and then click Folder Options), you need to include the extension in the file name.

You can save all your open files at once. You can save all your files at one time. Press and hold Shift, click the File menu, and then click Save All.

Save a File with Another Name

1. Click the File menu, and then click Save As.

2. Click an icon on the Places bar, or click the Save In list arrow, and then click the drive or folder where you want to save the file.

3. Type a new file name.

4. Click Save.

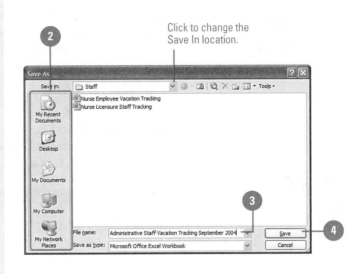

Click to change the Save In location.

Save a File in a New Folder

1. Click the File menu, and then click Save As.

2. Locate and select the drive and folder where you want to create the new folder.

3. Click the Create New Folder button.

4. Type the new folder name, and then click OK.

5. Type a name for the file, or use the suggested one.

6. Click Save.

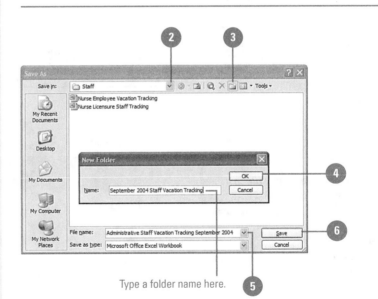

Type a folder name here.

Did You Know?

You can rename a folder in the Save As or Open dialog box. In the Save As or Open dialog box, right-click the folder you want to rename, click Rename, type a name, and then press Enter.

Saving a File with Different Formats

A file type specifies the document format (for example, a template) as well as the program and version in which the file was created (for example, Office Excel 2003). You might want to change the type if you're creating a custom template or sharing files with someone who has an earlier version of a program. You use the Save As dialog box to change the file type for a document. The Save As Type list arrow displays a list of the available formats for the program or current selection. In Office programs like Outlook and Access, which use different types of objects, you need to select the item before you can save it with a different format.

Save a File as a Different Type

1. Select the item you want to save (in Outlook or Access).

2. Click the File menu, and then click Save As.

3. Click the Save As Type list arrow.

4. Click the file type you want.

   You can select file types for previous versions of Office programs.

5. Click Save.

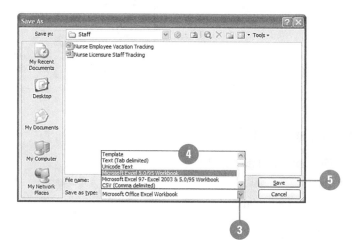

Did You Know?

You can delete or rename a file in a dialog box. In the Open or Save As dialog box, click the file, click the Tools list arrow, and then click Delete or Rename.

You can move or copy a file quickly in a dialog box. In the Open or Save As dialog box, right-click the file you want to move or copy, click Cut or Copy, open the folder where you want to paste the file, right-click a blank area, and then click Paste.

Common Formats	
Program	**Format**
Office	Template XML Web Page
Word	Rich Text Format (RTF)
Excel	Text (Tab delimited) or Text (MS-DOS) CSV (Comma delimited)
PowerPoint	Graphics: GIF, JPEG, PNG, and TIFF Outline/RTF PowerPoint Show
Publisher	Rich Text Format (RTF) Graphics: GIF, JPEG, PNG, and TIFF

Create a Template

1. Click the File menu, and then click Save As.

2. Click the Save As Type list arrow and then click a template.

3. Type a name for the new template, and then click Save.

4. In the new template, add the text and graphics you want to appear in all new office documents that you base on the template, and then delete any items you don't want to appear.

5. Make the changes you want to the margin settings, page size, and orientation styles, and other formats.

6. Click the Save button on the Standard toolbar.

7. Click the Close button.

Did You Know?

You can save multiple versions of a document in Word. Click the File menu, click Versions, click Save Now, enter comments about the document, and then click OK. In the Versions dialog box, you can also open, delete, and view comments from saved versions.

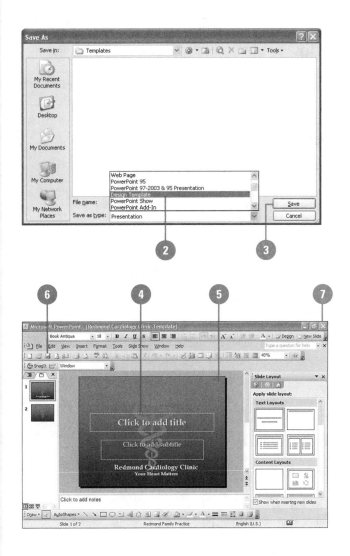

Opening an Existing File

You can open an existing file and its program at one time, or you can open the file from within its Office program. If you can't recall a file's name or location, use the Search feature in the Open dialog box to locate the file, based on the information (or **criteria**) you can recall, such as its creation date, content, author, size, and so forth.

Open an Existing File from Within an Office Program

1. Click the Open button on the Standard toolbar.

2. Click an icon on the Places bar to open a frequently used folder.

3. If necessary, click the Look In list arrow, and then click the drive where the file is located.

4. Double-click the folder in which the file is stored.

5. Click the file you want to open.

6. Click Open.

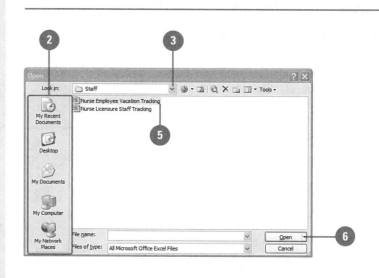

Click to find a file using the Open dialog box

Did You Know?

You can open a recent file quickly. Click the File menu, and then click the appropriate file name at the bottom of the menu.

You can open a recent file quickly from the Start menu. Click the Start button, point to My Recent Documents, and then click the file name you want to open.

You can open a copy of a file quickly. When opening a file from the Open dialog box, click the Open button list arrow, and then click Open As Copy. This creates a new copy of the file in the same folder with the file name Copy of [File name].

Finding a File or Text in a File ▶

The search feature available in the Open dialog box is also available using the Search task pane. You can use the Search task pane to find a file's name or location as well as search for specific text in a document. This becomes handy when you recall the content of a document, but not the name. When you perform a search, try to use specific or unique words to achieve the best results.

Find a File or Text in a File

1. Click the File menu, and then click File Search.

2. Type the name of the file you are looking for or any distinctive words or phrases in the document.

3. Click the Search In list arrow, and then select or clear the check boxes to indicate where you want the program to search.

   Click the plus sign (+) to expand a list.

4. Click the Results Should Be list arrow, and then select or clear the check boxes to indicate the type of files you want to find.

5. Click Go.

6. To revise the find, click Modify.

7. When the search results appear, point to a file, click the list arrow, and then click the command you want.

8. When you're done, click the Close button on the task pane.

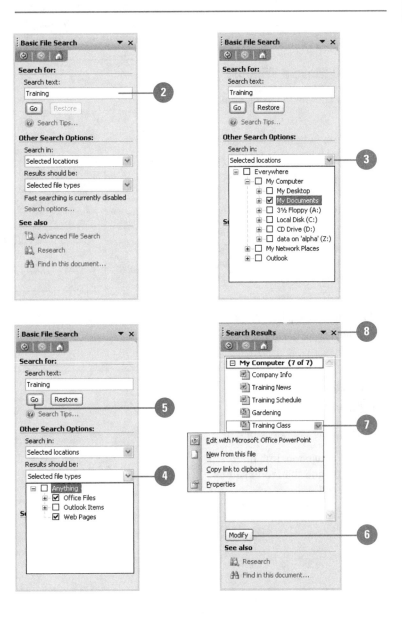

Arranging Windows

Every Office program and document opens inside a window, which contains a title bar, menus, toolbars and a work area, which is where you create and edit your documents. Most often, you'll probably fill the entire screen with one window. But when you want to move or copy information between programs or documents, it's easier to display several windows at once. You can arrange two or more windows from one program or from different programs on the screen at the same time. However, you must make the window active to work in it. You can also click the document buttons on the taskbar to switch between open Office documents.

Resize and Move a Window

All windows contain the same sizing buttons:

◆ **Maximize button.** Click to make a window fill the entire screen.

◆ **Restore Down button.** Click to reduce a maximized window to a reduced size.

◆ **Minimize button.** Click to shrink a window to a taskbar button. To restore the window to its previous size, click the appropriate taskbar button.

◆ **Close button.** Click to shut a window.

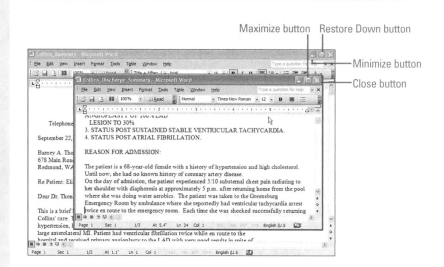

Maximize button   Restore Down button
Minimize button
Close button

Use the Mouse to Move a Window

1 Point to the window's title bar.

2 Drag the window to a new location, and then release the mouse button.

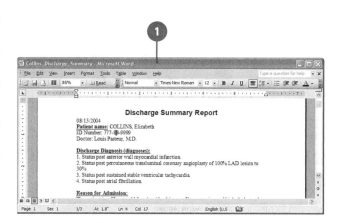

Use the Mouse to Resize a Window

1 If the window is maximized, click the Restore Down button.

2 Move the mouse over one of the borders of the window until the mouse pointer changes into a two-headed arrow.

The directions of the arrow-heads show you the directions in which you can resize the window.

3 Drag the window border until the window is the size you want.

Arrange Multiple Windows

1 Click the Window menu.

2 Click a window command (Office programs vary):

◆ Compare Side By Side With ... (in Word or Excel), click a document, and then click OK to tile two windows and scroll through both Office documents at the same time.

◆ Arrange All or Arrange to fit the windows on the screen.

Did You Know?

You can use the taskbar to arrange all open windows. Right-click a blank area on the taskbar, and then click Tile Windows Horizontally, Tile Windows Vertically, or Cascade Windows.

Compare two documents side by side.

Getting Help in an Office Program

At some point, everyone has a question or two about the program they are using. The Office online Help system provides the answers you need. You can search an extensive catalog of Help topics using a table of contents to locate specific information, or you can get context sensitive help in a dialog box.

Get Help Without the Office Assistant

1. Click the Help button on the Standard toolbar.

2. Locate the Help topic you want.

   ◆ Type one or more keywords in the Search For box, and then click the Start Searching button.

   ◆ Click Table Of Contents, and then click a topic.

   The topic you want appears in the right pane.

3. Read the topic, and then click any hyperlinks to get information on related topics or definitions.

4. When you are done, click the Close button.

5. Click the Close button on the task pane.

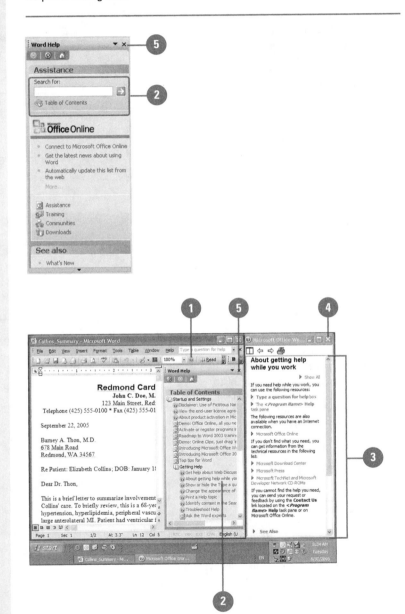

Get Help While You Work

1. Click the Type A Question For Help box.

2. Type your question, and then press Enter.

3. Click the topic that you want to read about.

4. When you're done, click the Close button on the task pane.

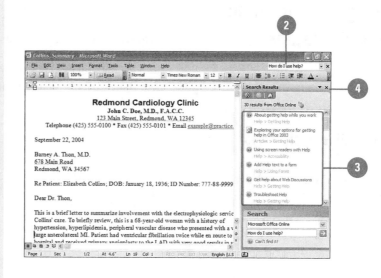

Get Help in a Dialog Box

1. Display the dialog box in which you want to get help.

2. Click the Help button.

3. Read the information in the Help window, and then click any links to display additional information.

4. When you're done, click the Close button.

Getting Help from the Office Assistant

Often the easiest way to learn how to accomplish a task is to ask someone who knows. Now, with Office, that knowledgeable friend is always available in the form of the Office Assistant. Using everyday language, just tell the Office Assistant what you want to do and it walks you through the process step by step. If the personality of the default Office Assistant—Clippit—doesn't appeal to you, choose from a variety of other Office Assistants.

Ask the Office Assistant for Help

1. Click the Help button on the Standard toolbar, or click the Office Assistant.

2. Click the Office Assistant, if necessary, to display the help balloon.

3. Type your question about a task you want help with.

4. Click Search.

5. Click the topic you want help with, and then read the information.

6. After you're done, click the Close button.

7. To refine the search, click the list arrow, select a search area, and then click the Start Searching button.

8. When you're done, click the Close button on the task pane.

9. Click the Help menu, and then click Hide the Office Assistant.

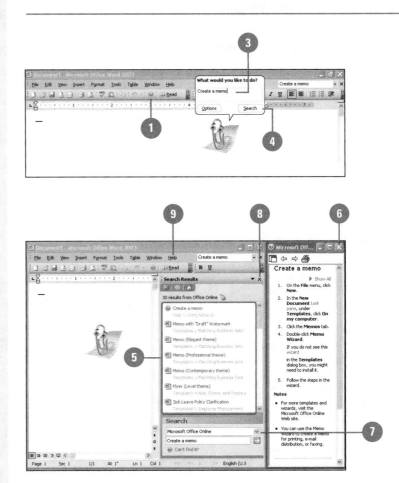

Did You Know?

You can use the Office Assistant to get help at any time. When you begin to create a common type of document (such as a letter), the Office Assistant appears and offers you help. You can have the Office Assistant walk you through the process, or you can complete the task alone.

Choose an Office Assistant

1. Right-click the Office Assistant and then click Choose Assistant.

2. Click the Gallery tab.

3. Click Next and Back to preview different Assistants.

4. Leave the Assistant you want to use visible.

5. Click OK.

   If you are prompted, insert the Office 2003 CD-ROM in your drive, and then click OK.

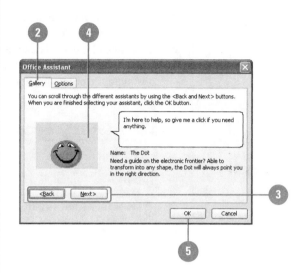

Turn Off the Office Assistant

1. Right-click the Office Assistant and then click Options, or click the Options button in the Assistant window.

2. Click the Options tab.

3. Clear the Use The Office Assistant check box.

4. Click OK.

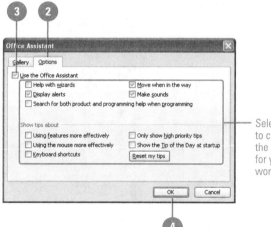

Select options to customize the Assistant for your working style.

Did You Know?

You can hide the Office Assistant while it is turned on. To hide the Office Assistant, right-click the Assistant, and then click Hide.

Closing a File

To conserve your computer's resources, close any files you are not working on. You can close open documents one at a time, or you can use one command to close all open files without closing the program. Either way, if you try to close a document without saving your final changes, a dialog box appears, prompting you to do so.

Close One File

1. Click the Close button.

2. If necessary, click Yes to save your changes.

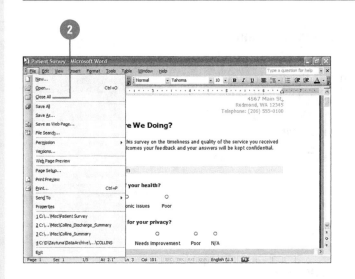

Close All Open Files

1. In Word or Excel, press and hold Shift.

2. Click the File menu, and then click Close All.

3. If necessary, click Yes to save your changes.

> ### Did You Know?
>
> **Microsoft Word uses one Close button.** When two or more documents are open in Word, the window contains one Close button. The Close button closes the document without exiting the program. You might need to click a Word document button on the taskbar to make it active before you click the Close button.

Getting Office Updates on the Web ▶

Microsoft continues to improve Office 2003 program with new features, security patches, or bug fixes. Microsoft Office Update allows you to keep your programs up-to-date with the latest software releases over the Internet. Microsoft Office Update scans your computer for any software components or fixes that need to be installed. Critical updates are important to install in order for your Office programs to run properly. By keeping your Office program updated with the latest security patches, you can protect your computer from the latest Internet threats.

Get Office Updates on the Web

1. Click the Help menu, and then click Check For Updates to open the Microsoft Online Web site.

2. Click Check For Updates to scan your system for any updates.

3. If necessary, click Yes to a security warning.

4. Follow the online instructions to download and install any updates.

Did You Know?

You can get Office information on the Web. Click the Help menu, and then click Microsoft Office Online. Your Web browser opens, displaying the Microsoft Office Online Web site.

You can get critical security updates on the Web. You can also check out Microsoft's Security's Web site for new announcements on the latest threats:

http://www.microsoft.com/security/

Repairing and Recovering Office Programs

Never again do you need to worry when Office stops working for no apparent reason. All the Office programs are now self-repairing, which means that Office checks to see if essential files are missing or corrupt as a program opens and fixes the files as needed. You may never even realize there was a problem. Other times, Office starts fine but might have another problem, such as a corrupted font file or a missing template. These kinds of problems used to take hours to identify and fix. Now Office does the work for you with the Detect And Repair feature, which locates, diagnoses, and fixes any errors in the program itself. If you need to add or remove features or remove Office entirely, you can use Office Setup's maintenance feature.

Detect and Repair Problems

1. Click the Help menu, and then click Detect And Repair.

2. Click Start.

   Insert the Office 2003 CD in your CD-ROM drive.

3. If the Detect And Repair command does not fix the problem, you might need to reinstall Microsoft Office.

4. Click Finish.

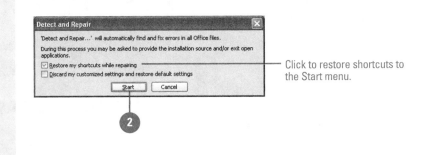

Click to restore shortcuts to the Start menu.

Recover an Office Program

1. Click the Start button on the taskbar, point to All Programs, point to Microsoft Office, point to Microsoft Office Tools, and then click Microsoft Office Application Recovery.

2. Select the application you want to recover.

3. Click Recover Application or End Application.

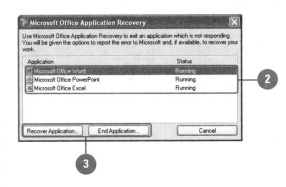

Perform Maintenance on Office Programs

1. In Windows Explorer, double-click the Setup icon on the Office CD.

2. Click one of the following maintenance buttons:

   ◆ Add Or Remove Features to determine which and when features are installed or removed

   ◆ Reinstall or Repair to repair or reinstall Office

   ◆ Uninstall to uninstall Office

3. Follow the wizard instructions to complete the maintenance.

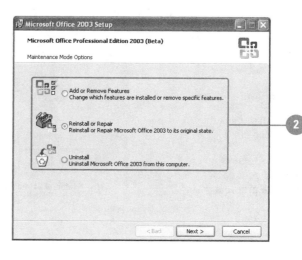

1

For Your Information

Recovering an Office File

If you are working on an Office document when there's a problem, you can recover the document in Word, Excel, and PowerPoint. Office saves files for recovery in case the program stops responding or you lose power. Office saves the changes in a recovery file based on the amount of time indicated in the AutoRecover option. To turn on the AutoRecover option and specify a time interval in which to save, click the Tools menu, click Options, click the Save tab, select the Save AutoRecover Info check box, specify the period of time, and then click OK. When you start the program after a problem, the Office program displays copies of the document in the Document Recover task pane where you can view, show repairs, and save the recovered file.

Quitting an Office Program

When you decide to stop working for the day, the last thing you must do is quit any running programs. All open documents close when you quit. If you haven't saved your final changes, a dialog box appears, prompting you to do so.

Quit an Office Program

1. Click the Close button, or click the File menu, and then click Exit.

2. If necessary, click Yes to save any changes you made to your open documents before the program quits.

Did You Know?

Microsoft Office Access 2003 compacts on close. Click the Tools menu, click Options, click the General tab, select the Compact On Close check box, and then click OK.

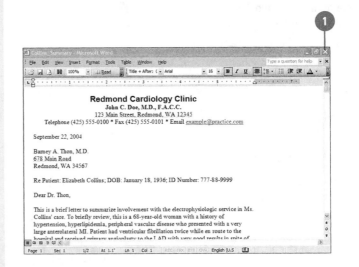

Click to close the document and program without saving your final changes.

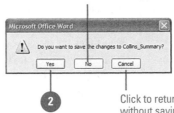

Click to return to the program and document without saving your latest changes.

Using Shared Office Tools

Introduction

The Microsoft Office 2003 programs are designed to work together so you can focus on what you need to do, rather than how to do it. In fact, the Office programs share tools and features for your most common tasks so you can work uninterrupted and move seamlessly from one program to another. All the Office programs work with text and objects in the same way. As a result, once you learn how to move, find, correct, and comment on text in one program, you can perform these tasks in every program. If you know how to perform a task in Word, you already know how to perform the same task in Excel, Access, Outlook, PowerPoint, and Publisher.

Editing Text

Before you can edit text, you need to highlight, or select, the text you want to modify. Then you can delete, replace, move (cut), or copy text within one document or between documents even if they're from different programs. In either case, the steps are the same. Text you cut or copy is temporarily stored in the Office Clipboard. When you paste the text, the Paste Options button appears below it. When you click the button, a menu appears with options to specify how Office pastes the information in the document. You can also move or copy selected text without storing it on the Clipboard by using drag-and-drop editing.

Select and Edit Text

1. Move the I-beam pointer to the left or right of the text you want to select.

2. Drag the pointer to highlight the text.

   TIMESAVER *Double-click a word to select it; triple-click a paragraph to select it.*

3. Perform one of the following editing commands:

   ◆ To replace text, type your text.

   ◆ To delete text, press the Backspace key or the Delete key.

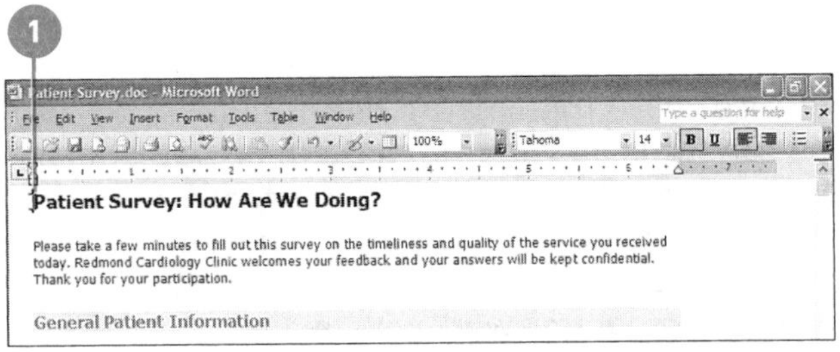

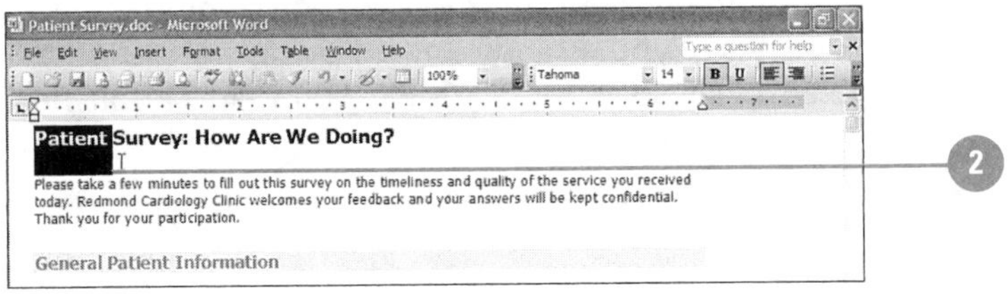

Insert and Delete Text

1. Click in the document to place the insertion point where you want to make the change.

   ◆ To insert text, type your text.

   ◆ To delete text, press the Backspace key or the Delete key.

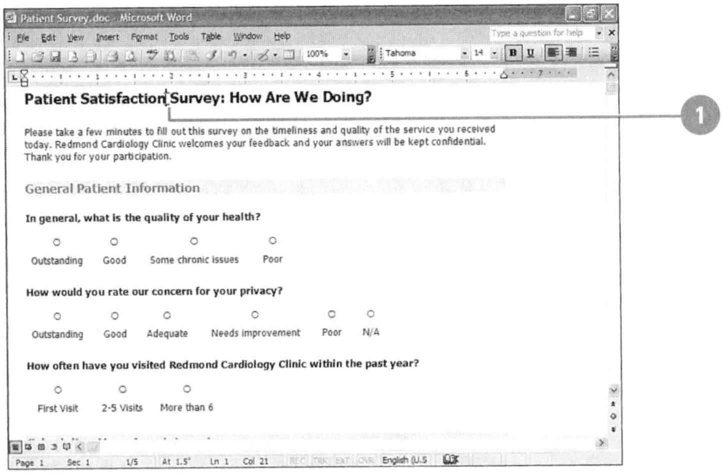

Move or Copy Text

1. Select the text you want to move or copy.

2. Click the Cut or Copy button on the Standard toolbar.

3. Click where you want to insert the text.

4. Click the Paste button on the Standard toolbar.

   To paste the text with another format, click the Edit menu, click Paste Special, click a format option, and then click OK.

5. Click the Paste Options button, and then click an option to customize the way the text appears.

Move or Copy Text Using Drag and Drop

1. If you want to drag text between programs or documents, display both windows.

2. Select the text you want to move or copy.

3. Point to the selected text, and then click and hold the mouse button.

   If you want to copy the text, also press and hold Ctrl. A plus sign (+) appears in the pointer box, indicating that you are dragging a copy of the selected text.

4. Drag the selected text to the new location, and then release the mouse button (and Ctrl, if necessary).

5. Click anywhere in the document to deselect the text.

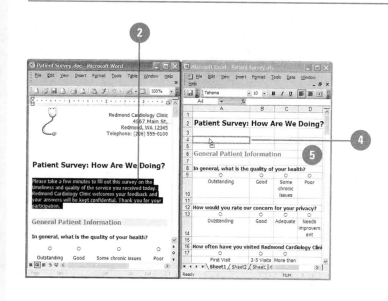

Working with the Clipboard

The **Office Clipboard** is available from within any Office program and holds up to 24 pieces of copied information, any or all of which you can paste to a new location. As you cut or copy information, Office collects it in the Office Clipboard. You can use the Office Clipboard task pane to manage the information and use it in documents. The Office Clipboard allows you to collect multiple items and paste them quickly. When you paste an item, the Paste Options button appears below it. When you click the button, a menu appears with options to specify how Office pastes the information. The available options differ depending on the content you are pasting.

Paste Items from the Office Clipboard

1. Click the Edit menu, and then click Office Clipboard.

   TIMESAVER *Press Ctrl+C twice to access the Office Clipboard.*

2. Click where you want to insert the text.

3. Click any icon on the Clipboard task pane to paste that selection. If there is more than one selection you can paste all the selections at once, by clicking Paste All.

4. When you're done, click the Close button on the task pane.

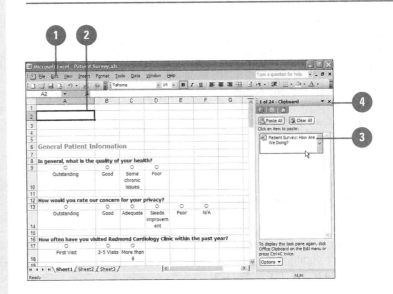

Did You Know?

You can turn on or off paste options. Click the Tools menu, click Options, click the Edit tab, select or clear the Show Paste Options Buttons check box, and then click OK.

You can paste information in a different format. Select the object or text, click the Copy button on the Standard toolbar, click to indicate where you want to paste the object, click the Edit menu, click Paste Special, click the object type you want, and then click OK.

Delete Items from the Office Clipboard

1. Click the Edit menu, and then click Office Clipboard.

2. Click the list arrow of the item you want to paste, and then click Delete.

3. To erase all items in the Office Clipboard, click Clear All.

4. When you're done, click the Close button on the task pane.

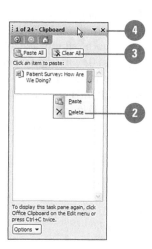

Change Clipboard Options

1. Click the Edit menu, and then click Office Clipboard.

2. Click Options, and then click any of the following options. (A check mark turns the feature on):

   - Show Office Clipboard Automatically

   - Show Office Clipboard When Ctrl+C Pressed Twice

   - Collect Without Showing Office Clipboard

   - Show Office Clipboard Icon On Taskbar

   - Show Status Near Taskbar When Copying

3. When you're done, click the Close button on the task pane.

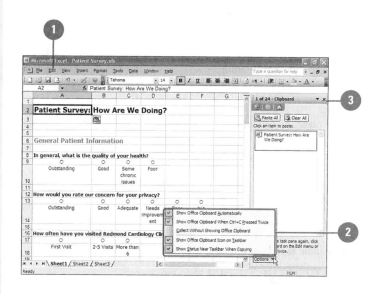

Finding and Replacing Text

The Find and Replace commands make it easy to locate or replace specific text or formulas in a document. For example, you might want to find each figure reference in a long report to verify that the proper graphic appears. Or you might want to replace all references to cell A3 in your Excel formulas with cell G3. The Find And Replace dialog boxes vary slightly from one Office program to the next, but the commands work essentially in the same way.

Find Text

1. Click at the beginning of the document, or select the text you want to find.

2. Click the Edit menu, and then click Find.

3. Type the text you want to find.

4. Select other options as appropriate.

5. Click Find Next until the text you want to find is highlighted.

   You can click Find Next repeatedly to locate each instance of the text.

6. If a message box opens when you reach the end of the document, click OK.

7. When you're done, click Close or Cancel.

You might need to drag the dialog box out of the way to see the selected text.

Replace Text

1. Click at the beginning of the document, or select the text you want to replace.

2. Click the Edit menu, and then click Replace.

3. Type the text you want to find.

4. Type the text you want to replace.

5. Select other options as appropriate. In Word, click More to display the additional options.

6. Click Find Next to begin the search and select the next instance of the search text.

7. Click Replace to substitute the replacement text, or click Replace All to substitute text throughout the entire document.

    You can click Find Next to locate the next instance of the search text without making a replacement.

8. If a message box appears when you reach the end of the document, click OK.

9. When you're done, click Close or Cancel.

Did You Know?

You can format text that you find and replace. In a Word document, you can search for and replace text with specific formatting features, such as a font and font size. Click More in the Find And Replace dialog box, click Format, click the formatting options you want, and then complete the corresponding dialog box.

Using Multiple Languages

International Microsoft Office users can change the language that appears on their screens by changing the default language settings. Users around the world can enter, display, and edit text in all supported languages, including European languages, Arabic, Chinese, Japanese, Korean, and Hebrew, just to name a few. You'll probably be able to use Office programs in your native language. If the text in your document is written in more than one language, you can automatically detect languages or designate the language of selected text so the spelling checker uses the right dictionary.

Add a Language to Office Programs

1 Click Start on the taskbar, point to All Programs, point to Microsoft Office, point to Microsoft Office Tools, and then click Microsoft Office 2003 Language Settings.

2 Click to select the languages you want to use.

3 Click Add.

4 Click OK, and then click Yes to quit and restart Office.

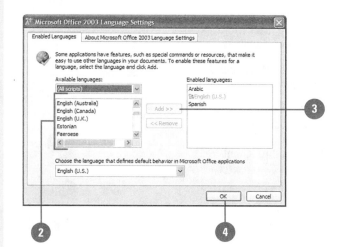

Did You Know?

There is a Multilingual AutoCorrect.
Office supports an AutoCorrect list for each language. For example, the English AutoCorrect list capitalizes all cases of the single letter "i;" in Swedish however, "i" is a preposition and is not capitalized.

You can check your keyboard layout.
After you enable editing for another language, such as Arabic, Cyrillic, or Greek, you might need to install the correct keyboard layout so you can enter characters for that language. In the Control Panel, double-click the Regional And Language icon, click the Language tab, and then click Details to check your keyboard.

Detect Languages Automatically in Word

1. In Word, click the Tools menu, point to Language, and then click Set Language.

2. Select the Detect Language Automatically check box.

3. If you want, select the Do Not Check Spelling Or Grammar check box to skip other language words while checking spelling and grammar.

4. Click OK.

Mark Text as a Language

1. In Word or PowerPoint, select the text you want to mark.

2. In Word, click the Tools menu, point to Language, and then click Set Language. In PowerPoint, click the Tools menu, and then click Language.

3. Click the language you want to assign to the selected text.

4. Click OK.

Did You Know?

You need to install other dictionaries. You must have the dictionaries for any language in order for Word to automatically detect the language and apply its spelling and proofing tools.

Correcting Text Automatically

Since the dawn of typing, people have consistently mistyped certain words or letter combinations. How many times do you misspell *and* or press and hold Shift too long? AutoCorrect fixes common misspellings and incorrect capitalization as you type. It also replaces typed characters, such as -- (two hyphens), with typographical symbols, such as — (an em dash). What's more, you can add your personal problem words to the AutoCorrect list. In most cases, AutoCorrect corrects errors after you press Enter or the Spacebar. When you point to a word that AutoCorrect changed, a small blue box appears under it. When you point to the small blue box, the AutoCorrect Options button appears, which gives you control over whether you want the text to be corrected. You can change it back to its original spelling, or you can stop AutoCorrect from automatically correcting text.

Replace Text as You Type

◆ To correct capitalization or spelling errors automatically, continue typing until AutoCorrect makes the required correction.

◆ To replace two hyphens with an em dash, turn ordinals into superscripts (for example, 1st to 1st), or stack a fraction (for example, 1/2), continue typing until AutoCorrect makes the appropriate change.

◆ To create a bulleted or numbered list, type **1.** or * (for a bullet), press Tab or Spacebar, type any text, and then press Enter. AutoCorrect inserts the next number or bullet. To end the list, press Backspace to erase the extra number or bullet.

Did You Know?

You can prevent automatic corrections. Click the Tools menu, click AutoCorrect Options, clear the Replace Text As You Type check box, and then click OK.

Examples of AutoCorrect Changes

Type of Correction	If You Type	AutoCorrect Inserts
Capitalization	cAP LOCK	Cap Lock
Capitalization	TWo INitial CAps	Two Initial Caps
Capitalization	ann Marie	Ann Marie
Capitalization	microsoft	Microsoft
Capitalization	thursday	Thursday
Common typos	accomodate	accommodate
Common typos	can;t	can't
Common typos	windoes	windows
Superscript ordinals	2nd	2nd
Stacked fractions	1/2	fi
Smart quotes	" "	" "
Em dashes	Madison--a small city in southern Wisconsin--is a nice place to live.	Madison—a small city in southern Wisconsin—is a nice place to live.
Symbols	(c)	©
Symbols	(r)	®
Hyperlinks	www.microsoft.com	www.microsoft.com

Change Correction as You Type

1. Point to the small blue box under the word Office changes.

2. Click the AutoCorrect Options button.

3. Click any of the following options:

   - Change Back To

   - Stop Automatically Correcting

   - Control AutoCorrect Options to change the AutoCorrect settings

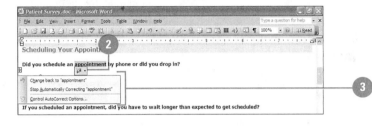

Add or Edit AutoCorrect Entries

1. Click the Tools menu, and then click AutoCorrect Options.

2. Click the AutoCorrect tab.

   To edit an AutoCorrect entry, select the entry you want to change.

3. Type the incorrect text you want AutoCorrect to correct.

4. Type the text or symbols you want AutoCorrect to use as a replacement.

5. Click Add or Replace.

6. When you're done, click OK.

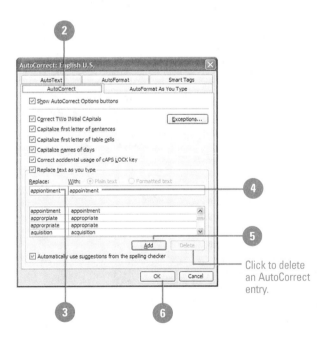

Click to delete an AutoCorrect entry.

Did You Know?

You can create exceptions to Auto-Correct. Specify abbreviations and terms that you don't want AutoCorrect to correct. Click Exceptions, and add these items to the list of exceptions.

Inserting Information the Smart Way

When you type certain information, such as the date and time, personal names, places, telephone numbers, or recent Office Outlook e-mail recipients, a purple dotted line appears under the item, which indicates a Smart Tag is available. A Smart Tag provides options for commonly performed tasks associated with the information. For example, you can add a name and address that you just typed in a Word document to your Contacts list in Office Outlook. When you point to the purple dotted line, the Smart Tags Option button appears below it. When you click the button, a menu appears with a list of available options. The available options differ depending on the Smart Tag content.

Insert Information Using Smart Tags

1. Point to the purple dotted line under an item.

2. Click the Smart Tags Actions button.

3. Click any of the available options:

   - Remove This Smart Tag

   - Smart Tag Options to change the smart tag settings

   - Additional options appear depending on the Smart Tag content

---

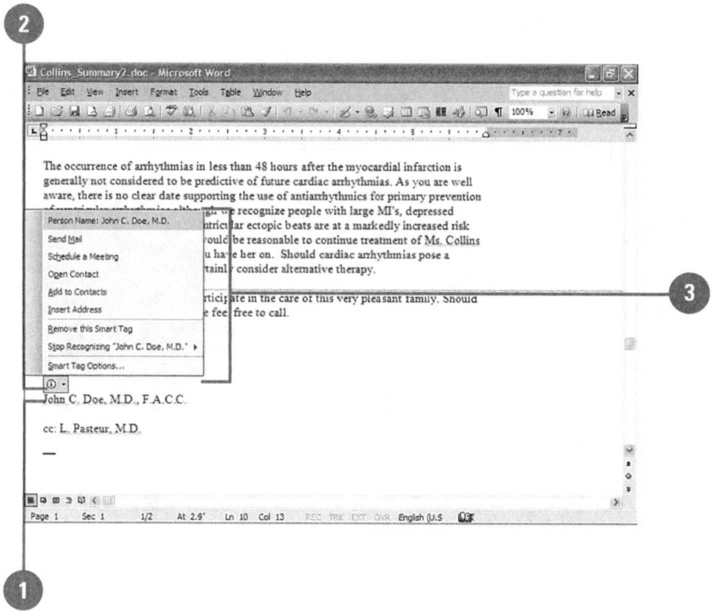

Did You Know?

You can turn off Smart Tags. Click the Tools menu, click AutoCorrect Options, click the Smart Tags tab, clear the Label Data With Smart Tags check box, and then click OK. There are vendors who offer healthcare-related Smart Tags. See Chapter 23, "Healthcare Products to Enrich Your Office Experience," for more information."

Change Smart Tag Options

1. Click the Tools menu, and then click AutoCorrect Options.

2. Click the Smart Tags tab.

3. Select the Label Text With Smart Tags check box.

4. Select the check boxes with the smart tags you want to use.

5. To check the active document for smart tags, click Check [Document, Workbook or Presentation], or click Recheck [Document, Workbook or Presentation].

6. To download new Smart Tag types from the Web, click More Smart Tags.

7. When you're done, click OK.

Did You Know?

Smart Tag options differ depending on the Office program. The Smart Tags tab in the AutoCorrect Options dialog box includes additional options depending on the Office program. For example, in Excel and PowerPoint, you can select the Embed Smart Tags In This [Workbook or Presentation] check box to save smart tags when you use the Save command. In Word, you can click Save As to embed smart tags.

Making Corrections

Everyone makes mistakes and changes their mind at some point, especially when creating or revising a document. With Office you can instantly correct typing errors by pressing a key. You can also reverse more complicated actions, such as typing an entire word, formatting a paragraph, or creating a chart. With the Undo button, if you change your mind, you can just as easily click the Redo button to restore the action you reversed.

Undo or Redo an Action

◆ Click the Undo button to reverse your most recent action, such as typing a word, formatting a paragraph, or creating a chart.

   TIMESAVER *Press Ctrl+Z to undo.*

◆ Click the Redo button to restore the last action you reversed.

   TIMESAVER *Press Ctrl+Y to redo your undo.*

◆ Click the Undo button list arrow, and then select the consecutive actions you want to reverse.

◆ Click the Redo button list arrow, and then select the consecutive actions you want to restore.

Did You Know?

You can use Undo to reverse an AutoCorrect change. To reverse an AutoCorrect change, click the Undo button on the Standard toolbar as soon as AutoCorrect makes the change.

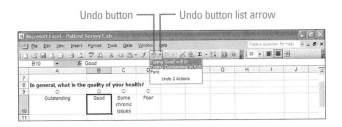

Undo button — Undo button list arrow

Redo button — Redo button list arrow

Correct Typing Errors Using the Keyboard

To Delete	Press
One character at a time to the left of the insertion point	Backspace
One word at a time to the left of the insertion point	Ctrl+Backspace
One character at a time to the right of the insertion point	Delete
One word at a time to the right of the insertion point	Ctrl+Delete
Selected text	Backspace or Delete

Inserting Comments

When you review an Office document, you can insert comments to the author or other reviewers. **Comments** are like electronic adhesive notes tagged with your name. They appear in yellow boxes in PowerPoint, as red triangles in Excel, or as selected text in Word. You can use comments to get feedback from others or to remind yourself of revisions you plan to make. A comment is visible only when you show comments and place the mouse pointer over the comment indicator.

Insert and Delete a Comment

1. Click where you want to insert a comment.

2. Click the Insert menu, and then click Comment.

3. Type your comment in the comment box or pane.

4. Click outside the comment box. In Word, click the Reviewing Pane button, if necessary, to close the pane.

5. To edit or delete a comment, right-click the comment, and then click Edit Comment or Delete Comment.

Read a Comment

1. Click the View menu, point to Toolbars, and then click Reviewing to display the toolbar.

2. On the Reviewing toolbar, click the Show/Hide Markup button in PowerPoint, or click Show, and then click Comments in Word.

3. Point to a red triangle in Excel or yellow box in PowerPoint.

4. Read the comment.

5. Click the Previous or Next button on the Reviewing toolbar to read another comment.

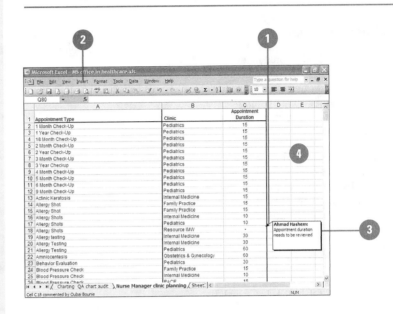

Using Track Changes

When multiple people are involved in the editing and preparation of a document, such as a policies and procedures document in a provider organization, the Track Changes feature will note who made any particular correction and save a record of all such changes for everyone who works on the document later. Each change can be either accepted or rejected by the person who has authority over the final form of the document. If you compare and merge two documents, you can review the changes and accept or reject the results.

Use Track Changes

1. In Excel, click the Tools menu, point to Track Changes, and then click Highlight Changes. Click the Track Changes While Editing check box to select it, and then click OK.

   In Word, click the Tools menu, click Track Changes, or double-click TRK on the status bar to turn tracking on or off. The Track Changes button on the Reviewing toolbar is active.

2. Make changes to the document.

Review Changes

1. Click the View menu, point to Toolbars, and then click Reviewing to display the toolbar.

2. Click the Previous or Next button on the Reviewing toolbar (Word or PowerPoint).

   In Excel, click the Tools menu, point to Track Changes, click Accept Or Reject Changes, specify which changes, and then click OK.

3. Click the Accept Change or Reject Change button (Word or Excel), or click the Apply or Unapply button (from a Compare and Merge in PowerPoint).

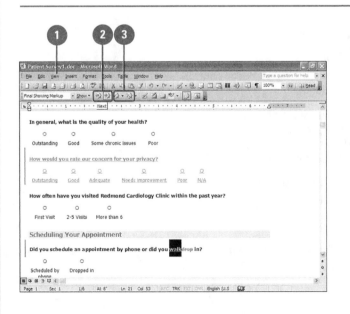

Comparing and Merging Documents

You can compare documents to graphically indicate changes between different versions of a document. The changes can be merged into one document or viewed for comparison. For example, you can compare a newer version of a document with an older one to view the differences. When you compare or merge documents, the text that differs between the two versions will be highlighted in a different color or with track reviewing marks.

Compare and Merge Documents

1. Open a document which you want to compare and merge.

2. Click the Tools menu, and then click Compare And Merge Documents (Word) or Compare And Merge Presentations (PowerPoint) or Compare And Merge Workbooks (Excel).

3. Select the document you want to compare and merge.

4. Click Merge or OK. In Word, you can also click the Merge button list arrow, and then click one of the following:

   ◆ Merge to display the results in the original document.

   ◆ Merge Into Current Document to display the results in the newer document that is currently open.

   ◆ Merge Into New Document to display the results in a new document.

Did You Know?

In Excel, you must share workbooks. Before you can merge a workbook with another workbook, you need to share the workbook. Click the Tools menu, click Share Workbook, select the sharing check box, and then click OK.

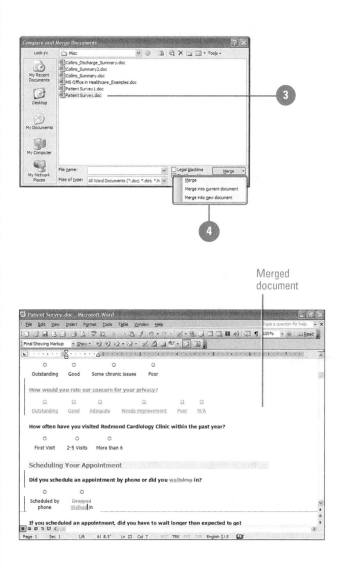

Merged document

Inserting Research Material

With the Research task pane, you can find research material and incorporate it into your work quickly and easily. The Research task pane allows you to access informational services, including healthcare ones provided through subscription, and insert the material right into your Office document without leaving your Office program. The Research task pane can help you access dictionaries, thesauruses, research sites, language translations, research journals, drug references, and stock quotes. You can also add and remove the services from the Research task pane.

Locate and Insert Research Material

1. Click the Tools menu, and then click Research.

2. Type the topic you want to research.

3. Click the Reference list arrow, and then select a reference source, or select All Reference Books.

4. Click the Start Searching button.

5. Copy and paste the material into your Office document.

6. When you're done, click the Close button on the task pane.

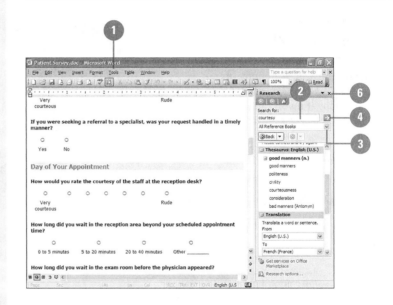

Use the Thesaurus

1. Press and hold the Alt key, and then click the word which you want to find a synonym.

2. Point to the word you want to use.

3. Click the list arrow, and then click Insert.

4. When you're done, click the Close button on the task pane.

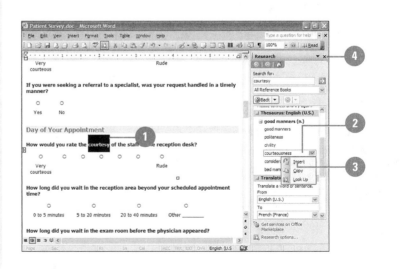

Translate a Word or Sentence

1. Click the Tools menu, and then click Research.

2. Type the word or sentence you want to translate.

3. Click the Reference list arrow, and then click Translation.

4. Select the language you want the word or sentence translated to.

5. Copy and paste the translated word or sentence into your Office document.

6. When you're done, click the Close button on the task pane.

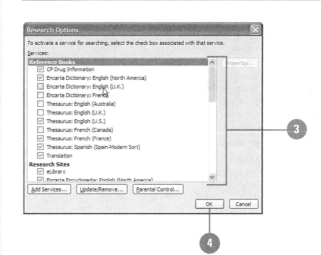

Change Research Options

1. Click the Tools menu, and then click Research.

2. Click Research Options.

3. Do one or more of the following:

   ◆ To activate or remove research services, select or clear the check boxes you want.

   ◆ To add research services, click Add Services, select or type the Internet address for a service you want, and then click Add.

   ◆ To remove a service provider, click Update/Remove, select a provider, click Remove, and then click Close.

   ◆ To turn on parental control, click Parental Controls, select the options you want, and then click OK.

4. Click OK.

5. When you're done, click the Close button on the task pane.

Controlling Programs with Your Voice

The Office Language bar allows you to dictate text directly into your document and also to control buttons, menus, and toolbar functions by using the Voice Command option. When you first install an Office program, the Language bar appears at the top of your screen. If you are using English as a default language, the toolbar is denoted by the letters EN. (Other languages have appropriate abbreviations as well.) Before you can use speech recognition, you need to install it first. You can choose the Speech command on the Tools menu in Word, or you can use Add Or Remove Programs in the Control Panel to change the Office 2003 installation. Before you can use the Language bar for either dictation or voice commands, you need to connect a microphone to your computer, and you must train your computer to your voice using the Speech Recognition Wizard.

Work with the Language Bar

◆ **Open.** Right-click a blank area on the taskbar, point to Toolbars, and then click Language Bar.

◆ **Minimize.** Right-click the Language bar, and then click Minimize. The Language bar docks in the taskbar at the bottom right of the screen, near the system clock.

◆ **Restore.** Right-click the Language bar, and then click Restore The Language Bar.

◆ **Display or hide option buttons.** Click the Options button (the list arrow at the right end of the toolbar), and then click an option to display or hide.

◆ **Change speech properties.** Click the Speech Tools button, and then click Options.

◆ **Change Language Bar properties.** Click the Options button (the list arrow at the right end of the toolbar), and then click Settings.

Train Your Computer to Your Voice

1. Click the Speech Tools button on the Language bar, and then click Training.

2. Click Next, read the instructions, ensure you are in a quiet place, and then click Next again.

3. Read the sentence provided to automatically set the proper volume of the microphone, and then click Next.

4. Read the text with hard consonants to help determine whether or not the microphone is positioned too closely to your mouth. Repeat the process until you have a clear, distinct audio playback, and then click Next.

5. After you are reminded to ensure that your environment is suitable for recording again, read the instructions, and then click Next.

6. Read the following series of dialog boxes. The words on the screen are highlighted as the computer recognizes them. As each dialog box is completed, the program will automatically move to the next one, and the process meter will update accordingly.

7. At the end of the training session, click Finish and your voice profile is updated and saved automatically.

Did You Know?

You can create additional speech profiles. Click the Speech Tools button on the Language bar, click Options, click New, and then follow the Profile Wizard instructions.

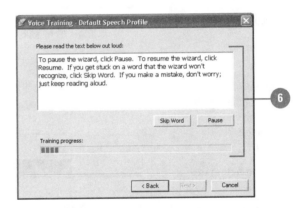

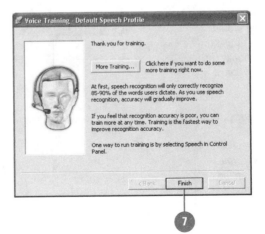

Executing Voice Commands

The two modes, Dictation and Voice Command, are mutually exclusive of one another. You do not want the word File typed, for example, when you are trying to open the File menu. Neither do you want the menu to open instead of the word File being typed when you are in the middle of a sentence where "patient file" is mentioned. As such, you must manually click either mode on the Language bar to switch between them. The Voice Command mode allows you to talk your way through any sequence of menus or toolbar commands, simply by reading aloud the appropriate text instead of clicking it. For example, if you wanted to print the current page of the document you are working on, you would simply say File, Print, Current Page, OK (without saying the commas between the words as written here). You need not worry about remembering every command sequence because as you say each word in the sequence, the corresponding menu or submenu appears onscreen for your reference.

Execute Voice Commands

① Display the Language bar, if necessary.

② Click the Microphone button on the Language bar. The toolbar expands so that the Voice Command button becomes available on the toolbar.

③ Click the Voice Command button to shift into that mode.

④ Work with your Office document normally. When you are ready to issue a command, simply speak the sequence just as you would click through it if you were using the menus or toolbar normally (ie. with the mouse or via keyboard shortcuts).

Say "Format" to display the menu.

> **Did You Know?**
>
> **You can have text read back to you.** Display the Speak Text button on the Language bar. Select the text you want read back to you, and then click Speak Text.

Dictating Text

Dictating the text of a patient record or referral letter using Office speech recognition functions may be easier for some users than typing, but don't think that it is going to be 100% accurate, particularly with specialized medical terms. This means you will need to clean up mistakes when they occur. Additionally, the Dictation function is not an entirely hands free operation. For example, you must manually click the Voice Command button when you want to format anything that has been input, and then click again on Dictation to resume inputting text. Finally, although you can say punctuation marks, such as comma and period, to have them accurately reflected in the document, all periods are followed by double spaces (which may not be consistent with the document formatting you want between sentences) and issues of capitalization remain as well. Nevertheless, it is fun and freeing to be able to get the first draft of any document on paper simply by speaking it.

Dictate Text

1. Display the Language bar, if necessary.

2. Click the Microphone button the Language bar. The toolbar expands so that the Dictation button becomes available on the toolbar.

3. Click to position the insertion point inside the Office document where you want the dictated text to appear, and then begin speaking normally into your microphone. As you speak, the words will appear on the page.

4. When you have finished dictating your text, click the Microphone button again to make the speech recognition functions inactive.

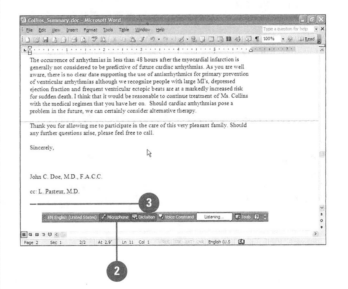

Recognizing Handwriting

Although entering information into an Office document through the keyboard is fast and efficient, you may find that you need to enter information in handwritten form. Office provides handwriting recognition to help you convert handwriting into text. Before you can insert handwritten text into a document, you need to have a mouse, a third party electronic stylus, an ink device, or a handwriting tablet, such as Tablet PC attached to your computer. Although you can use the mouse, for best results you should use a handwriting input device. When you insert handwritten text into a document that already contains typed text, the handwritten text is converted to typed text and then inserted in line with the existing text at the point of the cursor. The program recognizes the handwriting when there is enough text for it to do so, when you reach the end of the line, or if you pause for approximately two seconds. In addition, the converted text will take on the same typeface attributes as the existing text.

Insert Handwritten Text into a Document

1. Display the Language bar, if necessary.

2. Click the Handwriting button on the Language bar, and then click Write Anywhere.

3. Move the mouse over a blank area of your Office document, and then write your text.

   After recognition, the characters that you write appear as text in the Office document.

4. Use the additional handwriting tools to move the cursor, change handwriting modes, and correct text.

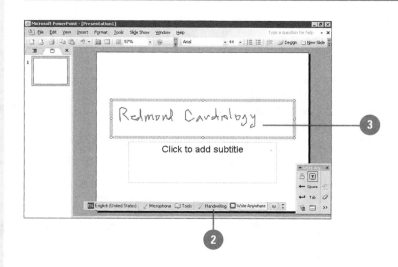

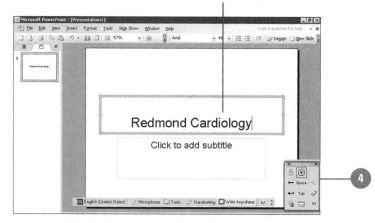

Handwriting changed to text

Insert Handwritten Text on a Writing Pad

① Display the Language bar, if necessary.

② Click the Handwriting button on the Language bar, and then click Writing Pad.

③ Move the cursor over the writing area of the Writing Pad dialog box. (The cursor turns into a pen.)

④ Write your text with the pen.

After recognition, the characters that you write appear in the Office document.

⑤ Use the additional handwriting tools to move the cursor, change handwriting modes, and correct text.

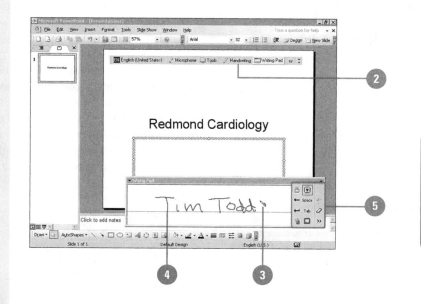

2

For Your Information

Using Additional Handwriting Tools

When you click the Handwriting button on the Language bar and then click the Writing Pad or Write Anywhere option, a dialog box opens on your screen with another toolbar. It has the same options that are available through the Handwriting button on the Language bar. In addition, the toolbar has the following buttons: Ink, Text, Backspace, Space, directional cursors, Enter, Tab, Recognize Now, and Write Anywhere. You use these buttons to control the input.

Automating Your Work with Macros

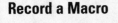

Do you often redo many tasks that require the same, sometimes lengthy, series of steps? Rather than repeat the same actions, you can work faster by recording the entire series of keystrokes and commands in a custom command, or **macro**. A macro is a sequence of commands and entries that can be activated collectively by clicking a toolbar button, clicking a menu command, typing a key combination, or clicking the Run command in the Macros dialog box. Macros are a perfect way to speed up routine formatting, combine multiple commands, and automate complex tasks. The macro recorder archives every mouse click and keystroke you make until you stop the recorder. Any time you want to repeat that series of actions, you "play," or run, the macro.

Record a Macro

1. Click the Tools menu, point to Macro, and then click Record New Macro.

2. Enter a macro name.

   Macro names must start with a letter and can be as many as 80 letters and numbers. Macro names cannot contain spaces, periods, or other punctuation.

3. Assign a toolbar button or keyboard shortcut key to the macro.

4. Select where you want to store the macro.

5. Enter a detailed description of the macro.

6. Click OK.

7. Perform each command or action to complete the task.

   The macro recorder doesn't record mouse movements within a document. For example, you cannot use the mouse to select, copy, or move objects. Instead, you must use keystrokes.

8. Click the Stop Recording button on the Stop Recording toolbar.

Run a Macro

1. Click the Tools menu, point to Macro, and then click Macros.

2. If necessary, click the Macros In list arrow, and then click the document that contains the macro you want to run.

3. Click the name of the macro you want to run.

4. Click Run.

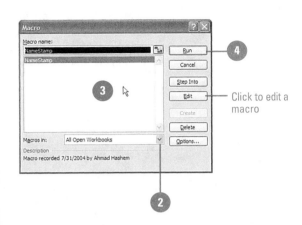

Click to edit a macro

Delete a Macro

1. Click the Tools menu, point to Macro, and then click Macros.

2. Select the macro you want to remove.

3. Click Delete, and then click Yes to confirm the deletion, and close the dialog box.

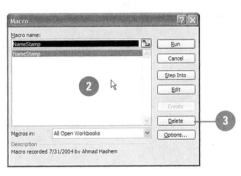

Did You Know?

There is an appropriate location to store macros. If you want a macro to be available in all your Word documents, store it in the Normal template. If you want a macro available in all your worksheets, store it in the Personal Workbook.

Modifying a Macro

If a macro doesn't work exactly the way you want it to, you can fix the problem without re-creating the macro. Instead of recording the macro over again, Office allows you to **debug**, or repair, an existing macro so that you change only the actions that aren't working correctly.

Debug a Macro Using Step Mode

1. Click the Tools menu, point to Macro, and then click Macros.

2. Click the name of the macro you want to debug.

3. Click Step Into.

4. Click the Debug menu, and then click Step Into to proceed through each action.

5. When you're done, click the File menu, and then click Close And Return To [Program name].

6. Click OK to stop the debugger.

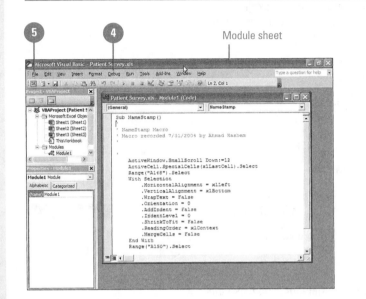

Module sheet

Did You Know?

You can re-record a macro. If you make a mistake as you record a macro, click the Stop Recording button on the Stop Recording toolbar, and then record the macro again using the same name. Click Yes in the dialog box to confirm that you want to replace the existing macro with the same name.

Adding Art to Office Documents

Introduction

Microsoft Office 2003 comes with common drawing and graphics tools that you can use with any of the Office programs. You can draw and modify shapes and lines, and you can insert several different types of graphics, such as pictures, clip art, stylized text, organization charts, diagrams, and Graph charts. Once you insert a graphic, you can modify it to create the look you want. All the Office programs work with drawing and graphics in a similar way, so once you learn how to draw a shape or insert a graphic in one program, you know how to perform the same task in another program.

When you need to manage all the pictures on your computer, Microsoft Office Picture Manager gives you a flexible way to organize, edit, and share your pictures. With Picture Manager, you can view all the pictures on your computer no matter where you store them. If you need to edit a picture, you can use Picture Manager to remove red eye and to change brightness, contrast, and color. You can also crop, rotate and flip, resize, and compress a picture. When you're done editing your pictures, you can share them with others using e-mail or the SharePoint Picture Library.

What You'll Do

Select, Move, and Resize Objects

Draw and Enhance Objects

Add WordArt

Insert Clip Art

Insert a Picture

Insert a Picture from a Scanner or Camera

Modify Pictures

Create an Organization Chart

Create a Diagram

Create a Graph Chart

Modify a Graph Chart

Manage Pictures

Share Pictures Using E-Mail

Selecting, Moving, and Resizing Objects

As you learn more about and use each Office program, you'll want to enhance your documents with more than just text or formulas. To do so, you can insert an object. An **object** is a picture or graphic image you create with a drawing program or insert from an existing file of another program. For example, you can insert the logo of your practice, or you can insert **clip art**—copyright-free pictures that come with Office. The word object can take on a new meaning with each program. For example, when you create an Access database, all tables, queries, forms, and reports are considered objects. To work with an object, you need to select it first. Then you can resize or move it with its selection **handles**, the little circles that appear on the edges of the selected object.

Select and Deselect an Object

◆ Click an object to display its handles.

To select more than one object at a time, hold down Shift as you click each object.

◆ Click elsewhere within the document window to deselect a selected object.

No handles appear around an unselected object.

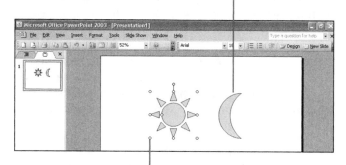

Circle white handles appear around a selected object.

Move an Object

1. Click an object to select it.

2. Drag the object to a new location indicated by the dotted outline of the object.

3. Release the mouse button to drop the object in the new location.

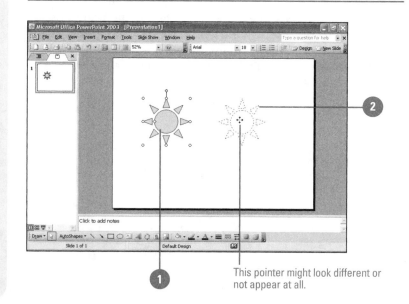

This pointer might look different or not appear at all.

Did You Know?

You can use the mouse button to select multiple objects. To select objects in the same area, drag a selection rectangle around the objects, and then release the mouse button.

Resize an Object

1. Click the object you want to resize.

2. To resize the object:

   ◆ Vertically or horizontally: drag a top, bottom, left, or right sizing handle.

   ◆ Proportionally in both the vertical and horizontal directions: drag a corner sizing handle.

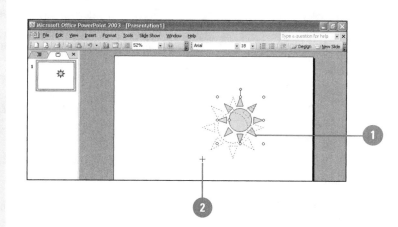

Resize an Object Precisely

1. Right-click the object you want to resize, and then click Format Object, Picture, AutoShape, or Text Box (depending on the program and object).

2. Click the Size tab.

3. Click to select the Lock Aspect Ratio check box to keep the object in its original proportion.

4. Click the Scale Height and Width up and down arrows to resize the object.

5. Click OK.

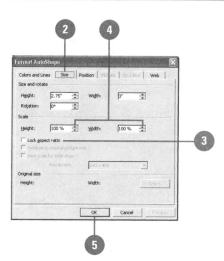

Drawing and Enhancing Objects

Drawn objects, like curved lines or lightning bolts, can enliven your document or help make your point. You can use the options on the Drawing toolbar to draw numerous objects without leaving your current program. After you add an object to your document, you can enhance it with a host of colors and special effects that reflect you, your practice, or your organization. Select the object you want to enhance, and then select the effect you prefer. To make your documents easy to read, don't add too many lines, shapes, or other objects to the same slide, spreadsheet, or page.

Draw Lines and Shapes

1. Display the Drawing toolbar, if necessary.

2. Click the AutoShapes button on the Drawing toolbar, point to Lines or Basic Shapes or any other option, and then select the line or shape you want.

3. Click in the document window, drag the pointer until the line or shape is the size you want, and then release the mouse button.

   When you draw some curvy lines, you need to click the mouse button once for every curve you want, and then double-click to end the line.

4. If you make a mistake, press Delete while the line or shape is still selected, and then try again.

Did You Know?

You can display the Drawing toolbar. Right-click any toolbar, and then click Drawing on the shortcut menu.

You can draw perfect squares or circles. Click the Rectangle or Oval button on the Drawing toolbar, and then press and hold Shift while you draw.

Click to draw a box.
Click to draw a circle.

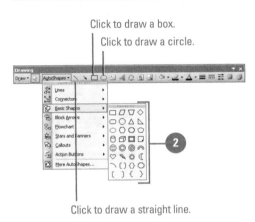

Click to draw a straight line.

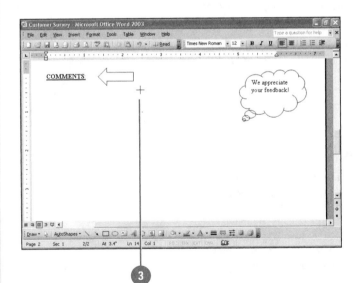

Add Color, Shadows, Line Styles, and 3-D Effects

1. Display the Drawing toolbar, if necessary.

2. Select the object in which you want to add an effect, and then select an option.

   ◆ To fill a shape with color, click the Fill Color button list arrow, and then select the color you want.

   ◆ To change the line color, click the Line Color button list arrow, and then select the color you want.

   ◆ To change the line style, click the Line Style button or the Dash Style button, and then select the style you want.

   ◆ To change the line arrow style, click the Arrow Style button, and then select the style you want.

   ◆ To add a shadow, click the Shadow button, and then select the shadow you want.

   ◆ To change an object to 3-D, click the 3-D button, and then select the 3-D effect you want.

Did You Know?

You can use the Drawing toolbar to align, group, or rotate objects. Click the Draw button on the Drawing toolbar to use commands to group, reorder, align or distribute, and rotate or flip objects.

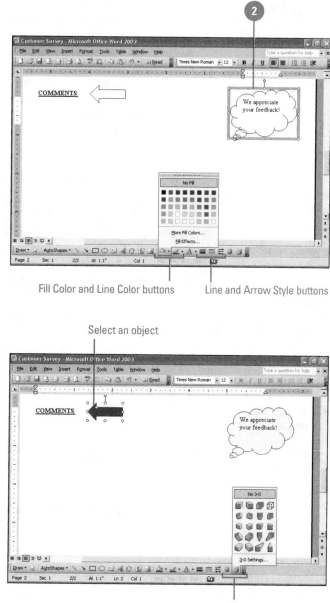

Fill Color and Line Color buttons   Line and Arrow Style buttons

Select an object

Shadow and 3-D buttons

3

Adding WordArt

To add life to your documents, you can add a WordArt object to your document. **WordArt** is an Office component that allows you to add visual enhancements to your text that go beyond changing a font or font size. You can select a WordArt style that stretches your text horizontally, vertically, or diagonally. You can also change the character spacing and reshape the text. Like many enhancements you can add to a document, WordArt is an object that you can move, resize, and even rotate. WordArt is a great way to enhance a newsletter or resume, jazz up an invitation or flyer, or produce a creative report cover or eye-catching envelope.

Create WordArt

1 Right-click any toolbar, and then click Drawing to display the Drawing toolbar.

2 Click the Insert WordArt button on the Drawing toolbar.

3 Double-click the style of text you want to insert.

4 Type the text you want in the Edit WordArt Text dialog box.

5 Click the Font list arrow, and then select the font you want.

6 Click the Size list arrow, and then select the font size you want.

7 If necessary, click the Bold button, the Italic button, or both.

8 Click OK.

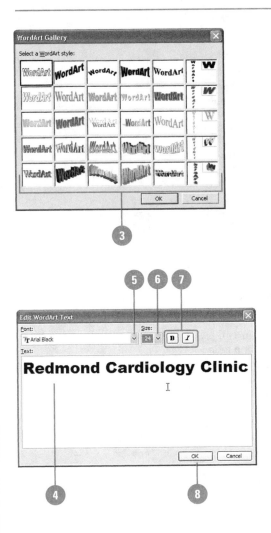

> ### Did You Know?
>
> **You can display the WordArt toolbar.** When you click a WordArt object, its selection handles and the WordArt toolbar reappear. If the toolbar doesn't appear, click the View menu, point to Toolbars, and then click WordArt.

9 With the WordArt object selected, drag any handle to reshape the object until the text is the size you want.

10 Use the WordArt toolbar buttons to format or edit the WordArt.

11 Drag the WordArt object to the location you want.

12 Click outside the WordArt text to deselect the object and close the toolbar.

Did You Know?

You can change the WordArt fill color to match the background. Click the WordArt object, click the Format WordArt button, click the Colors And Lines tab, click the Fill Color button list arrow, click Fill Effects, click the Patterns tab, click the Background list arrow, choose a background color, and then click OK.

You can add a fill effect to WordArt. To fill a WordArt object with a pattern or special effect, click the Fill Color button list arrow on the Drawing toolbar, click Fill Effects, and then click the fill effect you want.

Redmond Cardiology Clinic

9

10

Using WordArt Toolbar Buttons

Icon	Button Name	Purpose
	Insert WordArt	Create new WordArt
Edit Text...	Edit Text	Edit the existing text in a WordArt object
	WordArt Gallery	Choose a new style for existing WordArt
	Format WordArt	Change the attributes of existing WordArt
	WordArt Shape	Modify the shape of an existing WordArt object
	Free Rotate	Rotate an existing object
Aa	WordArt Same Letter Heights	Make uppercase and lowercase letters the same height
Ab b	WordArt Vertical	Change horizontal letters into a vertical formation
	WordArt Alignment	Modify the alignment of an existing object
AV	WordArt Character Spacing	Change the spacing between characters

3

Inserting Clip Art

You can insert clips from Microsoft's Clip Gallery or your own files. **Clips**—copyright-free images or pictures, sounds, and motion clips—enhance any Office document. A motion clip is an animated picture—also known as an animated GIF—frequently used in Web pages or videos. You can also insert your own files you scanned or created in a drawing program, and you can organize clip art in various collections using the Clip Art Organizer.

Insert a Clip

1. Click where you want to insert clip art.

2. Click the Insert menu, point to Picture, and then click Clip Art.

3. Type the word or phrase that describes the clip art you want to find.

4. Click the Search In list arrow, and then select the check boxes with the collection in which you want to search.

   Use the plus (+) and minus (-) signs to navigate the list.

5. Click the Results Should Be list arrow, and then select the check boxes with the type of media you want to search.

6. Click the Go button.

7. Click the clip art image you want to insert.

8. When you're done, click the Close button on the task pane.

Did You Know?

You can connect to the Web to access additional clip art, including medically related clip art. In the Clip Art task pane, click Clip Art On Office Online to open your Web browser and connect to a clip art Web site to download files.

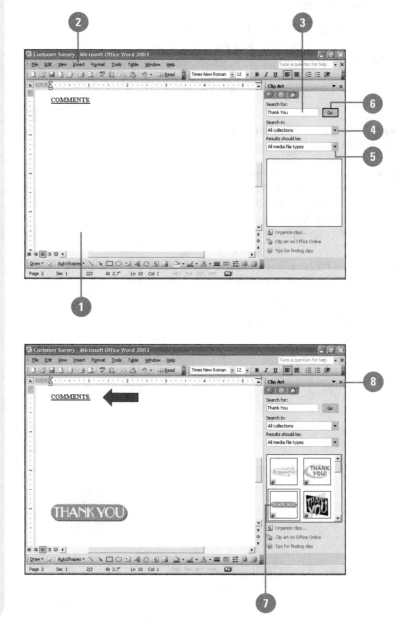

Add Your Own Picture to Clip Art

1. Click the Insert menu, point to Picture, and then click Clip Art.

2. Click Organize Clips, and then click Now, if necessary, to catalog all media files. (You only need to do this once.)

3. Select the collection where you want to place your picture.

4. Click the File menu, point to Add Clips To Organizer, and then click On My Own.

5. Select the picture file you want to add, and then click Add.

6. When you're done, click the Close button.

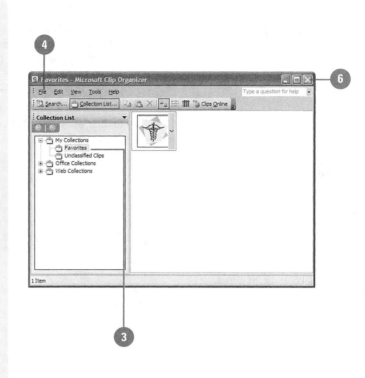

Organize Clip Art

1. Click the Insert menu, point to Picture, and then click Clip Art.

2. Click Organize Clips, and then click Now, if necessary, to catalog all media files. (You only need to do this once.)

3. Click the collection with the clip art in which you want to work.

4. Click the clip art list arrow, and then click the command you want, such as Delete From Clip Organizer, Edit Keywords (for searching), or Move To Collection.

5. When you're done, click the Close button.

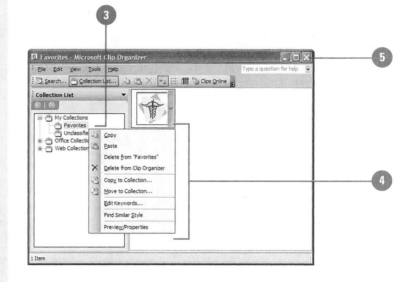

Inserting a Picture

You can add pictures, such as a patient photograph or the logo of your practice, into an Office document that you created in a drawing program. You can insert popular graphic formats, such as Windows Enhanced Metafile (.wmf), Windows Metafile (.emf), JPEG File Interchange format (.jpg), Portable Network Graphics (.png), Windows Bitmap, and Graphics Interchange Format (.gif), to name a few. When you insert a picture, the Picture toolbar appears, which you can use to modify the appearance of the picture.

Insert a Picture

1. Click where you want to insert a picture.

2. Click the Insert menu, point to Picture, and then click From File.

3. Open the folder with the picture you want to insert.

4. Click the picture you want to use.

5. Click Insert.

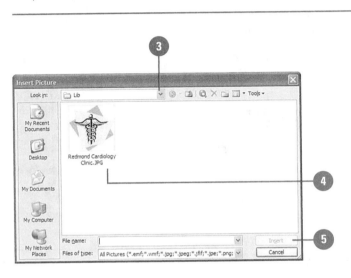

Did You Know?

You can display the Picture toolbar. If the Picture toolbar doesn't appear when you select a clip or picture, right-click any toolbar, and then click Picture.

You can add a border to a picture. Select the image, click the Line Style button on the Picture toolbar, and then click the line style you want.

See Also

See "Selecting, Moving, and Resizing Objects" on page 56 for information on working with pictures.

Inserted picture.

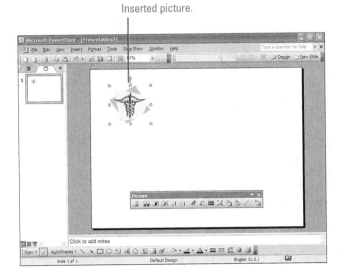

Inserting a Picture from a Scanner or Camera

If you have a scanner or digital camera connected to your computer, you can scan or download a picture, such as patient documents or photographs, into an Office document and you have the choice of storing it in the Clip Art Organizer. You can use a digital still or video camera, or a live Web camera. For a video or Web camera, you can capture an image and use it in an Office document. When you scan an image, you can use default or custom settings to scan and insert the image.

Insert a Picture from a Scanner or Camera

1. Click the Insert menu, point to Picture, and then click From Scanner Or Camera.

2. Click the Device list arrow, and then select the device connected to your computer.

3. Select the resolution (the visual quality of the image).

4. Select or clear the Add Pictures To Clip Organizer check box.

5. To use default settings, click Insert.

6. To specify your own settings to scan a picture or capture and select a camera image, click Custom Insert, and then follow the device instructions.

Customizing a scanned picture

3

Modifying Pictures

After you insert clip art or a picture, you can use the Picture toolbar to modify it. You can **crop**, or cut out, a section of the image. Cropping hides areas within a picture without eliminating them from the picture file. You can also add a border around a picture and change the picture's default colors to grayscale, black and white, or **washout**. Washout is a grayscale or pale hue version of an image that appears in the background of a page.

Crop a Picture

1. Click the picture or clip art image.

2. Click the Crop button on the Picture toolbar.

3. Drag the sizing handles until the borders surround the area you want to crop.

Did You Know?

You can reset a picture to original settings. Select the image, and then click the Reset Picture button on the Picture toolbar.

You can set an image color to transparent. Select the image, and then click the Set Transparent Color button on the Picture toolbar.

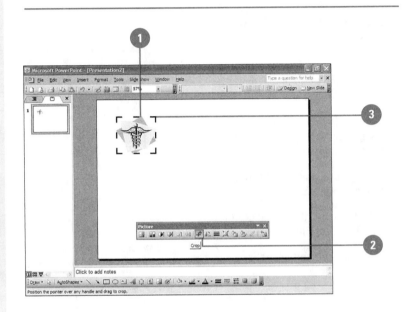

Add a Border Around a Picture

① Click the picture or clip art image.

② Click the Line Style button on the Picture toolbar.

③ Click the line style you want as a border around the picture.

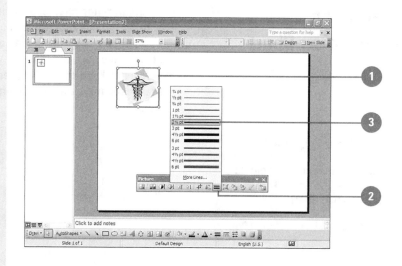

Choose a Color Type

① Click the object whose color type you want to change.

② Click the Color button on the Picture toolbar.

③ Click one of the Color options:

◆ Automatic (default coloring)

◆ Grayscale (whites, blacks, and grays)

◆ Black & White (white and black)

◆ Washout (whites and very light colors)

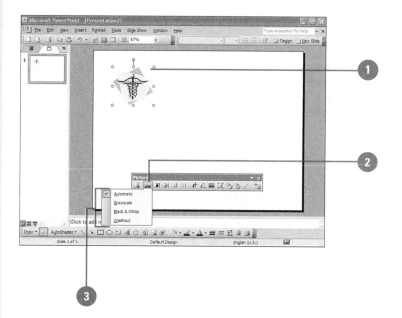

Did You Know?

You can change an image's brightness and contrast. Select the image, and then click the More Brightness or Less Brightness button on the Picture toolbar, or click the More Contrast or Less Contrast button on the Picture toolbar to achieve the desired effect.

Creating an Organization Chart

An **organization chart** shows the personnel structure in a hospital, company, or organization. You can create an organization chart, also known as an **org chart**, in any Office document. When you insert an org chart, **chart boxes** appear into which you enter the names and titles of personnel. Each box is identified by its position in the chart. For example, Managers are at the top, Subordinates are below, Coworkers are side to side, and so on.

Create a New Org Chart

1. Click the Insert menu, point to Picture, and then click Organization Chart.

2. Click a chart box, and then type a name.

3. Click the chart box to which you want to attach the new chart box.

4. Click the Insert Shape button list arrow on the Organization Chart toolbar, and then click a shape option.

5. When you're done, click anywhere outside the org chart to return to the Office document.

Did You Know?

You can edit an org chart. Double-click the organization chart, and then click the chart title or chart box you want to edit.

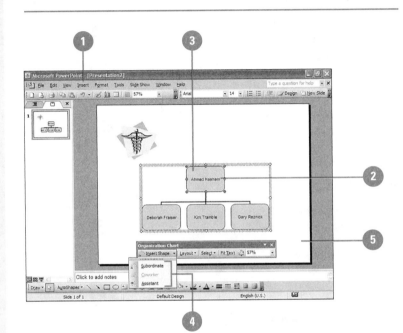

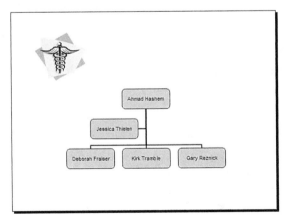

AutoFormat an Org Chart

1. Double-click the org chart, if necessary, to open the org chart.

2. Click the AutoFormat button on the Organization Chart toolbar.

3. Click an organization chart style.

4. Click OK.

5. When you're done, click anywhere outside the org chart to return to the Office document.

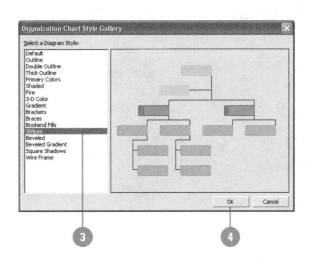

Change the Org Chart Layout

1. Double-click the org chart, if necessary, to open the org chart.

2. Click the Select button on the Organization Chart toolbar, and then click the selection option you want.

3. Click the Layout button on the Organization Chart toolbar, and then click a layout.

4. When you're done, click anywhere outside the org chart to return to the Office document.

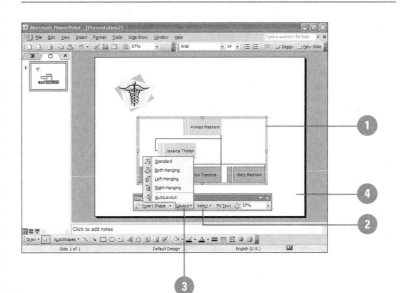

Creating a Diagram

A **diagram** is a collection of shapes that illustrates conceptual material. Office offers a variety of built-in diagrams from which to choose, including pyramid, cycle, radial, and Venn diagrams as well as organization charts. Using built-in diagrams makes it easy to create and modify charts without having to create them from scratch. You can customize different parts of the diagram the same way you modify the shapes you create using the Drawing toolbar.

Create a New Diagram

1. Click the Insert menu, and then click Diagram.

2. Select a diagram type.

3. Click OK.

4. Select a diagram element, and then use the Diagram toolbar to format the diagram with preset styles, add color and patterns, change line styles, add elements, and move them forward or backward.

5. When you're done, click anywhere outside of the diagram to return to the Office document.

> ### Did You Know?
>
> *You can edit a diagram.* Click the diagram, and then click the element you want to edit.
>
> *You can insert a diagram using the Drawing toolbar.* Click the Insert Diagram or Organization Chart button on the Drawing toolbar to insert a diagram.

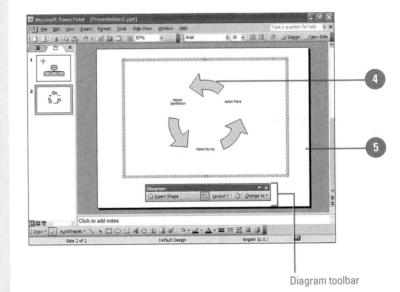

Diagram toolbar

Creating a Graph Chart

A **chart** is a graphical representation that makes numerical data, such as blood glucose levels of diabetic patients, more visual and easier to grasp. With Microsoft Graph Chart, you can create a chart in Office programs by entering your numbers and labels or by import data in the **datasheet**, a spreadsheet-like grid of rows and columns that holds your data in **cells** (intersections of rows and columns). Each **data series**, all the data from a row or column, has a unique color or pattern on the chart. The cell you select in the datasheet becomes the active cell, which appears with a heavy border. If you type data into a cell that already contains data, your entry replaces the active cell's contents.

Create a Graph Chart

1. Click where you want to insert the chart.

2. Start Microsoft Graph Chart.
   - Click the Insert menu, click Object, and then double-click Microsoft Graph Chart.
   - In Word, click the Insert menu, point to Picture, and then click Chart.
   - In PowerPoint, click the Insert menu, and then click Chart.

3. Click the datasheet's upper-left button to select all the cells, and then press Delete to erase the sample data.

4. Enter new data in each cell, or click the Import Data button on the Standard toolbar to insert data from another source, such as Excel.

5. Edit and format the data in the datasheet as you like.

6. Click the Close button on the datasheet to close it.

7. Click outside the chart to quit Microsoft Graph Chart and return to your Office document.

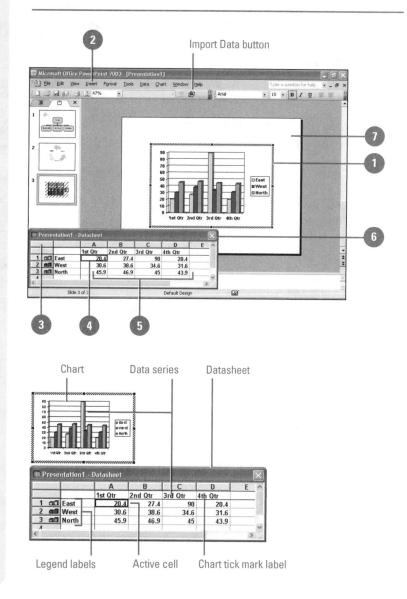

Import Data button

Chart   Data series   Datasheet

Legend labels   Active cell   Chart tick mark label

3

Modifying a Graph Chart

Once you enter data in the datasheet, you can easily modify and format the associated chart. Graph Chart comes with a gallery that lets you change the chart type and then format the chart to get the result that you want. There are 14 chart categories, each containing both two-dimensional and three-dimensional charts. To suit your needs, you can also format chart objects, individual elements that make up a chart, such as an axis, legend, or data series.

Change the Chart Type

1. Double-click the chart, if necessary, to open Graph Chart.

2. Click the Chart menu, and then click Chart Type.

3. Click the Standard Types or Custom Types tab.

4. Click a chart type, and then click a chart sub-type.

5. Click OK.

6. Click outside the chart to quit Microsoft Graph Chart and return to your Office document.

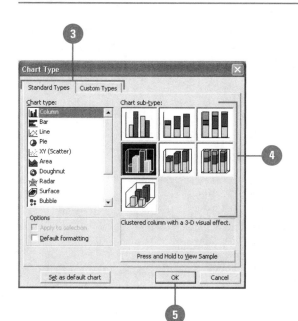

Did You Know?

You can edit a Graph chart. Double-click the Graph chart, and then click the datasheet or chart you want to edit.

Format a Chart Object

①	Double-click the chart, if necessary, to open Graph Chart.

②	Double-click the chart object you want to format, such as an axis, legend, or data series.

TROUBLE? *Click the Chart Objects button list arrow on the Standard toolbar, and then click the chart object you want to select.*

③	Click the tab (Patterns, Axis, Y Error Bars, Data Labels, or Options) corresponding to the options you want to change.

④	Select the options to apply.

⑤	Click OK.

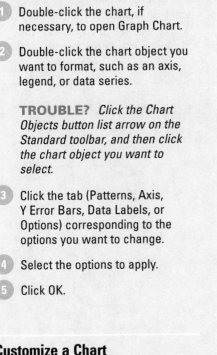

Customize a Chart

①	Double-click the chart, if necessary, to open Graph Chart.

②	Select the chart.

③	Click the Chart menu, and then click Chart Options.

④	Click the tab (Titles, Axes, Gridlines, Legend, Data Labels, or Data Table) corresponding to the chart object you want to customize.

⑤	Make your changes.

⑥	Click OK.

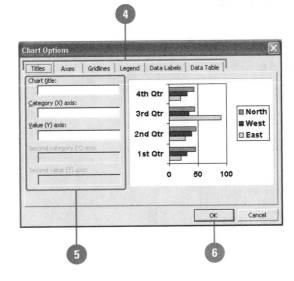

Managing Pictures

With Microsoft Office Picture Manager, you can manage, edit, and share your pictures. You can view all the pictures on your computer and specify which file type you want to open with Picture Manager. If you need to edit a picture, you can use Picture Manager to change brightness, contrast, and color, and to remove red eye. You can also crop, rotate and flip, resize, and compress a picture.

Open Picture Manager and Locate Pictures

1. Click the Start button, point to All Programs, point to Microsoft Office, point to Microsoft Office Tools, and then click Microsoft Office Picture Manager.

   The first time you start the program, it asks you to select the file types you want to open with Picture Manager. Select the check boxes with the formats you want, and then click OK.

2. Click Locate Pictures.

3. Click the Look In list arrow, and then click a drive location.

4. Click OK.

5. Use the View buttons to view your pictures.

6. When you're done, click the Close button.

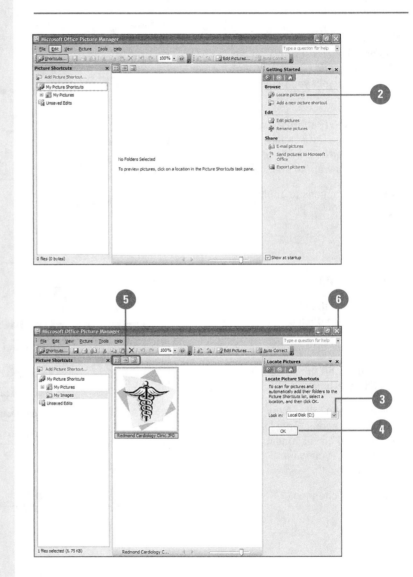

Did You Know?

You can export a folder of files with a new format or size. In Picture Manager, click the File menu, click Export, specify the folder with the pictures you want to change, select an export file format or select a size, and then click OK.

Edit Pictures

1. In Picture Manager, select the picture you want to edit.

2. Click the Edit Pictures button on the Standard toolbar.

3. Use the editing tools on the Edit Pictures task pane to modify the picture.

   ◆ Brightness And Contrast

   ◆ Color

   ◆ Crop

   ◆ Rotate And Flip

   ◆ Red Eye Removal

4. Use the sizing tools on the Edit Pictures task pane to change the picture size.

   ◆ Resize

   ◆ Compress Pictures

5. Click the Save button on the Standard toolbar.

6. When you're done, click the Close button.

Did You Know?

You can discard changes to a picture. If you don't like the changes you make to a picture, click the Edit menu, and then click Discard Changes to restore the picture.

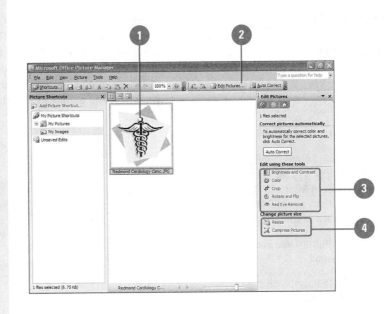

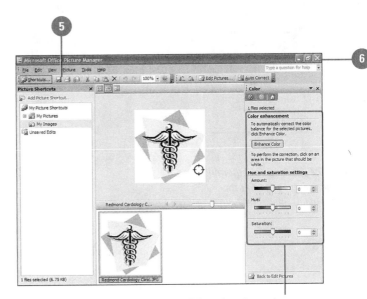

Color enhancing options

Sharing Pictures Using E-Mail

When you're done editing your pictures, you can share them with others using e-mail or the SharePoint Picture Library. When you send a picture using e-mail, Picture Manager opens your e-mail program and attaches the picture, where you can address and send the message. If you have an organization intranet with SharePoint services on a network server, you can share pictures using the SharePoint Picture Library.

Send a Picture in an E-Mail

1. Click the Start button, point to All Programs, point to Microsoft Office, point to Microsoft Office Tools, and then click Microsoft Office Picture Manager.

2. Select the picture you want to send via e-mail.

3. Click the Mail button on the Standard toolbar.

4. Select the settings you want.

5. Click Create Message to open Outlook and create a new message.

6. Address the e-mail, type a message, and then click Send.

See Also

See Chapter 20, "Working Together on Office Documents" on page 471 for information on using SharePoint services.

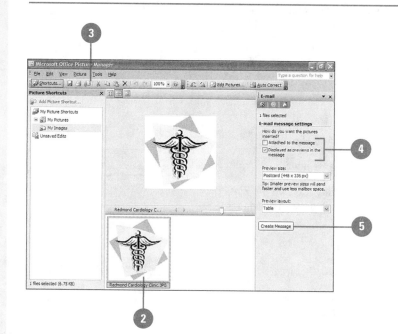

Creating a Document with Word

Introduction

Whether you're typing a carefully worded patient encounter summary, creating a professional research paper, or producing a promotional patient newsletter for your practice or department, Microsoft Office Word 2003 is the program for you. Word contains all the tools and features you need to produce interesting documents that say exactly what you mean and that have the look to match.

Microsoft Word is designed especially for working with text, so it's a snap to create and edit letters, reports, mailing lists, tables, or any other word-based communication. What makes Word perfect for your documents is its editing capabilities combined with its variety of views. For example, you can jot down your ideas in Outline view. Then switch to Normal view to expand your thoughts into complete sentences and revise them without retyping the entire page. When you're done revising the document, switch to Reading view to read and proof your work. Tools such as the Spelling and Grammar Checker and Thesaurus help you present your thoughts accurately, clearly, and effectively. Finally, in Print Layout view you can quickly add formatting elements, such as bold type and special fonts, to make your documents look professional.

Viewing the Word Window

Menu bar
The nine menus provide
access to all Word options.

Title bar
The document name and Microsoft
Word appear in the title bar.
Document1 is a temporary name
Word uses until you assign a new one.

Insertion point
The blinking
insertion point
(also called a
cursor) shows
you where the
next character
will appear.

**Standard and
Formatting
toolbars**
These and
other toolbars
contain buttons
that provide
quick access
to a variety of
commands
and features.

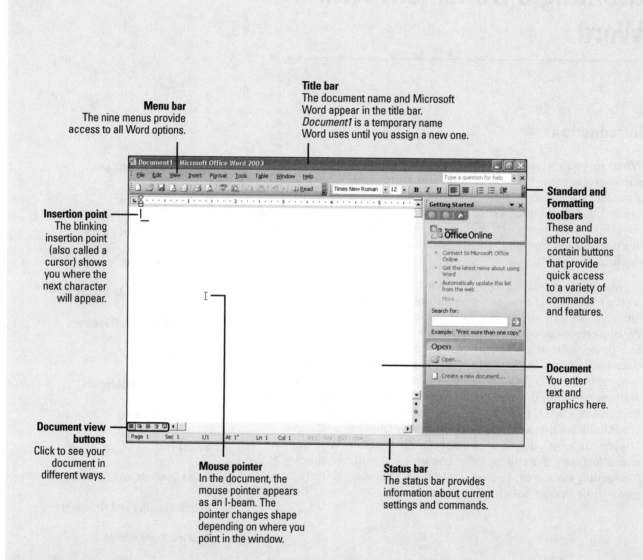

Document
You enter
text and
graphics here.

**Document view
buttons**
Click to see your
document in
different ways.

Mouse pointer
In the document, the
mouse pointer appears
as an I-beam. The
pointer changes shape
depending on where you
point in the window.

Status bar
The status bar provides
information about current
settings and commands.

Creating a Document

When you open a new Word document, it's blank, ready for you to enter text. By default, this document is titled Document1. You can create new documents in several ways: using the New command on the File menu, the New Blank Document button on the Formatting toolbar, and by the New Document task pane. Word numbers new documents consecutively. You can open and work on as many new documents as you'd like. The insertion point (blinking cursor bar) appears in the document where text will appear when you type. As you type, text moves, or **wraps**, to a new line when the previous one is full. You can move the insertion point anywhere within the document so that you can insert new text and **edit** (or insert, revise, or delete) existing text.

Create a Document

1. Click the File menu, and then click New.

2. Click Blank Document.

3. Click where you want to insert text, if necessary.

4. Begin typing, and then press Enter when you want to begin a new paragraph or insert a blank line.

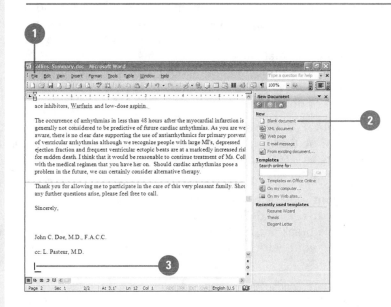

Edit Text in a Document

1. Click where you want to insert text, or select the text you want to edit.

2. Make the change you want:

   ◆ Type to insert new text.

   ◆ Press Enter to begin a new paragraph or insert a blank line.

   ◆ Press Backspace or Delete to erase text to the left or right of the insertion point.

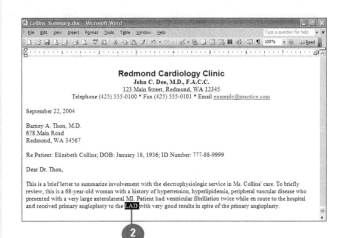

Changing Document Views

Word displays the contents of a document in different ways to help you work efficiently with your content. The available views include Normal, Web Layout, Print Layout, Outline, and Reading. You can change the window view from the View menu, or you can click a Document view button at the bottom left corner of the Word window.

Normal view displays the document as a single, long piece of "paper," divided into pages by perforation marks. Word displays each new document in Normal view by default. This view is fine for composition but inadequate for editing or previewing your work prior to printing or other publication.

Web Layout view displays the document as it will appear on the Web. You can save documents as HTML code to make Web content creation easy.

Print Layout view displays a gray gap between each page to clearly delineate where each actual page break occurs. This view is best for previewing your work before printing, and it

works well with the Zoom feature on the Standard toolbar to increase and decrease the page view size and display multiple pages of the same document simultaneously onscreen.

Outline view displays the document as an outline with headings and subheadings. When you shift to Outline view, each heading has a clickable plus or minus sign next to it to expand or collapse the content under the heading. You can drag a plus, or minus sign to move the heading and all of its associated text.

Reading Layout view displays the screen size and removes distracting screen elements to provide a more comfortable view to read your documents. You can also display the Thumbnail pane or the Document Map to quickly jump to different parts of your document.

Full Screen view displays the document using the entire screen without a window and toolbars. When you're done, you can use the Close Full Screen button on the toolbar. This view is only available on the View menu.

Normal view

Web Layout view

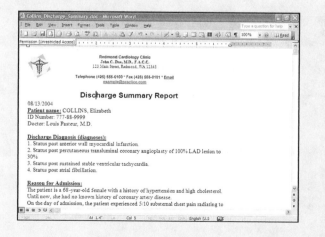

Print Layout view

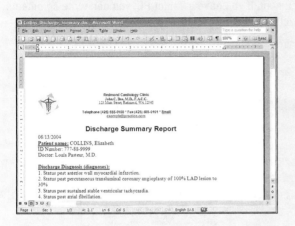

Print Layout view (with Zoom view)

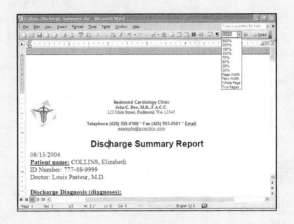

Outline view

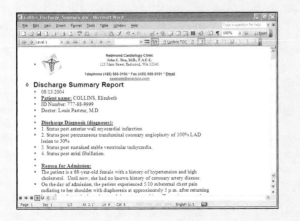

Reading Layout view

Reading a Document

You can avoid eye strain when you want to read a document with the Reading Layout view. The Reading Layout view is designed with tools optimized for reading a document. Word changes the screen size and removes distracting screen elements to provide a more comfortable view for reading your documents. In the Reading Layout view, you can display the Document Map or the Thumbnail pane to quickly jump to different parts of your document. If you have a Tablet PC, you can write comments and changes directly on the page using the tablet's stylus.

Read a Document

1. Click the Read button on the Standard toolbar.

   TIMESAVER *Press Alt+R to start reading.*

2. Click the Increase Text Size button or the Decrease Text Size button on the Reading Layout toolbar to display the text in a larger or smaller size.

3. Click the Allow Multiple Pages button or the Actual Page button on the Reading Layout toolbar to display two pages at once or a single page.

   TIMESAVER *Press Esc to deselect the document, type a number, and then press Enter to go to a page.*

4. When you're done, click the Close button on the Reading Layout toolbar.

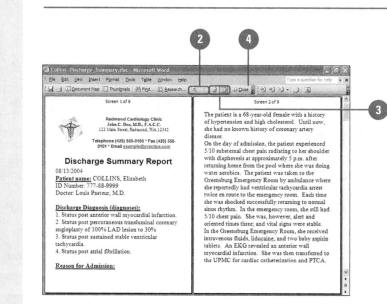

Did You Know?

You can highlight text and track changes in Reading Layout view. The Reviewing toolbar appears in Reading Layout view, where you can highlight text, track changes, insert comments, and use all the available commands.

Display Thumbnail View

① Click the Read button on the Standard toolbar.

② Click the Thumbnails button on the Reading Layout toolbar.

③ Click a thumbnail of a page to display the page.

④ Click the Thumbnails button on the Reading Layout toolbar again to turn it off.

⑤ When you're done, click the Close button on the Reading Layout toolbar.

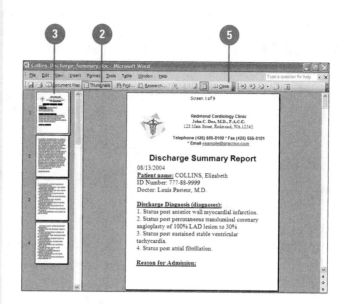

Display Document Map

① Click the Read button on the Standard toolbar.

② Click the Document Map button on the Reading Layout toolbar.

③ Click the part of the document you want to display.

④ Click the Document Map button on the Reading Layout toolbar again to turn it off.

⑤ When you're done, click the Close button on the Reading Layout toolbar.

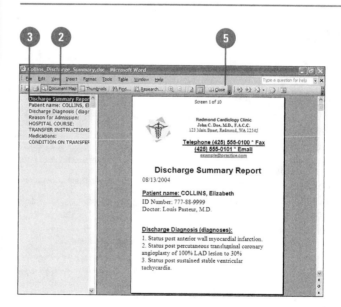

4

Working with Multiple Documents

Multiple open documents are handy if you want to refer to an old patient record or report or copy parts of one letter into another. You can view each document in its own window or all open documents in horizontally tiled windows. If you need to compare two documents, you can view them side by side and scroll through them at the same time. To view different parts of a document (convenient for summarizing a long report), you can split it into two windows that you view simultaneously but edit and scroll through independently.

Switch Between Documents

◆ Click the Word Document button on the taskbar you want to display.

◆ Click the Window menu, and then click the document on which you want to work.

Arrange Multiple Document Windows

1 Click the Window menu.

2 Click a window command.

◆ Arrange All to fit all open windows on the screen.

◆ Compare Side By Side With ..., click a document, and then click OK to tile two windows and scroll through both documents at the same time.

Did You Know?

You can move or copy text between documents. You can cut, copy, and paste text or drag text between two open windows or panes by having multiple windows open.

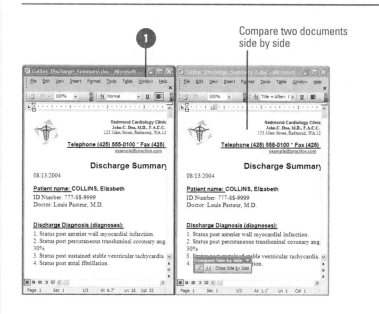

Compare two documents side by side

Work on Two Parts of the Same Document

1. Click the Window menu, and then click Split.

2. Drag the split bar until the two window panes are the sizes you want.

3. Click to set the split and display scroll bars and rulers for each pane.

4. Click to place the insertion point in each pane and scroll to the parts of the document you want to work on. Each pane scrolls independently. Edit the text as usual.

5. To return to a single pane, click the Window menu, and then click Remove Split.

Did You Know?

You can resize window panes. As you work in two parts of the same document, you can resize the window panes to fit your task. Drag the split bar between the two panes to resize the windows.

You can quickly change document interface settings. To change to a multiple document interface, click the Tools menu, click Options, click the View tab, and then clear the Windows In Taskbar check box.

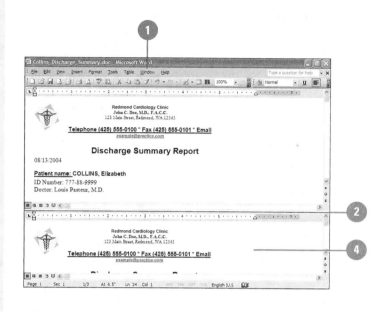

For Your Information

Working with Multiple Documents

When you create a new document, Word opens a separate instance of the document in a new window and displays an icon for that window on the taskbar. When Word creates new windows for each open document, it is a function of the single document interface. This feature was first introduced in Word 2000 so that users could easily navigate from Word to documents open in other programs. If you primarily work with several Word documents at the same time, you can turn off the single document interface and employ a multiple document interface. This enables you to shift between multiple documents in a single instance of Word using the Window menu. Each open document displays its own button on the Windows taskbar.

4

Moving Around in a Document

As your document gets longer, some of your work shifts out of sight. You can easily move any part of a document back into view. **Scrolling** moves the document line by line. **Paging** moves the document page by page. **Browsing** moves you through your document by the item you specify, such as to the next word, comment, picture, table, or heading. The tools described here move you around a document no matter which document view you are in.

Scroll, Page, and Browse Through a Document

◆ To scroll through a document one line at a time, click the up or down scroll arrow on the vertical scroll bar.

◆ To scroll quickly through a document, click and hold the up or down scroll arrow on the vertical scroll bar.

◆ To scroll to a specific page or heading in a document, drag the scroll box on the vertical scroll bar until the page number or heading you want appears in the yellow box.

◆ To page through the document one screen at a time, press Page Up or Page Down on the keyboard.

◆ To browse a document by page, edits, headings, or other items, click the Select Browse Object button, and then click that item. If a dialog box opens, enter the name or number of the item you want to find, and then click the Previous or Next button to move from one item to the next.

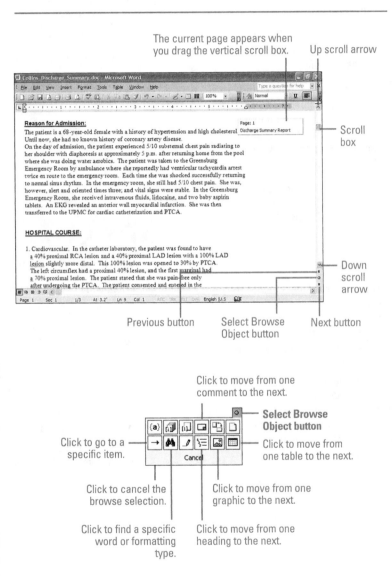

The current page appears when you drag the vertical scroll box.

Up scroll arrow

Scroll box

Down scroll arrow

Previous button

Select Browse Object button

Next button

Click to move from one comment to the next.

Select Browse Object button

Click to go to a specific item.

Click to move from one table to the next.

Click to cancel the browse selection.

Click to move from one graphic to the next.

Click to find a specific word or formatting type.

Click to move from one heading to the next.

Setting Up the Page

Every document you produce and print might need a different page setup. You can achieve the look you want by printing on a standard paper size (such as letter, legal, or envelope), international standard paper sizes, or any custom size that your printer accepts. The default setting is 8.5 x 11 inches, the most common letter and copy size. You can also print several pages on one sheet.

Set the Paper Size

① Click the File menu, and then click Page Setup.

② Click the Paper tab.

③ Click the Paper Size list arrow, and then select the paper size you want, or specify a custom size.

④ Select the paper source for the first page and other pages.

⑤ Click the Apply To list arrow, and then click This Section, This Point Forward, or Whole Document.

⑥ Verify your selections in the Preview box.

⑦ To make your changes the default settings for all new documents, click Default, and then click Yes.

⑧ Click OK.

Setting Up the Page Margins

Margins are the blank space between the edge of a page and the text. The default setting for Word documents is 1.25 inches on the left and right, and 1 inch on the top and bottom. You can use the mouse pointer to adjust margins visually for the entire document, or you can use the Page Setup dialog box to set precise measurements for an entire document or a specific section. You can also select the page orientation (portrait or landscape) that best fits the entire document or any section. **Portrait** orients the page vertically (taller than it is wide) and **landscape** orients the page horizontally (wider than it is tall). When you shift between the two, the margin settings automatically change. If you need additional margin space for binding pages into a book or binder, you can adjust the left or right gutter settings. Gutters allow for additional margin space so that all of the document text remains visible after binding. Unless this is your purpose, leave the default settings in place.

Adjust Margins Visually

1. Click the Print Layout View button.

2. Position the pointer over a margin boundary on the horizontal or vertical ruler.

3. Press and hold Alt, and then click a margin boundary to display the measurements of the text and margin areas as you adjust the margins.

4. Drag the left, right, top, or bottom margin boundary to a new position.

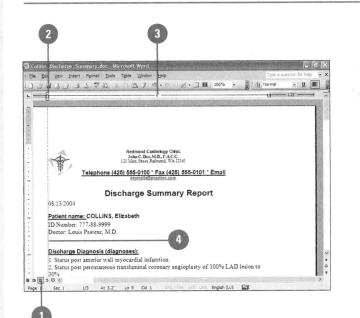

Did You Know?

You can turn off features not other-wise viewable in older versions. Click the Tools menu, click Options, click the Compatibility tab, click the Recommended Options For list arrow, and then click the version you want. Click to select the option check boxes you don't want, and then click OK.

Adjust Margins and Page Orientation Using Page Setup

1 Click the File menu, and then click Page Setup.

2 Click the Margins tab.

3 Type new margin measurements (in inches) in the Top, Bottom, Left, or Right boxes.

4 Click the page orientation you want.

5 Click the Apply To list arrow, and then click Selected Text, This Point Forward, or Whole Document.

6 To make the new margin settings the default for all new Word documents, click Default, and then click Yes.

7 Click OK.

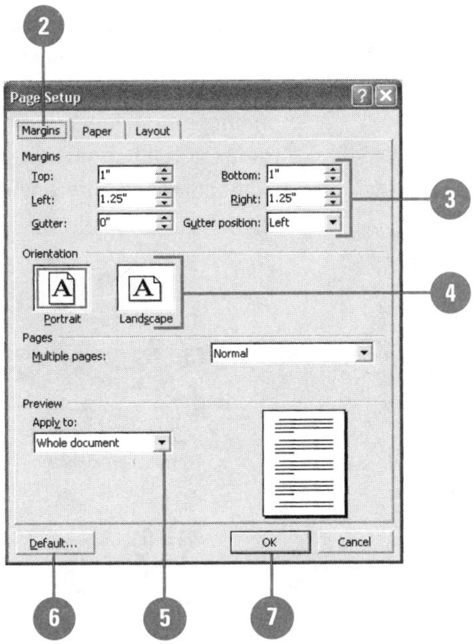

Did You Know?

You can preset gutter measurements.
To set the gutters for normal binding, display the Margins tab in the Page Setup dialog box, click the Multiple Pages list arrow, and then click Book Fold.

4

Creating an Outline

Outlines are useful for organizing information, such as topics in an essay. An outline typically consists of main headings and subheadings. You can create an outline from scratch in Outline view or change a bulleted or numbered list into an outline using the Bullets And Numbering command on the Format menu. In Outline view, you can use buttons on the Outlining toolbar or drag the mouse pointer to move headings and subheadings to different locations or levels.

Create an Outline from Scratch

1. In a new document, click the Outline View button.

2. Type each heading, and then press Enter.

3. To assign a heading to a different level and apply the corresponding heading style, place the insertion point in the heading, and then click the Promote or Demote button on the Outlining toolbar until the heading is at the level you want.

4. To move a heading to a different location, place the insertion point in the heading, and then click the Move Up or Move Down button on the Outlining toolbar until the heading is moved where you want it to go.

   The subordinate text under the heading moves with the heading.

5. When you're done, click the Normal view button.

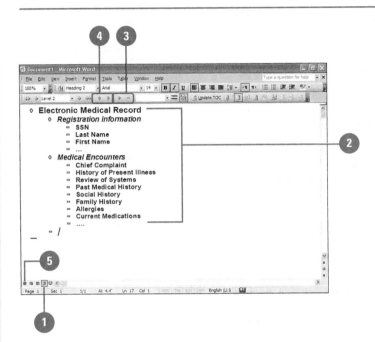

Did You Know?

You can create an outline in Normal view while you type. Click at the beginning of a line, type **1.**, press the Tab key, type a main heading, and then press Enter. You can type another main heading or press the Tab key to add a subheading under the main heading.

Selecting Text

The first step in working with text is to highlight, or **select**, the text you want. Once you've selected it, you can copy, move, format, and delete words, sentences, and paragraphs. When you finish with or decide not to use a selection, you can click anywhere in the document to **deselect** the text.

Select Text

1. Position the pointer in the word, paragraph, line, or part of the document you want to select.

2. Choose the method that accomplishes the task you want to complete in the easiest way.

   Refer to the table for methods to select text.

Did You Know?

AutoComplete finishes your words.
As you enter common text, such as your name, months, today's date, and common salutations and closings, Word provides the rest of the text in a ScreenTip. Press Enter to have Word complete your words.

Selecting Text	
To select	**Do this**
A single word	Double-click the word.
A single paragraph	Triple-click a word within the paragraph.
A single line	Click in the left margin next to the line.
Any part of a document	Click at the beginning of the text you want to highlight, and then drag to the end of the section you want to highlight.
A large selection	Click at the beginning of the text you want to highlight, and then press and hold Shift while you click at the end of the text that you want to highlight.
The entire document	Triple-click in the left margin.
An outline heading or subheading in Outline view	Click the bullet, plus sign, or minus sign.

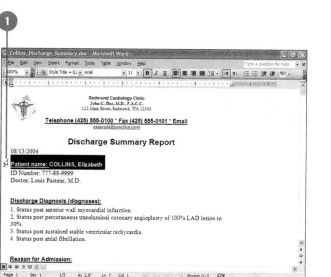

Inserting Symbols and AutoText

Word comes with a host of symbols and special characters for every need. Insert just the right one to keep from compromising a document's professional appearance with a hand-drawn arrow («) or missing mathematical symbol (å). **AutoText** stores text and graphics you want to reuse, such as commonly used medical phrases, a practice logo, boilerplate text, or formatted table. For example, you can use AutoText to quickly insert the text *Patient denies taking any prescription, OTC, herbal, or supplements* or a graphic of your signature. Use the AutoText entries that come with Word, or create your own.

Insert Symbols and Special Characters

1. Click the document where you want to insert a symbol or character.

2. Click the Insert menu, and then click Symbol.

3. Click the Symbols tab or the Special Characters tab.

4. To see other symbols, click the Font list arrow, and then click a new font.

5. Click a symbol or character.

6. Click Insert.

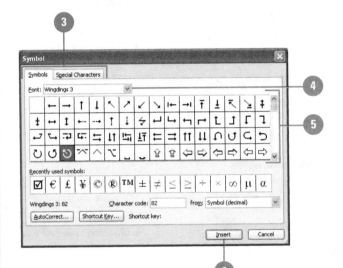

Did You Know?

You can assign a shortcut key to insert a symbol within the document. Click the Insert menu, click Symbol, click a symbol, click Shortcut Key, enter the shortcut key information requested, and then click Close.

Insert AutoText

1. Click where you want to insert AutoText.

2. Click the Insert menu, and then point to AutoText.

3. Point to an AutoText category.

4. Click the AutoText entry you want.

Did You Know?

You can use AutoText to store commonly used medical phrases. Follow the four steps outlined below.

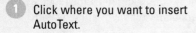

Create AutoText

1. Select the text or graphic in which you want to create an AutoText entry.

2. Click the Insert menu, point to AutoText, and then click New.

3. Type an AutoText name, or use the suggested one.

4. Click OK.

Did You Know?

You can delete an AutoText entry. Click the Insert menu, point to AutoText, click AutoText, select the AutoText entry you want to delete, click Delete, and then click OK.

You can use the AutoText toolbar for quick access. Click the View menu, point to Toolbars, and then click AutoText.

Checking Spelling and Grammar

As you type, a red wavy line appears under words not listed in Word's dictionary (such as misspellings or names) or duplicated words (such as *the the*). A green wavy underline appears under words or phrases with grammatical errors. You can correct these errors as they arise or after you finish the entire document. Before you print your final document, use the Spelling and Grammar checker to ensure that your document is error-free. You can also purchase and install a medical spell checker.

Correct Spelling and Grammar as You Type

1. Right-click a word with a red or green wavy underline.

2. Click a substitution, or click Ignore All (or Grammar) to skip any other instances of the word.

Did You Know?

You can purchase and add a medical spell checker. Several medical publishers offer medical spell checkers compatible with Microsoft Office Word 2003. See Chapter 23, "Healthcare Products to Enrich Your Office Experience," for more information.

Change Spelling and Grammar Options

1. Click the Tools menu, and then click Options.

2. Click the Spelling & Grammar tab.

3. Select or clear the spelling option check boxes you want.

4. Select or clear the grammar option check boxes you want.

5. If you want, click Settings, select or clear the advanced grammar and style option check boxes, and then click OK.

6. Click OK.

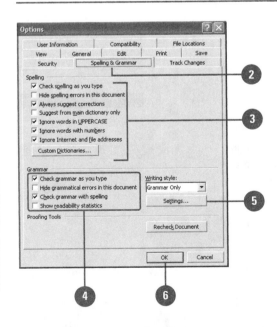

Correct Spelling and Grammar

1. Click at the beginning of the document or select the text you want to correct.

2. Click the Spelling And Grammar button on the Standard toolbar.

   As it checks each sentence in the document, Word selects misspelled words or problematic sentences and provides appropriate alternatives.

3. To check spelling only, clear the Check Grammar check box

4. Choose an option:

   - ◆ Click a suggestion, and then click Change to make a substitution.

   - ◆ Click Ignore Once to skip the word or rule, or click Ignore All or Ignore Rule to skip every instance of the word or rule.

   - ◆ If no suggestion is appropriate, click in the document and edit the text yourself. Click Resume to continue.

5. Click OK to return to the document.

Did You Know?

You can add a familiar word to your dictionary. Right-click the wavy line under the word in question, and then click Add To Dictionary.

You can hyphenate words. Click the Tools menu, point to Language, click Hyphenation, select the Automatically Hyphenate Document check box, and then click OK.

4

Finding the
Right Words

Repeating the same word in a document can reduce a message's effectiveness. Instead, replace some words with **synonyms**, words with similar meanings. Or find **antonyms**, words with opposite meanings. If you need help finding exactly the right word, use the shortcut menu to look up synonyms quickly or search Word's Thesaurus for more options. This feature can save you time and improve the quality and readability of your document. You can also install a thesaurus for another language.

Find a Synonym

1. Right-click the word for which you want a synonym.

2. Point to Synonyms.

3. Click the synonym you want to substitute.

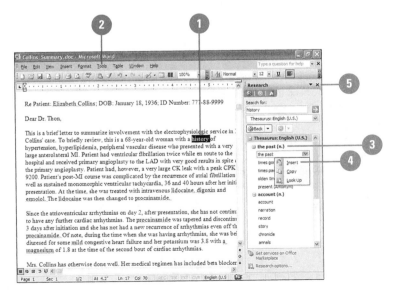

Click to open the Thesaurus and find other synonyms.

Use the Thesaurus

1. Select the word you want to look up.

2. Click the Tools menu, point to Language, and then click Thesaurus.

3. Click a word to find other synonyms.

4. Point to the word you want to use, click the list arrow, and then click Insert.

5. When you're done, click the Close button on the task pane.

Previewing a Document

Before printing, you should verify that the page looks the way you want. You save time, money, and paper by avoiding duplicate printing. Print Preview shows you exactly how your text will look on each printed page. This is especially helpful when you have a multi-page document divided into sections with different headers and footers. The Print Preview toolbar provides the tools you need to proof the look of each page.

Preview a Document

1. Click the Print Preview button on the Standard toolbar.

2. Preview your document.

   - To view one page at a time, click the One Page button.

   - To view multiple pages, click the Multiple Pages button, and then select the number of pages to view at a time.

   - To change the view size, click the Zoom list arrow to select a magnification percentage.

   - To shrink to fit a page, click the Shrink To Fit button to reduce the document to one page.

   - To display the full screen, click the Full Screen button to hide everything but the toolbar.

3. When you're done, click the Close Preview button on the Print Preview toolbar.

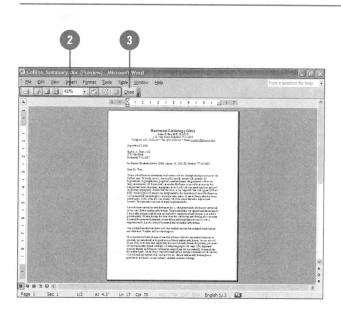

Did You Know?

You can edit while in Print Preview. Zoom the document to a closer view. Click the Magnify button on the Print Preview toolbar, click the document, and then edit as usual.

Printing a Document

Printing a paper copy is the most common way to share your documents. You can use the Print button on the Standard toolbar to print one copy of your document using the current settings, or you can open the Print dialog box to print your document and set how many copies to print, specify a series of pages to print, and choose what to print. Besides a document, you can also print comments, a list of styles used in the document, and AutoText entries. To review a long document on fewer pages, print multiple pages on one sheet with print zoom. The quality of print you achieve will be limited only by the quality of your printer or other output device, not by the limitations of the program itself.

Print All or Part of a Document

1. Click the File menu, and then click Print.

2. If necessary, click the Name list arrow, and then click the printer you want.

3. Type the number of copies you want to print.

4. Specify the pages to print:

   ◆ All prints the entire document.

   ◆ Current Page prints the page with the insertion point.

   ◆ Selection prints the selected text.

   ◆ Pages prints the specified pages.

5. Specify what you want to print.

6. Specify how many pages to print per sheet of paper, and then select the paper size to which to scale pages.

7. Click OK.

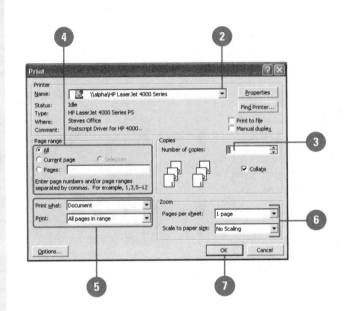

Formatting a Document with Word

Introduction

The text of your document is complete, but now you want others to notice your newsletter, think your document is professional, interesting, dynamic, or extraordinary. Try Microsoft Office Word 2003 to use extensive formatting features in order to lay out the information in your documents and create the exact look and mood you want.

Word documents are based on templates, which are pre-designed and preformatted files that serve as the foundation of the documents. Each template is made up of styles that have common design elements, such as coordinated fonts, sizes, and colors, as well as, page layout designs. Start with a Word template for memos, reports, fax cover pages, Web pages, and so on. Apply the existing styles for headings, titles, body text, and so forth. Then modify the template's styles, or create your own to better suit your needs. Make sure you get the look you want by adding emphasis using italics, boldface, and underline, changing text alignment, adjusting line and paragraph spacing, setting tabs and indents, and creating bulleted and numbered lists. When you're done, your document is sure to demand attention and convey your message in its appearance.

What You'll Do

Format Text for Emphasis

Format Text with Special Effects

Reveal Formatting

Find and Replace Formatting

Change Paragraph Alignment

Change Line Spacing

Display Rulers

Set Paragraph Tabs

Set Paragraph Indents

Change Character Spacing

Apply a Style

Create and Modify Styles

Create Bulleted and Numbered Lists

Insert New Pages and Sections

Add Headers and Footers

Insert Page Numbers and the Date and Time

Work with Templates

Hide Text

Formatting Text for Emphasis

You'll often want to format, or change the style of, certain words or phrases to add emphasis to parts of a document. **Boldface**, *italics*, <u>underlines</u>, highlights, and other text effects are toggle switches, which you simply click to turn on and off. For special emphasis you can combine formats, such as bold and italics. Using one **font**—a collection of characters, numbers, and symbols in the same letter design—for headings and another for main text adds a professional look to your document. You can also apply formatting effects to text, such as Strikethrough, Double Strikethrough, Superscript, Subscript, Shadow, Outline, Emboss, Engrave, Small Caps, All Caps, and Hidden.

Format Existing Text Quickly

1 Select the text you want to emphasize.

2 Click the Bold, Italic, Underline, or Highlight button on the Formatting toolbar.

You can add more than one formatting option at a time. For example, ***this text uses both boldface and italics.***

3 Click anywhere in the document to deselect the formatted text.

Change the Font or Size of Existing Text Quickly

1 Select the text you want to format.

2 Click the Font list arrow on the Formatting toolbar, and then click a new font.

3 Click the Font Size list arrow on the Formatting toolbar, and then click a new point size.

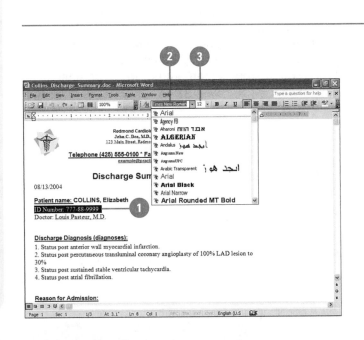

Highlight button

Apply Formatting Effects to Text

① Select the text you want to format.

② Click the Format menu, and then click Font.

③ Click the Font tab.

④ Click the formatting (Font, Font Style, Size, Font Color, Underline Style, and Underline Color) you want.

⑤ Click to select the effects (Strike-through, Double Strikethrough, Superscript, Subscript, Shadow, Outline, Emboss, Engrave, Small Caps, All Caps, and Hidden) you want.

⑥ Check the results in the Preview box.

⑦ To make the new formatting options the default for all new Word documents, click Default, and then click Yes.

⑧ Click OK.

Did You Know?

You can format text as you type. You can add most formatting options to text as you type. First select the formatting options you want, and then type the text. If necessary, turn off the formatting options when you're done.

You can use Word to format your document. Click the Format menu, and then click AutoFormat. Select a document type (General Document, Letter, Email) and indicate if you want to review each change, and then click OK.

Formatting Text with Special Effects

If you are using a document in an on-screen presentation, you can add animations effects to text. You can add animation effects, such as Las Vegas Lights, Marching Black Ants, and Sparkle Text to a title or heading. Animated effects appear only on the screen. When you select an animation, you can check the Preview box to make sure the animation is the one you want. When you printing a document with an animation effect, the text prints, but the animation does not. You can only apply one animation effect at a time.

Apply Special Effects to Text

1 Select the text you want to format.

2 Click the Format menu, and then click Font.

3 Click the Text Effects tab.

4 Click an animation.

5 Check the results in the Preview box.

6 To make the new formatting options the default for all new Word documents, click Default, and then click Yes.

7 Click OK.

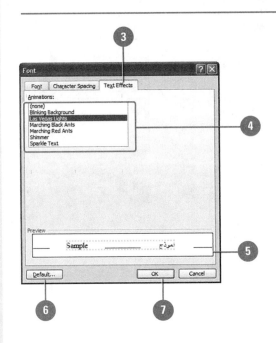

Did You Know?

You can view formatting marks.
Sometimes it's hard to see the number of spaces or tabs between words. You can change the view to display formatting marks, a period for space and an arrow for tabs. Click the Tools menu, click Options, click the View tab, select the formatting mark check boxes you want to view, and then click OK.

Revealing Formatting

Word uses wavy blue underlines to indicate possible instances of inconsistent formatting. If you see a wavy blue underline while formatting a document, you can open the Reveal Formatting task pane to display the format of selected text, such as its font and font effects. The Reveal Formatting task pane allows you to display, change, or clear formatting for the selected text. You can also select text based on formatting so that you can compare the formatting used in the selected text with formatting used in other parts of the documents.

Select or Clear Text Formatting

① Select the text whose formatting you want to select or clear away.

② Click the Format menu, and then click Reveal Formatting.

③ Point to the Selected Text box, click the down arrow, and then click either Select All Text With Similar Formatting or Clear Formatting.

   To apply formatting to surrounding text, click Apply Formatting Of Surrounding Text.

④ When you're done, click the Close button on the task pane.

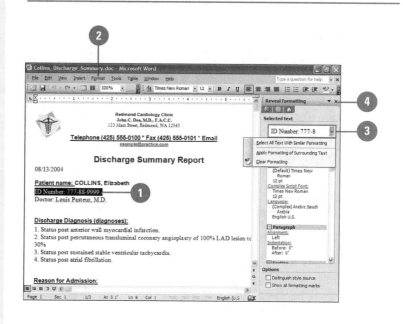

Compare Text Formatting

① Select the first instance of formatting you want to compare.

② Click the Format menu, and then click Reveal Formatting.

③ Select the Compare To Another Selection check box.

④ Select the second instance of formatting to compare.

⑤ When you're done, click the Close button on the task pane.

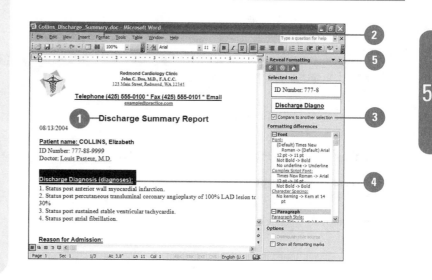

Finding and Replacing Formatting

Suddenly you realize all the bold text in your report would be easier to read in italics. Do you spend time making these changes one by one? No. The Find and Replace feature locates the formatting and instantly substitutes new formatting. If your search for a formatting change is an easy one, click Less in the Find And Replace dialog box to decrease the size of the dialog box. If your search is a more complex one, click More to display additional options. With the Match Case option, you can specify exact capitalization. The Go To tab quickly moves you to a place or item in your document.

Find Formatting

1. Click the Edit menu, and then click Find.

2. If you want to locate formatted text, type the word or words.

3. Click More, click Format, and then click the formatting you want to find.

4. Click Find Next to select the next instance of the formatted text.

5. Click OK to confirm Word finished the search.

6. Click Cancel.

Unless you search All, you may be asked whether to continue searching from the beginning of the document.

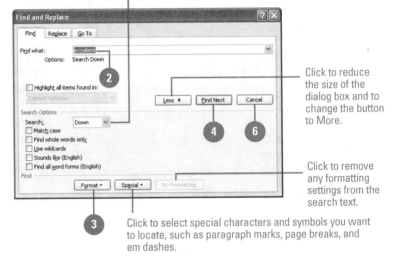

Click to reduce the size of the dialog box and to change the button to More.

Click to remove any formatting settings from the search text.

Click to select special characters and symbols you want to locate, such as paragraph marks, page breaks, and em dashes.

Find an Item or Location

1. Click the Edit menu, and then click Go To.

2. Click an item in the Go To What box.

3. Enter the item number or name.

4. Click Next, Previous, or Go To to locate the item.

5. When you're done, click Close.

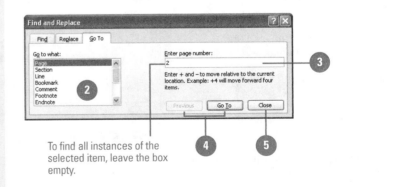

To find all instances of the selected item, leave the box empty.

Replace Formatting

1. Click the Edit menu, and then click Replace.

2. If you want to locate formatted text, type the word or words.

3. Click the More button, click Format, and then click the formatting you want to find. When you're done, click OK.

4. Press Tab, and then type any text you want to substitute.

5. Click Format, and then click the formatting you want to substitute. When you're done, click OK.

6. To substitute every instance of the formatting, click Replace All.

   To substitute the formatting one instance at a time, click Find Next, and then click Replace.

   If you want to cancel the replace, click Cancel.

7. If necessary, click Yes to search from the beginning of the document.

8. Click OK to confirm Word finished searching.

9. Click Close.

Did You Know?

You can find and replace special characters and document elements.
In Word, you can search for and replace special characters (for example, an em dash) and document elements (for example, a tab character). Click More in the Find And Replace dialog box, click Special, and then click the item you want from the menu.

Changing Paragraph Alignment

Text starts out positioned evenly along the left margin, and uneven, or **ragged**, at the right margin. Left-aligned text works well for body paragraphs in most cases, but other alignments vary the look of a document and help lead the reader through the text. **Right-aligned text**, which is even along the right margin and ragged at the left margin, is good for adding a date to a letter. **Justified text** spreads text evenly between the margins, creating a clean, professional look, often used in newspapers and magazines. **Centered text** is best for titles and headings. You can use Click-And-Type to quickly center titles or set different text alignment on the same line, or you can use the alignment buttons on the Standard toolbar to set alignment on one or more lines.

Align New Text with Click-And-Type

◆ Position the I-beam at the left, right, or center of the line where you want to insert new text.

When the I-beam shows the appropriate alignment, double-click to place the insertion point, and then type your text.

Click-And-Type Text Pointers

Pointer	Purpose
I	Left-aligns text
I	Right-aligns text
I	Centers text
I	Creates a new line in the same paragraph
I	Creates a text around a picture

Align Existing Text

① Position the I-beam, or select at least one line in each paragraph to align.

② Click the appropriate button on the Formatting toolbar.

◆ Align Left button

◆ Center button

◆ Align Right button

◆ Justify button

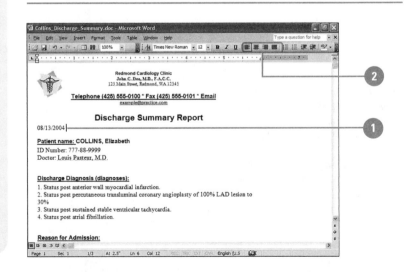

Changing Line Spacing

The lines in all Word documents are single-spaced by default, which is appropriate for letters and most documents. But you can easily change your document line spacing to double or 1.5 lines to allow extra space between every line. This is useful when you want to make notes on a printed document. Sometimes, you'll want to add space above and below certain paragraphs, for headlines, or indented quotations to help set off the text.

Change Line Spacing

1. Select the text you want to change.

2. On the Formatting toolbar, click the Line Spacing button list arrow, and then click a spacing option.

   ◆ To apply a new setting, click the number you want.

   TIMESAVER *Press Ctrl+1 for single-space, Ctrl+5 for 1.5 space, or Ctrl+2 for double-space.*

   ◆ Click More to enter precise parameters.

   ◆ To apply the setting you last used, click the Line Spacing button.

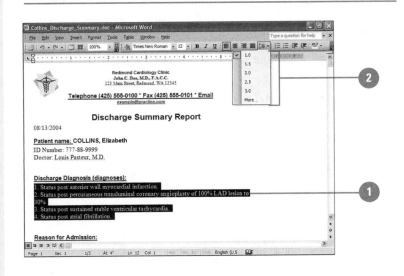

Change Paragraph Spacing

1. Choose the paragraph(s) whose spacing you want to change, and then select that text.

2. Click the Format menu, and then click Paragraph.

3. Click the Indents And Spacing tab.

4. Under the Spacing header, enter the custom spacing parameters you want both before and after the paragraph(s), and then click OK.

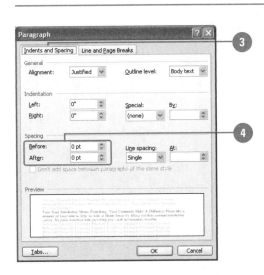

5

Displaying Rulers

Word rulers do more than measure. The **horizontal ruler** above the document shows the length of the typing line and lets you quickly adjust left and right margins and indents, set tabs, and change column widths. The **vertical ruler** along the left edge of the document lets you adjust top and bottom margins and change table row heights. You can hide the rulers to get more room for your document. As you work with long documents, use the document map to jump to any heading in your document. Headings are in the left pane and documents in the right.

Show and Hide the Rulers

1. Click the View menu, and then click Ruler.

   ◆ To view the horizontal ruler, click the Normal View button.

   ◆ To view the horizontal and vertical rulers, click the Print Layout View button.

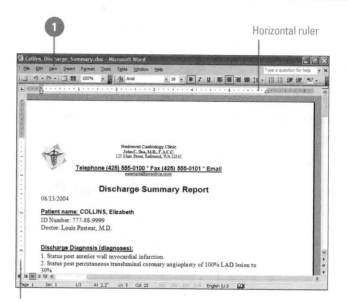

Horizontal ruler

Vertical ruler

Did You Know?

You can change the ruler measurements. Change the ruler to show inches, centimeters, millimeters, points, or picas. Click the Tools menu, click Options, click the General tab, click the Measurement Units list arrow, and then select the measurement you want.

You can set your text to be hyphenated. Hyphenation prevents ugly gaps and short lines in text. Click the Tools menu, point to Language, click Hyphenation, select the Automatically Hyphenate Document check box, set the hyphenation zone and limit the number of consecutive hyphens (usually two), and then click OK.

Setting Paragraph Tabs

In your document, **tabs** set how text or numerical data aligns in relation to the document margins. A **tab stop** is a predefined stopping point along the document's typing line. Default tab stops are set every half-inch, but you can set multiple tabs per paragraph at any location. Choose from four text tab stops: left, right, center, and decimal (for numerical data). The bar tab inserts a vertical bar at the tab stop. You can use the Tab button on the horizontal ruler to switch between the available tabs.

Create and Clear a Tab Stop

1. Select one or more paragraphs in which you want to set a tab stop.

2. Click the Tab button on the horizontal ruler until it shows the type of tab stop you want.

3. Click the ruler where you want to set the tab stop.

4. If necessary, drag the tab stop to position it where you want.

   To display a numerical measurement in the ruler where the tab is placed, press and hold Alt as you drag.

5. To clear a tab stop, drag it off the ruler.

> **Did You Know?**
>
> ***You can display tab characters.*** If you don't see a tab character, that looks like an arrow when you press Tab, click the Show/Hide ¶ button on the Standard toolbar.

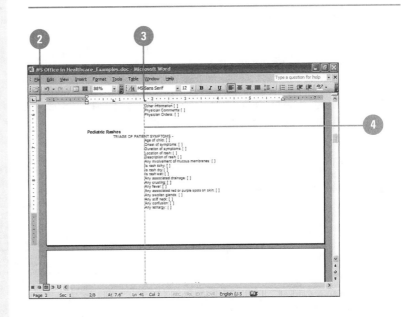

Tab Stops	
Tab Stop	**Purpose**
∟	Aligns text to the left of the tab stop
⅃	Aligns text to the right of the tab stop
⊥	Centers text on the tab stop
⊥·	Aligns numbers on the decimal point
I	Inserts a vertical bar at the tab stop

5

Setting Paragraph Indents

Quickly indent lines of text to precise locations from the left or right margin with the horizontal ruler. Indent the first line of a paragraph (called a **first-line indent**) as books do to distinguish paragraphs. Indent the second and subsequent lines of a paragraph from the left margin (called a **hanging indent**) to create a properly formatted bibliography. Indent the entire paragraph any amount from the left and right margins (called **left indents** and **right indents**) to separate quoted passages.

Indent Paragraph Lines Precisely

Click the paragraph or select multiple paragraphs to indent:

◆ To change the left indent of the first line, drag the First-line Indent marker.

◆ To change the indent of the second and subsequent lines, drag the Hanging Indent marker.

◆ To change the left indent for all lines, drag the Left Indent marker.

◆ To change the right indent for all lines, drag the Right Indent marker.

As you drag a marker, the dotted guideline helps you position the indent accurately. You can also press and hold Alt to see a measurement in the ruler.

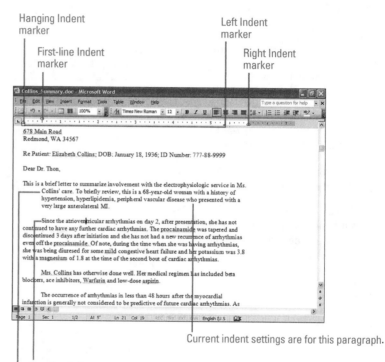

Current indent settings are for this paragraph.

Did You Know?

You can indent using the Tab key. You can indent the first line of a paragraph by clicking at the beginning of the paragraph, and then pressing Tab. You can indent the entire paragraph by selecting it, and then pressing Tab.

Indent a Paragraph

1 Click the paragraph, or select multiple paragraphs to indent.

2 Click the Increase Indent button or Decrease Indent button on the Formatting toolbar to move the paragraph right or left one-half inch.

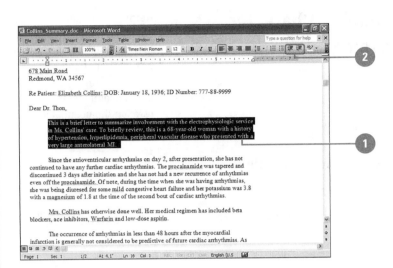

Set Indentation Using the Tab Key

1 Click the Tools menu, and then click AutoCorrect Options.

2 Click the AutoFormat As You Type tab.

3 Select the Set Left- And First-Indent With Tabs And Backspaces check box.

4 Click OK.

5

Changing Character Spacing

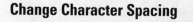

Kerning is the amount of space between each individual character that you type. Sometimes the space between two characters is larger than others, which makes the word look uneven. You can use the Font dialog box to change the kerning setting for selected characters. Kerning works only with TrueType or Adobe Type Manager fonts. You can expand or condense the character spacing to create a special effect for a title, or re-align the position of characters to the bottom edge of the text—this is helpful for positioning the copyright or trademark symbols.

Change Character Spacing

1. Select the text you want to format.

2. Click the Format menu, and then click Font.

3. Click the Character Spacing tab.

4. Click the Spacing list arrow, click an option, and then specify a point size to expand or condense spacing by the amount specified.

5. Click the Position list arrow, click an option, and then specify a point size to raise or lower the text in relation to the baseline (bottom of the text).

6. Select the Kerning For Fonts check box, and then specify a point size.

7. Check the results in the Preview box.

8. To make the new formatting options the default for all new Word documents, click Default, and then click Yes.

9. Click OK.

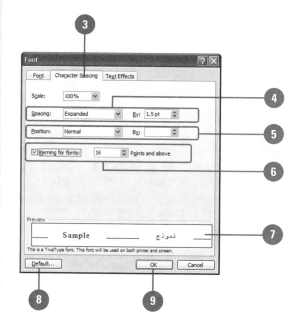

Applying a Style

The **Format Painter** copies and pastes formatting from one batch of selected text to another without copying the text. When you want to apply multiple groupings of formatting, save each as a style. A **style** is a collection of formatting settings saved with a name in a document or template that you can apply to text at any time. If you modify a style, you make the change once, but all text tagged with that style changes to reflect the new format.

Copy a Style with the Format Painter

1. Select the text with the formatting you want to copy.

2. Click the Format Painter button on the Standard toolbar.

3. Select the text you want to format with the Format Painter pointer.

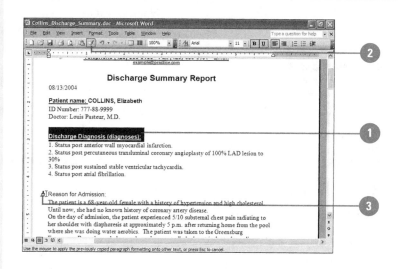

Apply a Style

1. Select the text to which you want to apply a style.

2. Click the Styles And Formatting button on the Formatting toolbar.

3. Click the style you want to apply.

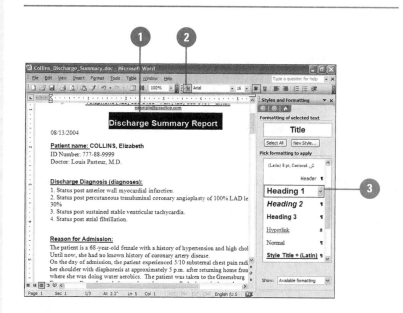

Did You Know?

Additional styles are available within a document. Open the Styles And Formatting task pane, click the Show list arrow, and then click All Styles.

You can also request a style by name. Click or type a style name in the Style box on the Formatting toolbar.

5

Creating and Modifying Styles

Word provides a variety of styles to choose from. But sometimes you need to create a new style or modify an existing one to get the exact look you want. When you create a new style, specify if it applies to paragraphs or characters, and give the style a short, descriptive name that describes its purpose so you and others recall when to use that style. A **paragraph style** is a group of format settings that can be applied only to all of the text within a paragraph (even if it is a one-line paragraph), while a **character style** is a group of format settings that is applied to any block of text at the user's discretion. To modify a style, adjust the formatting settings of an existing style.

Create a New Style

1. Select the text whose formatting you want to save as a style.

2. Click the Format menu, click Styles And Formatting, and then click New Style.

3. Type a short, descriptive name.

4. Click the Style Type list arrow, and then click Paragraph to include the selected text's line spacing and margins in the style, or click Character to include only formatting, such as font, size, and bold, in the style.

5. Click the Style For Following Paragraph list arrow, and then click the name of style you want to be applied after a paragraph with the new style.

6. To add the style to the document template, select the Add To Template check box.

7. Click OK.

8. When you're done, click the Close button on the task pane.

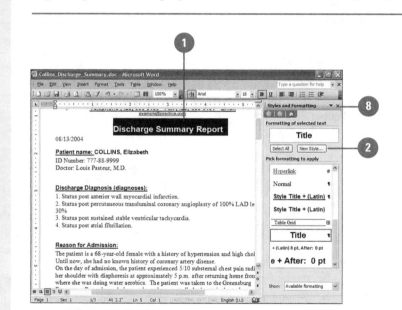

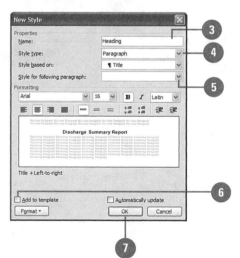

Modify a Style

1. Click the Format menu, and then click Styles And Formatting.

2. Click the style list arrow you want to modify.

3. Click Modify.

4. Click Format, and then click the type of formatting you want to modify:

   ◆ To change character formatting, such as font type and boldface, click Font.

   ◆ To change line spacing and indents, click Paragraph.

5. Select the formatting options you want.

6. Check the Preview box, and review the style description. Make any formatting changes necessary.

7. Click OK.

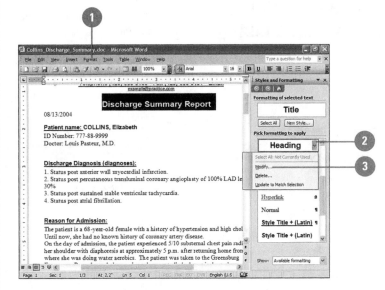

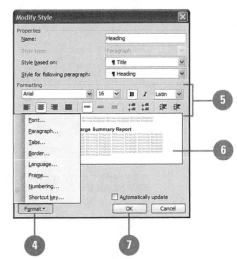

Did You Know?

You can save time by using the Styles feature. Once you format a document with styles, you can try different looks quickly. Modify each style, and then watch all text tagged with that style change automatically.

You can view different style lists. When looking at the list of styles in the Styles And Formatting task pane, you can select what types of styles to view from the Show list arrow: Available Formatting, Formatting In Use, Available Styles, and All Styles.

5

Creating Bulleted and Numbered Lists

The best way to draw attention to a list is to format the items with bullets or numbers. You can even create multi-level lists. For different emphasis, change any bullet or number style to one of Word's many predefined formats. For example, switch round bullets to check boxes or Roman numerals to lowercase letters. You can also customize the list style or insert a picture as a bullet. If you move, insert, or delete items in a numbered list, Word sequentially renumbers the list for you.

Create a Bulleted List

1. Click where you want to create a bulleted list.

2. Click the Bullets button on the Formatting toolbar.

3. Type the first item in your list, and then press Enter.

4. Type the next item in your list, and then press Enter.

5. Click the Bullets button on the Formatting toolbar, or press Enter again to end the list.

Create a Numbered List

1. Click where you want to create a numbered list.

2. Click the Numbering button on the Formatting toolbar.

3. Type the first item in your list, and then press Enter.

4. Type the next item in your list, and then press Enter.

5. Click the Numbering button on the Formatting toolbar, or press Enter again to end the list.

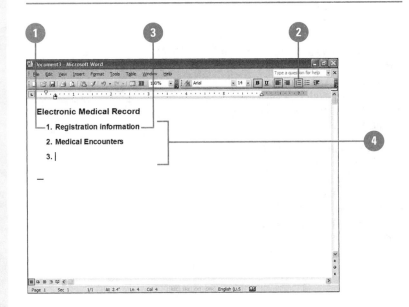

Change Bullet or Number Styles

1. Select the list, click the Format menu, and then click Bullets And Numbering.

2. Click the Bulleted tab or the Numbered tab.

3. Click a predefined format.

4. Click Customize to change the format style. You can change the Bullet (or Number) Position and Text Position options to specify where you want the bullet (or number) to appear and how much to indent the text.

5. To add a graphic bullet, click Picture, and then select the picture you want.

6. Click OK.

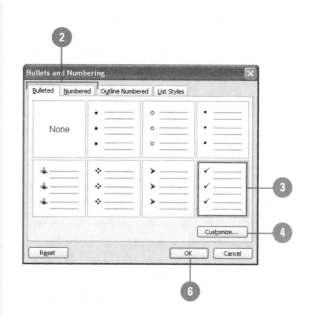

Create a Multi-Level Bulleted or Numbered List

1. Start the list as usual.

2. Press Tab to indent a line to the next level bullet or number, type the item, and then press Enter to insert the next bullet or number.

3. Press Shift+Tab to return to the previous level bullet or number.

4. End the list as usual.

> ### Did You Know?
>
> **You can quickly create a numbered list.** Click to place the insertion point at the beginning of a line, type **1.**, press the Spacebar, type the first item, and then press Enter. Press Enter or Backspace to end the list.

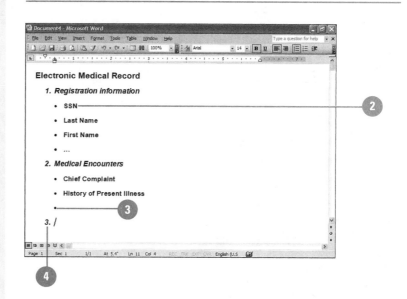

Inserting New Pages and Sections

When you fill a page, Word inserts a page break and starts a new page. As you add or delete text, this **soft page break** moves. A soft page break appears as a dotted gray line in Normal view. To start a new page before the current one is filled, insert a **hard page break** that doesn't shift as you edit text. A hard page break appears as a dotted gray line with the text *Page Break* centered in Normal view. A **section** is a mini-document within a document that stores margin settings, page orientation, page numbering, and so on. In Page Layout view, you can show or hide the white space on the top and bottom of each page and the gray space between pages.

Insert and Delete a Hard Page Break

1. Click where you want to insert a hard page break.

2. Click the Insert menu, and then click Break.

   TIMESAVER *Press Ctrl+Enter to insert a page break.*

3. Click the Page Break option.

4. Click OK, and the page break appears.

5. To delete a page break, click the page break in Normal view, and then press the Delete key.

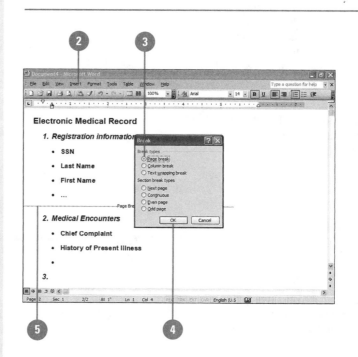

Did You Know?

You can move a page or section break. Click the View menu, click Normal to switch to Normal view, select the break you want to move, and then drag the break to its new location and release the mouse button.

You can opt to start a new line, but not a new paragraph. Insert a text wrapping break to force text to the next line in the same paragraph—the perfect tool to make a phrase fall on one line. Press Shift+Enter where you want to insert a text wrapping break.

Insert and Delete a Section Break

1. Click where you want to insert a section break.

2. Click the Insert menu, and then click Break.

3. Click the type of section break you want.

   ◆ **Next Page.** Starts the section on a new page.

   ◆ **Continuous.** Starts the section wherever the point is located.

   ◆ **Even Page.** Starts the section on the next even-numbered page.

   ◆ **Odd Page.** Starts the section on the next odd-numbered page.

4. Click OK.

5. To delete a section break, click the section break in Normal view, and then press Delete.

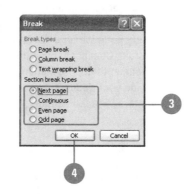

Show or Hide White Space Between Pages

1. Click the Print Layout button.

2. Scroll to the bottom of a page, and then point to the gap between two pages. (The Hide White Space cursor or Show White Space cursor appears.)

3. Click the gap between the pages to show or hide the white space.

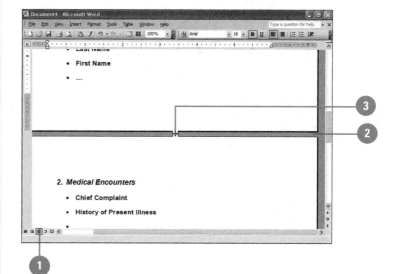

Adding Headers and Footers

Most books, including this one, use headers and footers to help you keep track of where you are. A **header** is text printed in the top margin of every page within a document. **Footer** text is printed in the bottom margin. Commonly used headers and footers contain your name, the document title, the filename, the print date, and page numbers. If you divide your document into sections, you can create different headers and footers for each section.

Create and Edit Headers and Footers

1. Click the View menu, and then click Header And Footer.

2. If necessary, click the Switch Between Header And Footer button on the Header And Footer toolbar to display the footer text area.

3. Click the header or footer box, and then type the text you want.

4. To insert common phrases, click the Insert AutoText button on the Header And Footer toolbar, and then click the text you want.

5. Edit and format header or footer text as usual.

6. When you're done, click the Close button on the Header And Footer toolbar.

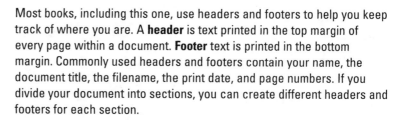

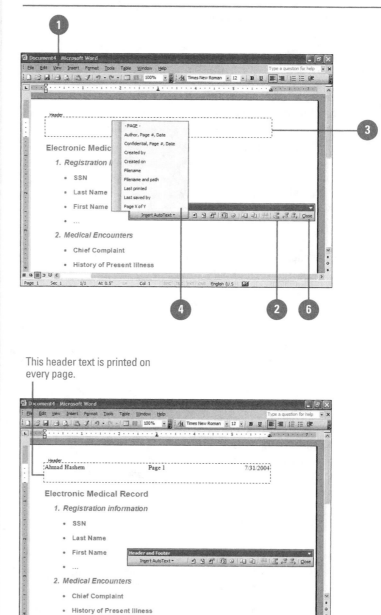

This header text is printed on every page.

Did You Know?

There are default tab stops used to align header and footer text. Headers and footers have two default tab stops. The first, in the middle, centers text. The second, on the far right, aligns text on the right margin. To left align text, don't press Tab. You can add and move the tab stops as needed. In addition, you can use the alignment buttons on the Formatting toolbar.

Create Different Headers and Footers for Different Pages

1. Click the View menu, and then click Header And Footer.

2. Click the Page Setup button on the Header And Footer toolbar.

3. Click the Layout tab.

4. To create different headers or footers for odd and even pages, click to select the Different Odd And Even check box.

   To create a unique header or footer for the document's first page, click to select the Different First Page check box.

5. Click OK.

6. Click the Show Previous and Show Next buttons to move from one header to the next; enter and format the text in the remaining headers and footers.

   To move between the header and footer, click the Switch Between Header And Footer button.

7. Click the Close button on the Header And Footer toolbar.

Did You Know?

There is a format difference between even and odd pages. As in books, odd pages appear on the right, and even pages appear on the left.

You can add a graphic to either a header or footer, such as a practice logo. Click the header or footer to position the insertion point, click the Insert menu, click Picture, and then click the type of file and the location of the file on the submenus that follow.

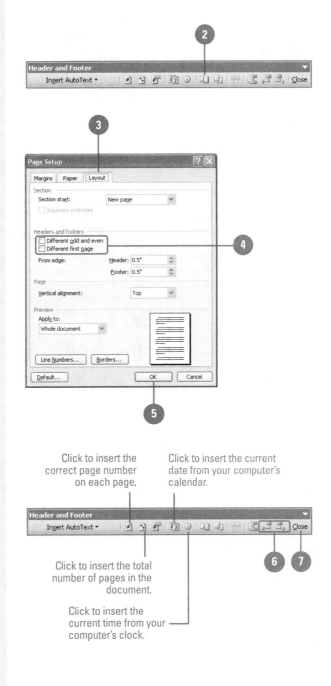

Click to insert the correct page number on each page.

Click to insert the current date from your computer's calendar.

Click to insert the total number of pages in the document.

Click to insert the current time from your computer's clock.

5

Inserting Page Numbers and the Date and Time

Page numbers help you keep your document in order or find a topic from the table of contents. Number the entire document consecutively or each section independently; pick a numbering scheme, such as roman numerals or letters. When you insert page numbers, you can select the position and alignment of the numbers on the page. The date and time field ensures you know which printout is the latest. Word uses your computer's internal calendar and clock as its source. You can insert the date and time for any installed language. Add page numbers and the date in a footer to conveniently keep track of your work.

Insert Page Numbers

1. Click the Insert menu, and then click Page Numbers.

2. Click the Position list arrow, and select a location.

3. Click the Alignment list arrow, and then select the horizontal placement.

4. Click Format.

5. Click the Number Format list arrow, and then select a numbering scheme.

6. Select the starting number.

7. Click OK.

8. Click OK.

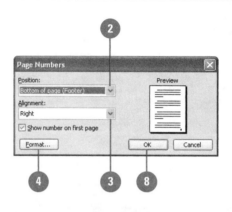

Did You Know?

You can format page numbers in headers and footers. Click the View menu, click Header And Footer, select the text you want to format in the header or footer, and then use the formatting tools on the Formatting toolbar to customize the text.

Insert the Date or Time

1. Click the Insert menu, and then click Date And Time.

2. If necessary, click the Language list arrow, and then select a language.

3. Select the Update Automatically check box.

4. Click the date and time format you want.

5. Click OK.

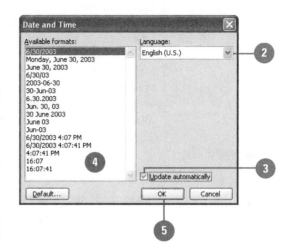

Did You Know?

You can set the current date and time as the default. In the Date And Time dialog box, click the Default button, and then click Yes.

5

Working with Templates

When you start Word, a blank document opens based on a default template. The default template defines the page margins, default font, and other settings. Instead of using the default template, you can create your own template. A custom template can store text, styles, formatting, macros, and page information for use in other documents. Start with a predefined Word template, or use one you created. Quickly try a new look by attaching a different template to your current document. The attached template's styles replace the styles in your document.

Save a Document as a Template

1. Open a new or existing document.

2. Add any text, graphics, and formatting you want to appear in all documents based on this template. Adjust margin settings and page size, and create new styles as necessary.

3. Click the File menu, and then click Save As.

4. Click the Save As Type list arrow, and then click Document Template.

5. Make sure the Templates folder (usually located in the Microsoft Office folder in the Programs folder) or one of its subfolders appears in the Save In box.

6. Type a name for the new template.

7. Click Save.

   You can open the template and make and save other changes just as you would in any other document.

See Also

See "Creating a New File" on page 8 for information on creating a new file using a template.

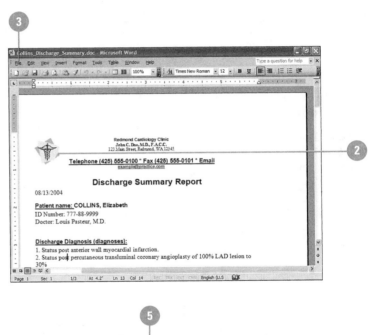

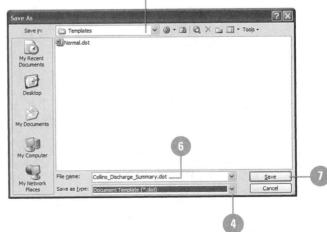

Attach a Template to an Existing Document

1. Open the document to which you want to apply a new template.

2. Click the Format menu, click Theme, and then click Style Gallery.

3. Click a template name to preview it.

4. Click OK to add the template styles to the document.

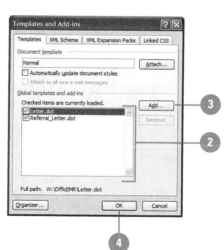

Click the option you want to see in the Preview box.

Load an Add-In

1. Click the Tools menu, and then click Templates And Add-Ins.

2. Click the add-in you want to load.

3. To add one to the list, click Add, switch to the folder that contains the add-in, click the Files Of Type list arrow, select Word Add-Ins, click the add-in, and then click Click OK.

4. Click OK.

Did You Know?

You are probably using the Normal template. By default, all Word documents use the Normal template, which formats text in 12-point Times New Roman and offers three different heading styles.

Hiding Text

If you have confidential information in a document or text that you don't want others to see, you can hide the text. When you hide text, you can't view or print the text unless you select the Hidden Text option in the Options dialog box. When you display or print hidden text, the characters appear with a dotted lined underneath. Hiding text does not protect your text from being seen, but it does conceal it from others.

Hide or Unhide Text

1. Select the text you want to hide or the hidden text.

2. Click the Format menu, and then click Font.

3. Click the Font tab.

4. Select or clear the Hidden check box.

5. Click OK.

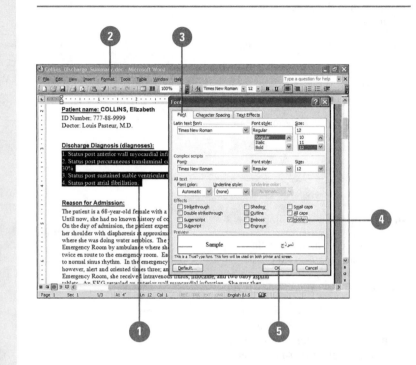

Display or Print Hidden Text

1. Click the Tools menu, and then click Options.

2. Click the View tab.

3. Select the Hidden Text check box.

4. Click the Print tab.

5. Select the Hidden Text check box.

6. Click OK.

Enhancing a Document with Word

Introduction

Once you've mastered the basics, Microsoft Office Word 2003 has plenty of advanced features to enhance your documents. Whether it's a single-page patient flyer or a twenty-page scientific report, you can arrange the text and add enhancements that make your document appealing and easy to read.

After you create your basic document, consider how you can improve its appearance and communicate its message more effectively. For example, if your document is a brochure or newsletter, arrange the text in columns and add an enlarged capital letter to the first word in each paragraph to convey expertise and quality. Or organize information in a table to draw attention to important data or clarify the details of a complicated paragraph.

Another way to impress patients, business associates, social groups, or even family members is to create personalized form letters for any occasion—an upcoming meeting, a holiday greeting, or an important announcement. Create a formatted document and enter text that doesn't change. Any data that changes from person to person (such as names) goes into another file, which you merge with the form letter. In a snap, you've got personalized letters that show you care.

What You'll Do

Add Desktop Publishing Effects

Arrange Text in Columns

Create a Table

Enter Text in a Table

Modify a Table

Adjust Table Cells

Format a Table

Create a Form Letter

Create Labels

Address Envelopes and Labels

Insert a Table of Contents

Create Multiple Document Versions

Modify the Document Summary

Protect a Document

Adding Desktop Publishing Effects

A few simple elements—drop caps, borders, and shading—make your newsletters and brochures look like a professional produced them. A **drop cap** is the enlarged first letter of a paragraph. **Borders** are lines or graphics that appear around a page, paragraph, selected text, or table cells. For borders, you can change the line style, width, and colors, and you can add shadows and 3D effects. **Shading** is a color that fills the background of selected text, paragraphs, or table cells. For more attractive pages, add clips or columns.

Add a Dropped Capital Letter

1. Click the Print Layout View button.

2. Click the paragraph where you want the drop cap.

3. Click the Format menu, and then click Drop Cap.

4. Click a drop cap position.

5. Change the drop cap font.

6. Change the drop cap height.

7. Enter the distance between the drop cap and paragraph.

8. Click OK.

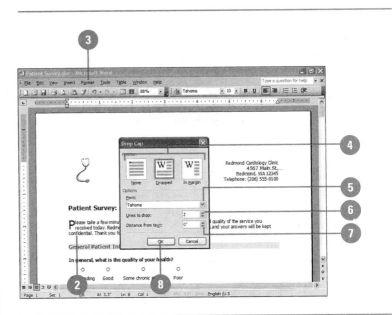

Add Shading

1. Select the text you want to shade.

2. Click the Format menu, and then click Borders And Shading.

3. Click the Shading tab.

4. Click a color.

5. Select a color style percentage.

6. Click OK.

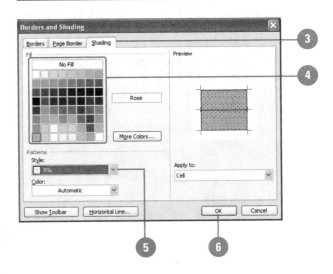

Add a Page Border

1. Click the Format menu, click Borders And Shading, and then click the Page Border tab.

2. Click a box setting.

3. Click a line style or click the Art list arrow, and then select a line or art style.

4. Enter a border width.

5. Select the pages you want to have borders.

6. Click OK.

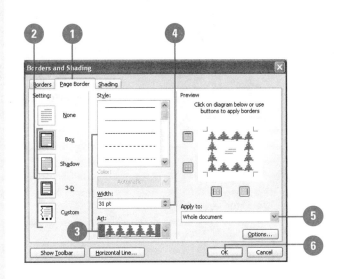

Add Borders

1. Select the text you want to have a border.

2. Click the Format menu, and then click Borders And Shading.

3. Click the Borders tab.

4. Click a box setting.

5. Click a border style.

6. Select a border width.

7. Click OK.

Did You Know?

You can add a border quickly. Click the Border button on the Formatting toolbar, and then select a common border.

You can use the Tables And Border toolbar to modify borders. Click the View menu, point to Toolbar, and then click Tables And Borders.

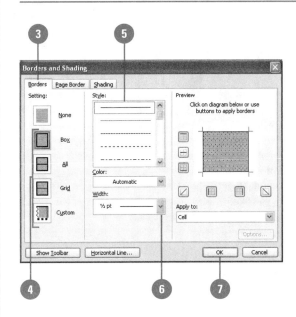

6

Arranging Text in Columns

Newspaper-style columns can give newsletters and brochures a more polished look. You can format an entire document, selected text, or individual sections into columns. You can create one, two, or three columns of equal size. You can also create two columns and have one column wider than the other. Word 2003 fills one column with text before the other, unless you insert a column break. **Column breaks** are used in two-column layouts to move the text after the insertion point to the top of the following column. You can also display a vertical line between the columns. To view the columns side by side, switch to print layout view.

Create Columns

1. Click the Print Layout View button.

2. Select the text you want to arrange in columns.

3. Click the Columns button on the Standard toolbar.

4. Drag to select the number of columns you want.

Did You Know?

You can remove columns quickly. Select the columns, click the Columns button on the Standard toolbar, and then click the first column.

You can align text in a column. Click the Align Left, Center, Align Right, or Justify button on the Formatting toolbar to align paragraphs in columns.

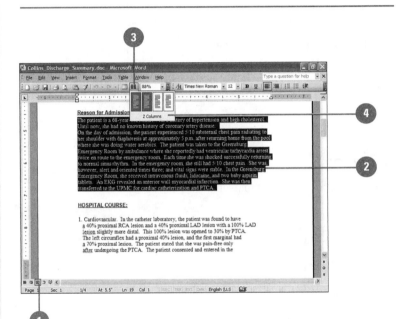

Modify Columns

1. Click the Print Layout View button, and then click in the columns you want to modify.

2. Click the Format menu, and then click Columns.

3. Click a column format.

4. If necessary, enter the number of columns you want.

5. Enter the width and spacing you want for each column.

6. To place a vertical line between columns, select the Line Between check box.

7. Click OK.

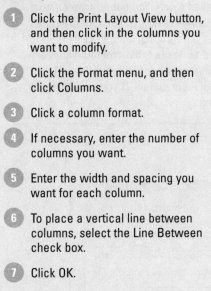

Insert a Column Break

1. Click where you want to insert a column break.

2. Click the Insert menu, and then click Break.

3. Click the Column Break option.

4. Click OK.

5. To delete a column break, click the page break in Normal view, and then press the Delete key.

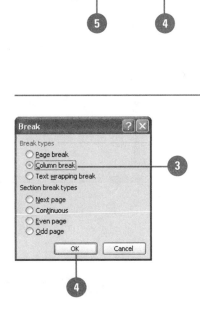

6

Creating a Table

A **table** organizes information neatly into rows and columns. The intersection of a row and a column is called a **cell**. You can draw a custom table with various sized cells and then enter text, or you can create a table from existing text separated by paragraphs, tabs, or commas. In addition, now you can create **nested tables** (a table created within a table cell), **floating tables** (tables with text wrapped around them), or **side-by-side** tables (separate but adjacent tables). If you decide not to use a table, you can convert it to text.

Draw a Custom Table

1. Click the View menu, point to Toolbars, and then click Tables And Borders.

2. Click the Draw Table button on the Tables And Borders toolbar to select it.

3. Draw the table.

   ◆ A rectangle creates individual cells or the table boundaries.

   ◆ Horizontal lines create rows.

   ◆ Vertical lines create columns.

   ◆ Diagonal lines split cells.

4. If necessary, press and hold Shift, and then click one or more lines to erase them.

Create a Table from Existing Text

1. Select the text for the table.

2. Click the Table menu, point to Convert, and then click Text To Table.

3. Enter the number of columns.

4. Select a column width option.

5. Click a symbol to separate text into cells.

6. Click OK.

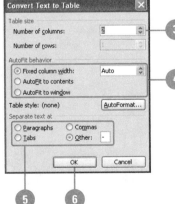

Entering Text in a Table

Once you create your table, you enter text into cells just as you would in a paragraph, except pressing Tab moves you from cell to cell. As you type in a cell, text wraps to the next line, and the height of a row expands as you enter text that extends beyond the column width. The first row in the table is good for column headings, whereas the left-most column is good for row labels. Before you can modify a table, you need to know how to select the rows and columns of a table.

Enter Text and Move Around a Table

1 The insertion point shows where text that you type will appear in a table. After you type text in a cell:

◆ Press Enter to start a new paragraph within that cell.

◆ Press Tab to move the insertion point to the next cell to the right (or to the first cell in the next row).

◆ Press the arrow keys or click in a cell to move the insertion point to a new location.

Press Tab to move to the next cell.

Press Tab to move to the first cell in the next row.

Type and format text just as you would in a paragraph.

Press Tab to create a new row.

Select Table Elements

Refer to this table for methods of selecting table elements, including:

◆ The entire table

◆ One or more rows and columns

◆ One or more cells

Did You Know?

You can delete contents within a cell. Select the cells whose contents you want to delete, and then press Backspace or Delete.

Selecting Table Elements

To Select	Do This
The entire table	Click ⊞ next to the table, or click anywhere in the table, click the Table menu, point to Select, and then click Table.
One or more rows	Click in the left margin next to the first row you want to select, and then drag to select the rows you want.
One or more columns	Click just above the first column you want to select, and then drag with ↓ to select the columns you want.
The column or row with the insertion point	Click the Table menu, point to Select, and then click Column or Row.
A single cell	Drag a cell or click the cell with ➦.
More than one cell	Drag with ➦ to select a group of cells.

6

Modifying a Table

As you begin to work on a table, you might need to modify its structure by adding more rows, columns, or cells to accommodate new text, graphics, or other tables. The table realigns as needed to accommodate the new structure. When you insert rows, columns, or cells, the existing rows shift down, the existing columns shift right, and you choose what direction the existing cells shift. Similarly, when you delete unneeded rows, columns, or cells from a table, the table realigns itself.

Insert Additional Rows

1. Select the row above which you want the new rows to appear.

2. Drag to select the number of rows you want to insert.

3. Click the Table menu, point to Insert, and then click Rows Above or Rows Below.

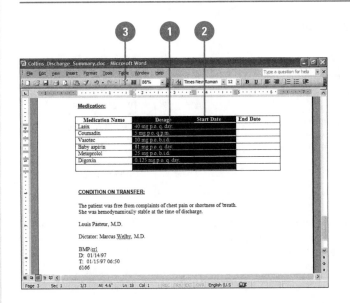

Insert Additional Columns

1. Select the column to the left of which you want the new columns to appear.

2. Drag to select the number of columns you want to insert.

3. Click the Insert Columns button on the Standard toolbar.

Did You Know?

You can choose what direction existing rows or columns shift. Decide where the new rows and columns appear in your table. Click the Table menu, point to Insert, and then click Columns To The Left, Columns To The Right, Rows Above, or Rows Below.

Insert Additional Cells

1. Select the cells where you want the new cells to appear.

2. Click the Insert Cells button on the Standard toolbar.

3. Select the direction in which you want the existing cells to shift.

4. Click OK.

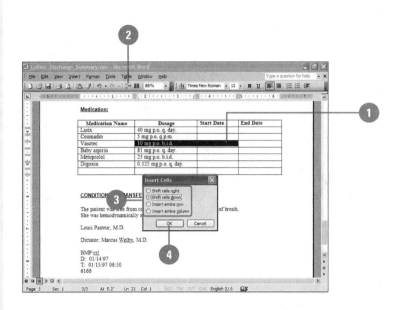

Delete Rows, Columns, or Cells

1. Select the rows, columns, or cells you want to delete.

2. Click the Table menu, point to Delete, and then click Columns, Rows, or Cells.

3. If necessary, select the direction in which you want the remaining cells to shift to fill the space, and then click OK.

Did You Know?

You can set column widths to fit text.
Word can set the column widths to fit the cells' contents or to fill the space between the document's margins. Click in the table, click the Insert Table button list arrow on the Tables And Borders toolbar, and then click AutoFit To Contents or AutoFit To Window.

6

Adjusting Table Cells

Often there is more to modifying a table than adding or deleting rows or columns; you need to make cells just the right size to accommodate the text you are entering in the table. For example, a title in the first row of a table might be longer than the first cell in that row. To spread the title across the top of the table, you can merge (combine) the cells to form one long cell. Sometimes, to indicate a division in a topic, you need to split (or divide) a cell into two. You can also split one table into two at any row. Moreover, you can modify the width of any column and height of any row to better present your data.

Merge and Split Table Cells and Tables

◆ To merge two or more cells into a single cell, select the cells you want to merge, click the Table menu, and then click Merge Cells.

◆ To split a cell into multiple cells, click the cell you want to split, click the Table menu, and then click Split Cells. Enter the number of rows or columns (or both) you want to split the selected cell into, clear the Merge Cells Before Split check box, and then click OK.

◆ To split a table into two tables separated by a paragraph, click in the row that you want as the top row in the second table, click the Table menu, and then click Split Table.

◆ To merge two tables into one, delete the paragraph between them.

> ### Did You Know?
>
> **You can quickly adjust columns and rows.** Position the pointer over the boundary of the column or row you want to adjust until it becomes a resize pointer. Drag the boundary to a new location.

The four cells in this row will be combined into one.

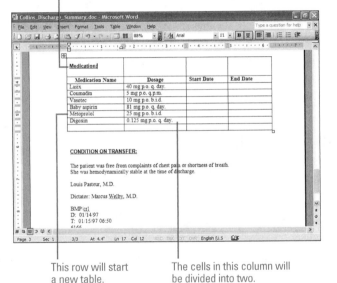

This row will start a new table.

The cells in this column will be divided into two.

Merged cells   Split cells

Split tables

Adjust Column Widths and Row Heights

1. Select the columns or rows you want to change.

2. Click the Table menu, and then click Table Properties.

3. Click the Column tab.

4. To specify an exact width, click the Measure In list arrow, and then click Inches.

5. Type an inch measurement.

6. Click the Row tab.

7. Click the Row Height Is list arrow, and then click Exactly or At Least.

8. Type an inch measurement.

9. Click OK.

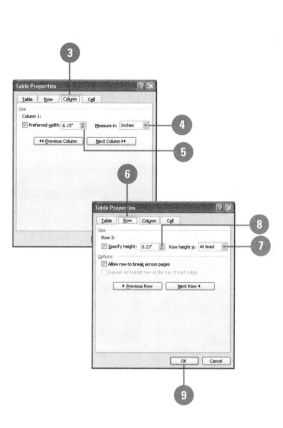

Change Table Properties

1. Select the rows to change.

2. Click the Table menu, and then click Table Properties.

3. Click an alignment option, and then specify an indent from the left (when you select the Left alignment option).

4. Click a text wrapping option.

5. Click OK.

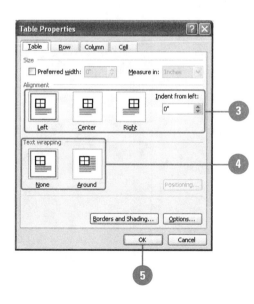

6

Formatting a Table

Tables distinguish text from paragraphs. In turn, formatting, alignment, and text direction distinguish text in table cells. Start by applying one of Word's predesigned table formats using AutoFormat. Then customize your table by realigning the cells' contents both horizontally and vertically in the cells, changing the direction of text within selected cells, such as the column headings, and resizing the entire table. You can modify borders and shading using the Tables And Borders toolbar to make printed tables easier to read and more attractive.

Format a Table Automatically

1. Select the table you want to format.

2. Click the Table menu, and then click Table AutoFormat.

3. Click a format.

4. Preview the results.

5. When you find a format you like, click Apply.

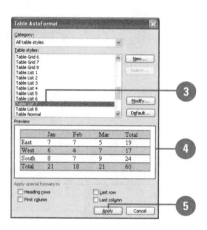

Align Text Within Cells

1. Click the View menu, point to Toolbars, and then click Tables And Borders.

2. Select the cells, rows, or columns you want to align.

3. Click the Cell Alignment button list arrow on the Tables And Borders Toolbar.

4. Click one of the alignment buttons.

Did You Know?

You can create nested tables. Select the table or cells, click the Edit menu, click Cut or Copy, right-click the table cell, and then click Paste As Nested Table.

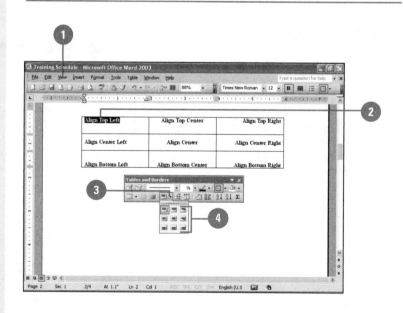

Change Text Direction Within Cells

1. Click the View menu, point to Toolbars, and then click Tables And Borders.

2. Select the cells you want to change.

3. Click the Change Text Direction button on the Tables And Borders toolbar until the text is the direction you want.

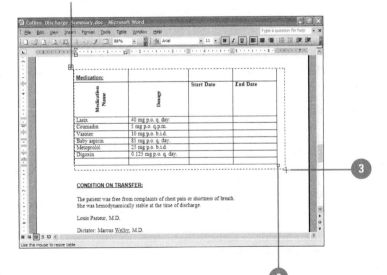

Drag the table from here to move it to a new location.

Resize the Entire Table Proportionally

1. Click to place the insertion point in the table.

2. Position the pointer over the table resize handle in the lower-right corner of the table.

3. Drag the resize handle until the table is the size you want.

Did You Know?

You can sort entries in a table column. Display the Tables And Borders toolbar, select the cells in the column you want to sort, and then click the Sort Ascending or Sort Descending button.

You can calculate the sum of a table column. Display the Tables And Borders toolbar, click in the blank cell in the bottom of the column you want to total, and then click the AutoSum button.

6

Creating a Form Letter

Did you ever send the same letter to several people and spend a lot of time changing personal information, such as names and addresses? If so, form letters will save you time. **Mail merge** is the process of combining names and addresses stored in a data file with a main document (usually a form letter) to produce customized documents. There are four main steps to merging. First, select the document you want to use. Second, create a data file with the variable information. Third, create the main document with the boilerplate (unchanging information) and merge fields. Each merge field corresponds to a piece of information in the data source and appears in the main document with the greater than and less than characters around it. For example, the <<Address Block>> merge field corresponds to name and address information in the data source. Finally, merge the main document with the data source to create a new document with all the merged information.

Create a Form Letter Using Mail Merge

1. Click the Tools menu, point to Letters And Mailings, and then click Mail Merge. The Mail Merge task pane opens. Step 1 of 6 appears on the task pane.

2. Click a document type option (such as Letters), and then click Next at the bottom of the task pane. Step 2 of 6 appears on the task pane.

3. Click a starting document option (such as Use The Current Document), and then click Next at the bottom of the task pane. Step 3 of 6 appears on the task pane.

4. Click a recipient option (such as Use An Existing List or Type A New List), click Browse, double-click a data document, click OK to select the mail recipients, and then click Next at the bottom of the task pane. Step 4 of 6 appears on the task pane.

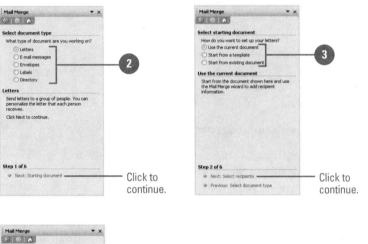

Click to continue.

Click to continue.

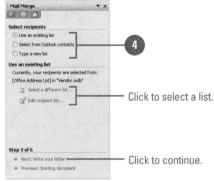

Click to select a list.

Click to continue.

5. Type your letter, click a location in the document, and then click one of the field items on the task pane (such as Address Block or Greeting Line), select the options you want, click OK, and then click Next at the bottom of the task pane. Step 5 of 6 appears on the task pane.

6. Preview the data in the letter and make any changes, and then click Next at the bottom of the task pane. Step 6 of 6 appears on the task pane.

7. Click Edit Individual Letters.

8. Click the All option, and then Click OK.

9. When you're done, click the Close button on the task pane, and then save the form letter.

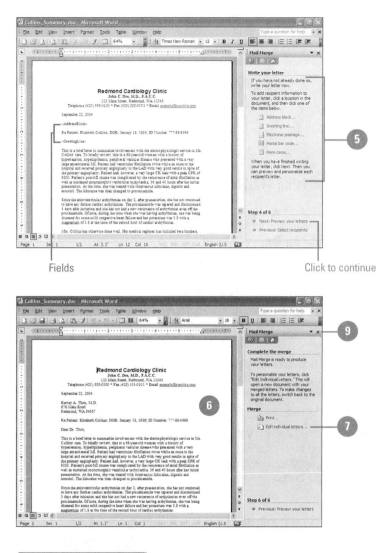

Fields

Click to continue

Did You Know?

You can have common words used as field names. Information in a data file is stored in merge fields, labeled with one-word names, such as FirstName, LastName, City, and so on. You insert merge field names in the main document as blanks, or placeholders, for variable information. When you merge the data file and main document, Word fills in the blanks with the correct information.

You should beware of those extra spaces. Don't press the Spacebar after entering data in a field. Extra spaces will appear in the document between the data and the next word or punctuation, leaving ugly gaps or floating punctuation. Add spaces and punctuation to your main document instead.

6

Creating Labels

You can use a data document to create more than one kind of merge document. For example, you can use a data document to print mailing labels or envelopes to use with your mailing. The process for creating mailing labels is similar to the mail merge process for form letters, except that you insert the merge field into a main document that contains a table with cells in a specific size for labels. During the process for creating mailing labels, you can select brand-name labels in a specific size, such as Avery Standard 1529. After you merge the data into the main document with the labels, you can print the labels on a printer.

Create Labels Using Mail Merge

1. Click the Tools menu, point to Letters And Mailings, and then click Mail Merge. The Mail Merge task pane opens. Step 1 of 6 appears on the task pane.

2. Click the Labels option, and then click Next at the bottom of the task pane. Step 2 of 6 appears on the task pane.

3. Click a starting document option button (such as Change Document Layout), and then click Label Options.

4. Select the label options you want, click OK, and then click Next at the bottom of the task pane. Step 3 of 6 appears on the task pane.

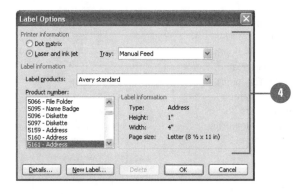

Click to continue

Click to continue

5. Click a recipient option button (such as Use An Existing List or Type A New List), click Browse, double-click a data document, click OK to select the mail recipients, and then click Next at the bottom of the task pane. Step 4 of 6 appears on the task pane.

6. Click in the first label of the document, and then click one of the field items on the task pane (such as Address Block or Greeting Line), select the options you want, and then click OK.

7. Click Update All Labels, and then click Next at the bottom of the task pane. Step 5 of 6 appears on the task pane.

8. Preview the data in the letter and make any changes, and then click Next at the bottom of the task pane. Step 6 of 6 appears on the task pane.

9. Click Print.

10. Click a Print Records option and then click OK.

11. When you're done, click the Close button on the task pane, and then save the form letter.

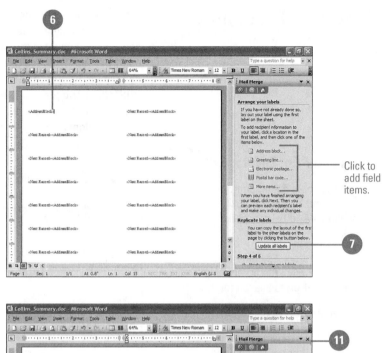

Click to add field items.

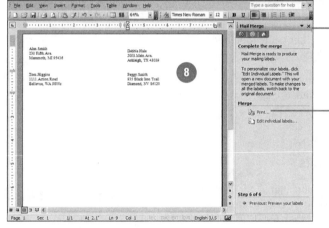

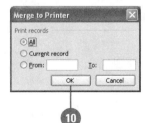

6

Addressing Envelopes and Labels

When you write a letter, you can use Word to print an address on an envelope or mailing label. Word scans your document to find a delivery address. You can use the one Word finds, enter another one, or select one from your Address Book. You can specify a return address, or you can omit it. Addresses can contain text, graphics, and bar codes. The POSTNET bar code is a machine-readable depiction of a U.S. zip code and delivery address; the FIM-A code identifies the front of a courtesy reply envelope. You can print a single label or multiple labels.

Address and Print Envelopes

1. Click the Tools menu, point to Letters And Mailings, click Envelopes And Labels, and then click the Envelopes tab.

2. Type the recipient's name and address, or click the Insert Address button to search for it.

3. Type your name and address.

4. Click Options, select a size, placement, bar code, font, and then click OK.

5. Insert an envelope in your printer, and then click Print.

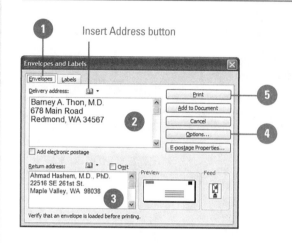

Address and Print Mailing Labels

1. Click the Tools menu, click Letters And Mailings, click Envelopes And Labels, and then click the Labels tab.

2. Type the recipient's name and address, or the Insert Address button to search for it.

3. Select which labels to print.

4. Click Options, select a type or size, and then click OK.

5. Insert labels in your printer, and then click Print.

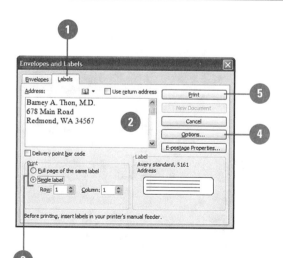

Inserting a Table of Contents

A **table of contents** provides an outline of main topics and page locations. Word builds a table of contents based on the styles in a document that you choose. By default, Heading 1 is the first-level entry, Heading 2 the second level, and so on. In a printed table of contents, a **leader**, a line whose style you select, connects an entry to its page number. In Web documents, entries become hyperlinks. Hide nonprinting characters before creating a table of contents so text doesn't shift to other pages as you print.

Insert a Table of Contents

1. Click the Insert menu, point to Reference, and then click Index And Tables.

2. Click the Table Of Contents tab.

3. Select the Show Page Numbers and the Right Align Page Numbers check boxes.

4. Click the Tab Leader list arrow, and then select a leader style.

5. Click the Formats list arrow, and then select a table of contents style.

6. Enter the number of heading levels you want.

7. Click Options.

8. If necessary, delete any numbers, and then type **1** next to the first-level style, **2** next to the second-level style, and so on.

9. Click OK.

10. Click OK.

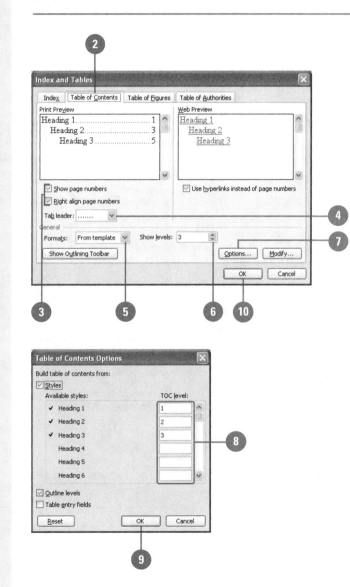

Did You Know?

You can create an index of figures and legal notations. Use the Index and Tables dialog box to create an index, table of figures, or table of authorities, which tracks legal notations.

Creating Multiple Document Versions

If you want a record of changes made to a document, you can save different versions of a document within the same document. When you save different versions within Word, you also save disk space because Word saves only the differences between versions, not an entire copy of each document. After you've saved several version of the document, you can go back and review, open, print, and delete earlier versions. Before you can modify an earlier version, you must open that version and use the Save As command to save it as a separate file. You can also have Word save a version of your document each time you close the document. You cannot access this feature when you save a document as a Web page.

Create Document Versions Automatically

1. Click the File menu, and then click Versions.

2. Select the Automatically Save A Version On Close check box.

3. Click Close.

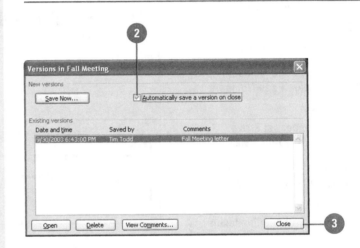

Save a Document Version

1. Click the File menu, and then click Versions.

2. Click Save Now.

3. In the Comments On Version box, type descriptive information about the version you're saving.

4. Click OK.

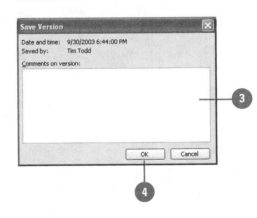

Modifying the Document Summary

If you're not sure of the version of a document, or if you need statistical information about a document, such as the number of pages, paragraphs, lines, words, and characters to fulfill a requirement, you can use the Properties dialog box to quickly find this information. If you need a word count for a paragraph or a select portion of text, you can use the Word Count dialog box or toolbar. You can also create custom file properties, such as client or project, to help you manage and track files. If you associate a file property to an item in the document, the file property updates when you change the item.

Display and Modify Document Properties

1. Click the File menu, and then click Properties.

2. Click the tabs (General, Summary, Statistics, Contents or Custom) to view information about the document.

3. To add title and author information for the document, click the Summary tab.

4. To add and modify tracking properties, click the Custom tab.

5. Click OK.

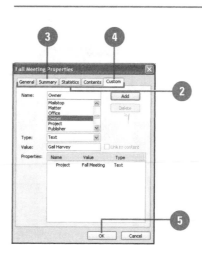

Find Out the Word Count

1. Select the text you want to count.

2. Click the Tools menu, and then click Word Count.

3. To display the Word Count toolbar, click Show Toolbar.

4. Click Close.

Word Count toolbar

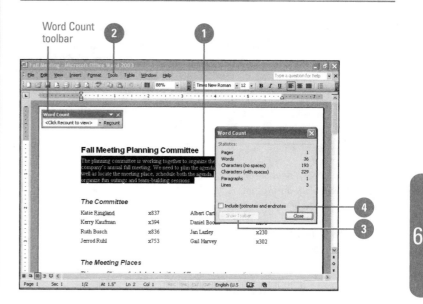

6

Protecting a Document

You can use the security options in Word to protect the integrity of your documents as others review it. At times, you will want the information in a document to be used, but not changed; at other times, you might want only specific people in your office to be able to view the document. When you set a password to a document, make sure you memorize it or write it down exactly as it was entered; the password is case-sensitive. Word doesn't keep a list of passwords. If you lose or forget the password for a protected document, you will not be able to open it.

Protect a Document

1. Click the Tools menu, and then click Protect Document.

2. Select or clear the Limit Formatting To A Selection Of Styles check box.

3. Select the Allow Only This Type Of Editing In The Document check box.

4. Click the Editing Restrictions list arrow, and then select an editing restriction.

5. Select the groups you want to edit the document and any document area restrictions.

6. Click Yes, Start Enforcing Protection.

7. Type a password, and then type the password again to confirm it.

8. Click OK.

9. When you're done, click the Close button on the task pane.

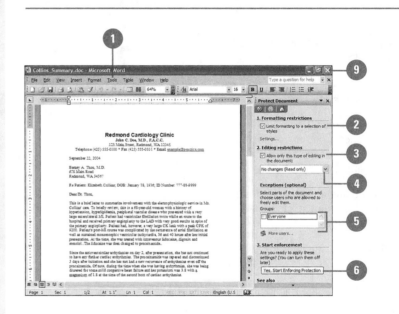

Creating a Worksheet with Excel

7

Introduction

Are you spending too much time number-crunching, rewriting department budgets, drawing charts, or searching for your calculator to figure out a pediatric dosage? Throw away your pencil, graph paper, and calculator, and start using Microsoft Office Excel 2003.

Excel is a **spreadsheet program**, designed to help you record, analyze, and present quantitative information. With Excel, you can track and analyze nurse productivity, organize your department expenses, create budgets, and accomplish a variety of tasks in a fraction of the time it takes using pen and paper. With Excel, you can create a variety of documents for analysis and record keeping, such as monthly statistics on DRGs or length of stay, charts displaying annual quality improvement, an inventory of supplies, or a payment schedule for a capital expenditure.

Excel offers several tools that make your worksheets look more attractive and professional. Without formatting, a worksheet can look like nothing more than meaningless data. To highlight important information, you can change the appearance of selected numbers and text by adding dollar signs, commas, and other numerical formats, or by applying attributes such as boldface and italics.

The file you create and save in Excel is called a **workbook**. It contains a collection of **worksheets**, which look similar to an accountant's ledger sheets with lines and grids, but can perform calculations and other tasks automatically.

Viewing the Excel Window

Cell address
Each cell has a unique address determined by the column letter and row number. For example, the cell B4 is the intersection of column B and row 4.

Title bar
The title bar contains the name of the active workbook.

Menu bar
The nine menus give you access to all Excel commands.

Formula bar
Any data contained in the active cell appears in the formula bar.

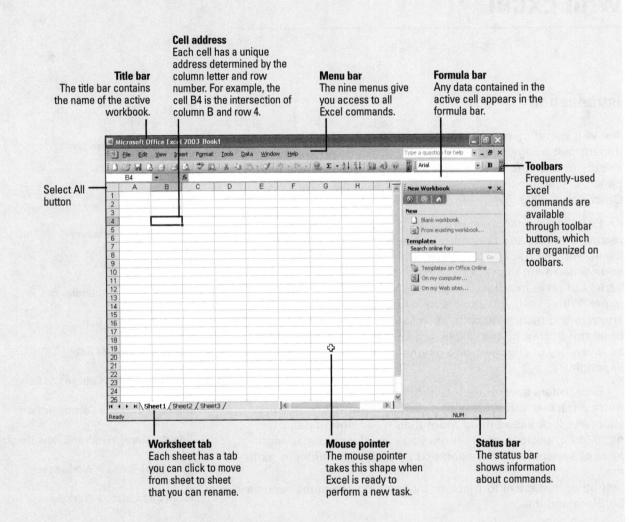

Select All button

Toolbars
Frequently-used Excel commands are available through toolbar buttons, which are organized on toolbars.

Worksheet tab
Each sheet has a tab you can click to move from sheet to sheet that you can rename.

Mouse pointer
The mouse pointer takes this shape when Excel is ready to perform a new task.

Status bar
The status bar shows information about commands.

Selecting Cells

A **cell** is the intersection of a column and a row. You must select a cell and make it **active** to work with it. A range is one or more selected cells that you can edit, delete, format, print, or use in a formula just like a single cell. The active cell has a dark border; selected cells have a light shading called a see-through selection. A range can be **contiguous** (all selected cells are adjacent) or **noncontiguous** (selected cells are not all adjacent). As you select a range, you can see the range reference in the Name box. A range reference lists the upper-left cell address, a colon (:), and the lower-right cell address. Commas separate noncontiguous cells. For example, B4:D10,E7,L24. You can click any cell to deselect a range.

Select a Cell

1. Click a cell to select it.

Select a Range

1. Click the first cell you want to include in the range.

2. Drag to the last cell you want to include in the range. The upper-left cell of a selected range is active and the others are highlighted.

Select a Noncontiguous Range

1. Click the first cell, or select the first contiguous range you want to include.

2. Press and hold Ctrl while you click additional cells and select other ranges.

Moving Around Cells

You can move around a worksheet or workbook using your mouse or the keyboard. You might find that using your mouse to move from cell to cell is most convenient, while using various keyboard combinations is easier for covering large areas of a worksheet quickly. However, there is no right way; whichever method feels the most comfortable is the one you should use.

Use the Mouse to Navigate

Using the mouse, you can navigate to:

◆ Another cell

◆ Another part of the worksheet

◆ Another worksheet

Did You Know?

Microsoft IntelliMouse users can roll from cell to cell with IntelliMouse. If you have the new Microsoft IntelliMouse—with the wheel button between the left and right buttons— you can click the wheel button and move the mouse in any direction to move quickly around the worksheet.

You can quickly zoom in or out using IntelliMouse. Instead of scrolling when you roll with the IntelliMouse, you can zoom in or out. To turn on this feature, click the Tools menu, click Options, click the General tab, click to select the Zoom On Roll With IntelliMouse check box, and then click OK.

To move from one cell to another, point to the cell you want to move to, and then click.

When you click the wheel button on the IntelliMouse, the pointer changes shape. Drag the pointer in any direction to move to a new location quickly.

To see more sheet tabs without changing the location of the active cell, click a sheet scroll button.

To move from one worksheet to another, click the tab of the sheet you want to move to.

Use the Keyboard to Navigate

Using the keyboard, you can navigate to:

◆ Another cell

◆ Another part of the worksheet

Refer to the table for keyboard shortcuts for navigating around a worksheet.

Did You Know?

You can change or move cell selections after pressing Enter. When you press Enter, the active cell moves down one cell. To change the direction, click the Tools menu, click Options, click the Edit tab, click the Direction list arrow, select a direction, and then click OK.

Keys For Navigating in a Worksheet

Press This Key	To Move
Left arrow	One cell to the left
Right arrow	One cell to the right
Up arrow	One cell up
Down arrow	One cell down
Enter	One cell down
Tab	One cell to the right
Shift+Tab	One cell to the left
Page Up	One screen up
Page Down	One screen down
End+arrow key	In the direction of the arrow key to the next cell containing data or to the last empty cell in the current row or column
Home	To column A in the current row
Ctrl+Home	To cell A1
Ctrl+End	To the last cell in the worksheet containing data

Go To a Specific Location

1 Click the Edit menu, and then click Go To.

2 Type the cell address to the cell location where you want to go.

3 To go to other locations (such as comments, blanks, last cell, objects, formulas, etc.), click Special, select an option, and then click OK.

4 Click OK.

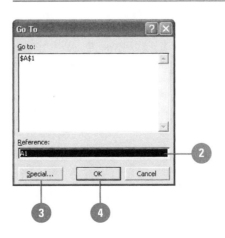

Entering Text and Numbers

You can enter values as whole numbers, decimals, percentages, or dates. You can enter values using either the numbers on the top row of your keyboard, or the numeric keypad on the right side of your keyboard. When you enter a date or the time of day, Excel recognizes these entries (if entered in an acceptable format) as numeric values and changes the cell's format to a default date, currency, or time format. The AutoFill feature fills in data based on the data in adjacent cells. Using the fill handle, you can enter data in a series, or you can copy values or formulas to adjacent cells. The entry in a cell can create an AutoFill that repeats a value or label, or the results can be a more complex extended series, such as days of the week, months of the year, or consecutive numbering.

Enter a Value

1. Click the cell where you want to enter a value.

2. Type a value.

   To simplify your data entry, type the values without commas and dollar signs, and then apply a numeric format to them later.

3. Press Enter, or click the Enter button on the formula bar.

Did You Know?

You can use the numeric keypad like a calculator to enter numbers on your worksheet. Before using the numeric keypad, make sure NUM appears in the lower-right corner of the status bar. If NUM is not displayed, you can turn on this feature by pressing the Num Lock key on the numeric keypad.

You can quickly select all data within a worksheet. To select all the cells in the worksheet, including those cells that do not contain data, click the Select All button.

Enter Repeating Data Using AutoFill

1. Select the first cell in the range you want to fill.

2. Enter the starting value or label that you want to repeat.

3. Position the mouse pointer on the lower-right corner of the selected cell. The fill handle (a small black box) changes to the fill handle pointer (a black plus sign).

4. Drag the fill handle pointer over the range where you want to repeat the value. The fill handle ScreenTip indicates what is being repeated.

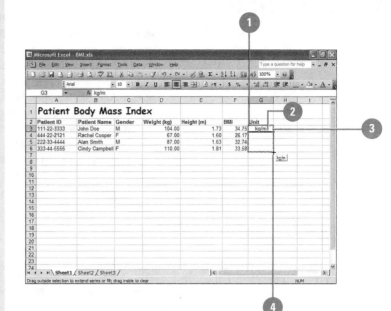

Create a Complex Series Using AutoFill

1. Select the first cell in the range you want to fill.

2. Enter the starting value for the series, and then click the Enter button on the formula bar.

3. Position the mouse pointer on the lower-right corner of the selected cell, and then hold down Ctrl. The pointer changes to the fill handle pointer (a black plus sign with a smaller plus sign).

4. Drag the fill handle pointer over the range where you want the value extended. The destination value appears in a small box.

5. Click the AutoFill Options button, and then click an option that specifies how you want to fill in the data.

Making Label Entries

Excel has three types of cell entries: labels, values, and formulas. Excel uses values and formulas to perform its calculations. A label is text in a cell that identifies the data on the worksheet so readers can interpret the information, such as titles or column headings. A label is not included in calculations. A value is a number you enter in a cell. To enter values easily and quickly, you can format a cell, a range of cells, or an entire column with a specific number-related format. Labels turn a worksheet full of numbers into a meaningful report by identifying the different types of information it contains. You use labels to describe or identify the data in worksheet cells, columns, and rows. You can enter a number as a label (for example the year 2003), so that Excel does not use the number in its calculations. To help keep your labels consistent, you can use Excel's **AutoComplete** feature, which completes your entries based on the format of previously entered labels.

Enter a Text Label

① Click the cell where you want to enter a text label.

② Type a label.

A label can include uppercase and lowercase letters, spaces, punctuation, and numbers.

③ Click the Enter button on the formula bar, or press Enter.

What you type in the cell also appears in the formula bar.

Did You Know?

You can enter labels quickly using AutoComplete. Type the first few characters of a label. If a previous entry in that column begins with the same characters, AutoComplete displays the entry. Press Enter or click the Enter button on the formula bar to accept the entry. Resume typing to ignore the AutoComplete suggestion.

You can enable AutoComplete for cell values. Click the Tools menu, click Options, click the Edit tab, click to select the Enable AutoComplete For Cell Values check box, and then click OK.

Enter a Number as a Label

1. Click the cell where you want to enter a number label.

2. Type ' (apostrophe).

   The apostrophe is a label prefix and does not appear on the worksheet.

3. Type a number.

   Examples of number labels include a year, social security number, or telephone number.

4. Click the Enter button on the formula bar, or press Enter or Tab.

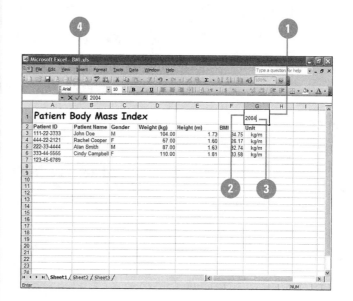

Enter a Label from the PickList

1. Right-click the cell at the bottom of a list where you want to enter a label, and then click Pick From Drop-Down List.

2. Click an entry from the list.

Did You Know?

Using long labels might appear truncated. When you enter a label wider than the cell it occupies, the excess text appears to spill into the next cell to the right—unless there is data in the adjacent cell. If the adjacent cell contains data, the label appears truncated—you see only the portion of the label that fits in the cell's current width.

Editing Cell Contents

No matter how much you plan, you can count on having to make changes on a worksheet. Sometimes you'll need to correct an error; other times, you'll want to add new information or see the results for different conditions, such as higher insurance reimbursements, reduced blood pressure levels, or other variables. You edit data just as easily as you enter it, using the formula bar or directly in the active cell.

Edit Cell Contents

1. Double-click the cell you want to edit.

   The status bar displays Edit instead of Ready.

2. Use the mouse pointer or the Home, End, and arrow keys to position the insertion point in the cell.

3. To erase characters, press Backspace or Delete.

4. To enter characters, type new characters.

5. Press Enter or click the Enter button on the formula bar to accept the edit, or click the Cancel button on the formula bar to cancel it.

Click to edit the cell content in the formula bar.

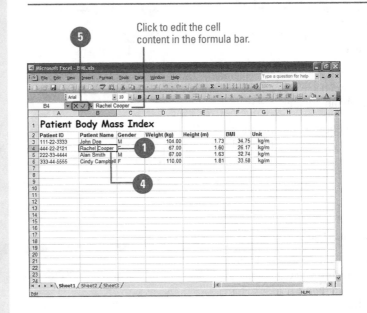

Did You Know?

You can change editing options. Click the Tools menu, click Options, click the Edit tab, change the editing options you want, and then click OK.

By deleting a cell, you remove the cell completely from the worksheet. When you choose Delete from the Edit menu or from the shortcut menu, you must choose to move the remaining cells left or up, or to remove the entire row or column.

Clearing Cell Contents

You can clear a cell to remove its contents. Clearing a cell does not remove the cell from the worksheet; it just removes from the cell whatever elements you specify: data, comments (also called cell notes), or formatting instructions. When clearing a cell, you must specify whether to remove one, two, or three of these elements from the selected cell or range.

Clear the Contents of a Cell

1. Select the cell or range you want to clear.

2. Click the right mouse button, and then click Clear Contents on the shortcut menu, or press Delete.

Clear Cell Contents, Formatting, and Comments

1. Select the cell or range you want to clear.

2. Click the Edit menu, and then point to Clear.

3. Click All.

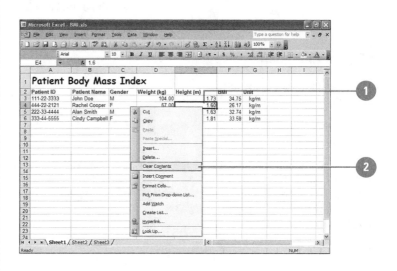

See Also

See "Inserting Comments" on page 41 for information on inserting comments.

Inserting and Deleting Cells

You can insert new, blank cells anywhere on the worksheet so you can enter new data exactly where you want it. Inserting cells moves the remaining cells in the column or row to the right or down as you choose and adjusts any formulas so they refer to the correct cells. You can also delete cells if you find you don't need them; deleting cells shifts the remaining cells to the left or up a row—just the opposite of inserting cells. Deleting a cell is different from clearing a cell. Deleting a cell removes the actual cell from the worksheet whereas clearing a cell erases the cell contents, the cell format, or both.

Insert One or More Cells

1. Select one or more cells where you want to insert new cell(s).

2. Click the Insert menu, and then click Cells.

3. To move the contents of the cells right, click the Shift Cells Right option; to move the contents of the cells down, click the Shift Cells Down option.

4. Click OK.

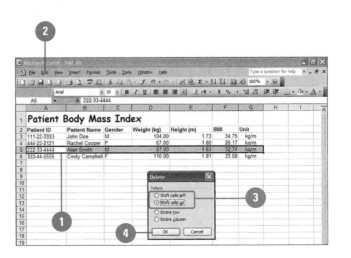

Delete One or More Cells

1. Select one or more cells you want to delete.

2. Click the Edit menu, and then click Delete.

3. To move the remaining cells left, click the Shift Cells Left option; to move the remaining cells up, click the Shift Cells Up option.

4. Click OK.

Selecting a Column or Row

You can select one or more columns or rows in a worksheet in order to apply formatting attributes, insert or delete columns or rows, or perform other group actions. The header buttons above each column and to the left of each row indicate the letter or number of the column or row. You can select multiple columns or rows even if they are non-contiguous—that is, not next to one another in the worksheet.

Select a Column or Row

1. Click the column or row header button of the column or row you want to select.

Select Multiple Columns or Rows

1. Drag the mouse over the header buttons of any contiguous columns or rows you want to select.

2. To select noncontiguous columns or rows, press and hold Ctrl while clicking each additional column or row header button.

Did You Know?

You can select the entire worksheet quickly. Click the Select All button located above the row number 1 and the left of column A.

Inserting and Deleting Columns or Rows

You can insert one or more blank columns and rows on a worksheet between columns or rows that are already filled. The header buttons above each column and to the left of each row indicate the letter or number of the column or row. Inserted columns are added to the left of the selected columns. Inserted rows are added above the selected rows. Excel repositions existing cells to accommodate the new columns and rows and adjusts any existing formulas so that they refer to the correct cells. The Insert menu can change depending on the selection. When you select a column, only the Columns command appears on the Insert menu. When you select a row, only the Rows command appears.

Insert One or More Columns or Rows

① To insert a column, click the column header button directly to the right of where you want to insert the new column.

To insert a row, click the row header button directly below where you want to insert the new row.

② To insert multiple columns or rows, drag to select the header buttons for the number of columns or rows you want to insert.

③ Click the Insert menu, and then click Columns or Rows.

Row header button   ①   Column header button

Delete One or More Columns or Rows

① Select the columns or rows you want to delete.

② Click the Edit menu, and then click Delete.

Hiding and Unhiding a Column or Row

Not all the data on a worksheet should be available to everyone. You can hide sensitive information without deleting it by hiding selected columns or rows. For example, you can hide the patient name and address columns so that they are not readily displayed. Hiding columns and rows does not affect calculations in a worksheet; all data in hidden columns and rows is still referenced by formulas as necessary. Hidden columns and rows do not appear in a printout either. When the hidden data is needed, you (or other users) can unhide the sensitive information.

Hide a Column or Row

1. Click the column or row header button of the column or row you want to hide. (Drag to select multiple header buttons to hide more than one column or row.)

2. Click the Format menu, point to Column or Row, and then click Hide.

Header button

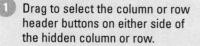

Unhide a Column or Row

1. Drag to select the column or row header buttons on either side of the hidden column or row.

2. Click the Format menu, point to Column or Row, and then click Unhide.

Adjusting Column Width and Row Height

You've entered labels and values, constructed formulas, and even formatted the cells, but now some of your data isn't visible; the value displays as ##### in the cell. Also, some larger-sized labels are cut off. You can narrow or widen each column width to fit its contents and adjust your row heights as needed. As you build your worksheet, you can change the default width of some columns or the default height of some rows to accommodate long strings of data or larger font sizes. You can manually adjust column or row size to fit data you have entered, or you can use AutoFit to resize a column or row to the width or height of its largest entry.

Adjust Column Width or Row Height

1. Click the column or row header button for the first column or row you want to adjust.

2. If you want, drag to select more columns or rows.

3. Right-click the selected column(s) or row(s), and then click Column Width or Row Height.

4. Type a new column width or row height in points.

5. Click OK.

Adjust Column Width or Row Height Using the Mouse

1. Position the mouse pointer on the right edge of the column header button or the bottom edge of the row header button for the column or row you want to change.

2. When the mouse pointer changes to a double-headed arrow, click and drag the pointer to a new width or height.

Change Column Width or Row Height Using AutoFit

1. Position the mouse pointer on the right edge of the column header button or the bottom edge of the row header button for the column or row you want to change.

2. When the mouse pointer changes to a double-headed arrow, double-click the mouse.

Selecting and Naming a Worksheet

Each new workbook opens with three worksheets (or sheets), in which you store and analyze values. You work in the active, or selected, worksheet. The default worksheet names are Sheet1, Sheet2, and Sheet3, which appear on the sheet tab, like file folder labels. As you create a worksheet, give it a meaningful name to help you remember its contents. The sheet tab size adjusts to fit the name's length. If you work on a project that requires more than three worksheets, add additional sheets to the workbook so all related information is stored in one workbook.

Select a Worksheet

1. If necessary, click a sheet tab scroll button to display other tabs.

2. Click a sheet tab to make it the active worksheet.

3. To select multiple worksheets, press and hold Ctrl as you click other sheet tabs.

Name a Worksheet

1. Double-click the sheet tab you want to name.

2. Type a new name.

   The current name, which is selected, is replaced when you begin typing.

3. Press Enter.

Inserting and Deleting a Worksheet

You can add or delete sheets in a workbook. If, for example, you are working on a project that requires more than three worksheets, you can insert additional sheets in one workbook rather than open multiple workbooks. You can insert as many sheets in a workbook as you want. If, on the other hand, you are using only one or two sheets in a workbook, you can delete the unused sheets to save disk space. Before you delete a sheet from a workbook, make sure you don't need the data. You cannot undo the deletion.

Insert a Worksheet

1. Click the sheet tab to the right of where you want to insert the new sheet.

2. Click the Insert menu, and then click Worksheet.

   A new worksheet is inserted to the left of the selected worksheet.

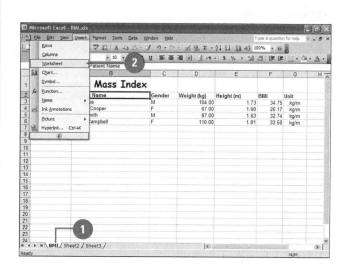

Delete a Worksheet

1. Click the sheet tab of the worksheet you want to delete.

2. Click the Edit menu, and then click Delete Sheet.

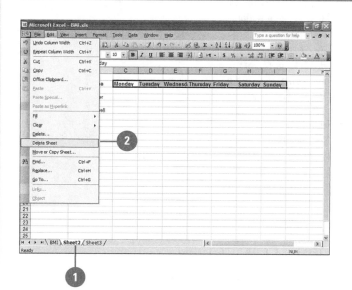

7

Moving and Copying a Worksheet

After adding several sheets to a workbook, you might want to reorganize them. You can arrange sheets in chronological order or in order of their importance. You can easily move or copy a sheet within a workbook or to a different open workbook. Copying a worksheet is easier and often more convenient than reentering similar information on a new sheet. If you are moving or copying a worksheet a short distance, you should use the mouse. For longer distances, you should use the Move Or Copy Sheet command on the Edit menu.

Move a Worksheet Within a Workbook

1 Click the sheet tab of the worksheet you want to move, and then hold down the mouse button.

2 When the mouse pointer changes to a sheet of paper, drag it to the right of the sheet tab where you want to move the worksheet.

3 Release the mouse button.

Did You Know?

You can use the Create A Copy check box to move a worksheet. Clear the Create A Copy check box in the Move Or Copy dialog box to move a worksheet rather than copy it.

You can give your worksheet a different background. Click the tab of the sheet on which you want to insert a background, click the Format menu, point to Sheet, and then click Background. Select the picture you want to use as a background, and then click Insert.

Copy a Worksheet

1. Click the sheet tab of the worksheet you want to copy.

   TIMESAVER *Press and hold the Ctrl key while you drag a sheet name to copy a worksheet.*

2. Click the Edit menu, and then click Move Or Copy Sheet.

3. If you want to copy the sheet to another open workbook, click the To Book list arrow, and then select the name of that workbook. The sheets of the selected workbook appear in the Before Sheet list.

   TROUBLE? *If the workbook you want to copy to does not show up in the To Book drop-down list, you must first open the other workbook.*

4. Click a sheet name in the Before Sheet list. Excel inserts the copy to the left of this sheet.

5. Select the Create A Copy check box.

6. Click OK.

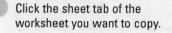

Did You Know?

You can use groups to affect multiple worksheets. Click a sheet tab, press and hold the Shift key, and click another sheet tab to group worksheets. Right-click a grouped sheet tab, and then click Ungroup Sheet on the shortcut menu.

Hiding and Unhiding Worksheets and Workbooks

Not all worksheets and workbooks should be available to everyone. You can hide sensitive information without deleting it by hiding selected worksheets or workbooks. For example, if you want to share a workbook with others, but it includes confidential employee salaries, you can simply hide a worksheet. Hiding worksheets does not affect calculations in the other worksheets; all data in hidden worksheets is still referenced by formulas as necessary. Hidden worksheets do not appear in a printout either. When you need the data, you can unhide the sensitive information.

Hide or Unhide a Worksheet

◆ **Hide.** Click the sheet tab you want to hide, click the Format menu, point to Sheet, and then click Hide.

◆ **Unhide.** Click the Format menu, point to Sheet, click Unhide, select the worksheet you want to unhide, and then click OK.

Click to hide or unhide a worksheet.

Hide or Unhide a Workbook

◆ **Hide.** Open the workbook you want to hide, click the Window menu, and then click Hide.

◆ **Unhide.** Click the Window menu, click Unhide, select the workbook you want to unhide, and then click OK.

Select a workbook to unhide it.

Splitting a Worksheet in Panes

If you are working on a large worksheet, it can be time consuming and tiring to scroll back and forth between two parts of the worksheet. You can split the worksheet into four panes and two scrollable windows that you can view simultaneously but edit and scroll independently. As you work in two parts of the same worksheet, you can resize the window panes to fit your task. Drag the split bar between the panes to resize the windows. No matter how you display worksheets, Excel's commands and buttons work the same as usual.

Split a Worksheet in Panes

◆ **Split.** Click the Window menu, and then click Split.

◆ **Remove Split.** Click the Window menu, and then click Remove Split.

Did You Know?

You can search for a value or data in a cell and then replace it with different content. Click the cell or cells containing content you want to replace. Click the Edit menu, click Find, and then click the Replace tab for additional options.

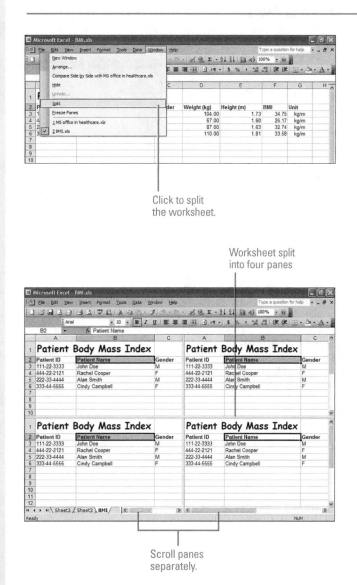

Click to split the worksheet.

Worksheet split into four panes

Scroll panes separately.

Freezing Panes

Once you've finished creating the worksheet structure—labels and formulas—you're ready to enter data. The first six columns and twelve rows or so are just fine, but as you scroll to enter data in later columns or rows, the labels for the column headings shift out of view. Instead of memorizing the headings, freeze the label columns and rows so they remain visible as you scroll through the rest of the worksheet. You can freeze a row, a column, or a pane from a split worksheet.

Freeze Columns and Rows

1. Click the cell that intersects the rows and columns you want to remain visible on the screen.

   To freeze panes from a split window, skip step 1.

2. Click the Window menu, and then click Freeze Panes.

3. Edit and scroll the worksheet as usual.

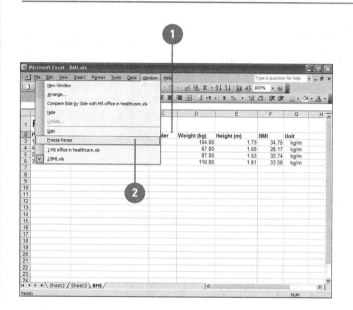

Unfreeze Columns and Rows

1. Click the worksheet that you want to unfreeze.

2. Click the Window menu, and then click Unfreeze Panes.

Building a Worksheet with Excel

Introduction

Once you enter the data on a worksheet, you'll want to add formulas to calculate values such as pediatric dosages. With Microsoft Office Excel 2003, you can create your own formulas or insert built-in formulas, called functions, for more complex computations.

In addition to using a worksheet to calculate values, you can also use it to manage a list of information, called a list or database. You can use an Excel worksheet to keep an inventory of supplies, a nursing vacation schedule, or a patient database. You can enter information directly on a worksheet, or use a Data Form, which lets you quickly enter information by filling in blank text boxes, similar to a paper form. Excel provides a variety of tools that make it easy to keep lists up-to-date and analyze them to get the information you want quickly. Excel's data analysis tools include alphabetical organizing (called sorting), and collecting information that meets specific criteria (called filtering).

When you're ready to share data with others, a worksheet might not be the most effective way to present the information. Excel makes it easy to create and modify a chart, also called a graph, which is a visual representation of selected data in your worksheet.

What You'll Do

Create a Simple Formula

Edit and Copy a Formula

Name a Range

Simplify a Formula with Ranges

Understand Cell Referencing

Use Absolute Cell References

Perform Calculations Using Functions

Calculate Results

Correct Calculation Errors

Create and Edit a Chart

Change a Chart Type

Add and Delete a Data Series

Enhance a Data Series

Format a Chart

Enhance a Chart

Understand Lists

Create a List

Sort and Work with Data in a List

Creating a Simple Formula

A formula calculates values to return a result. All formulas begin with the equal sign (=) followed by arguments—values (such as 147 or $10.00) and cell references (such as B3:F20)—connected by arithmetic operators (+, -, *, and /). You enter and edit formulas just as you do labels and values—in the formula bar or in the cell. By default, Excel displays the results of the formula in a cell, but you can change your view of the worksheet to display formulas instead of results.

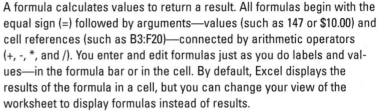

Formula bar

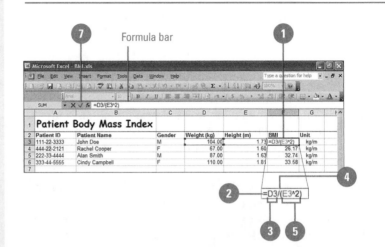

Enter a Formula

1. Click a cell where you want to enter a formula.

2. Type an equal sign (=) to begin the formula. If you do not begin a formula with an equal sign, Excel displays the information you type; it does not perform the calculation.

3. Enter the first argument (a number or a cell reference). If the argument is a cell reference, type the cell reference, or click the cell.

   If the formula can accept cell references, the cursor changes to a light gray cell-like shape.

4. Enter an arithmetic operator, such as +, -, *, or /.

5. Enter the next argument.

6. Repeat steps 4 and 5 to complete the formula.

7. Click the Enter button on the formula bar, or press Enter.

   The cell displays the formula result, and the formula bar displays the formula.

Did You Know?

You can select a cell to enter its address. To avoid careless typing mistakes, click a cell to insert its cell reference in a formula rather than typing its address.

For Your Information

Understanding Order of Precedence

Formulas containing more than one operator follow the order of precedence: exponentiation, multiplication and division, and then addition and subtraction. So, in the formula 5 + 2 * 3, Excel performs multiplication first and addition next for a result of 11. Excel calculates operations within parentheses first. The result of the formula (5 + 2) * 3 is 21.

Editing and Copying a Formula

You can edit formulas just as you do other cell contents: use the formula bar or work in the cell. When you select a cell to edit a formula, the status bar displays Edit Mode, indicating that you can edit the contents of a cell. You can select, cut, copy, paste, delete, and format cells that contain formulas, just as you do cells that contain labels or values. Using AutoFill, you can quickly copy formulas to adjacent cells. If you need to copy formulas to different parts of a worksheet, use the Office Clipboard.

Edit a Formula Using the Formula Bar

1. Select the cell that contains the formula you want to edit.

2. Press the F2 key to change to Edit Mode.

3. If necessary, use the Home, End, and arrow keys to position the cursor within the cell contents.

4. Use any combination of Backspace and Delete to erase unwanted characters, and then type new characters as needed.

5. Click the Enter button on the formula bar, or press Enter.

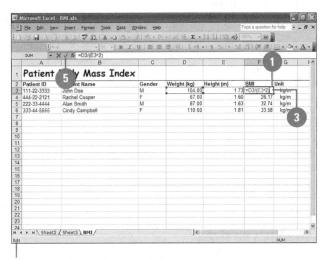

The mode indicator changes to Edit.

Copy a Formula Using AutoFill

1. Select the cell that contains the formula you want to copy.

2. Point to the fill handle in the lower-right corner of the selected cell. (The pointer changes to a black plus sign.)

3. Drag to select the adjacent cells where you want to paste the formula, and then release the mouse button.

4. Click the AutoFill Options button, and then click an option that specifies how you want to fill in the data.

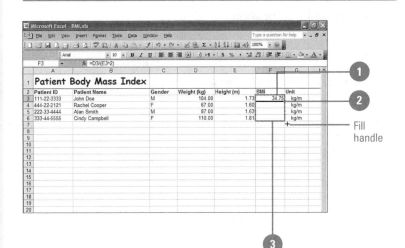

Fill handle

8

Naming a Range

To make working with ranges easier, Excel allows you to name them. The name Doses, for example, is easier to remember than the coordinates B4:D10. You can use named ranges in formulas the same way you use cell references and range addresses. Named ranges can be helpful when navigating larger worksheets.

Name a Cell or Range

1. Select the cell or range you want to name.

2. Click the Name box on the formula bar.

3. Type a name for the range.

   A range name can include uppercase or lowercase letters, numbers, and punctuation. A range name cannot include spaces in the name. Try to use a simple name that reflects the information in the range, such as VendorNames.

4. Press Enter. The Name box shows the name whenever you select the range.

Select a Named Cell or Range

1. Click the Name box list arrow on the formula bar.

2. Click the name of the cell or range you want to use.

   The range name appears in the Name box, and all cells included in the range are highlighted on the worksheet.

Did You Know?

You can delete a named range. Click the Insert menu, point to Name, click Define, click the name you want to delete, click Delete, and then click OK.

Simplifying a Formula with Ranges

You can simplify formulas by using ranges and range names. For example, if 12 cells on your worksheet contain monthly budget amounts and you want to multiply each amount by 10 percent, you can insert one range address in a formula instead of inserting 12 different cell addresses, or you can insert a range name. Using a range name in a formula helps to identify what the formula does; the formula =2003 EXPENSES *1.10, for example, is more meaningful than =D7:O7*1.10.

Use a Range in a Formula

1. Type an equal sign (=), and then type a function (such as SUM).

2. Click the first cell of the range, and then drag to select the last cell in the range. Excel enters the range address for you.

3. Complete the formula, and then click the Enter button on the formula bar, or press Enter.

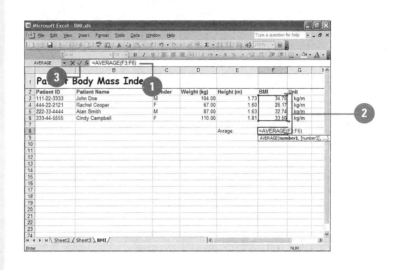

Use a Range Name in a Formula

1. Type an equal sign (=), and then type the function you want to use.

2. Press F3 to display a list of named ranges.

3. Click the name of the range you want to insert.

4. Click OK.

5. Complete the formula, and then click the Enter button on the formula bar or press Enter.

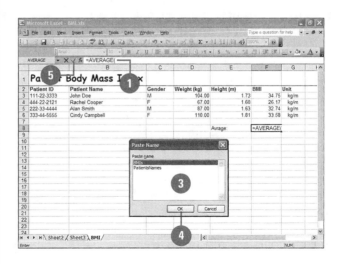

Understanding Cell Referencing

Each cell, the intersection of a column and a row on a worksheet, has a unique address, or **cell reference**, based on its column letter and row number. For example, the cell reference for the intersection of column D and row 4 is D4.

Cell References in Formulas

The simplest formula refers to a cell. If you want one cell to contain the same value as another cell, type an equal sign followed by the cell reference, such as =D4. The cell that contains the formula is known as a **dependent cell** because its value depends on the value in another cell. Whenever the cell that the formula refers to changes, the cell that contains the formula also changes. The formula =D4*7 multiplies the value in cell D4 by 7. The formula recalculates whenever the value in cell D4 changes.

Depending on your task, you can use either relative cell references, which are references to cells relative to the position of the formula, or absolute references, which are cell references that always refer to cells in a specific location.

Relative Cell References

When you copy and paste or move a formula that uses relative references, the references in the formula change to reflect cells that are in the same relative position to the formula. The formula is the same, but it uses the new cells in its calculation. For example, when you copy the formula =D3+D4 in cell D5 to cell E5, the cell references change automatically: the formula becomes =E3+E4. Relative

addressing eliminates the tedium of creating new formulas for each row or column in a worksheet filled with repetitive information.

Absolute Cell References

If you don't want a cell reference to change when you copy a formula, make it an absolute reference by typing a dollar sign ($) before each part of the reference that you don't want to change. For example, the formula =D4 changes as you copy it from cell to cell, but the formula =D4 always references the same cell. You can add a $ before the column letter, the row number, or both. To ensure accuracy and simplify updates, enter constant values (such as medical insurance deductible, hourly rates, and so on) in a cell, and then use absolute references to them in formulas.

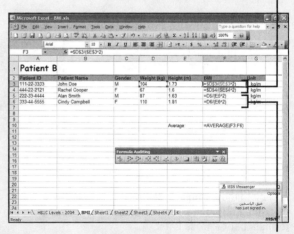

Absolute cell references

Relative cell references

Using Absolute Cell References

When you want a formula to consistently refer to a particular cell, even if you copy or move the formula elsewhere on the worksheet, you need to use an absolute cell reference. An absolute cell reference is a cell address that contains a dollar sign ($) in the row or column coordinate, or both. When you enter a cell reference in a formula, Excel assumes it is a relative reference unless you change it to an absolute reference. If you want part of a formula to remain a relative reference, remove the dollar sign that appears before the column letter or row number.

Use an Absolute Reference

1. Click a cell where you want to enter a formula.

2. Type = (an equal sign) to begin the formula.

3. Select a cell, and then type an arithmetic operator (+, -, *, or /).

4. Select another cell, and then press the F4 key to make that cell reference absolute.

5. If necessary, continue entering the formula.

6. Click the Enter button on the formula bar, or press Enter.

> ### Did You Know?
>
> ***You can change an absolute reference back to a relative reference.*** In the cell with the absolute formula, press F4 repeatedly until all the dollar signs are removed from the reference.

Even if you move or copy this formula to another location, this cell reference will not change.

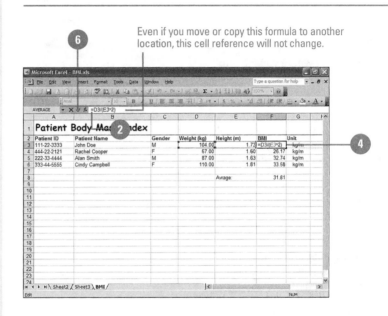

Performing Calculations Using Functions

Functions save you time and trouble of creating commonly used or complex equations. Functions are pre-designed formulas that involve one or more values, performing an operation, and returning one or more values. Excel includes hundreds of functions that you can use alone or in combination with other formulas or functions. Functions perform a variety of calculations, from adding, averaging, and counting to more complicated tasks, such as calculating the monthly payment amount of a loan. You can enter a function manually if you know its name and all the required arguments, or you can easily insert a function using Insert Function.

Enter a Function

1. Click the cell where you want to enter the function.

2. Type an equal sign (=), type the name of the function, and then type (, an opening parenthesis. For example, to insert the AVERAGE function, type =**AVERAGE(**.

3. Type the argument or click the cell or range you want to insert in the function.

4. Click the Enter button on the formula bar, or press Enter. Excel adds the closing parenthesis to complete the function.

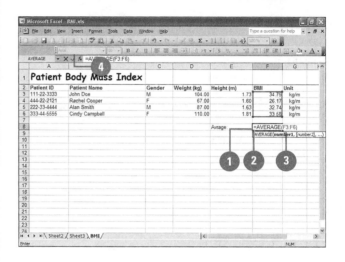

Did You Know?

You can use data from a different workbook. Open both workbooks, arrange them side by side, type an equal sign in the cell that you want to contain a reference to the other worksheet, type the formula as usual, click the cell in the other worksheet, complete the formula, and then press Enter. The formula includes the name of the workbook, the name of the worksheet, and the cell reference.

Commonly Used Excel Functions

Function	Description	Sample
SUM	Calculates the sum of the argument	=SUM(*argument*)
AVERAGE	Calculates the average value of the argument	=AVERAGE(*argument*)
COUNT	Calculates the number of values in the argument	=COUNT(*argument*)
MAX	Displays the largest value in the argument	=MAX(*argument*)
MIN	Displays the smallest value in the argument	=MIN(*argument*)
PMT	Determines the monthly payment in a loan	=PMT(*argument*)

Enter a Function Using the Insert Function

1 Click the cell where you want to enter a formula.

2 Click the Insert Function button on the formula bar.

3 Click a function you want to use. A description of the selected function appears at the bottom of the Insert Function dialog box.

4 Click OK.

5 Enter the cell addresses in the text boxes. Type them or click the Collapse Dialog button to the right of the text box, select the cell or range using your mouse, and then click the Expand Dialog button. In many cases, the Insert Function might try to "guess" which cells you want to include in the function.

6 Click OK.

Did You Know?

You can enter a function with the Insert Function. Select the cell where you want to enter a function, click the Paste Function button on the Standard toolbar, click a function category, click a function, click OK, select cell references, and then click OK.

You can use Paste Special to copy only formulas. Select the cells containing the formulas you want to copy, click where you want to paste the data, click the Edit menu, click Paste Special, click the Formulas option, and then click OK.

Collapse Dialog button
(changes to Expand Dialog button)

Calculating Results

You can verify or check your work without inserting a formula into your worksheet by using the AutoCalculate feature. Because AutoCalculate is not a formula that you've inserted, the results do not appear on the worksheet when you print it. AutoCalculate can give you quick answers while you work. You can easily total a range of cells by using the AutoSum button on the Standard toolbar. AutoSum suggests a range to sum, but you can modify this range if you want a different range. You can calculate subtotals for data ranges using the Tools menu and the Subtotals dialog box. You can select where Excel performs the subtotals and the function type.

Calculate a Range Automatically

1. Select the range (contiguous or noncontiguous). The sum of the selected cells appears in the status bar.

2. To change the type of calculation, right-click the AutoCalculate button in the status bar.

3. Click the type of calculation you want.

Calculate Totals with AutoSum

1. Click the cell where you want to display the calculation.

2. Click the AutoSum button.

3. Click the Enter button on the formula bar, or press Enter.

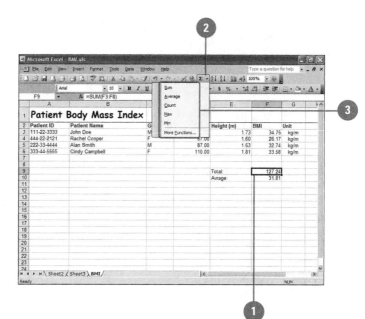

Calculate with Extended AutoSum

1. Click the cell where you want to display the calculation.

2. Click the AutoSum button list arrow.

3. Click the function you want to use.

Did You Know?

Select additional AutoFill commands. Click the Edit menu, and then click Fill to select additional commands such as Up, Down, Left, Right, Series, or Justify.

Correcting Calculation Errors

When Excel finds a possible error in a calculation, it displays a green triangle in the upper left corner of the cell. If Excel can't complete a calculation, it displays an error message, such as "#DIV/0!" You can use the Error smart tag to help you fix the problem. In a complex worksheet, it can be difficult to understand the relationships between cells and formulas. Auditing tools enable you to clearly determine these relationships. When the Auditing feature is turned on, it uses a series of arrows to show you which cells are part of which formulas. When you use the auditing tools, tracer arrows point out cells that provide data to formulas and the cells that refer to the cells. A box is drawn around the range of cells that provide data to formulas.

Review and Correct Errors

1. Select a cell that contains a green triangle in the upper left corner.

2. Click the Error Smart Tag button.

3. Click one of the troubleshooting options. (Menu options vary depending on the error.)

   ◆ To have Excel fix the error, click one of the available options specific to the error.

   ◆ To find out more about an error, click Help On This Error.

   ◆ To remove the error alert, click Ignore Error.

   ◆ To fix the error manually, click Edit In Formula Bar.

Did You Know?

You can check for errors in the entire worksheet. Click the Tools menu, and then click Error Checking.

You can change error checking options. Click the Tools menu, click Options, click the Error Checking tab, select or clear the options you want to change, and then click OK.

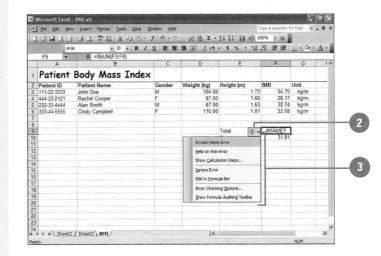

Audit a Formula

1. Click the Tools menu, point to Formula Auditing, and then click Show Formula Auditing Toolbar.

2. To find cells that provide data to a formula, select the cell that contains the formula, and then click the Trace Precedents button.

3. To find out which formulas refer to a cell, select the cell, and then click the Trace Dependents button.

4. If a formula displays an error value, such as #DIV/0!, click the cell, and then click the Trace Error button to locate the problem.

5. To remove arrows, click the Remove Precedent Arrows, Remove Dependent Arrows, or Remove All Arrows button.

6. Click the Close button on the Formula Auditing toolbar.

Did You Know?

You can have Excel circle invalid data. Click the Circle Invalid button on the Auditing toolbar. Click the Clear Validation Circles button to clear the circles.

Creating a Chart

A **chart** provides a visual, graphical representation of numerical data. Whether you turn numbers into a bar, line, pie, surface, or bubble chart, patterns become more apparent. For example, the trend of controlling blood glucose levels of diabetic patients becomes powerful in a line chart. A second line showing reduced microvascular and neuropathic complications creates an instant map of the success of your care. **Titles** on the chart, horizontal (x-axis), and vertical (y-axis) identify the data. A legend connects the colors and patterns in a chart with the data they represent. **Gridlines** are horizontal and vertical lines to help the reader determine data values in a chart. Excel simplifies the chart-making process with the **Chart Wizard**, a series of dialog boxes that leads you through all the steps to create an effective chart on a new or an existing worksheet. When you choose to place the chart on an existing sheet, rather than on a new sheet, the chart is called an embedded object. You can then resize or move it just as you would any graphic object.

Create a Chart Using the Chart Wizard

1. Select the data range you want to chart.

   Make sure you include the data you want to chart and the column and row labels in the range. The Chart Wizard expects to find this information and incorporates it in your chart.

2. Click the Chart Wizard button on the Standard toolbar.

   To move backward or forward in the Chart Wizard, click Back or Forward. You can click Finish at any time.

3. Click a chart type.

4. Click a chart sub-type.

5. Click the Press And Hold To View Sample button to preview your selection.

6. Click Next to continue.

7. Verify the data range, and then select to plot the data series in rows or in columns.

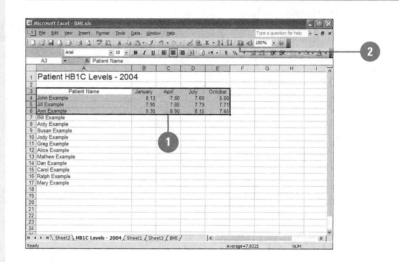

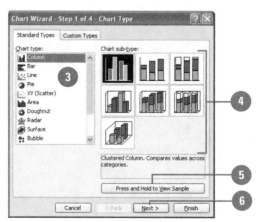

8 Click Next to continue.

9 Click a chart options tab.

♦ **Titles tab.** Type titles for the chart, x-axis, and y-axis in the appropriate text boxes.

♦ **Axes tab.** Select the axes you want to display for the data.

♦ **Gridlines tab.** Select the type of gridlines you want for the x-axis and y-axis.

♦ **Legend tab.** Select options to display a legend and its location.

♦ **Data Labels tab.** Select the labels you want for the data.

♦ **Data Table tab.** Click to add a table to the chart.

10 Preview the options, and then click Next to continue.

11 Select to place the chart on a new sheet or as an embedded object.

12 Click Finish.

13 Drag the chart to a new location if necessary.

Did You Know?

The difference between major and minor gridlines. Major gridlines occur at each value on an axis; minor gridlines occur between values on an axis. Use gridlines sparingly and only when they improve the chart's readability.

You can change chart options. You can revise titles, gridlines, and legends at any time. Select the chart, click the Chart menu, click Chart Options, click the appropriate tab, select or change options, and then click OK.

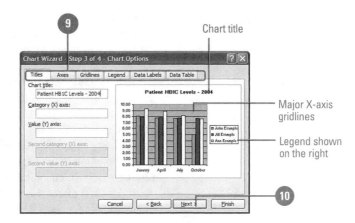

Chart title

Major X-axis gridlines

Legend shown on the right

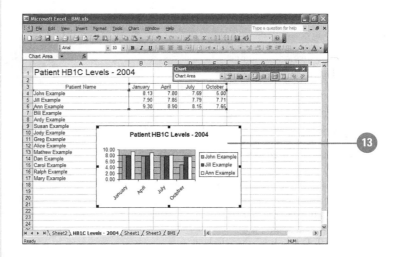

Selecting and Editing a Chart

When you edit a chart, you alter its features, which can include selecting data or formatting elements. For example, you might want to use different colors or patterns in a data series. To change the type of chart or any element in it, you must first select the chart or element. When you select a chart, handles (small black squares) display around the window's perimeter, and the Chart toolbar displays on screen (docked or floating). When you select a chart, all of the buttons on this toolbar become active. You can use the ScreenTip feature to display the data value and the name of any object or area on a chart. When you select an object in a chart, the name of the object appears in the Chart Objects list box on the Chart toolbar, which indicates that you can now edit the object. Editing a chart does not affect the data used to create it. You don't need to worry about updating a chart if you change data in the worksheet because Excel automatically updates the chart. You can change the data range at any time. If you want to plot more or less data in a range, you can select the data series on the worksheet and then drag the range to the chart.

Select and Edit a Chart Object

1. Select a chart. The Chart toolbar appears.

2. Position the mouse pointer over a chart object, click the object to select it.

3. To edit the object, double-click it, make changes, and then click OK.

4. Click another area of the chart, or press Esc to deselect a chart object.

Did You Know?

You can use the Chart toolbar to select chart elements. Select a chart element by clicking the Chart Objects list arrow on the Chart toolbar. Once an element is selected, double-click it to open a corresponding Format dialog box.

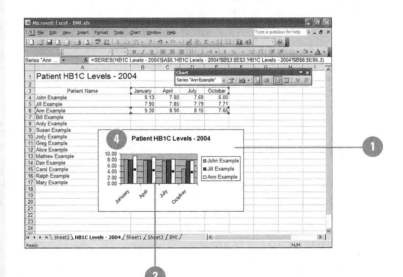

Changing a Chart Type

Excel's default chart type is the column chart, although there are many other types from which to choose. A column chart might adequately display your data, but you should experiment with a variety of chart types to find the one that shows your data in the most effective way. A pie chart is an effective and easily understood chart type for comparing parts that make up a whole entity, such as departmental percentages of a hospital budget. You can call attention to individual pie slices that are particularly significant by moving them away from the other pieces, called exploding the pie.

Change a Chart Type Quickly

1. Select the chart you want to change.

2. Click the Chart Type button list arrow on the Chart toolbar.

3. Select a chart type. Excel changes the chart type when you release the mouse button.

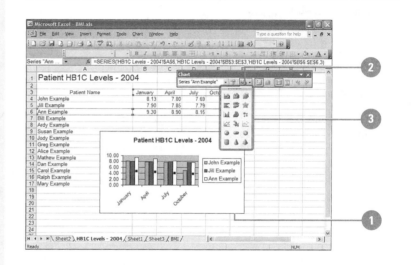

Explode a Pie Slice

1. Select a pie chart.

2. Click to select the pie slice you want to explode.

3. Drag the slice away from the pie.

Did You Know?

You can move and resize a chart. Drag the selected chart from its center to a new location. Drag a resize handle to enlarge or shrink the chart's size.

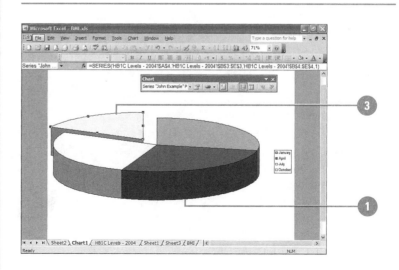

Adding and Deleting a Data Series

Many components make up a chart. Each range of data that comprises a bar, column, or pie slice is called a **data series**; each value in a data series is called a **data point**. The data series is defined when you select a range on a worksheet and then open the Chart Wizard. But what if you want to add a data series once a chart is complete? Using Excel, you can add a data series by using the mouse, the Chart menu, or the Chart Wizard. As you create and modify more charts, you might also find it necessary to delete or change the order of one or more data series. You can delete a data series without re-creating the chart.

Add a Data Series Quickly

1 Select the range that contains the data series you want to add to your chart.

2 Drag the range into the existing chart.

3 Release the mouse button to display the chart with the added data series.

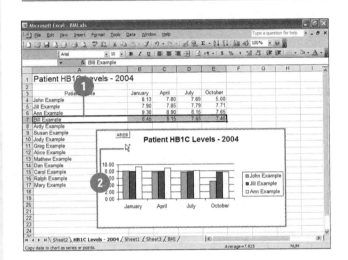

Delete a Data Series

1 Select the chart that contains the data series you want to delete.

2 Click any data point in the data series to select the series in the chart and the worksheet.

To delete one data point but keep the rest of the series in the chart, click the data point twice.

3 Press Delete.

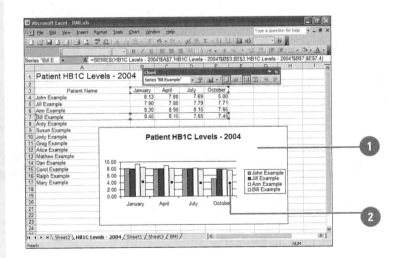

Change a Data Series

1. Select the chart that contains the data series you want to change.

2. Click the Chart menu, and then click Source Data.

3. Click the Series tab.

4. Click the series name you want to change.

5. Click the Name or Values Collapse Dialog button to change the name or value, make the change, and then click the Expand Dialog button.

6. Click OK.

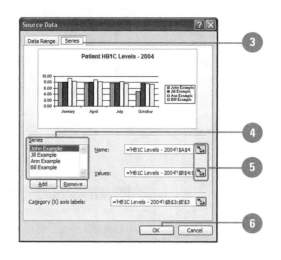

Change Data Series Order

1. Select the chart and the data series you want to change.

2. Click the Format menu, and then click Selected Data Series.

3. Click the Series Order tab.

4. Click the series you want to reorder.

5. Click Move Up or Move Down.

6. Click OK.

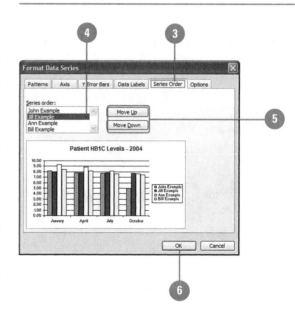

Did You Know?

You can add a trendline. A trendline helps you analyze problems of prediction. Select the chart to which you want to add a trendline, click the Chart menu, click Add Trendline, select a trend type, select a series, and then click OK.

8

Enhancing a Data Series

When you initially use the Chart Wizard, Excel automatically selects the colors that it will use to represent each data series. You can change one or all of the default colors. You may want more dynamic colors—adding patterns and texture to further enhance a data series. Or, perhaps you'll be printing your charts in black and white and you want to ensure the readability of each data series. You can also insert a picture in a chart so that its image occupies a bar or column.

Change a Data Series Color or Pattern

1. Click any data point in a data series to select it.

2. Double-click a data point in the selected data series.

3. Click the Patterns tab.

4. Click a color in the Area palette. The selected color displays in the Sample box.

5. If you want to add effects, such as textures, patterns, gradients, or pictures, click the Fill Effects button.

6. Click the Gradient, Texture, or Pattern tab to change the qualities of the data series color.

7. When you're done, click OK.

8. Click OK if you're satisfied with the results shown in the Sample box, or select different options.

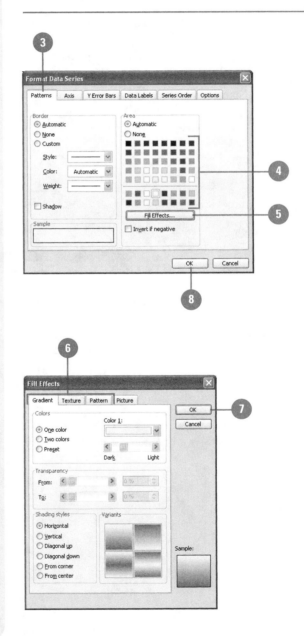

Formatting a Chart

You can format or change any chart object—such as titles, legends, gridlines, data labels, data tables, and text annotations—to enhance the appearance of the chart and increase its overall effectiveness. A chart title identifies its purpose and axis titles identify the plotted data. Titles can be multiple lines and formatted like other worksheet text.

Format a Chart Object

1. Double-click the chart element you want to format.

2. Click the tab that corresponds to the type of change you want to make.

3. Select the formatting options you want to change or apply.

4. Click OK.

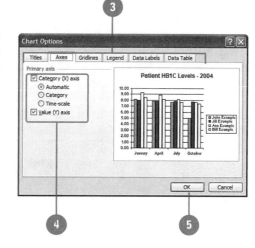

Change Chart Options

1. Select a chart you want to change.

2. Click the Chart menu, and then click Chart Options.

3. Click the chart option tab (Titles, Axes, Gridlines, Legend, Data Labels, or Data Table) you want to change.

4. Enter information, and then select the options you want.

5. Click OK.

Did You Know?

You can add a text annotation. A text annotation is separate text. Select the chart, type the annotation text, and then press Enter. You can drag the text box to a new location.

8

Enhancing a Chart

Add chart options to enhance the appearance of the chart and increase its overall effectiveness. Chart options include chart objects such as titles, legends, text annotations, and gridlines. A chart title identifies the primary purpose of the chart; adding a title for each axis also clarifies the data that you're plotting. Titles can be any length, and you can format them just like other worksheet text. A legend associates the colors and patterns in a chart with the data they represent. Legend text is derived from the data series plotted within a chart. You can rename an item within a legend by changing the text in the data series. Gridlines are horizontal and vertical lines that help the reader determine data point values in a chart. You can modify legends and gridlines at any time.

Add a Title

1. Select a chart to which you want to add one or more titles.

2. Click the Chart menu, click Chart Options, and then click the Titles tab.

3. Type the text you want for the title of the chart.

4. Type title text for the x-axis and y-axis.

5. If you want a second line for the x-axis or y-axis, type the title text (if available).

6. Click OK.

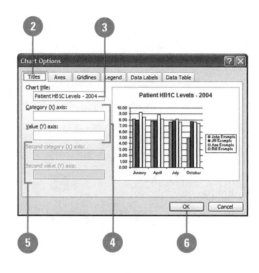

Add or Delete a Legend

1. Select the chart to which you want to add or delete a legend.

2. Click the Legend button on the Chart toolbar. You can drag the legend to move it to a new location.

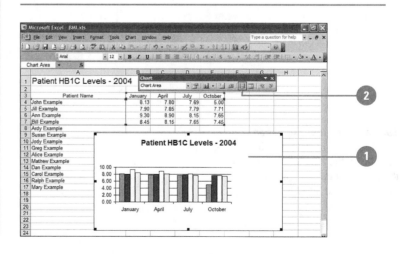

Understanding Lists

A **database** is a collection of related records.
Examples of databases are an address book,
a list of patients or services, and a staff directory. In Excel, a database is referred to as a **list**.

Record
One set of related fields, such as all the fields
pertaining to one patient or service. In a
worksheet, each row represents a unique record.

List range
The block of
cells that
contains some
or all of the list
you want to
analyze. The
list range
cannot occupy
more than one
worksheet.

	A	B	C	D	E	F	G	H	I
1	**Patient List**								
2									
3	ID	Patient Name	Birthdate	Patient Age	Patient Sex	Blood Pressure	Weight	Height	
4									
5	1	John Example	1959	44	Male	120/75	210	71	
6	2	Jill Example	1936	67	Female	114/60	160	60	
7	3	Ann Example	1958	45	Female	180/95	123	61	
8	4	Bill Example	1952	51	Male	132/75	185	68	
9	5	Ardy Example	1941	62	Male	166/81	190	67	
10	6	Susan Example	1945	58	Female	155/95	122	61	
11	7	Jody Example	1944	59	Female	130/80	144	64	
12	8	Greg Example	1933	70	Male	144/90	178	69	
13	9	Alice Example	1948	55	Female	115/60	114	61	
14	10	Mathew Example	1942	61	Male	172/91	150	64	
15	11	Dan Example	1936	67	Male	155/79	156	68	
16	12	Carol Example	1942	61	Female	199/100	189	69	
17	13	Ralph Example	1947	56	Male	120/68	135	62	
18	14	Mary Example	1940	63	Female	123/85	177	65	

Field name
The title of a field.
In an Excel list,
the first row
contains the
names of each
field. Each field
name can have
up to 255
characters,
including
uppercase and
lowercase letters
and spaces.

Field
One piece of information, such as patient's last name or an ICD-9
number. On a worksheet, each cell represents a field.

Creating a List

To create a list in Excel, you can enter data on worksheet cells, just as you do any other worksheet data, but the placement of the field names and list range must follow these rules: (1) Enter field names in a single row that is the first row in the list (2) Enter each record in a single row (3) Do not include any blank rows within the list range (4) Do not use more than one worksheet for a single list range. You can enter data directly in the list or in a data form, a dialog box in which you can view, change, add, or delete records in a list. Don't worry about entering records in any particular order; Excel tools organize an existing list alphabetically, by date, or in almost any order you can imagine.

Create a List

1 Open a blank worksheet, or use a worksheet that has enough empty columns and rows for your list.

2 Enter a label for each field in adjacent columns across the first row of the list.

3 Enter field information for each record in its own row; start with the row directly below the field names.

4 Select the range of cells for the list.

5 Click the Data menu, point to List, and then click Create List.

6 Click OK.

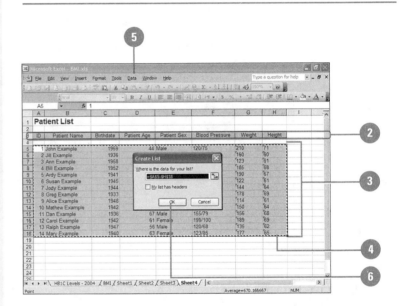

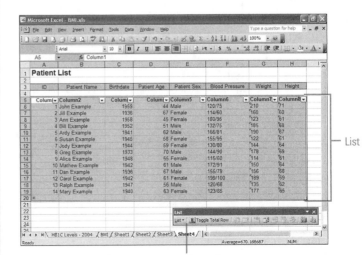

List toolbar

Enter Records with a Data Form

1. Enter a descriptive label for each field in adjacent columns across the first row of the list.

2. Click the Data menu, and then click Form.

3. Click OK to set the row as the column labels.

4. Enter information for each field, pressing Tab to move from one field to the next.

5. Click New, and then enter field information for each additional record.

6. When you're done, click Close.

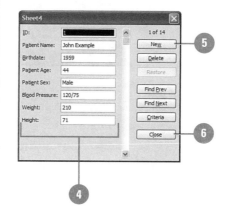

Did You Know?

You can publish a list to a SharePoint server. Click a cell in the list, click the Data menu, point to List, click Publish List, type the URL of the server, type the name of the list, type a description, click Next, inspect the data for an accurate layout, and then click Finish. To view a published list on SharePoint Services, click List on the List toolbar, and then click View List On Server.

You can unlink a list to a SharePoint server. Click a cell in the list, click List on the List toolbar, and then click Unlink.

8

Sorting Data in a List

After you enter records in a list, you can reorganize the information by sorting the records. For example, you might want to sort records in a patient list alphabetically by last name or numerically by their age. **Ascending order** lists records from A to Z, earliest to latest, or lowest to highest. **Descending order** lists records from Z to A, latest to earliest, or highest to lowest. You can sort the entire list or use **AutoFilter** to select the part of the list you want to display in the column. You can also sort a list based on one or more **sort fields**— fields you select to sort the list. A sort, for example, might be the telephone directory numerically by area code and then alphabetically by last name.

Sort Data Quickly

1. Click the field name by which you want to sort.

2. Click the Sort Ascending or the Sort Descending button on the Standard toolbar.

Did You Know?

You can sort data in rows. If the data you want to sort is listed across a row instead of down a column, click Options in the Sort dialog box, and then click the Sort Left To Right option.

Display Parts of a List

1. Click in the list range.

2. Click the Data menu, point to Filter, and then click AutoFilter.

3. Click the list arrow of the field you want to use.

4. Select the item that the records must match to be displayed.

5. To redisplay all records in the list, click the Data menu, point to Filter, and then click Show All.

6. To remove the field list arrows, click the Data menu, point to Filter, and then click AutoFilter.

198

Sort a List Using More Than One Field

1. Click anywhere within the list range.

2. Click the Data menu, and then click Sort.

3. Click the Sort By list arrow, and then click the field on which the sort is based (the *primary sort field*).

4. Click the Ascending or Descending option.

5. Click the top Then By list arrow, select a second sort field, and then click Ascending or Descending.

6. If you want, click the lower Then By list arrow, select a third sort field, and then click Ascending or Descending.

7. If available, click the Header Row option to *exclude* the field names (in the first row) from the sort, or click the No Header Row option to *include* the field names (in the first row) in the sort.

    The header row is the first row in your list that contains the column names or field labels.

8. Click OK.

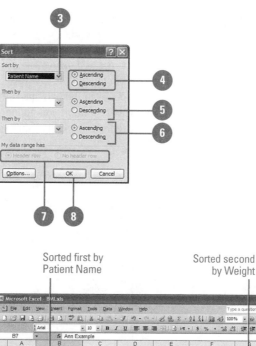

Sorted first by Patient Name

Sorted second by Weight

Did You Know?

You can protect your original list order. So you can always sort a list to restore its original order, include an index field, a field that contains consecutive numbers (1, 2, 3, and so on). For example, name the first field "Number," and then consecutively number each record as you enter it.

Working with Lists

After you create a list, you can sort the entries, add new entries, and display totals. You can insert rows anywhere in a list or add rows at the bottom of the list. The last row of the list is a blank row with a blue asterisk (*) inside the left-most cell. You can type a new entry in the list directly into the last row. When the list is inactive, the asterisk does not appear in the list, and the list border shifts up to the bottom of the last row of data. If you no longer need the data in list form, you can convert the list back to normal Excel data.

Insert a Row in a List

① Click a cell in the list where you want to insert a row.

② Click the List button on the List toolbar, point to Insert, and then click Row.

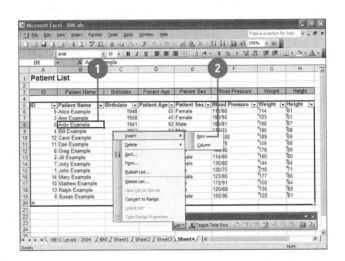

Convert a List to a Range

① Click a cell in the list.

② Click the List button on the List toolbar, and then click Convert To Range.

③ Click OK.

Designing a Worksheet with Excel

9

Introduction

Microsoft Office Excel 2003 offers several tools that make your worksheets look attractive and professional. Without formatting, a worksheet can look confusing with meaningless data. To highlight important information, such as insurance co-payment or staff hourly rate, you can change the appearance of selected numbers and text by adding dollar signs, commas, and other numerical formats, or by applying attributes such as boldface and italics. You can change font and font size, adjust the alignment of data in cells, and add colors, patterns, borders, and pictures. By using AutoFormats and styles to apply multiple changes, you can speed up the formatting process and ensure a greater degree of consistency among your worksheets.

You can also modify the look of your printouts by adjusting a variety of print settings, including page orientation, margins, headers and footers, and other elements that enhance the readability of your worksheets and workbooks. When you're ready to print your workbook, you can choose to print all or part of the worksheets.

Formatting Text and Numbers

Sometimes you want to format cells with labels differently from cells with totals. You can change the appearance of data in selected cells without changing its actual label or value. Format text and numbers by using **font attributes**, such as boldface, italics, or underlines, to enhance data to catch the readers' eye and focus their attention. You can also apply **numeric formats** to values to better reflect the type of information they present—dollar amounts, dates, decimals, or percentages.

Format Text Quickly

1. Select a cell or range with the text you want to format.

2. Click one of the buttons on the Formatting toolbar to apply that attribute to the selected range:

   ◆ Bold

   ◆ Italic

   ◆ Underline

3. Click the Font or Font Size list arrow, and then select a font or size.

   You can apply multiple attributes to the range.

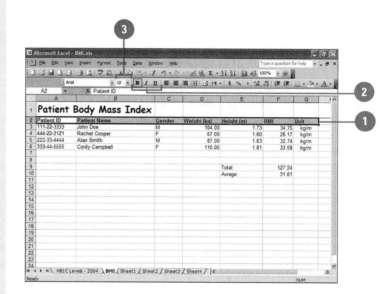

Format Numbers Quickly

1. Select a cell or range with the numbers to format.

2. Click one of the buttons on the Formatting toolbar to apply that attribute to the selected range.

   ◆ Currency Style

   ◆ Percent Style

   ◆ Comma Style

   ◆ Increase Decimal

   ◆ Decrease Decimal

   You can apply multiple attributes to the range.

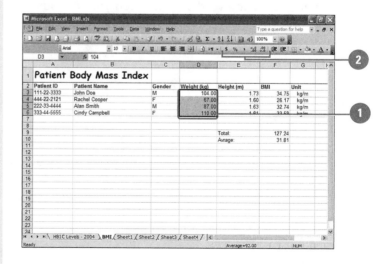

Apply Numeric, Date, and Time Formats

1. Select a cell or range with the numbers to format.

2. Click the Format menu, and then click Cells.

3. Click the Number tab.

4. Click a numeric, date, or time category.

5. Select the formatting type options you want to apply.

6. Preview the sample.

7. Click OK.

Did You Know?

Excel has formatting intelligence. As you type at the end of a column or row, Excel extends the formatting and formulas you are using in that column or row.

You can use AutoFormat to save time. An AutoFormat is a combination of ready-to-use, designed formats. Select the cell or range you want to format, click the Format menu, click AutoFormat, click a format style, and then click OK.

Changing Data Alignment

When you enter data in a cell, Excel aligns labels on the left edge of the cell and aligns values and formulas on the right edge of the cell. Horizontal alignment is the way in which Excel aligns the contents of a cell relative to the left or right edge of the cell; vertical alignment is the way in which Excel aligns cell contents relative to the top and bottom of the cell. Excel also provides an option for changing the character flow and rotation of text in a cell. You can select the rotate text in horizontal orientation up or down. The default orientation is 0 degrees—the text is level in a cell.

Change Alignment Using the Formatting Toolbar

1. Select a cell or range containing the data to be realigned.

2. Click the Align Left, Center, or Align Right button on the Formatting toolbar.

3. To center cell contents across selected columns, click the Merge And Center button on the Formatting toolbar.

Change Alignment Using the Format Dialog Box

1. Select a cell or range containing the data to be realigned.

2. Click the Format menu, and then click Cells.

3. Click the Alignment tab.

4. Click the Horizontal list arrow or the Vertical list arrow, and then select an alignment.

5. Select an orientation. Click a point on the map, or click the Degrees up or down arrow.

6. If you want, select one or more Text Control check boxes.

7. Click OK.

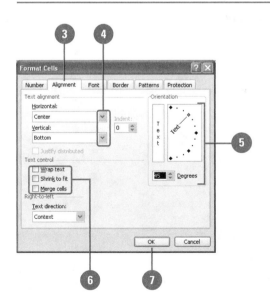

Changing Data Font and Color

You can change the color of numbers and text on a worksheet. The strategic use of font color can be an effective way of visually uniting similar values. For example, on a lab results worksheet you might want to display normal values in blue and abnormal ones in red. The Font Color button on the Formatting toolbar displays the last font color you used. To apply this color to another selection, simply click the button. To apply a different color, click the Font Color button list arrow, and then select a color.

Change Font Color Using the Formatting Toolbar

1 Select a cell or range that contains the text you want to change.

2 Click the Font Color list arrow on the Formatting toolbar.

3 Click a color.

Change Font, Font Style, and Font Size

1 Select a cell or range that contains the font you want to change.

2 Click the Format menu, and then click Cells.

3 Click the Font tab.

4 Select a font.

5 Select a font style.

6 Select a font size.

7 Select any additional formatting effects.

8 Click OK.

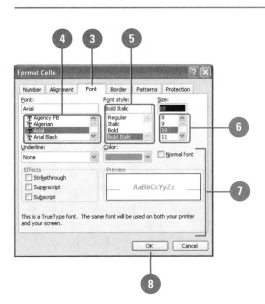

Designing Conditional Formatting

You can make your worksheets more powerful by setting up conditional formatting. Conditional formatting lets the value of a cell determine its formatting. For example, you might want the current blood glucose level of a diabetic patient to be displayed in red italic if it's higher than the previous level, but in green and bold if it's less.

Establish a Conditional Format

1. Select a cell or range you want to conditionally format.

2. Click the Format menu, and then click Conditional Formatting.

3. Select the operator and values you want for condition 1.

4. Click the Format button, select the attributes you want applied, and then click OK.

5. Click Add to include additional conditions, and then repeat steps 3 and 4.

6. Click OK.

Delete a Conditional Format

1. Click the Format menu, and then click Conditional Formatting.

2. Click Delete.

3. Select the check box for the condition(s) you want to delete.

4. Click OK.

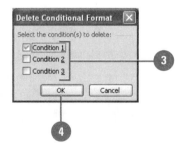

Adding Color and Patterns to Cells

Colors and patterns added to the worksheet's light gray grid help identify data and streamline entering and reading data. If your data spans many columns and rows, color every other row light yellow to help readers follow the data. Or add a red dot pattern to cells with totals. Color adds background shading to a cell. Patterns add dots or lines to a cell in any color you choose. You can use the Format Cells dialog box to add color and patterns to a worksheet. However, if you want to add color to cells quickly, you can use the Fill Color button on the Formatting toolbar.

Apply Color and Patterns

1. Select a cell or range to which you want to apply colors and patterns.

2. Click the Format menu, and then click Cells.

3. Click the Patterns tab.

4. To add shading to the cell, click a color in the palette.

5. To add a pattern to the cell, click the Pattern list arrow, and then click a pattern and color in the palette.

6. Click OK.

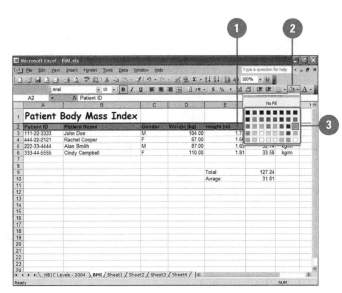

Apply Color Using the Formatting Toolbar

1. Select a cell or range.

2. Click the Fill Color list arrow on the Formatting toolbar.

   If necessary, click the Toolbar Options list arrow to display the button.

3. Click a color.

9

Adding Borders to Cells

The light gray grid that appears on the worksheet helps your eyes move from cell to cell. Although you can print these gridlines, sometimes a different grid pattern better emphasizes your data. For example, you might put a decorative line border around the title, a double-line bottom border below cells with totals, or a thick border between sections of a complicated worksheet. You can add borders of varying colors and widths to any or all sides of a single cell or range.

Apply a Border

1. Select a cell or range to which you want to apply borders.

2. Click the Format menu, and then click Cells.

3. Click the Border tab.

4. Select a line style.

5. Click the Color list arrow, and then click a color for the border.

6. If you want a border on the outside of a cell or range, click Outline. If you want a border between cells, click Inside. If you want to remove a border, click None.

7. To set a custom border, click a Border button, or click the Preview Border box where you want to add a border.

8. Click OK.

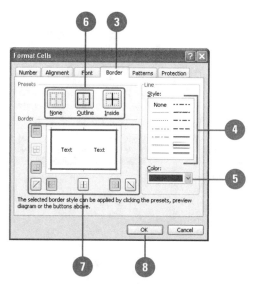

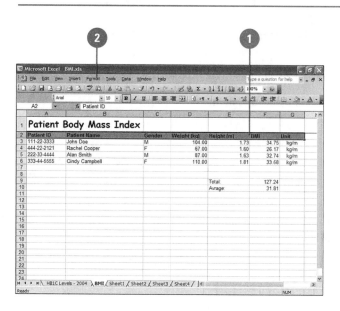

> ### Did You Know?
>
> ***You can apply a border using the Formatting toolbar.*** Select a cell or range to which you want to apply a border, Click the Borders button list arrow on the Formatting toolbar to select a border. The most recently selected style displays on the Borders button.

Formatting Data with AutoFormat

Formatting worksheet data can be a lot of fun but also time consuming, especially for busy healthcare professionals. To make formatting data more efficient, Excel includes 18 AutoFormats. An AutoFormat includes a combination of fill colors and patterns, numeric formats, font attributes, borders, and font colors that are professionally designed to enhance your worksheets. If you don't select any cells before choosing the AutoFormat command, Excel will "guess" which data should it should format.

Apply an AutoFormat

1. Select a cell or range to which you want to apply an AutoFormat, or skip this step if you want Excel to "guess" which cells to format.

2. Click the Format menu, and then click AutoFormat.

3. Click an AutoFormat in the list.

4. Click Options.

5. Select one or more Formats To Apply check boxes to turn a feature on or off.

6. Click OK.

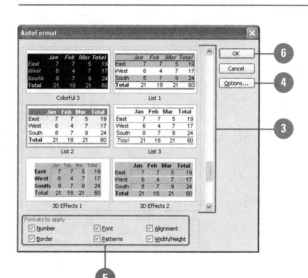

Creating and Applying Styles to Cells

A **style** is a defined collection of formats—font, font size, attributes, numeric formats, and so on—that you can store as a set and later apply to other cells. For example if you always want subtotals to display in blue 14-point Times New Roman, bold, italic, with two decimal places and commas, you can create a style that includes all these formats. If you plan to enter repetitive information, such as a list of dollar amounts in a row or column, it's often easier to apply the desired style to the range before you enter the data. That way you can simply enter each number, and Excel formats it as soon as you press Enter. You can also copy styles from one workbook to another. Once you create a style, it is available to you in every workbook.

Create a New Style

1. Select a cell or range that you want to create a style.

2. Click the Format menu, and then click Style.

3. Type the name of the new style.

4. Clear the check boxes with the options you do not want.

5. Click Modify.

6. Click any of the formatting tabs, and make additional formatting changes to the style.

7. Click OK.

8. Click OK.

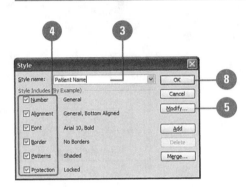

> ### Did You Know?
>
> *You can merge a style from another workbook.* Click the Format menu, click Style, click Merge, click the workbook that contains the style you want, click OK, and then click OK.

Apply a Style

1. Select a cell or range to which you want to apply a style.

2. Click the Format menu, and then click Style.

3. Click the Style Name list arrow, and then select the style you want to apply.

4. Click OK.

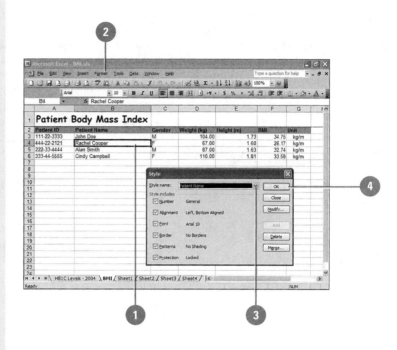

Delete a Style

1. Click the Format menu, and then click Style.

2. Click the Style Name list arrow, and then click the style you want to delete.

3. Click Delete.

4. Click OK.

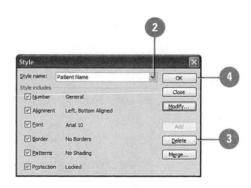

Formatting Tabs and the Background

Depending on your screen size, the sheet tabs at the bottom of your workbook can be hard to view. You can add color to the sheet tabs to make them more distinguishable. If you want to add artistic style to your workbook or you are creating a Web page from your workbook, you can add a background picture. When you add a background to a worksheet, the background does not print, and it's not included when you save an individual worksheet as a Web page. You need to publish the entire workbook as a Web page to include the background.

Add Color to Worksheet Tabs

1. Click the sheet tab you want to color.

2. Click the Format menu, point to Sheet, and then click Tab Color.

3. Click a tab color.

4. Click OK.

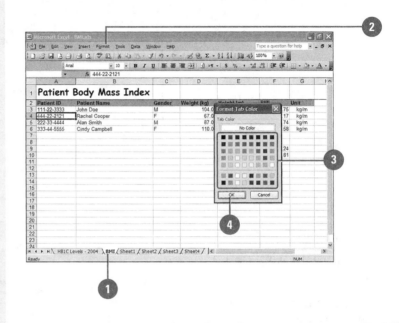

Add or Remove a Background

1. Click the sheet tab you want to add a background to.

2. Click the Format menu, point to Sheet, and then click Background.

3. Select the folder with the graphic file you want to use.

4. Select the graphic you want.

5. Click Insert.

6. To remove the background, click the Format menu, point to Sheet, and then click Remove Background.

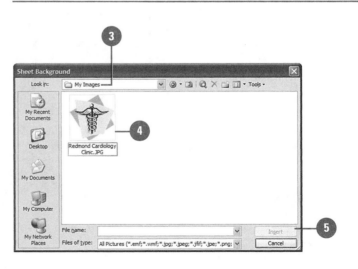

Inserting Page Breaks

If you want to print a worksheet that is larger than one page, Excel divides it into pages by inserting **automatic page breaks**. These page breaks are based on paper size, margin settings, and scaling options you set. You can change which rows or columns are printed on the page by inserting **horizontal** or **vertical page breaks**. In page break preview, you can view the page breaks and move them by dragging them to a different location on the worksheet.

Insert a Page Break

① To insert a horizontal page break, click the row where you want to insert a page break.

To insert a vertical page break, click the column where you want to insert a page break.

② Click the Insert menu, and then click Page Break.

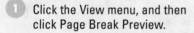

Preview and Move a Page Break

① Click the View menu, and then click Page Break Preview.

② Drag a page break (a thick blue line) to a new location.

③ When you're done, click the View menu, and then click Normal.

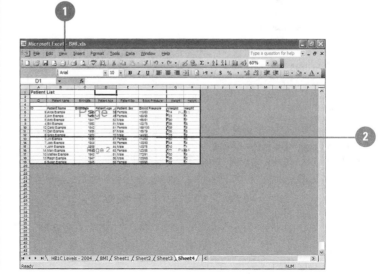

Setting Up the Page

You can set up the worksheet page to print just the way you want. With the Page Setup dialog box, you can choose the page orientation, which determines whether Excel prints the worksheet data portrait (vertically) or landscape (horizontally). You can also adjust the print scaling (to reduce or enlarge the size of printed characters), change the paper size (to match the size of paper in your printer), and resize or realign the left, right, top, and bottom margins (the blank areas along each edge of the paper). Changes made in the Page Setup dialog box are not reflected in the worksheet window. You can see them only when you preview or print the worksheet.

Change Page Orientation

1. Click the File menu, and then click Page Setup.

2. Click the Page tab.

3. Click the Portrait (8.5 x 11 inches) option (the default) or click the Landscape (11 x 8.5 inches) option to select page orientation.

4. Click OK.

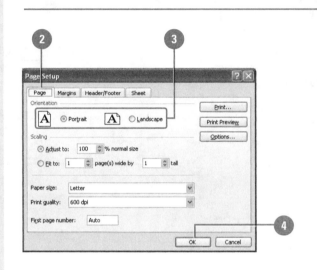

Change the Margin Settings

1. Click the File menu, and then click Page Setup.

2. Click the Margins tab.

3. Click the Top, Bottom, Left, and Right up or down arrows to adjust the margins.

4. Select the Center On Page check boxes to automatically center your data.

5. Click OK.

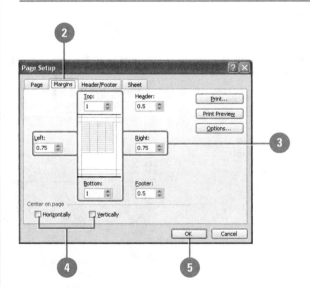

Adding Headers and Footers

Adding a header or footer to a workbook is a convenient way to make your printout easier for readers to follow. Using the Page Setup command, you can add information such as page numbers, the worksheet title, or the current date at the top and bottom of each page or section of a worksheet or workbook. Using the Custom Header and Custom Footer buttons, you can include information such as your computer system's date and time, the name of the workbook and sheet, a graphic, or other custom information.

Change a Header or Footer

1. Click the File menu, and then click Page Setup.

2. Click the Header/Footer tab.

3. If the Header box doesn't contain the information you want, click Custom Header.

4. Type the information in the Left, Center, or Right Section text boxes, or click a button to insert built-in header information. If you don't want a header to appear at all, delete the text and codes in the text boxes.

5. Select the text you want to format, click the Font button, make font changes, and then click OK. Excel will use the default font, Arial, unless you change it.

6. Click OK.

7. If the Footer box doesn't contain the information that you want, click Custom Footer.

8. Type information in the Left, Center, or Right Section text boxes, or click a button to insert the built-in footer information.

9. Click OK.

10. Click OK.

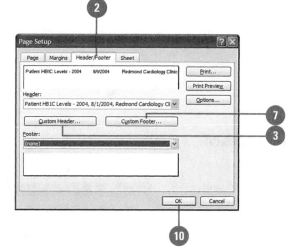

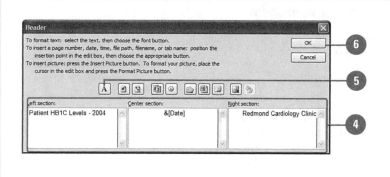

9

Customizing Worksheet Printing

At some point you'll want to print your worksheet so you can distribute it to others or use it for other purposes. You can print all or part of any worksheet, and you can control the appearance of many features, such as whether gridlines are displayed, whether column letters and row numbers are displayed, or whether to include print titles, columns and rows that are repeated on each page. If you have already set a print area, it will appear in the Print Area box on the Sheet tab of the Page Setup dialog box. You don't need to re-select it.

Print Part of a Worksheet

1. Click the File menu, and then click Page Setup.

2. Click the Sheet tab.

3. Click in the Print Area box, and then type the range you want to print. Or click the Collapse Dialog button, select the cells you want to print, and then click the Expand Dialog button to restore the dialog box.

4. Click OK.

Collapse Dialog button

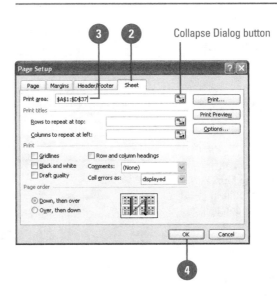

Print Row and Column Titles on Each Page

1. Click the File menu, and then click Page Setup.

2. Click the Sheet tab.

3. Enter the number of the row or the letter of the column that contains the titles. Or click the Collapse Dialog button, select the row or column with the mouse, and then click the Expand Dialog button to restore the dialog box.

4. Click OK.

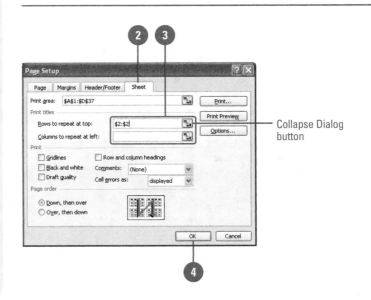

Collapse Dialog button

Print Gridlines, Column Letters, and Row Numbers

1. Click the File menu, and then click Page Setup.

2. Click the Sheet tab.

3. Select the Gridlines check box.

4. Select the Row And Column Headings check box.

5. Click OK.

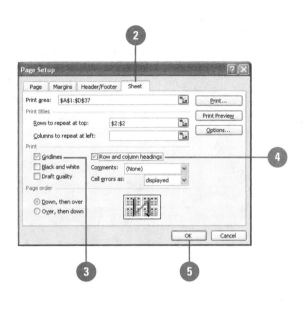

Fit Your Worksheet on a Specific Number of Pages

1. Click the File menu, and then click Page Setup.

2. Click the Page tab.

3. Select a scaling option.

   ◆ Click the Adjust To option to scale the worksheet using a percentage.

   ◆ Click the Fit To option to force a worksheet to be printed on a specific number of pages.

4. Click OK.

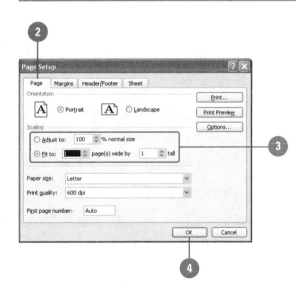

9

Setting the Print Area

When you're ready to print your worksheet, you can choose several printing options. The print area is the section of your worksheet that Excel prints. You can set the print area when you customize worksheet printing or any time when you are working on a worksheet. For example, you might want to print a different range in a worksheet for different people. In order to use headers and footers, you must first establish, or set, the print area. You can design a specific single cells or a contiguous or non-contiguous range.

Set the Print Area

1. Select the range of cells you want to print.

2. Click the File menu, and then point to Print Area.

3. Click Set Print Area.

Clear the Print Area

1. Click the File menu, and then point to Print Area.

2. Click Clear Print Area.

Previewing a Worksheet

Before printing, you should verify that the page looks the way you want. You save time, money, and paper by avoiding duplicate printing. Print Preview shows you the exact placement of your data on each printed page. You can view all or part of your worksheet as it will appear when you print it. The Print Preview toolbar makes it easy to zoom in and out to view data more comfortably, set margins and other page options, preview page breaks, and print.

Preview a Worksheet

1. Click the Print Preview button on the Standard toolbar, or click the File menu, and then click Print Preview.

2. Click the Zoom button on the Print Preview toolbar, or position the Zoom pointer anywhere on the worksheet and click it to enlarge a specific area of the page.

3. If you do not want to print from Print Preview, click the Close button to return to the worksheet.

4. If you want to print from Print Preview, click the Print button on the Print Preview toolbar.

5. Click OK.

Did You Know?

You can preview your work from the Print dialog box. In the Print dialog box, click Preview. After previewing you can click the Print button on the Print Preview toolbar to print the worksheet or click the Close button to return to your worksheet.

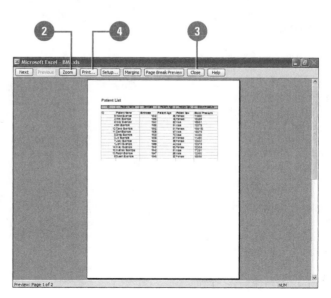

Printing a Worksheet

Printing a paper copy is a common way to review and share a document. You can print a copy of your worksheet by clicking the Print button on the Standard toolbar or on the Print Preview toolbar. When you use the Print button, Excel prints the selected worksheet with the current Print dialog box settings. You can open the Print dialog box to specify several print options, such as choosing a new printer, selecting the number of pages in the worksheet you want printed, and specifying the number of copies.

Print a Worksheet Quickly

1. Click the Print button on the Standard toolbar.

   Excel prints the selected worksheet with the current Print dialog box settings.

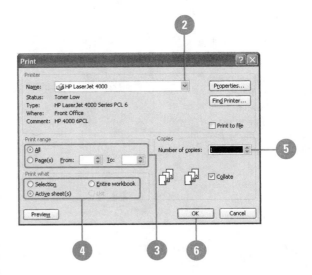

Specify Print Options

1. Click the File menu, and then click Print.

2. If necessary, click the Name list arrow, and then click the printer you want to use.

3. Select whether you want to print the entire worksheet or only the pages you specify.

4. Select whether you want to print the selected range, the active worksheet(s), or all the worksheets in the workbook with data.

5. Select the number of copies you want.

6. Click OK.

Creating a Presentation with PowerPoint

Introduction

Whether you need to put together a quick presentation for a brown-bag series in your department or create a polished slide show for a professional conference, Microsoft Office PowerPoint 2003 can help you present your information efficiently and professionally.

PowerPoint is a **presentation graphics program**—software that helps you create a slide show presentation. A slide show presentation is made up of a series of slides that can contain charts, graphs, bulleted lists, eye-catching text, multimedia video and sound clips, and more. PowerPoint makes it easy to generate and organize ideas, and it provides tools for creating the parts of an effective slide show presentation.

To help you create a presentation, PowerPoint features two kinds of templates. **Design templates** include professionally designed colors, graphics, and other visual elements you can apply to your presentation. **Content templates**, on the other hand, contain both designs and content. **Masters** contain the formatting information for each slide in your presentation and are available for each part of your presentation—slides, handouts, and speaker notes. A presentation's **color scheme** is a set of eight balanced colors that coordinates your presentation's text, borders, fills, backgrounds, and so on.

Creating a Presentation Using the AutoContent Wizard

Often the most difficult part of creating a presentation is knowing where to start. PowerPoint solves this problem for you. The **AutoContent Wizard** helps you develop presentation content on a variety of business and personal topics walking you through a step-by-step process. The wizard prompts you for presentation information, starting with the type of presentation that you want to give and output that you will use and ending with the title slide, which is the first slide in the presentation. When you finish, the wizard provides you with suggested content on 5 to 10 logically organized slides, which you can modify to meet your specific needs. Many AutoContent presentations are available in Standard and Online formats.

Create a Presentation Using the AutoContent Wizard

1. Click the File menu, and then click New.

2. Click From AutoContent Wizard on the task pane.

3. Read the first Wizard dialog box, and then click Next to continue.

4. Click the presentation type you want to use. If you want to focus on one set of presentations, such as sales presentations, click the appropriate category button, and then click the presentation type you want.

5. Click Next to continue.

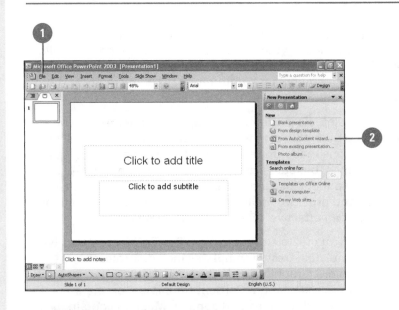

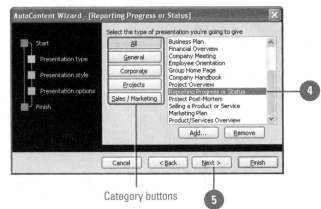

Category buttons

6. Click the presentation output option you want to use.

7. Click Next to continue.

8. Enter a presentation title and any items you want to include on each slide.

9. If you want, enter a presentation footer.

10. Select or clear the Date Last Updated check box.

11. Select or clear the Slide Number check box.

12. Click Next to continue.

13. Read the last Wizard dialog box, and then click Finish.

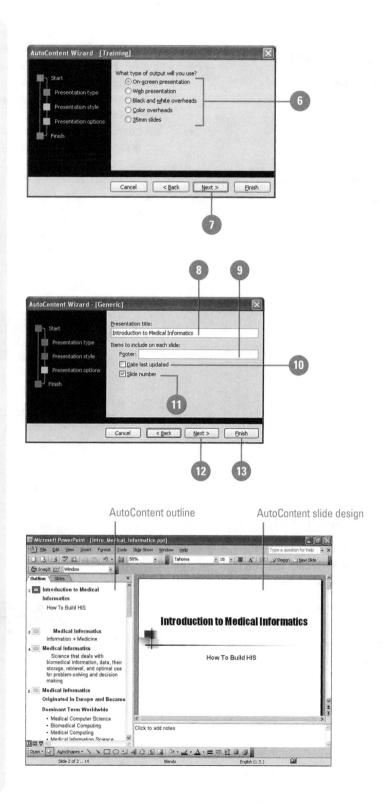

AutoContent outline

AutoContent slide design

Applying a Design Template

PowerPoint provides a collection of professionally designed templates that you can use to create effective presentations. Start with a template when you have a good idea of your content but want to take advantage of a template's professional design and formatting. Each template provides a format and color scheme so you only need to add text. You can choose a new template for your presentation at any point, either when you first start your presentation or after you've developed the content.

Create a New Presentation with a Template

1. Click the File menu, and then click New.

2. Click From Design Template on the task pane.

3. Click the slide design you want to apply to your slides.

   PowerPoint applies the design to the new presentation.

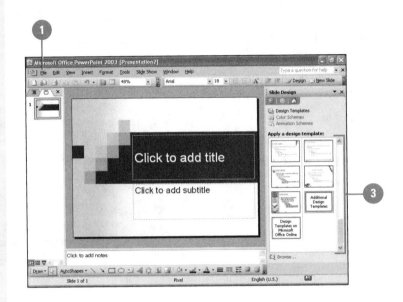

Apply a Template to an Existing Presentation

1. Click the Slide Design button on the Formatting toolbar.

2. Point to the design you want.

3. Click the list arrow, and then click Apply To All Slides, or Apply To Selected Slides.

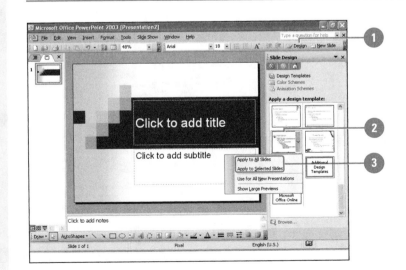

Viewing the PowerPoint Window

Title bar

Task pane

Menu bar

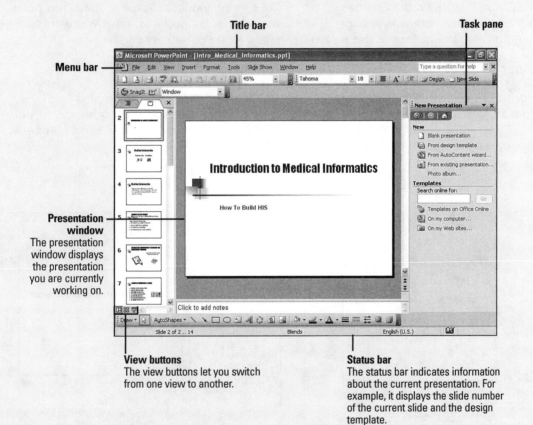

Presentation window
The presentation window displays the presentation you are currently working on.

10

View buttons
The view buttons let you switch from one view to another.

Status bar
The status bar indicates information about the current presentation. For example, it displays the slide number of the current slide and the design template.

Understanding the PowerPoint Views

To help you during all phases of developing a presentation, PowerPoint provides three different views: Normal, Slide Sorter, and Slide Show. You can switch from one view to another by clicking a view button located next to the horizontal scroll bar. In any view, you can use the Zoom feature on the Standard toolbar to increase and decrease the page view size and display the slide to fit the screen.

your presentation and let you work on all of its parts. You can adjust the size of the panes by dragging the pane borders. You can use the Outline pane to develop and organize your presentation's content. Use the Slide pane to add text, graphics, movies, sounds, and hyperlinks to individual slides, and the Notes pane to add speaker notes or notes you want to share with your audience.

Normal view

Use the Normal view to work with the three underlying elements of a presentation—the outline, slide, and notes—each in its own pane. These panes provide an overview of

Outline pane

Use the Outline pane in Normal view to develop your presentation's content. Individual slides are numbered and a slide icon appears for each slide.

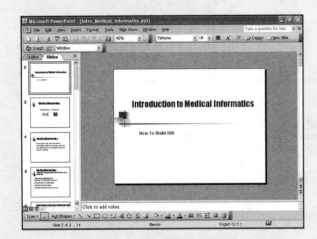

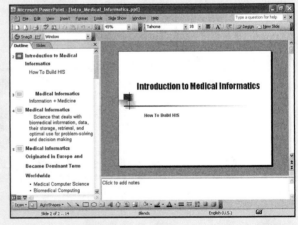

Slide pane

Use the Slides pane in Normal view to preview each slide. Click the slide you want to view. You can also move through your slides using the scroll bars or the Previous Slide and Next Slide buttons. When you drag the scroll box up or down on the vertical scroll bar, a label appears that indicates which slide will be displayed if you release the mouse button.

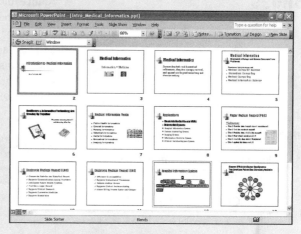

Slide Show view

Slide Show view presents your slides one at a time. Use this view when you're ready to rehearse or give your presentation. To move through the slides, click the screen, or press Enter to move through the show.

Slide Sorter view

Use the Slide Sorter view to organize your slides, add actions between slides—called slide transitions—and apply other effects to your slide show. The Slide Sorter toolbar helps you to add slide transitions and to control your presentation. When you add a slide transition, you see an icon that indicates an action will take place as one slide replaces another during a show. If you hide a slide, you see an icon that indicates the slide will not be shown during the presentation.

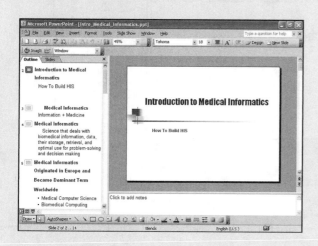

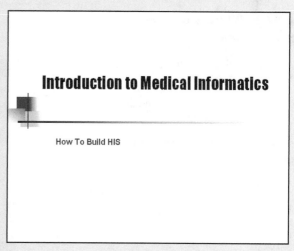

Creating Consistent Slides

You need to arrange the objects on your slides in a visually meaningful way so that others can understand your presentation. PowerPoint's **AutoLayout** feature helps you arrange objects on your slide in a consistent manner. When you create a new slide, you apply an AutoLayout to it. You see design elements and placeholders for text and other objects. You can also apply an AutoLayout to an existing slide at any time. When you change a slide's AutoLayout, you keep existing information. PowerPoint applies the new AutoLayout, and you can arrange the placeholders the way you want them.

Insert a New Slide

1. Click the New Slide button on the Formatting toolbar.

2. Click the AutoLayout you want to use.

> **Did You Know?**
>
> *You can delete a slide quickly.* In Outline or Slides pane or Slide Sorter view, select the slide you want to delete, and then press Delete.

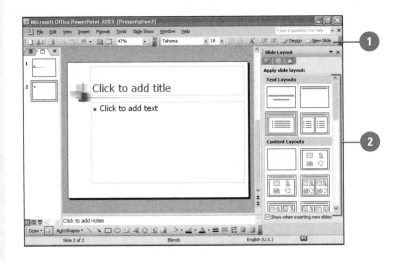

Apply an AutoLayout to an Existing Slide

1. In Normal view, display the slide you want to change.

2. Click the Format menu, and then click Slide Layout.

3. Click the AutoLayout you want.

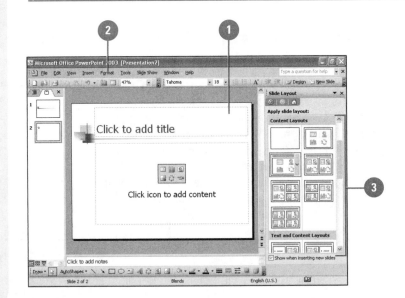

Enter Information in a Placeholder

◆ For text placeholders, click the placeholder, and then type the text.

◆ For other objects, click the placeholder, and then work with the accessory that PowerPoint starts.

Did You Know?

You can duplicate a slide. In the Outline or Slide pane of Normal view, click the slide you want to duplicate, Click the Edit menu, and then click Duplicate.

You can hide master background objects on a slide. Display the slide whose background object you want to hide, click the Format menu, click Background, select the Omit Background Graphics From Master check box, and then click Apply or Apply To All.

AutoLayout Placeholders

A placeholder is a border that defines the size and location of an object.

AutoLayout Placeholders

Placeholder	Description
Bulleted List	Displays a short list of related items
Clip Art	Inserts a picture from the Clip Organizer
Chart	Inserts a chart
Diagram or Organization Chart	Inserts an organizational chart
Table	Inserts a table from Microsoft Word
Media Clip	Inserts a music, sound, or video clip
Picture	Inserts a picture from a file

10

Entering and Deleting Text

In Normal or Slide view, you type text directly into the text placeholders. A **text placeholder** is an empty text box. If you type more text than fits in the placeholder, the text is resized to fit on the slide. The **AutoFit** Text feature changes the line spacing—or **paragraph spacing**—between lines of text and then changes the font size to make the text fit. You can also manually increase or decrease the line spacing or font size of the text. The insertion point (the blinking vertical line) indicates where text will appear when you type. To place the **insertion point** into your text, move the pointer arrow over the text. The pointer changes to an I-beam to indicate that you can click and then type.

Enter Text into a Placeholder

1. In Normal view, click the text placeholder if it isn't already selected.

2. Type the text you want to enter.

3. Click outside the text object to deselect the object.

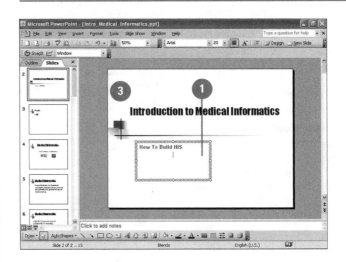

Insert and Delete Text

1. Click to place the insertion point where you want to insert text.

2. Type the text.

3. To delete text, press the Backspace key (deletes left) or the Delete key (deletes right).

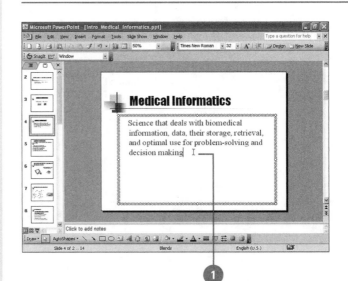

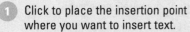

Enter Text in a Bulleted List

1. In Normal view, click in the bulleted text placeholder.

2. Type the first bulleted item.

3. Press Enter.

4. Type the next bulleted item.

5. Repeat steps 3 and 4 until you complete the list.

   If you type more text than can fit on a slide, the AutoFit button appears.

6. Click the AutoFit button, and then click the option you want to fit the text on the slide.

Did You Know?

You can use the insertion point to determine text location. When entering bulleted text, be sure the insertion point is at the beginning of the line, and then press Tab to indent a level, or press Shift+Tab to move back out a level.

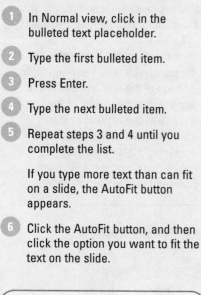

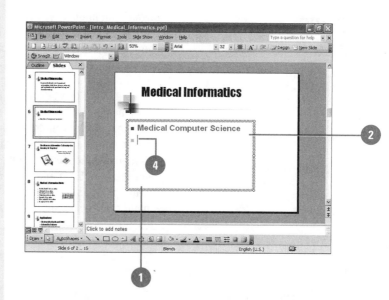

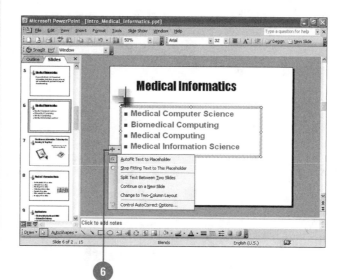

10

Aligning and Spacing Text

PowerPoint enables you to control the way text lines up on the slide. You can align text to the left or right or to the center in a text object. You can also adjust the alignment of text in an object by selecting the object and clicking an alignment button (Align Left, Center, or Align Right) on the Formatting toolbar. The Align Left button aligns text evenly along the left edge of the text box and is useful for paragraph text. The Align Right button aligns text evenly along the right edge of the text box and is useful for text labels. The Center button aligns text in the middle of the text box and is useful for titles and headings. Adjust the vertical space between selected lines and the space before and after paragraphs by selecting the object and clicking a line spacing button (Increase Paragraph Spacing or Decrease Paragraph Spacing) on the Formatting toolbar or by using the Line Spacing command on the Format menu.

Change Text Alignment

1. Select the text box.

2. On the Formatting toolbar, click an alignment button (Align Left, Center, or Align Right).

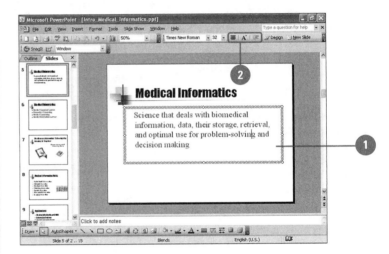

Adjust Line Spacing

1. Select the text object with the dotted selection box or click anywhere in the paragraph you want to adjust.

2. On the Format menu, click Line Spacing.

3. Click the Before Paragraph or After Paragraph arrows to select a setting.

4. Click OK.

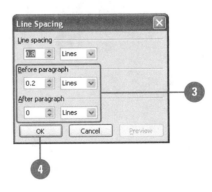

Modifying Page Setup ▶

Before you develop a presentation, you should use the Page Setup dialog box to set the proportions of your presentation slides and their orientation on the page. The presentation size and orientation affects how much information you can put on a slide. The standard size for an on-screen presentation is 10 by 7.5 inches. If you are creating a presentation for print purposes, the 8.5 by 11 inch letter paper size works the best. You can also control slide numbering from the Page Setup dialog box.

Modify Page Setup

1. Click the File menu, and then click Page Setup.

2. Click the Slides Sized For list arrow, and then select the size you want.

   To customize the slide size, click the Width and Height up and down arrows to enter a specific width and height in inches.

3. Click the Portrait or Landscape option to orient your slides.

4. Click the Portrait or Landscape option to orient your notes, handouts, and outline.

5. To specify the starting page number, click the Number Slides From up and down arrows.

6. Click OK.

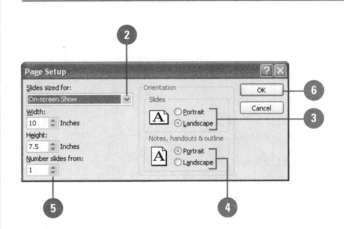

10

Developing an Outline

If you create your presentation using an AutoContent Wizard, Power-Point generates an outline. If you prefer to develop your own outline, you can create a blank presentation and then type your outline. As you develop an outline, you can add new slides and duplicate existing slides in your presentation. You can also insert an outline you created in another program, such as Microsoft Word. Make sure the document containing the outline is set up using outline heading styles. When you insert the outline in PowerPoint, it creates slide titles, subtitles, and bulleted lists based on those styles.

Enter Text in Outline Pane

1. In the Outline pane of Normal view, click to position the insertion point where you want the text to appear.

2. Type the text you want to enter, pressing Enter after each line.

3. Press Tab to indent the text in one level, or press Shift+Tab to indent the text out one level.

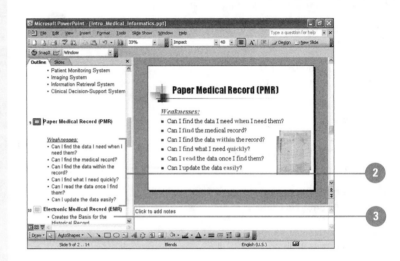

Add a Slide in Outline Pane

1. In the Outline pane of Normal view, click at the end of the slide text where you want to insert a new slide.

2. Click the New Slide button on the Formatting toolbar, and double-click a layout, or press Ctrl+Enter to insert a new slide.

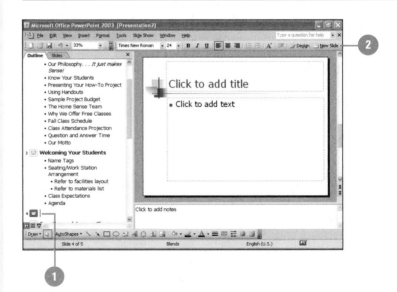

Move Text to Different Levels in an Outline

1. In the Outline pane in Normal view, click in the line you want to indent.

2. If necessary, click the View menu, point to Toolbars, and then click Outlining to display the Outlining toolbar.

3. Click the button you want:

    ◆ To indent the line in one level, click the Promote button.

    ◆ To indent the line out one level, click the Demote button.

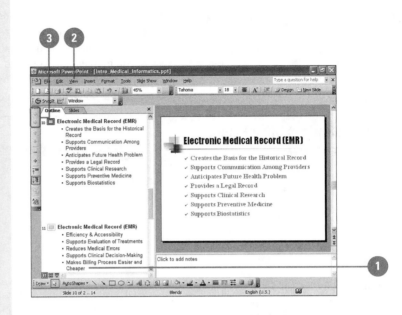

Insert an Outline from Another Program

1. In the Outline pane of Normal view, click the slide after which you want to insert an outline.

2. Click the Insert menu, and then click Slides From Outline.

3. Locate and then select the file containing the outline you want to insert.

4. Click Insert.

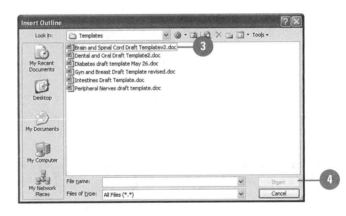

Did You Know?

You can open an outline from another program in PowerPoint. Click the Open button on the Standard toolbar, click the Files Of Type list arrow, click All Outlines, and then double-click the outline file you want to open.

10

Rearranging Slides

You can instantly rearrange slides in Outline or Slide pane or in Slide Sorter view. You can use the drag-and-drop method or the Cut and Paste buttons to move slides to a new location. In the Outline pane of Normal view, you can use the Move Up and Move Down buttons to move selected slides within the outline. You can also collapse the outline to its major points so you can more easily see its structure.

Rearrange a Slide in Slide Pane or Slide Sorter View

① Click the Slide pane in Normal view, or click the Slide Sorter View button.

② Select the slide(s) you want to move.

③ Drag the selected slide to a new location. A vertical bar appears where the slide(s) will be moved when you release the mouse button.

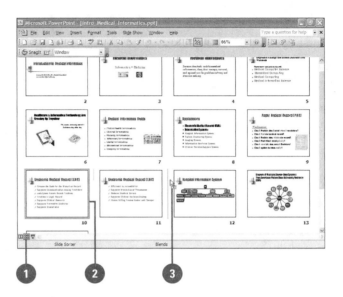

Rearrange a Slide in the Outline Pane

① In the Outline pane in Normal view, click the slide icon you want to move.

TIMESAVER *Drag the slide up or down to move it in Outline pane.*

② If necessary, click the View menu, point to Toolbars, and then click Outlining to display the Outlining toolbar.

③ Click the Move Up button, or click the Move Down button.

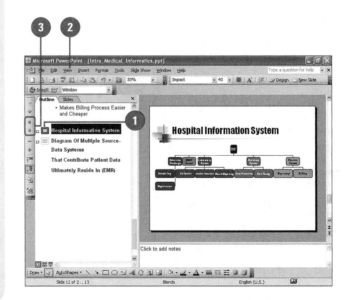

Move a Slide Using Cut and Paste

1. In the Outline or Slide pane or in Slide Sorter view, select the slide(s) you want to move.

2. Click the Cut button on the Standard toolbar.

3. Click the new location.

4. Click the Paste button on the Standard toolbar.

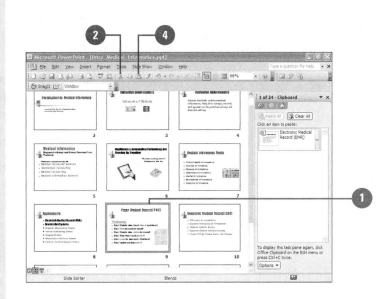

Collapse and Expand Slides in the Outline Pane

1. In the Outline pane in Normal view, select the slide you want to work with, and then click the button you want:

   ◆ To collapse the selected slides, click the Collapse button.

   A horizontal line appears below a collapsed slide in Outline view.

   ◆ To expand the selected slides, click the Expand button.

   ◆ To collapse all slides, click the Collapse All button.

   ◆ To expand all slides, click the Expand All button.

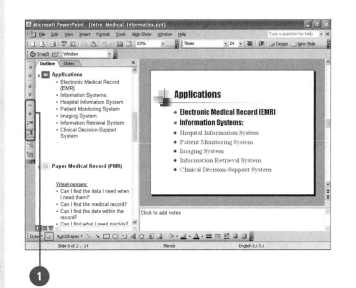

10

Controlling Slide Appearance with Masters

If you want an object, such as a hospital logo or clip art, to appear on every slide in your presentation (except the title slide), place it on the **Slide Master**. All of the characteristics of the Slide Master (background color, text color, font, and font size) appear on every slide. The title slide has its own master, called the **Title Master**. Each master contains placeholders. You can modify and arrange placeholders for the date and time, footers, and slide numbers. The Slide Master View toolbar contains several buttons to insert, delete, rename, duplicate, and preserve masters. When you preserve a master, you protect it from being deleted.

Include an Object on Every Slide

1. Click the View menu, point to Master, and then click Slide Master.

   TIMESAVER *Press and hold Shift, and then click the Normal view button to view the Slide Master.*

2. Add the object you want, and then modify its size and placement.

3. Click the Close Master View button on the Slide Master View toolbar.

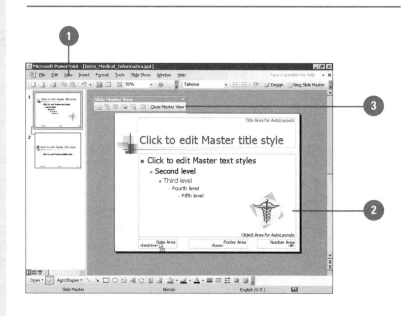

Insert a New Master

1. Click the View menu, point to Master, and then click Slide Master.

2. To insert a new master, click the Insert New Slide Master button, or click the Insert New Title Master button on the Slide Master View toolbar.

3. To lock a master, click the Preserve Master button.

4. Click the Close Master View button on the Slide Master View toolbar.

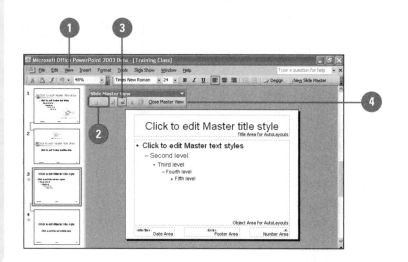

Apply a Design Template to a Master

1. Click the View menu, point to Master, and then click Slide Master.

2. Select the master slide you want to apply a design.

3. Click the Slide Design button on the Formatting toolbar.

4. Point to the design you want, click the list arrow, and then click Replace Selected Designs.

5. Click the Close Master View button on the Slide Master View toolbar.

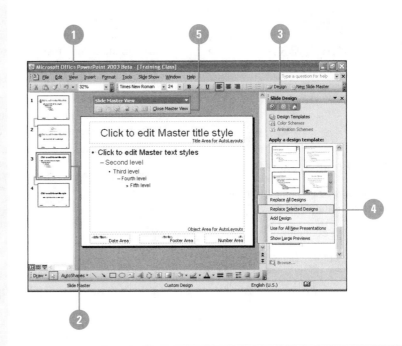

Modify Placeholders

1. Click the View menu, point to Master, and then click Slide Master.

2. Select the master slide with the placeholder you want to change.

3. Select the placeholder you want to change.

4. To format the placeholder, use the formatting tools on the Formatting toolbar.

5. To delete the placeholder, press the Delete key.

6. To add placeholders, click the Master Layout button on the Slide Master View toolbar, select the check boxes with the placeholders you want to add, and then click OK.

7. Click the Close Master View button on the Slide Master View toolbar.

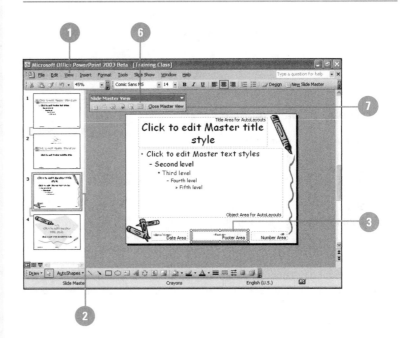

10

Working with Color Schemes

Every presentation, even a blank one, contains a set of colors called a color scheme. A **color scheme** is a set of eight colors designed to be used as the colors in slide presentations. The color scheme determines the colors for the background, text, lines, shadows, fills, and accents of slides. You can apply a color scheme to one slide or all slides in a presentation. You can choose from one or more standard color schemes in each template. You can also create your own color schemes and save them so you can apply them to other slides and presentations.

Choose a Color Scheme

1. Click the Slide Design button on the Formatting toolbar.

2. Click Color Schemes.

3. Click the color scheme you want.

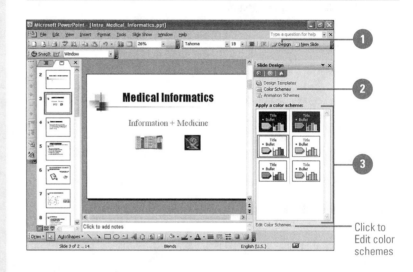

Click to Edit color schemes

Edit or Delete a Color Scheme

1. Click the Slide Design button on the Formatting toolbar.

2. Click Edit Color Schemes.

3. To edit a color scheme, click the Custom tab, double-click a color, click a new color, and then click OK.

4. To delete a color scheme, click the Standard tab, click the scheme that you want to delete, and then click Delete Scheme.

5. Click Apply.

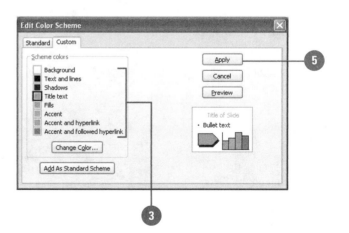

Apply the Color Scheme of One Slide to Another Slide

① Click the Slide Sorter View button.

② Click the slide with the color scheme you want to apply.

③ Click the Format Painter button on the Standard toolbar to apply the color scheme to one slide, or double-click the button to apply the color scheme to multiple slides.

④ Click the slides to which you want to apply the color scheme. The slides can be in the current presentation or in another open presentation.

⑤ If you are applying the scheme to more than one slide, press Esc to cancel Format Painter. If you are applying the scheme to only one slide, Format Painter is canceled automatically.

Did You Know?

You can save a changed color scheme. Click the Format menu, click Slide Design, click Edit Color Schemes, and then click the Custom tab. Change the color scheme until all eight colors are as you want them, and then click Add As Standard Scheme.

10

Applying Color and Effects to an Object

When you want to change the color of only one element in your presentation on only one slide, you don't need to use the Color Scheme dialog box. Instead, you can select the object and open the Color dialog box for the color you want to change—the fill, border, line, text, and so on. The fill is the inside pattern or color of an object or background. For example, if you have drawn a square, the fill is the color inside the border. PowerPoint fill effects include gradients, textures, patterns, and pictures. The Color dialog box looks the same from one element to another. When you work with color, you should keep in mind whether you'll be printing handouts in black and white. PowerPoint makes it easy to preview color presentations in grayscale and black and white.

Change an Object's Color

1. Click the object(s) whose color you want to change.

2. Click the Fill Color, Line Color, or Text Color button on the Drawing toolbar to change an object's color.

3. Click a color from the color scheme, or click More Fill Colors, and then select a color.

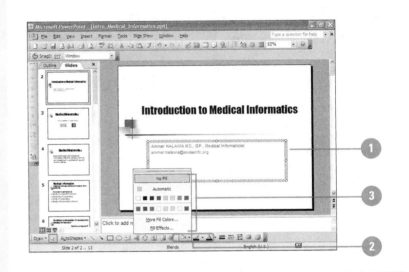

Change an Object's Fill Effect

1. Click the object(s) whose color you want to change.

2. Click the Fill Color button on the Drawing toolbar.

3. Click Fill Effects.

4. Click the tab (Gradient, Texture, Pattern, or Picture) with the fill effect you want.

5. Select the options for the fill effect you want.

6. Click OK.

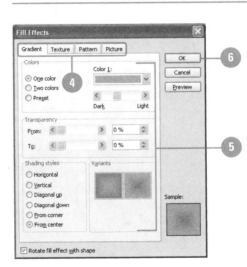

Change the Slide Background

1. Display the slide whose background you want to change.

2. Click the Format menu, and then click Background.

3. Click the Background Fill list arrow.

4. Select the color you want.

5. Click Apply, or click Apply To All.

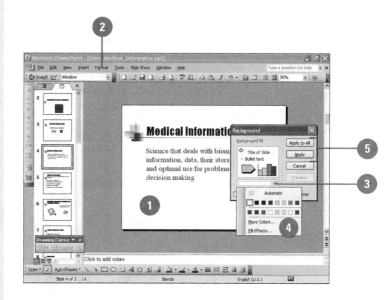

View a Presentation in Black and White

1. Click the Color/Grayscale button on the Standard toolbar.

2. Click Grayscale or Pure Black And White.

3. Click the Close Grayscale View button on the Grayscale View toolbar.

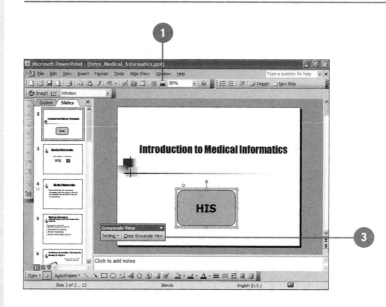

10

Working with Objects ▶

If you create a collection of objects that work together, you can group them to create a new drawing object that you can move, resize, or copy as a single unit. If you need to change the orientation of a drawing object, you can rotate or flip it. For example, if you want to create a mirror image of your object, you can flip it, or if you want to turn an object on its side, you can rotate it 90 degrees. Rotating and flipping tools work with drawing and text objects. You can join two shapes together with a connecting line to create a flow chart or diagram. Once two shapes are joined, the connecting line moves when you move either shape.

Group Objects Together

1. Select the objects you want to group together.

2. Click the Draw button on the Drawing toolbar, and then click Group.

Did You Know?

You can regroup an object quickly. Select one of the objects in the group of objects you want to regroup, click the Draw button on the Drawing toolbar, and then click Regroup.

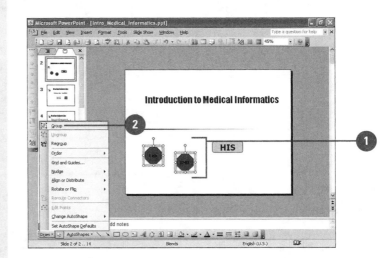

Ungroup a Drawing

1. Select the grouped object you want to ungroup.

2. Click the Draw button on the Drawing toolbar, and then click Ungroup.

Did You Know?

You can use the Tab key to select objects in order. Move between the drawing objects on your slide (even those hidden behind other objects) by pressing the Tab key.

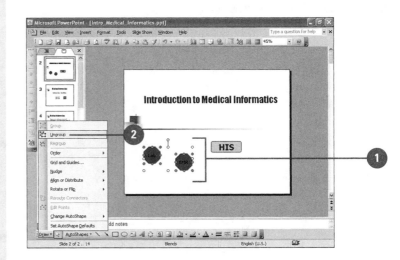

Rotate or Flip an Object

1. Click the object you want to rotate.

2. Click the Draw button on the Drawing toolbar.

3. Point to Rotate Or Flip, and then click the option you want.

   If you click Free Rotate, drag the rotation handle to rotate the object.

Did You Know?

You can orient text vertically. Select the text object, click the Format menu, click Text Box, select the Rotate Text Within AutoShape By 90° check box, and then click OK.

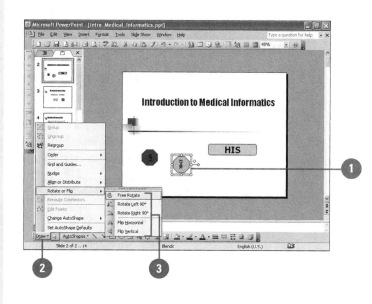

Connect Shapes

1. Click AutoShapes on the Drawing toolbar, point to Connectors, and then click a connection option.

2. Position the pointer over a small blue handle on a shape, and then click the object to select a connection.

3. Position the pointer over a small blue handle on another shape, and then click the object.

   Red handles appear at each end of the line, indicating the objects are connected. A yellow, diamond-shaped handle appears in the middle of the connector lines so that you can resize the curve of the line.

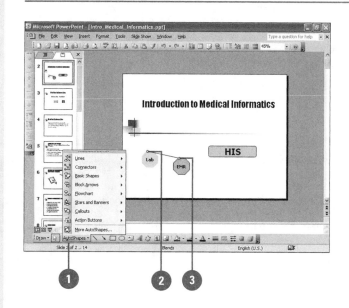

Aligning and Arranging Objects

PowerPoint offers several tools for controlling where you place objects on the slide. One tool is the **grid**, an invisible matrix of lines. When the Snap Objects To Grid option is on, an object snaps, or aligns, to the nearest point on the grid. You can also use **alignment guides**—horizontal and vertical lines superimposed on the slide to help manually align objects. When an object is close to a guide, its edge or center, whichever is closer, snaps to the guide. PowerPoint also lets you distribute objects evenly horizontally and vertically across the slide. If multiple objects overlap, the most recently created drawing is placed on top of older drawings. You can change the order of this stack of objects.

Display the Grid and Guides

1. Click the Draw button on the Drawing toolbar, and then click Grids And Guides.

2. Select or clear the Snap Objects To Grid check box.

3. Select or clear the Display Grid On Screen check box.

   TIMESAVER *Click the Show/Hide Grid button on the Standard toolbar.*

4. Select or clear the Display Drawing Guides On Screen check box.

5. Click OK.

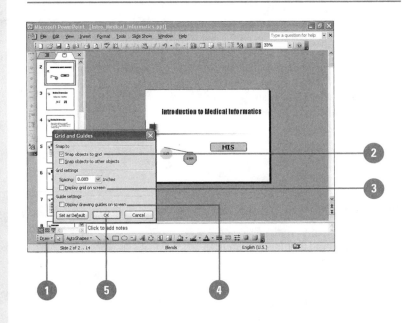

Align an Object to a Guide

1. Display the Guides.

2. Position the pointer over a guide, and then drag to change its position.

3. Drag the object's center or edge near the guide. PowerPoint aligns the center or edge to the guide.

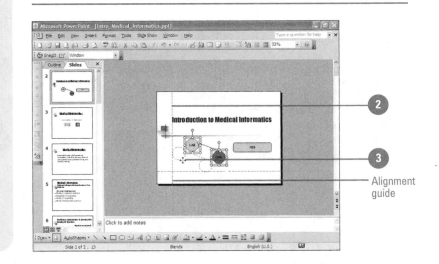

Alignment guide

Align or Distribute Objects

① Select the objects you want to align or distribute.

② Click the Draw button on the Drawing toolbar, point to Align Or Distribute, and then click the command you want:

◆ Click Align Left, Align Center, Align Right, Align Top, Align Middle, or Align Bottom.

◆ Click Distribute Horizontally or Distribute Vertically.

◆ Select Relative To Slide if you want the objects to align relative to the slide, or deselect it if you want the objects to align relative to each other.

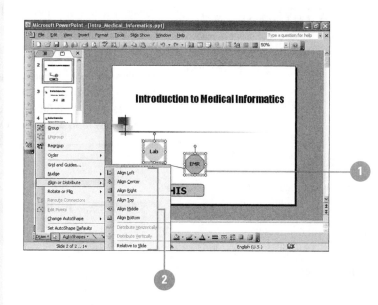

Arrange a Stack of Objects

① Select the objects you want to arrange.

② Click the Draw button on the Drawing toolbar, point to Order, and then click the command you want:

◆ Click Bring To Front or Bring Forward to move a drawing to the top of the stack or up one location in the stack.

◆ Click Send To Back or Send Backward to move a drawing to the bottom of the stack or back one location in the stack.

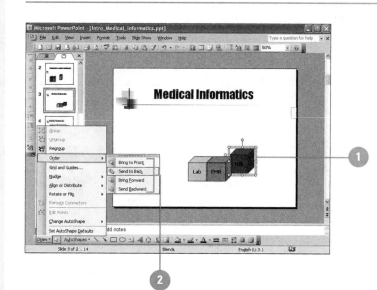

10

Creating a Text Box

Usually you use the title, subtitle, and bulleted list placeholders to place text on a slide. However, when you want to add text outside one of the standard placeholders, you can create a text box. Your text box doesn't have to be rectangular—you can also use one of PowerPoint's **AutoShapes**, a collection of shapes that range from rectangles and circles to arrows and stars. When you place text in an AutoShape, the text becomes part of the AutoShape. Text boxes appear in the Slide pane of Normal view or in Slide Sorter view, but not in the Outline pane.

Create a Text Box

1. In Normal view, click the View menu, point to Toolbars, and then click Drawing to display the Drawing toolbar, if necessary.

2. Click the Text Box button on the Drawing toolbar.

3. To add text that wraps, drag to lengthen the box, and then start typing.

   To add text that doesn't wrap, click and then start typing.

4. Click outside the text box to deselect it.

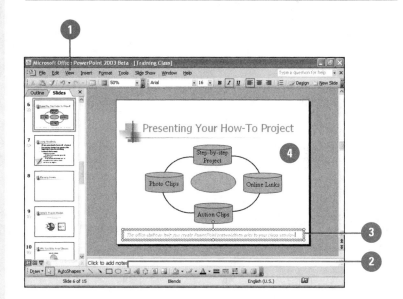

Add Text to an AutoShape

1. Select the AutoShape to which you want to add text.

2. Type the text.

Did You Know?

You can wrap text in an AutoShape or resize it. Right-click the AutoShape, click Format AutoShape, click the Text Box tab, select the Word Wrap In AutoShape check box or select the Resize To Fit Text check box, and then click OK.

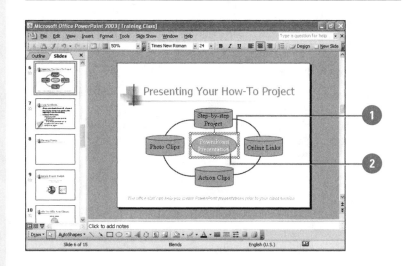

Inserting Slides from Other Presentations

To insert slides from other presentations in a slide show, you can open the presentation and copy and paste the slides you want, or you can use the **Slide Finder** feature. With Slide Finder, you don't have to open the presentation first; instead, you view a **miniature** of each slide in a presentation, and then insert only the ones you select. With Slide Finder, you can also create a list of favorite presentations for use in future slide shows.

Insert Slides Using the Slide Finder

1. Click the Insert menu, and then click Slides From Files.

2. Click the Find Presentation tab.

3. Click Browse, locate and select the file you want, and then click Open.

4. If necessary, click Display to display a miniature of each slide.

5. Select the slides you want to insert.

   ◆ To insert just one slide, click the slide, and then click Insert.

   ◆ To insert multiple slides, click each slide you want to insert, and then click Insert.

   ◆ To insert all the slides in the presentation, click Insert All.

6. Click Close.

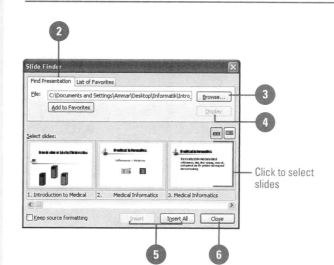

Click to select slides

Did You Know?

You can add or remove a slide presentation from your list of favorites. Click the Insert menu, click Slides From Files, locate the presentation you want to add, click Add To Favorites, and then click OK. Click the List Of Favorites tab, select the presentation you want to remove, and then click Remove.

10

Inserting a Table

A table organizes information neatly into rows and columns. The intersection of a column and row is called a cell. You enter text into cells just as you would anywhere else in PowerPoint, except that pressing the Tab key moves you from one cell to the next. PowerPoint tables behave much like tables in Word. After you create a table or begin to enter text in one, you can use the Tables and Borders toolbar to add more rows or columns, align cell contents, and format the table.

Insert a Table Quickly

1. In Normal or Slide view, display the slide to which you want to add a table.

2. Click the Insert Table button on the Standard toolbar.

3. Drag to select the number of rows and columns you want.

4. Release the mouse button to insert a blank table. Press Esc to cancel the selection.

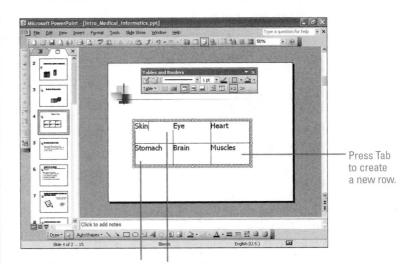

The first number indicates the number of rows. The second number indicates the number of columns.

Enter Text and Move Around in a Table

Click in a cell to place the insertion point, type your text, and then choose one of the following:

- Press Enter to start a new paragraph within that cell.

- Press Tab to move the insertion point to the next cell to the right (or to the first cell in the next row).

- Use the arrow keys or click in a cell in the table to move around.

Press Tab to create a new row.

Press Tab to move from here to the next cell to the right.

Type and format text just as you would in an object.

> ### See Also
>
> See "Modifying a Table" on page 134 and "Formatting a Table" on page 138 for information on working with tables.

Inserting and Playing Media

You can insert movies or sounds into a presentation by inserting them from the Clip Organizer or a file. Movies can be either animated pictures, also known as animated GIFs, such as cartoons, or they can be digital videos prepared with digitized video equipment. Movies and sounds are inserted as PowerPoint objects. When you insert a sound, a small icon appears representing the sound file, which you can hide during a slide show. You can modify videos and sounds so they play continuously or just one time. You can also view and play movies using the full screen. When Windows Media Player 8 or later is installed on your computer, PowerPoint supports its file formats. To play sounds, or sounds from video, you need a sound card and speakers.

Insert a Movie or Sound

1. Click the Insert menu, point to Movies And Sound, and then click a command to insert a movie or sound from the Clip Organizer or a file.

2. Locate the movie or sound you want to insert from the Clip Organizer or a folder.

3. Click the movie or sound you want in the Clip Organizer or click one from the dialog box, and then click OK.

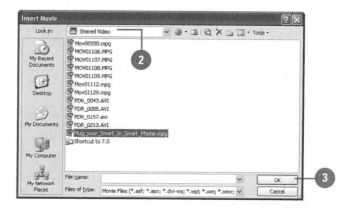

Change Play Options

1. Right-click the sound icon or movie object, and then click Edit Sound Object or Edit Movie Object.

2. Change the sound or movie settings.

   ◆ To play continuously, select the Loop Until Stopped check box.

   ◆ For a movie, select the Rewind Movie When Done Playing check box, or select the Zoom To Full Screen check box.

   ◆ For a sound, select the Hide Sound Icon During Slide Show check box.

3. Click OK.

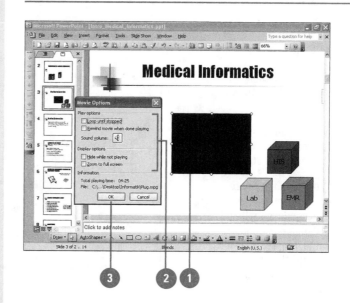

10

Checking Style and Spelling

PowerPoint's spelling checker checks the spelling of the entire presentation, including all slides, outlines, notes pages, and handout pages. You can correct misspelled words in your presentation two different ways. Use the Spelling button on the Standard toolbar to check the entire presentation, or when you encounter a wavy red line under a word, you can right-click the word and choose the correct spelling from the list. PowerPoint's style checker works with the Office Assistant to help you correct common presentation style mistakes, such as incorrect font size, inconsistent punctuation, and other readability problems.

Set Style Options

1. Click the Tools menu, and then click Options.

2. Click the Spelling And Style tab.

3. Select the Check Style check box.

4. Click Style Options.

5. Click the Case And End Punctuation tab or the Visual Clarity tab.

6. Select the style options you want to set.

7. Click OK twice.

Check Style or Spelling

◆ If a light bulb appears, click the light bulb, and then click an option on the Office Assistant.

◆ If a red wavy line appears under a word as you type, right-click it, and then click the correct spelling.

◆ If you want to check the entire presentation, click the Spelling button on the Standard toolbar. If the Spelling dialog box appears, use the Change, Ignore, and Add buttons to change the spelling, ignore the word, or add it to the dictionary.

Style Options

Case and End Punctuation | Visual Clarity

Case
☑ Slide title style: Title Case
☑ Body text style: Sentence case

End punctuation
☐ Slide title punctuation: Paragraphs have punctuation
☑ Body punctuation: Paragraphs have consistent punctuation

To check for the consistent use of end punctuation other than periods, enter characters in the edit boxes below:
Slide title: [ ]   Body text: [ ]

OK   Cancel   Defaults

Click the light bulb to correct style.

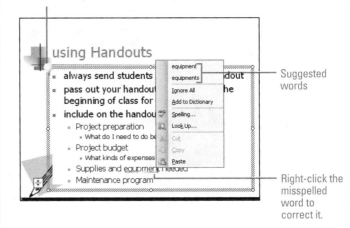

using Handouts
- always send students ... dout
- pass out your handou ... he beginning of class for
- include on the handou
  - Project preparation
    - What do I need to do be
  - Project budget
    - What kinds of expenses
  - Supplies and equipment needed
  - Maintenance program

equipment
equipments
Ignore All
Add to Dictionary
Spelling...
Look Up...
Cut
Copy
Paste

Suggested words

Right-click the misspelled word to correct it.

Delivering a Presentation with PowerPoint

Introduction

Microsoft Office PowerPoint 2003 provides many tools to help make your slide show a complete multimedia production.

Before you can deliver a slide show, you need to set up for the type of show you want. Some presentations include slides that are appropriate for one audience but not for another. PowerPoint lets you create custom slide shows that include only a selection of slides, in whatever order you want, intended for a given audience.

A slide show can feature special visual, sound, and animation effects. For example, you can include special **transitions**, or actions, between slides. Using **animations**—effects that animate your slide elements such as text flying in from the right—you can also control how the audience first sees each element of the slide. PowerPoint includes tools that let you time your presentation to make sure that it is neither too long nor too short. You can also make a PowerPoint presentation come alive with the proper use of narration and music.

As you deliver your slide show, it's helpful to have speaker notes and handouts for your audience to follow. PowerPoint makes it easy to create and print presentation supplements, such as speaker notes, handouts, and transparencies.

Adding Action Buttons

When you create a self-running presentation to show at a conference kiosk, you might want a user to be able to move easily to specific slides or to a different presentation altogether. To give a user this capability, insert **action buttons**, which are onscreen objects that users can click to control a presentation. Clicking an action button activates a **hyperlink**, a connection between two locations in the same document or in different documents.

Insert an Action Button

1. Click the Slide Show menu.

2. Point to Action Buttons, and then choose the action button you want.

3. Drag the pointer to insert the action button, and then release the mouse button when the action button is the size you want.

4. If necessary, fill out the Action Settings dialog box, and then click OK.

5. If the button is custom, right-click the button, click Add Text, and then type a name.

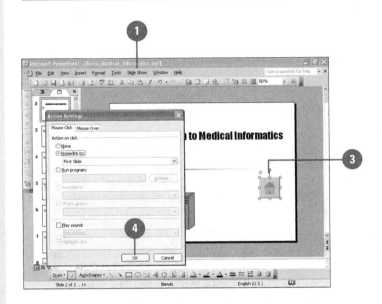

Test an Action Button

1. Click the Slide Show View button.

2. Display the slide containing the action button.

3. Click the action button.

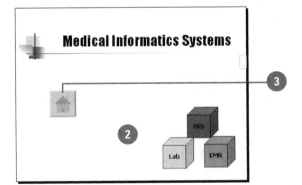

Create an Action to Go to a Specific Slide

1. Select the text or object in which you want to apply an action.

2. Click the Slide Show menu, and then click Action Settings.

3. Click the Mouse Click tab or the Mouse Over tab, which determines how the action behaves.

4. Click the Hyperlink To option, click the list arrow, and then click Slide from the list of hyperlink destinations.

5. Select the slide you want the action button to jump to.

6. Click OK.

7. Click OK.

8. Click outside the action button to deselect it.

9. Run the slide show, and test the action button.

Did You Know?

You can create a hyperlink to external places. In the Action Settings dialog box, click the Hyperlink To list arrow, and then click a place where you want to go, such as a URL, a PowerPoint presentation, or another slide show.

You can insert the Return action button to help navigate the slide show. If you want to return to the slide you were previously viewing, regardless of its location in the presentation, insert the Return action button.

Creating Slide Transitions

If you want to give your presentation more visual interest, you can add transitions between slides. For example, you can create a **fading out** effect so that one slide fades out as it is replaced by a new slide, or you can have one slide appear to push another slide out of the way. When you add a transition effect to a slide, the effect takes place between the previous slide and the selected slide. You can also add sound effects to your transitions, although you need a sound card and speakers to play them.

Apply a Transition

1. Click the Slide Sorter View button.

2. Click the slide(s) to which you want to add a transition effect.

   TIMESAVER *In Normal view, click the Slide Show menu, and then click Slide Transition to add a transition to a slide.*

3. Click the Slide Transition button on the Slide Sorter toolbar.

4. Click the transition effect you want.

5. To apply the transition to all slides, click Apply To All Slides.

6. When you're done, click the Close button on the task pane.

Did You Know?

You can view a slide's transition quickly in Slide Sorter view. In Slide Sorter view, click a slide's transition icon to view the transition effect.

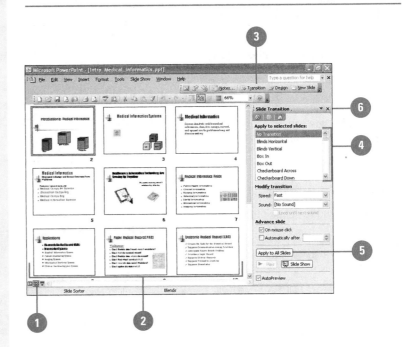

Set Transition Effect Speeds

1. In Normal or Slide Sorter view, click or display the slide(s) whose transition effect you want to edit.

2. Click the Slide Show menu, and then click Slide Transition.

3. Click the Speed list arrow, and then click Slow, Medium, or Fast.

4. To apply the transition effect to all slides, click Apply To All Slides.

5. When you're done, click the Close button on the task pane.

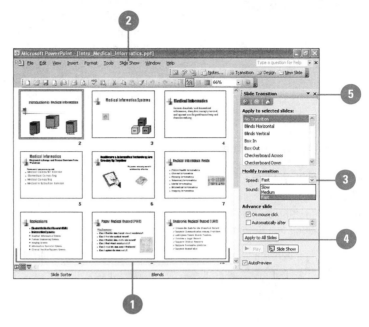

Add Sound to a Transition

1. In Normal or Slide Sorter view, click or display the slide to which you want to add a transition sound.

2. Click the Slide Show menu, and then click Slide Transition.

3. Click the Sound list arrow, and then click the sound you want.

4. To apply the transition effect to all slides, click Apply To All Slides.

5. When you're done, click the Close button on the task pane.

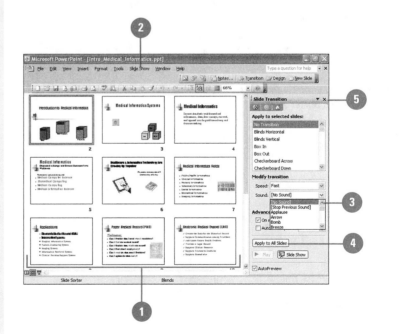

11

Adding Animation

You can use animation to introduce objects onto a slide one at a time or with special animation effects. For example, a bulleted list can appear one bulleted item at a time, or a picture or chart can fade gradually into the slide's foreground. You can use many kinds of animations with PowerPoint. Some are called **animations schemes**—animation effects that PowerPoint has designed for you. Many of the preset animations contain sounds. You can also design your own **customized animations**, including those with your own special effects and sound elements.

Apply an Animation Scheme

1. Select the slide or object you want to animate.

2. Click the Slide Show menu, and then click Animation Schemes.

3. Click the animation you want.

4. To apply the animation scheme to all slides, click Apply To All Slides.

5. To preview the animation, click Play.

6. When you're done, click the Close button on the task pane.

Did You Know?

You can view a slide's animation quickly in Slide Sorter view. In Slide Sorter view, click a slide's animation icon to view the animation.

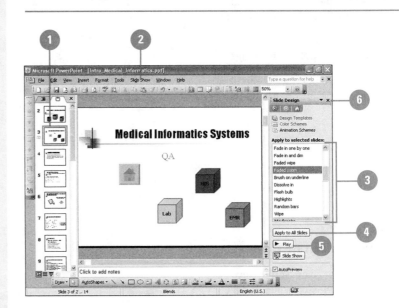

Remove an Animation Scheme

1 Select the slide or object you want to animate.

2 Click the Slide Show menu, and then click Animation Schemes.

3 Click No Animation.

4 When you're done, click the Close button on the task pane.

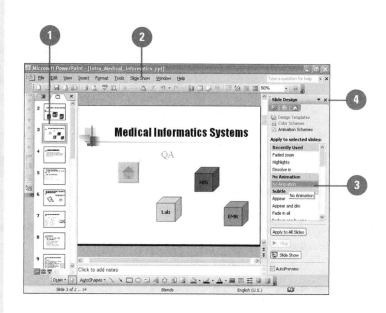

Change an Animation Scheme

1 In Normal, right-click the object, and then click Custom Animation.

2 Click the animation scheme item you want to change.

3 To remove it, click Remove.

4 To modify it, click a list arrow (Start, Direction, or Speed), and then click an option.

5 To preview it, click Play.

6 When you're done, click the Close button on the task pane.

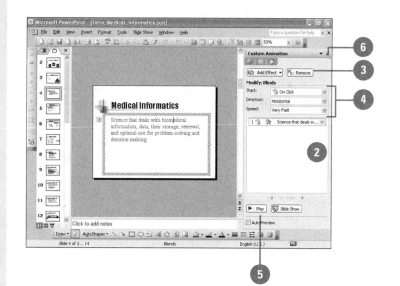

11

Using Specialized Animations

Using specialized animations, you can apply animations specific to certain objects. For example, for a text object, you can introduce the text on your slide all at once or by word or letter. Similarly, you can introduce bulleted lists one bullet item at a time and apply different effects to older items, such as graying out the items as they are replaced by new ones. You can animate charts by introducing chart series or chart categories one at a time.

Animate Text

① In Normal view, right-click the selected text object, and then click Custom Animation.

② Click Add Effect, and then choose an effect from the list of animation effects.

③ When you're done, click the Close button on the task pane.

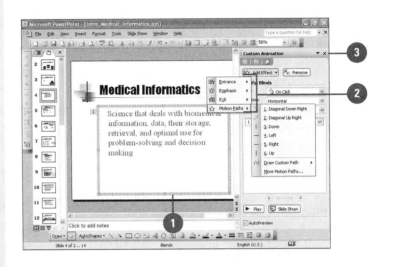

Modify the Animation Order

① In Normal view, display the slide with the animation, click the Slide Show menu, and then click Custom Animation.

② Click the animation effect whose animation order you want to change.

③ Click the Re-Order Up or Re-Order Down arrow button.

④ When you're done, click the Close button on the task pane.

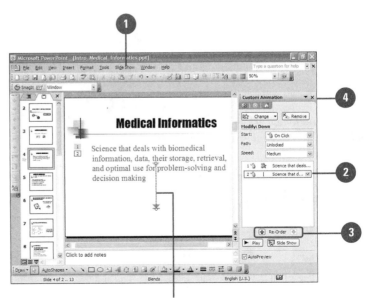

Animation effect

Animate Bulleted Lists

1. In Normal view, right-click the bulleted text, and then click Custom Animation.

2. Click Add Effect, and then choose an effect from the list of animation effects.

3. Click the animation effect, click the list arrow, and then click Effect Options.

4. Click the Text Animation tab.

5. Click the Group Text list arrow, and then click at what paragraph level bulleted text will be animated.

6. To reverse the order of the text, select the In Reverse Order check box.

7. To dim text after it's animated, click the Effect tab, click the Dim list arrow, and then click an option.

8. Click OK.

9. When you're done, click the Close button on the task pane.

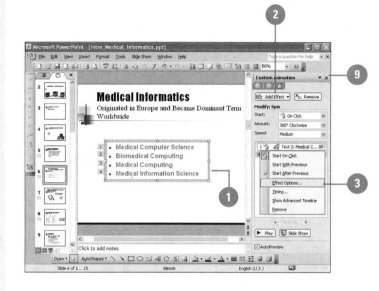

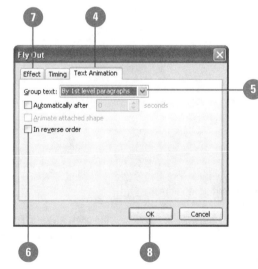

Did You Know?

You can set and show animation timing. In the Custom Animation task pane, select an animated item, click the list arrow, and then click Timing to set animation timings or click Show Advanced Timeline to display a time-line where you can click Play to view the animation effect and its progress. Click the list arrow, and then click Hide Advanced Timeline to hide it again.

Timing a Presentation ▶

If you have a time limit for presenting your slide show, you can use PowerPoint's timing features to make sure that your presentation is not taking too long or going too fast. You can specify the amount of time given to each slide and test yourself during rehearsal using the **slide meter**, which ensures that your timings are workable. By rehearsing timings, you can vary the amount of time each slide appears on the screen. If you want the timings to take effect, make sure the show is set to use timings in the Set Up Show dialog box.

Set Timings Between All Slides

① Click the Slide Show menu, and then click Slide Transition.

② Select the Automatically After check box.

③ Enter the time (in seconds) before the presentation automatically advances to the next slide after displaying the entire slide.

④ Click Apply To All Slides.

⑤ When you're done, click the Close button on the task pane.

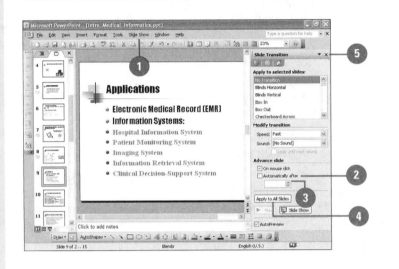

Create Timings Through Rehearsal

① Click the Slide Show menu, and then click Rehearse Timings.

② As the slide show runs, rehearse your presentation by clicking the mouse or pressing Enter to go the next slide.

③ Click Yes to accept the timings you just recorded.

④ Review the timings in Slide Sorter view.

Time, in seconds, spent on this slide

Time for the entire presentation

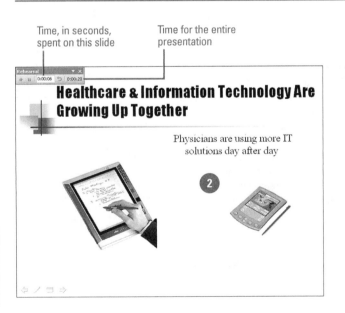

Setting Up a
Slide Show

PowerPoint offers several types of slide shows appropriate for a variety of presentation situations, from a traditional full-screen slide show to a show that runs automatically on a computer screen at a conference kiosk. When you don't want to show all of the slides in a PowerPoint presentation to a particular audience, you can specify only a range of slides to show, or you can hide individual slides.

Set Up a Show

1 Click the Slide Show menu, and then click Set Up Show.

2 Choose the show type you want:

◆ Click the Presented By A Speaker option to run a traditional full-screen slide show, where you can advance the slides manually or automatically.

◆ Click the Browsed By An Individual option to run a slide show in a window and allow access to some PowerPoint commands.

◆ Click the Browsed At A Kiosk option to create a self-running, unattended slide show for a booth or kiosk. The slides will advance automatically, or a user can advance the slides or activate hyperlinks.

3 Change additional show options as appropriate.

◆ Loop Continuously Until 'Esc'

◆ Show Without Narration

◆ Show Without Animation

4 Click OK.

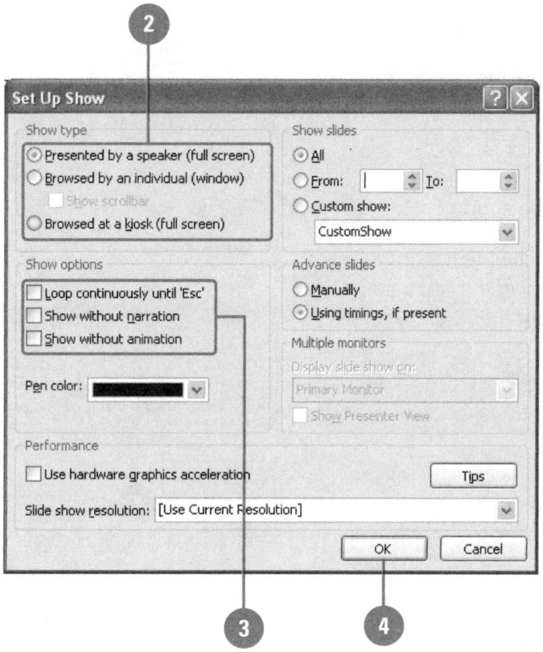

11

Creating a Custom Slide Show

If you plan to present a slide show to more than one audience, you don't have to create a separate slide show for each audience. Instead, you can create a **custom slide show** that allows you to specify which slides from the presentation you will use and the order in which they will appear. You can also customize a presentation for a specific audience by using the Hide Slide command. You can hide the slides that you don't want to use during a slide show but still want to keep.

Create a Custom Slide Show

1. Click the Slide Show menu, and then click Custom Shows.

2. Click New.

3. Type a name for the show.

4. Double-click the slides you want to include in the show in the order you want to present them.

5. Click OK.

6. Click Close.

Show a Custom Slide Show

1. Click the Slide Show menu, and then click Custom Shows.

2. Click the custom slide show you want to run.

3. Click Show.

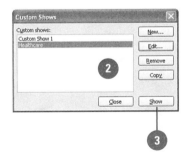

Did You Know?

You can use the Set Up Show command to display a custom slide show. Click the Slide Show menu, click Set Up Show, click the Custom Show option, click the Custom Show list arrow, select the custom slide show, and then click OK.

Hide and Display a Slide

1. Display the slide you want to hide in Normal view or select the slide in Slide Sorter view.

2. Click the Slide Show menu, and then click Hide Slide.

3. To display a hidden slide, click the Slide Show menu, and then click Hide Slide again.

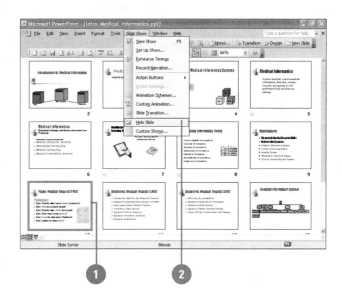

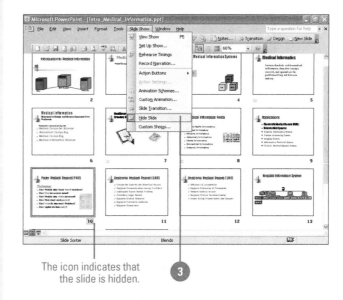

The icon indicates that the slide is hidden.

Starting a Slide Show

Once you have set up your slide show, you can start the show at any time. As you run your slide show, you can use the Slide Show view popup menu to access certain PowerPoint commands without leaving Slide Show view. If your show is running at a kiosk, you might want to disable this feature.

Start a Slide Show and Display the Popup Toolbar

1. Click the Slide Show menu, and then click View Show.

2. Move the mouse pointer to display the Popup toolbar.

3. Click a button on the Popup toolbar to move to the next or previous slide, or navigate the slide show, or end the show.

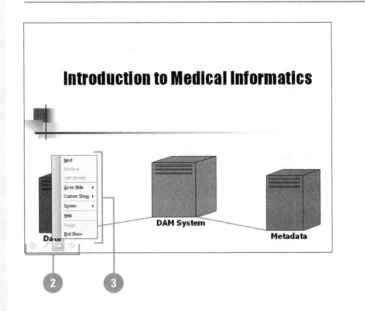

Set Slide Show Options

1. Click the Tools menu, and then click Options.

2. Click the View tab.

3. Select the slide show and popup toolbar options you want.

4. Click OK.

> ### Did You Know?
>
> **You can start a slide show quickly from the current slide.** Click the Slide Show button.

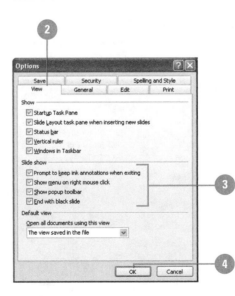

Navigating a Slide Show

In Slide Show view, you advance to the next slide by clicking the mouse button, pressing the Spacebar, or pressing Enter. In addition to those basic navigational techniques, PowerPoint provides keyboard shortcuts that can take you to the beginning, the end, or any particular slide in your presentation. You can also use the navigation commands on the shortcut menu to access slides in custom slide shows. After a period of inactivity during a normal full-screen slide show, PowerPoint hides the pointer and Slide Show icon.

Go to a Specific Slide

1. In Slide Show view, right-click a slide.

2. Point to Go To Slide.

3. Click the title of the slide you want to go to.

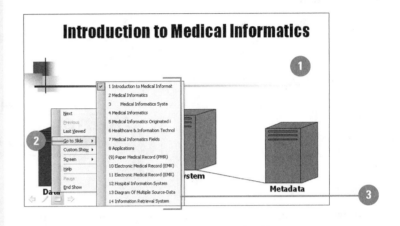

Use Slide Show View Navigation Shortcuts

1. Refer to the adjacent table for information on Slide Show view navigation shortcuts.

Did You Know?

You can add speaker notes in Slide Show. In Slide Show view, right-click a blank area on the slide, point to Screen, click Speaker Notes, type your notes, and then click OK.

You can switch to another program in Slide Show. In Slide Show view, right-click a blank area on the slide, point to Screen, and then click Switch Programs. Use the taskbar to switch between programs.

Slide Show View Shortcuts

Action	Result
Mouse click	Moves to the next slide
Right-mouse click	Moves to previous the slide (only if the Shortcut Menu On Right-Click option is disabled)
Press Enter	Moves to the next slide
Press Home	Moves to the first slide in the show
Press End	Moves to the last slide in the show
Press Page Up	Moves to the previous slide
Press Page Down	Moves to the next slide
Enter a slide number and press Enter	Moves to the slide number you specified when you press Enter
Press B	Displays a black screen; press again to return
Press W	Displays a white screen; press again to return
Press Esc	Exits Slide Show view

Annotating a Slide Show

When you are presenting your slide show, you can turn your mouse pointer or Tablet PC pen into a light pen to highlight and circle your key points. If you decide to use a light pen, you might want to set its colors to match the colors in your presentation. Marks you make in a slide with the light pen during a slide show are not permanent. If you don't need to display the pointer, you can change pointer options to automatically hide the mouse or Tablet PC pen until you move it or permanently display or hide it.

Change Pointer Options

1. In Slide Show view, move the mouse to display slide show buttons.

2. Click the Pen button, point to Arrow Options, and then click a pointer option.

   ◆ Automatic hides the pointer until you move the mouse.

   ◆ Visible makes the pointer visible.

   ◆ Hidden makes the pointer invisible throughout the presentation.

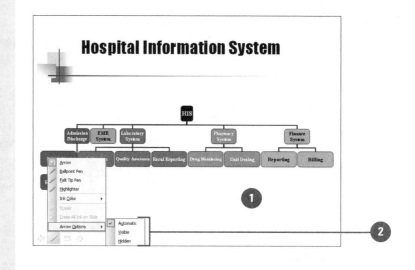

Use a Pen During the Slide Show

1. In Slide Show view, move the mouse to display slide show buttons.

2. Click the Pen button, and then click or point to an option.

   ◆ A writing tool (Ballpoint Pen, Felt Tip Pen, or Highlighter).

   ◆ Ink Color to select an ink color.

3. Drag the mouse pointer to draw on your slide presentation with the pen or highlighter.

4. Click the Pen button, and then click Eraser to remove individual ink or Erase All Ink On Slide.

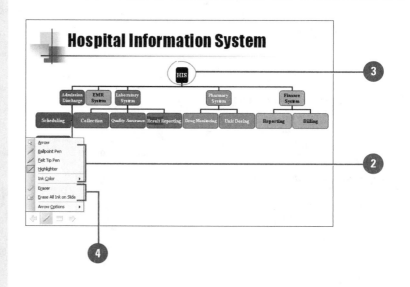

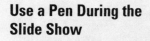

Adding a Header and Footer

A header and footer appear on every slide. You can choose not to have them appear on the title slide. They often include information such as the presentation title, slide number, date, and name of the presenter. Use the masters to place header and footer information on your slides, handouts, or notes pages. Make sure your header and footer don't make your presentation look cluttered. Their default font size is usually small enough to minimize distraction, but you can experiment by changing their font size and placement to make sure.

Add a Header and Footer

1. Click the View menu, and then click Header And Footer.

2. Click the Slide or Notes And Handouts tab.

3. Enter or select the information you want to include on your slide or your notes and handouts.

4. Click Apply to apply your selections to the current slide, or click Apply To All to apply the selections to all slides.

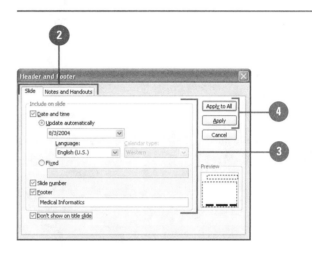

See Also

See "Controlling Slide Appearance with Masters" on page 238 for information on changing the look of a header or footer.

Did You Know?

You don't have to show a header or footer on the title slide. Click the View menu, click Header And Footer, click the Slide tab, select the Don't Show On Title Slide check box, and then click Apply To All.

11

Preparing Speaker Notes and Handouts

You can add speaker notes to a slide in Normal view using the Notes pane. Also, every slide has a corresponding **notes page** that displays a reduced image of the slide and a text placeholder where you can enter speaker notes. Once you have created speaker notes, you can reference them as you give your presentation, either from a printed copy or from your computer. You can enhance your notes by including objects on the notes master. The objects that you add to the notes master will appear when you print the notes pages. They do not appear in the Notes pane of Normal view or when you save your presentation as a Web page. The dotted rectangles on the master are placeholders for slides and for header and footer information.

Enter Notes in Normal View

1. In Normal view, switch to the slide for which you want to enter notes.

2. Click in the Notes pane, and then type your notes.

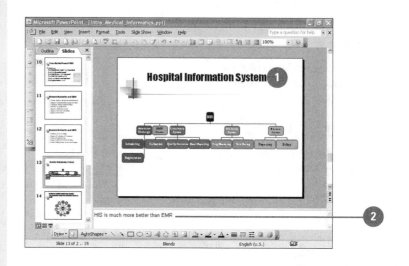

Enter Notes in Notes Page View

1. Switch to the slide for which you want to enter notes.

2. Click the View menu, and then click Notes Page.

3. If necessary, click the Zoom list arrow, and then increase the zoom percentage to better see the text you type.

4. Click the text placeholder.

5. Type your notes.

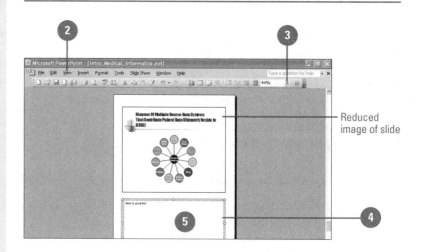

Reduced image of slide

Format the Notes Master

1. Click the View menu, point to Master, and then click Notes Master.

2. Use the Formatting and Drawing toolbar buttons to format the master.

3. If you want, add a header, footer, date, or page numbering.

4. Click the Close Master View button on the Notes Master View toolbar.

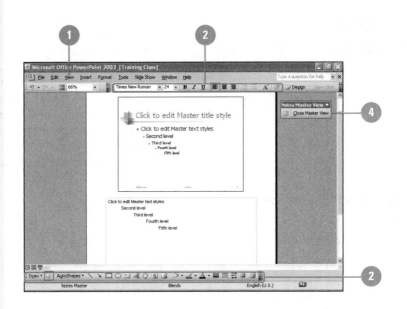

Format the Handout Master

1. Click the View menu, point to Master, and then click Handout Master.

2. Click a button to specify how many slides you want per page.

3. Use the Formatting and Drawing toolbar buttons to format the master.

4. If you want, add a header, footer, date, and page numbering.

5. Click the Close Master View button on the Handout Master View toolbar.

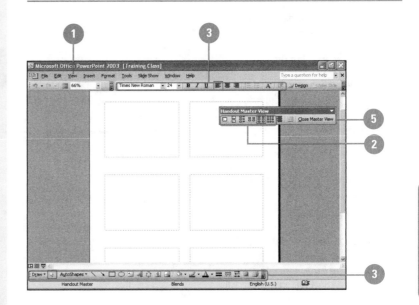

11

Previewing and Printing a Presentation

Before printing, you should verify that the slides look the way you want. You save time, money, and paper by avoiding duplicate printing. Print Preview shows you exactly how your slides will look on each printed page. The Print Preview toolbar provides the tools you need to proof the look of each slide. You can print all the elements of your presentation—the slides, outline, notes, and handouts—in either color or black and white. The Print dialog box offers standard Windows features, giving you the option to print multiple copies, specify ranges, access printer properties, and print to a file. When you print an outline, PowerPoint prints the presentation outline as shown in Outline view.

Preview a Presentation

1. Click the Print Preview button on the Standard toolbar.

2. Click the Print What list arrow, and then select the item (slides, handouts, notes pages, or outline) you want to preview.

3. Click the Options button on the Print Preview toolbar, and then click or point to an option.

   ◆ Header And Footer

   ◆ Color/Grayscale

   ◆ Scale To Fit Paper

   ◆ Frame Slides

   ◆ Print Hidden Slides

   ◆ Print Comments And Ink Mark UP

   ◆ Printing Order

4. To change the orientation of the previewed item, click the Landscape button or Portrait button on the Print Preview toolbar.

5. Click the Next Page button or Previous Page button on the Print Preview toolbar to display pages.

6. When you're done, click the Close button on the Print Preview toolbar.

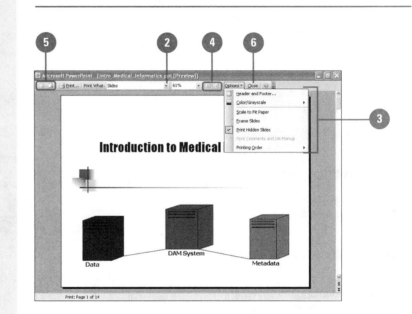

Print a Presentation

1. Click the File menu, and then click Print.

2. Click the Name list arrow, and then click a printer.

3. Click the Print What list arrow, and then click what you want to print.

4. Select a print range.

5. Specify the number of copies.

6. If necessary, specify the handout settings.

7. Click OK.

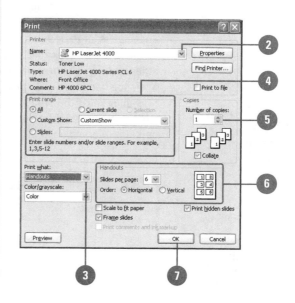

Print an Outline

1. In Outline view, display the outline the way you want it to be printed.

   ◆ Display only slide titles or all text levels

   ◆ Display with or without formatting

   ◆ Display with a small or large view percentage

2. Click the File menu, and then click Print.

3. Click the Print What list arrow, and then click Outline View.

4. Click OK.

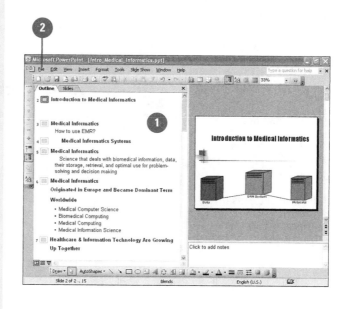

11

Broadcasting a Presentation

With online broadcasting, you can give or view a slide show over a computer network or on the Internet. Broadcasting is useful when your audience is large or at remote locations. Using an e-mail program, such as Microsoft Outlook 2003, you can schedule the broadcast just like any other meeting. The presentation saves as a Web page so that all your audience needs is a Web page browser to see the presentation. After the presenter starts the broadcast, each member of the audience needs to join the broadcast. After joining, each member sees a lobby page that contains information about the broadcast before it starts.

Set up and Schedule a New Broadcast

1. Open the presentation you want to broadcast.

2. Click the Slide Show menu, point to Online Broadcast, and then click Schedule A Live Broadcast.

3. Click Settings.

4. Click Browse, navigate to a shared folder, and then click Select.

5. Click OK.

6. Type your description.

7. Click Schedule.

8. Enter schedule information.

9. Enter e-mail addresses for the participants you want to invite to the online broadcast.

10. Click Send, and then click Yes to continue.

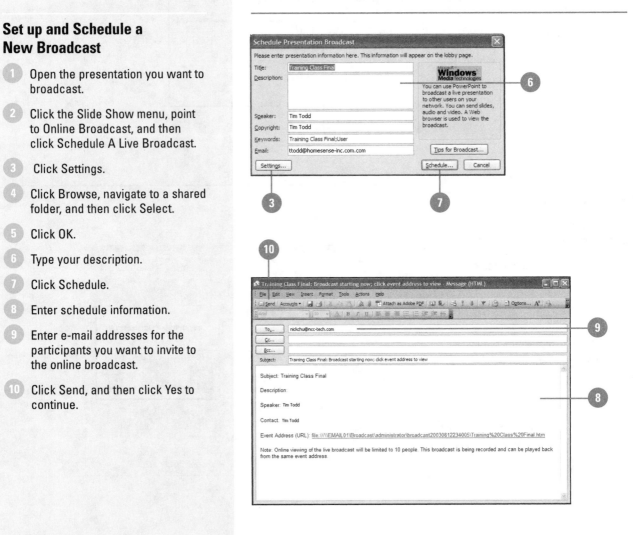

Start a Broadcast

1. Open and save the presentation that you want to broadcast.

2. Click the Slide Show menu, point to Online Broadcast, and then click Start Live Broadcast Now.

3. Select the broadcast presentation you want to present.

4. Click Broadcast.

   Your presentation saves as a Web page, at the location that you designated.

5. When you are ready to begin, click Start.

Did You Know?

You can join a broadcast. You need Internet Explorer 5.01 or later. Open the e-mail message that contains the broadcast invitation, and then click the URL for the broadcast.

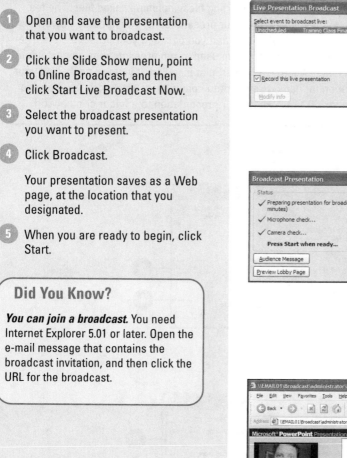

Online broadcast for the audience

11

Packaging a Presentation on CD

The Package for CD feature allows you to copy on CD one or more presentations and all of the supporting files, including linked files. The feature also automatically runs your presentations. The updated PowerPoint viewer is included on the CD when you package your presentations. The PowerPoint Viewer is a program used to run presentations on computers that don't have Microsoft PowerPoint installed. If you are packaging your presentation for use on your laptop computer or a network, you can use Package for CD to package your presentation to a folder or a network.

Package a Presentation on CD

1. Click the File menu, and then click Package For CD.

2. Type a name for the CD.

3. To add additional files to the CD, click Add Files, select the files you want, and then click Add.

4. Click Options.

5. To include the PowerPoint Viewer, select the PowerPoint Viewer check box, and then select a play option from the list arrow.

6. To link any external files (such as movies), select the Linked Files check box.

7. To make sure fonts are available on the play back computer, select the Embedded TrueType Fonts check box.

8. If you want, type a password to open or modify the presentation.

9. Click OK.

10. To copy to a folder, click Copy To Folder, specify a folder location, and then click OK.

11. Click Copy To CD, and then follow the CD writer instructions for your operating system.

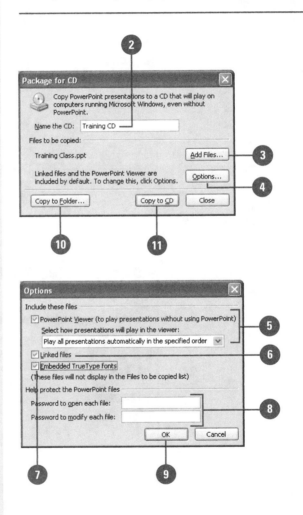

Creating a Database with Access

Introduction

Few fields are as information-intensive as healthcare. The practice of healthcare is characterized as one where information is processed, reprocessed, retrieved, and communicated. Microsoft Office Access 2003 helps you organize large amounts of healthcare information and build connections among them with ease. For example, you can create a database of your patients and the medications they are on, to track progress of hypertensive patients and how effective their medications are relative to the patient age and gender. You can easily generate mailing labels to communicate with the patients in your database that are due for a follow up. And much, much more.

You can start working with databases right away by looking at the sample database applications provided with Access, which you can use to store your own personal or practice data. Access also offers a set of database wizards that aid you in creating common business databases. These sample databases can give you some ideas for designing your own database for storing types of data not covered by the existing samples and wizards.

When you are working with an existing database, however, you don't need to worry about the complexities of database design. You just need to know how to move around the database you are using. The tasks that you are likely to perform with an existing database include entering and viewing data or subsets of data, creating and printing reports, and working efficiently with all the windows in front of you.

Understanding How Databases Store Data

Storing Data on a Computer

Some lists can serve a much more useful purpose when stored on a computer. For example, the patient names, addresses, and phone numbers you jot down on cards or in a paper address book are used only when you have the paper list in your hand. Suppose you currently store names and addresses on cards. All the information about a particular person is stored in one place.

If you store that list on a computer, however, you can do much more with it than just refer to it. For example, you can generate lists of all diabetic patients, you can print mailing labels for visit reminder cards, you can create lists of this month's birthdays for pediatric patients, and so on.

There are a number of ways to store lists on a computer. For example, you can store a list in a Microsoft Word table or on a Microsoft Excel spreadsheet.

If you place this information in a Word table or on an Excel spreadsheet, you are faced with a problem: you end up repeating some of the information. Consider what happens if a family moves or a last name is changed. You have to ensure that information is updated everywhere it's stored. For a small list that might not matter, but for a large list with information that requires constant updating (such as an address list), it is a huge task to keep data up-to-date in this way.

Storing Data in a Database

If, on the other hand, you save address information in an Access database, you can ensure that each piece of information is entered only once.

An Access database consists of objects, such as tables, forms, queries, reports, pages, macros, and modules.

- A **table** is a collection of related information about a topic, such as names and addresses. A table consists of fields and records. A field stores each piece of information in a table, such as first name, last name, or address. A record is a collection of all the fields for one patient.

- A **form** provides an easy way to view and enter information into a database. Typically, forms display one record at a time.

- A **query** is a method to find information in a database. The information you find with a query is based on conditions you specify.

- **Reports** are documents that summarize information from the database.

- **Pages** enable you to access a database on the Internet using a Web browser.

- A **macro** saves you time by automating a series of actions into one action.

- **Modules** are programs you create in a programming language called Visual Basic for Applications (VBA), which extend the functionality of a database.

A database table with fields and records

Frequently Asked Questions

What Is a Microsoft Access Project?

A Microsoft Office Access project is an Access data file that provides access to a Microsoft SQL Server database through the OLE DB component architecture, which provides network and Internet access to many types of data sources. An Access project is called a project because it contains only code-based or HTML-based database objects: forms, reports, the name and location of data access pages, macros, and modules. Unlike an Access database, an Access project doesn't contain any data or data objects, such as tables, views, database diagrams, stored procedures, or user-defined functions. Working with an Access project is virtually the same as working with an Access database, except you need to connect to an SQL Server database, which stores the data.

Creating a Database

You can use a wizard to create a database, or you can create a custom database from scratch. The Access database wizards help you create databases suited to your specific needs. Each wizard guides you through the process of selecting and creating fields, tables, queries, reports, and forms, which makes it easier to use the database. When you create a database, you need to assign a name and location to your database, and then you can create the tables, forms, and reports that make up the inner parts of the database.

Create a Blank Database

1. Click the New button on the Standard toolbar.

2. Click Blank Database.

3. Click the Save In list arrow, and then select the location where you want to save the new database.

4. Type in a name for the database, and then click Create.

5. To close the database, click the Close button in the database window.

Did You Know?

You can open a sample database. Click the Help menu, point to Sample Databases, and then click a sample database from the list.

See Also

See "Stepping Through a Database Wizard" on page 282 for information on using database wizards.

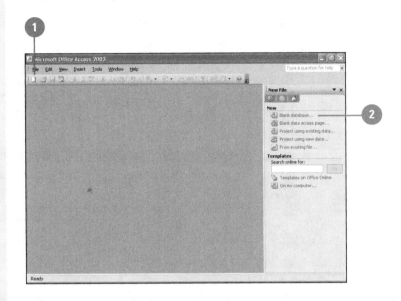

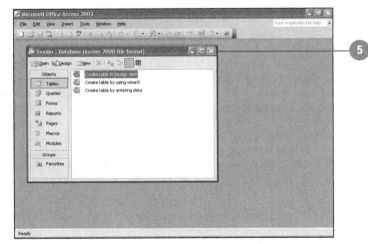

Create a Database Using a Wizard

1. Click the New button on the Standard toolbar.

2. Click On My Computer.

3. Click the Databases tab.

4. Click the database wizard you want.

5. Click OK.

6. Click the Save In list arrow, and then select the location where you want to save the new database.

7. Type in a name for the database, and then click Create.

8. Read the introduction, and then click Next to continue.

9. Click a table to display the fields in the table, select the check boxes with the fields you want, and then click Next.

10. Select the style you want to use for screen displays, and then click Next.

11. Select the report style you want, and then click Next.

12. Type a name for the database, and then click Next.

13. Click Finish.

Access creates the database based on your responses to the wizard. Enter any additional information requested during the final process.

When Access finishes creating all the database objects, the Main Switchboard appears, where you can use the database.

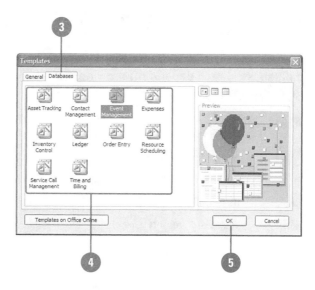

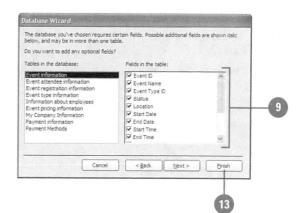

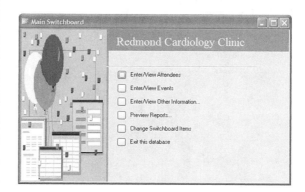

Stepping Through a Database Wizard

The choices that appear as you progress through a database wizard depend on the kind of information the database is designed to manage. All the wizards, however, share certain features.

Database Wizard Choices

Wizard Choice	Description
Field selection	The wizard presents a list of tables it will include in the database. Each table requires certain fields. You can click a table to see which fields it includes. Required fields are checked; optional fields appear in italics. To include an optional field in your database, click its check box.
Report style	You can choose from a set of report styles, such as Bold, Casual, or Corporate. Report styles give printed reports a professional look.
Screen style	Access offers a set of visual styles for on-screen database objects that use a variety of color, font, and background enhancements. Click the style you want to see a sample of.
Name and picture	Access provides a default name for its wizard databases, but you can enter your own. You can also include a picture with your database.

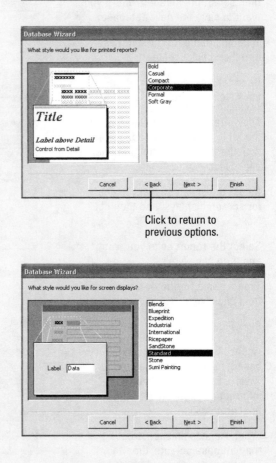

Click to return to previous options.

Viewing the Access Window

Parts of the Access Window

- The **database title bar** displays the name of the open database.

- The **menu bar** contains menus that represent groups of related commands.

- The **Database toolbar** contains buttons that you can click to carry out commands.

- The **status bar** displays information about the items you click or the actions you take.

Did You Know?

You can customize Access startup.
Click the Tools menu, click Startup, set the startup options you want, and then click OK. Close and open the database to see the new startup.

You can view the Database window.
All the databases that come with Access 2003 open with a switchboard. You can open the Database window by clicking the Window menu and then clicking the name of the database.

When you open a database, the Access program window opens and displays either the Database window or a switchboard. The **Database window** displays the database objects. A **switchboard** is a window that gives easy access to the most common actions a database user might need to take.

Access title bar   Database title bar   Menu bar

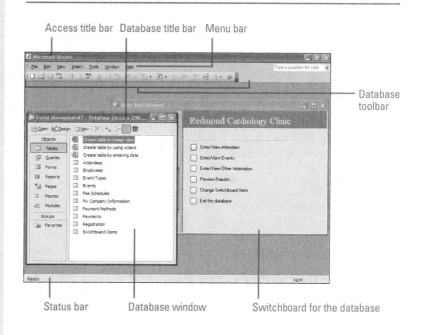

Database toolbar

Status bar   Database window   Switchboard for the database

Viewing Database Objects

When you open an existing database, the first thing you usually see is the Database window. However, if the database was created with a switchboard, you must close the switchboard before you can view the Database window. Access databases can contain seven database object types. The table on this page identifies the database objects that you use when creating a database.

View the Database Window

1. Open the database.

   If no special startup options are specified, the Database window opens automatically.

2. If necessary, click the Window menu, and then click the name of the database to open the Database window.

   Databases with multiple users might have security measures in effect that prevent some users from accessing the Database window.

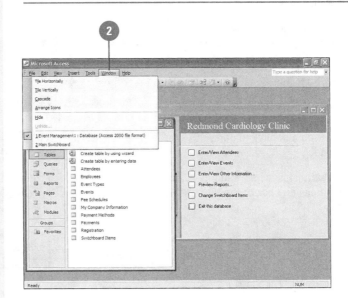

Did You Know?

You can switch between Datasheet and Design view. For many of the tasks you do in Access, you will switch back and forth between Design and Datasheet view. In Design view, you format and set controls for queries, reports, forms, or tables that you are creating from scratch or modifying from an original wizard design. In Datasheet view, you observe the result of the modifications you have made in Design view. To switch between the two, click the View button on the toolbar, and then select the appropriate view.

View a List of Database Objects

1. Open the database whose objects you want to view.

2. If necessary, click the Window menu, and then click the name of the database.

3. Click Tables, Queries, Forms, Reports, Pages, Macros, or Modules on the Objects bar.

   ◆ The **Database window toolbar** contains buttons for commands that allow you to create, open, and manage database objects.

   ◆ The **Objects bar** lists the types of objects in a database.

   ◆ The **Groups bar** allows you to group database objects the way you want them, creating shortcuts to objects of different types.

Objects bar

Database window toolbar

List of objects for the selected type

Groups bar

Database Objects

Database Object	Description
Tables	Grids that store related information, such as a list of patient addresses
Queries	A question you ask a database to help locate specific information
Forms	A window that is designed to help you enter information easily and accurately
Reports	Summaries of information that are designed to be readable and accessible
Pages	Separate files outside the Access data base in HTML format that can be placed on the Web to facilitate data sharing with the world-wide Internet community
Macros	Stored series of commands that carry out an action
Modules	Programs you can write using Microsoft Visual Basic

12

Working with Database Objects

The Database window is the container for all the objects in a database, including tables, forms, reports, queries, pages, macros, and modules. These database objects work together to help you store and manage your data. Objects are organized by object type on the Objects bar. You can open, group, rename, and delete database objects from the Database window. You use the Open button in the Database window to view and enter object data and the Design button to create the layout for the object data.

Open and View a Database Object

1. If necessary, click the Objects bar in the Database window.

2. Click the object type icon on the Objects bar.

3. Click the object you want to open.

4. Click the Open button on the Database window toolbar to view the object's data, or click the Design button to work with the object's design.

5. To close the object, click the Close button in the upper-right corner.

Did You Know?

You can switch to the Database window. You can press F11 to switch to the Database window from a switchboard or any other window.

You can delete or rename a group. In the Database window, click the Groups bar, right-click anywhere under the Groups bar, and then click Delete Group or Rename Group. When you rename a group, type a new name, and then click OK.

Manage Database Objects

◆ To create a new object, click the type of object you want to create on the Objects bar, and then click the New button on the Database window toolbar.

◆ To delete an object, right-click it in the Object list and then click Delete.

◆ To rename a database object, right-click the object in the Object list, click Rename, and then type a new name.

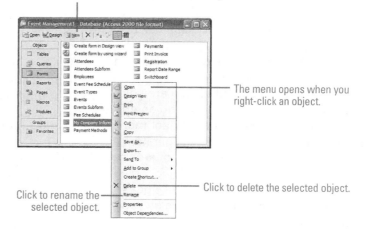

Click to create a new database object.

The menu opens when you right-click an object.

Click to delete the selected object.

Click to rename the selected object.

Create a Group of Database Objects

1 In the Database window, click the Groups bar.

2 Right-click anywhere under the Groups bar.

3 Click New Group, type a name for your group, and then click OK.

4 Drag an object from the Object list to the group.

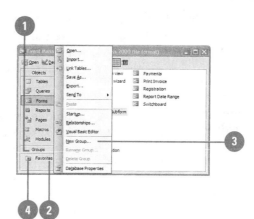

Did You Know?

You can use AutoCorrect to rename objects. When you rename a database object, you don't have to worry about other Access objects that use the object you just renamed. The Name AutoCorrect feature automatically fixes common side effects that occur when a user makes name changes. Click the Tools menu, click Options, click the General tab, and then work with the Name AutoCorrect settings to enable this feature.

12

Planning Tables

Although you can always make changes to your database when necessary, a little planning before you begin can save time later on. When you plan a database, consider how you will use the data. What kind of data are you collecting? What kind of data are you entering? How are data values related to one another? Can your data be organized into separate, smaller groups? What kinds of safeguards can you create to ensure that errors do not creep into your data? As you consider these questions, you should apply the answers as you structure your database.

Plan Tables

Tables are one of the fundamental building blocks of a database. Database planning begins with deciding how many and what kinds of tables your database will contain. Consider organizing your database information into several tables—each one containing fields related to a specific topic—rather than one large table containing fields for a large variety of topics. For example, you could create a Patients table that contains only patient information and an Encounters table that contains only information about the encounters you have with patients. By focusing each table on a single task, you greatly simplify the structure of those tables and make them easier to modify later on.

Choose Data Types

When you create a table, you must decide what fields to include and the appropriate format for those fields. Access allows you to assign a data type to a field, a format that defines the kind of data the field can accept. Access provides a wide variety of data types, ranging from text and number formats to object-based formats for images, sound, and video clips. Choosing the correct data type helps you manage your data and reduces the possibility of data-entry errors.

Specify a Primary Key

You should also identify which field or fields are the table's primary keys. Primary keys are those fields whose values uniquely identify each record in the table. A social security number field in a personnel table could be used as a primary key, since each employee has a unique social security number. Although primary keys are not required, using them is one way of removing the possibility of duplicate records existing within your tables.

Creating a Table by Entering Data

Access allows you to display many of its objects in multiple viewing modes. Datasheet view displays the data in your tables, queries, forms, and reports. Design view displays options for designing your Access objects. You can create a new table in both views. When you create a table in Datasheet view, you enter data and Access creates the table as you type. Access determines the data type of each field based on the data you enter. When you finish entering data, Access will prompt you for the name of the table you've just created.

Enter Data to Create a Table

1. In the Database window, click Tables on the Objects bar.

2. Double-click the Create Table By Entering Data icon.

3. Enter the data.

   Press Tab to move from field to field or click in a cell.

4. To change a field name, double-click the field name, type the new name, and then press Enter.

5. Click the Save button on the toolbar.

6. Type a table name, and then click OK.

7. To have Access set the primary key, click Yes.

8. Close the Table window.

Did You Know?

You can select or resize a column or row like in Excel. To select a column or row in a table, click the Column or Row selector. To resize a column or row, drag the border between the Column or Row selector.

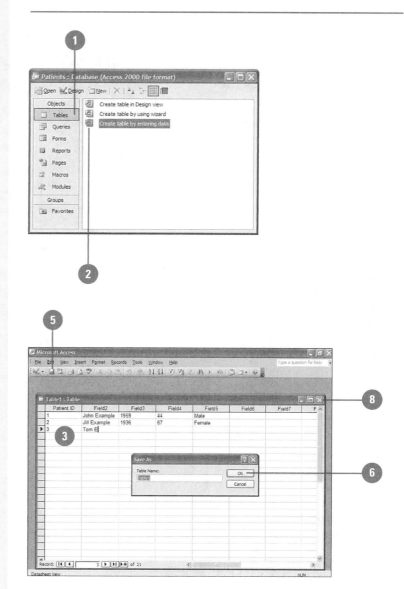

Creating a Table Using a Wizard

One of the easiest ways to create a table is to use the Table Wizard. The **Table Wizard** walks you through a series of dialog boxes that help you choose the types of tables your database will contain and the fields present in each table. You can change table names, field names, and properties as you proceed through the wizard. The wizard also makes it easy to create a primary key for your table and to establish relationships between the new table and other tables in the database.

Create a Table Using the Table Wizard

1. In the Database window, click Tables on the Objects bar, and then double-click the Create Table By Using Wizard icon.

2. Click the Business or Personal option.

3. Scroll thru the list to find the table that best matches your needs.

4. Double-click each field you want to include in the table. Click Next to continue.

5. Type a new name for the table, or accept the suggested name.

6. Click the Yes option to have the Table Wizard assign the primary key, or click the No option to assign your own primary key. Click Next to continue.

> ### Did You Know?
>
> **You can select fields in the order you want them to appear in the table.** In the Sample Fields list, you can choose the fields you want to include in your table in any order. The fields you choose will appear in the table in the order you chose them.

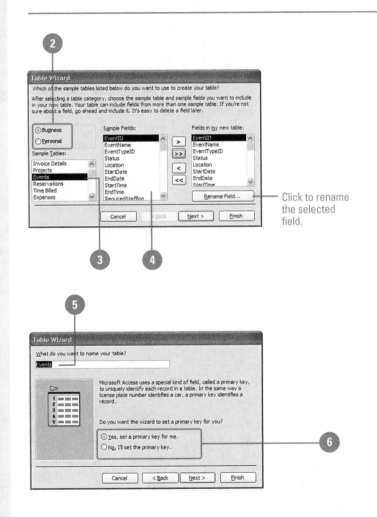

Click to rename the selected field.

This dialog box appears only if your database already contains at least one table.

⑦ If you chose to set the primary key, select the field and data type. Click Next to continue.

⑧ If your database already contains at least one table and you want to make changes, select the relationship you want to change, click Relationships, specify the new table relationships, and then click OK. Click Next to continue.

⑨ In the final wizard dialog box, click one of the options, either to modify the table design (in Design view) before entering data, to enter data directly (in Datasheet view), or to enter data in a form that the wizard creates for you.

⑩ Click Finish.

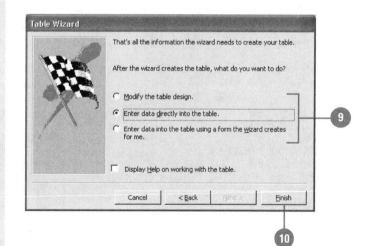

Click to specify table relationships.

Did You Know?

You can insert a subdatasheet in a table. In the Datasheet view of a table, click the Insert menu, and then click Sub-Datasheet. Click the Tables tab, click the table you want to insert, specify the foreign key in the Link Child Fields box and the primary key in the Link Master Fields box, and then click OK.

You can view a subdatasheet. In the Datasheet view of a table, click the plus box next to the record to display the subdatasheet. Click the minus box to hide the subdatasheet.

12

Working with a Table

A **database** is made up of groups of fields organized into tables. A **field** is a specific category of information, such as a name or a diagnosis. Related fields are grouped in tables. You usually enter data into fields one entity at a time (one patient at a time, one encounter at a time, and so on). Access stores all the data for a single entity in a record. You can view a table in Datasheet or Design view. Design view allows you to work with your table's fields. Datasheet view shows a grid of fields and records. The fields appear as columns and the records as rows. The first field in a table is often an **AutoNumber** field, which Access uses to assign a unique number to each record. You can't select or change this value.

Enter a New Record and Move Around in a Table

1. In the Database window, click Tables on the Objects bar, and then double-click the table.

2. Click the New Record button.

3. Press Tab to accept the AutoNumber entry.

4. Enter the data. If you make a typing mistake, press Backspace.

5. Press Tab to move to the next field or Shift+Tab to move to the previous field.

6. When you reach the end of the record, click one of the Record buttons:

   ◆ First Record button.

   ◆ Previous Record button.

   ◆ Specific Record box. Enter a record number in the box, and then press Enter.

   ◆ Next Record button.

   ◆ Last Record button.

Find Records

1. In the Database window, click Tables on the Objects bar, and then double-click the table.

2. If you want, click in the table field in which you want to search.

3. Click the Edit menu, and then click Find.

4. Type the text you want to find.

5. Click the Look In list arrow, and then select a search location.

6. Click the Match list arrow, and then select an option.

7. Click the Search list arrow, and then select a search direction.

8. To match upper and lower case, select the Match Case check box.

9. Click Find Next.

10. When you're done, click Cancel.

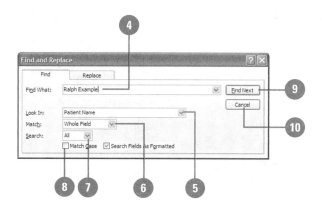

Delete a Record from a Table

1. In the Database window, click Tables on the Objects bar, and then double-click the table.

2. Right-click the row selector.

3. Click Delete Record.

4. Click Yes.

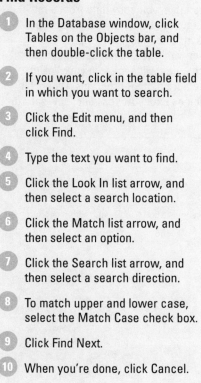

Did You Know?

You might want to delete related data. When you delete a record, such as a supplier, you might want to also delete the products the supplier supplies.

12

Importing Data into Tables

You can create new tables from other Access databases by importing and linking tables. When you import a table, you copy data from a table in one Access database and place it in a new table in your database. When you link a table, the data stays in its original location, but you can display and access that data from within your database. If data in the original database changes, the changes will appear in your linked database, too. You can also import data from other programs. When you import data from some programs, such as Excel, Access uses a wizard to help you set up the data as a table.

Import a Table from a Database

1. In the Database window, click the New button.

2. Double-click Import Table.

3. Locate and select the database file that contains the data you want to import, and then click Import.

4. Click the tables you want to import. To deselect a table, click the table again.

5. Click OK.

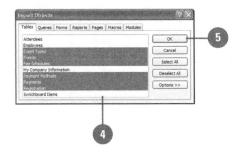

Allows you to link a table rather than import one

Import Data from Another Program

1. In the Database window, click the File menu, point to Get External Data, and then click Import.

2. Click the Files Of Type list arrow, and then click the type of file you want to import.

3. Locate and select the file, and then click Import.

4. If necessary, follow the instructions in the wizard.

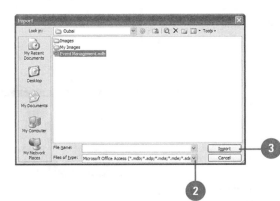

Working with a Table in Design View

Most Access objects are displayed in Design view, which allows you to work with the underlying structure of your tables, queries, forms, and reports. To create a new table in Design view, you define the fields that will comprise the table before you enter any data. In Design view for tables, each row corresponds to a field. You can edit, insert, and delete fields in your database tables in Design view. You insert a field by adding a row, while you delete a field by removing a row. You can also change field order by dragging a row selector to a new position.

Create or Modify a Table in Design View

1. In the Database window, click Tables on the Objects bar.

2. Double-click the Create Table In Design View icon, or click the table you want to modify, and then click the Design button.

3. Click in a Field Name cell, and then type a modified field name.

4. Click in a Data Type cell, click the Data Type list arrow, and then click a data type.

5. Click in a Description cell, and then type a description. If the Property Update Options button appears, select an option, if necessary.

6. To insert a field, click the row selector below where you want the field, and then click the Insert Rows button on the Table Design toolbar.

7. To delete a field, click the row selector for the field you want to delete, and then click the Delete Rows button on the Table Design toolbar.

8. Click the Save button on the toolbar, and then if necessary, enter a table name and click OK.

9. When you're done, click the Close button in the Table window.

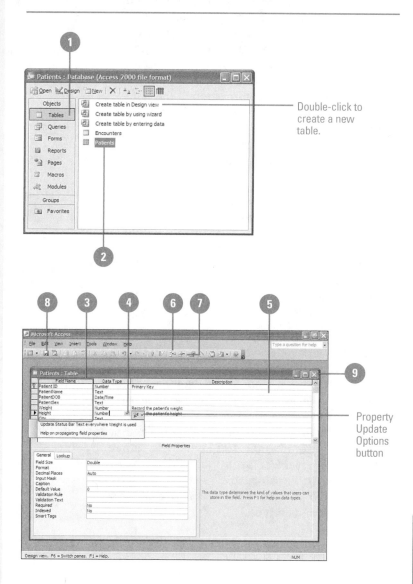

Double-click to create a new table.

Property Update Options button

Specifying Data Types and Field Properties

Access provides different **data types**— field formats that define the kind of data the field can accept—which cover a wide variety of data. When you choose a data type for a field, Access will accept data entered only in the format specified by the data type. Selecting the appropriate data type makes it easier for users to enter and retrieve information in the database tables. It also acts as a check against incorrect data being entered. For example, a field formatted to accept only numbers removes the possibility that a user will erroneously enter text into the field.

You can change the data type for a field even after you have entered data in it. However, you might need to perform a potentially lengthy process of converting or retyping the field's data when you save the table. If the data type in a field conflicts with a new data type setting, you may lose some or all of the data in the field.

Once you've selected a data type, you can begin to work with field properties. A **field property** is an attribute that defines the field's appearance or behavior in the database. The number of decimal places displayed in a numeric field is an example of a property that defines the field's appearance. A property that forces the user to enter data into a field rather than leave it blank controls that field's behavior. In Design view for tables, Access provides a list of field properties, called the **properties list**, for each data type.

Data Types

Data Type	Description
Text (default)	Text or combinations of text and numbers, as well as numbers that don't require calculations, such as phone numbers. Limited to 255 characters.
Number	Numeric data used in mathematical calculations.
Date/Time	Date and time values for the years 100 through 9999.
Currency	Currency values and numeric data used in mathematical calculations involving data with one to four decimal places. Values are accurate to 15 digits on the left side of the decimal separator.
AutoNumber	A unique sequential number (incremented by 1) or a random number Access assigns whenever you add a new record to a table. AutoNumber fields can't be changed.
Yes/No	A field containing only one of two values (for example, Yes/No, True/False, On/Off).
OLE Object	An object (such as a Microsoft Excel spreadsheet) linked to or embedded in an Access table.
Hyperlink	A link that, when clicked, takes the user to another file, a location in a file, or a site on the Web.
Lookup Wizard	A wizard that helps you to create a field whose values are chosen from the values in another table, query, or list of values.

Changing Field Properties

After you create fields in a table, you can specify properties that define the field's appearance or behavior in the database. In Design view for tables, Access provides a list of field properties for each data type. The properties list changes depending on the data type. Some of the field text properties include Field Size, Format, Input Mask, Caption, Default Value, Validation Rule, Validation Text, Required, Allow Zero Length, and Smart Tags.

Change Field Properties

1. Display the table in Design view.

2. Click the field you want to change.

3. Click the field property box you want to change.

4. Type or change the value, or click the list arrow, and then select a value or option.

5. Click the Save button on the toolbar.

6. When you're done, click the Close button in the Table window.

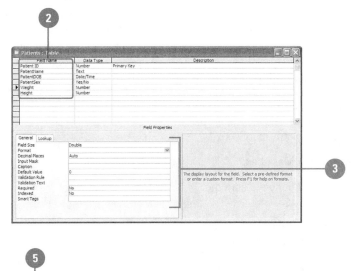

Did You Know?

You can set the number of decimal places. Another way to set the number of decimal places for numeric fields is to specify the number of decimal places in the Decimal Places box in the list of field properties.

You can use different formats for different values. Access allows you to specify different formats for positive, negative, zero, and null values within a single field. Use online Help for more information.

12

Creating Input Masks

An **input mask** allows you to control what values a database user can enter into a field. Input masks consist of literal characters, such as spaces, dots, parentheses, and placeholders. A **placeholder** is a text character, such as the underline symbol (_), that indicates where the user should insert values. An input mask for a phone number field might appear as follows: (_ _ _) _ _ _ - _ _ _ _ . The parenthesis and dash characters act as literal characters, and the underscore character acts as a placeholder for the phone number values. Access provides several predefined input masks, which cover most situations, but you can create your own customized masks, if necessary. The **Input Mask Wizard** is available only for text and date fields. If you want to create an input mask for numeric fields, you must enter the formatting symbols yourself.

Specify an Input Mask

1. Display the table in Design view, and then click a field for which you want to specify an input mask.

2. Click the Input Mask box.

3. Click the Build button to start the Input Mask Wizard.

4. Scroll thru the predefined list to find an input mask form.

5. Type some sample values to see how the input mask affects your sample values, and then click Next.

6. If you change the input mask, type new formatting codes.

7. If you want to display a different placeholder, click the Placeholder list arrow, and select the placeholder you want to use.

8. Enter values to test the final version of your input mask, and then click Next.

9. Indicate whether you want to store the input mask symbols along with the data values.

10. Click Next, and then click Finish.

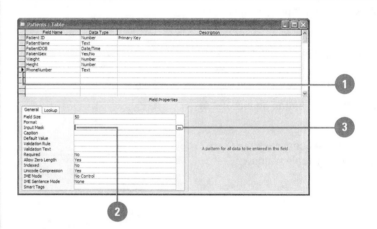

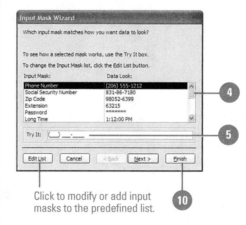

Click to modify or add input masks to the predefined list.

Creating a Lookup Field

The **Lookup Wizard** helps you create a field that displays either of two kinds of lists during data entry: a **Lookup** list that displays values looked up from an existing table or query, or a **Value** list that displays a fixed set of values you enter when you create the field. Because values are limited to a predefined list, using Lookup fields helps you avoid data entry errors in situations where only a limited number of possible values are allowed. The lists are not limited to a single column. You can include additional columns that could include descriptive information for the various choices in the list. However, only a single column, called the **bound column**, contains the data that is extracted from the list and placed into the Lookup field.

Create a Field Based on a Lookup List

1. Display the table in Design view, enter a new field, click the Data Type list arrow, and then click Lookup Wizard.

2. Click the I Will Type In The Values That I Want option button. Click Next to continue.

3. Specify the number of columns you want in the Value list.

4. Enter the values in the list. Resize the column widths, if necessary. Click Next to continue.

5. Choose which column will act as the bound column. Click Next to continue.

6. Enter a label for the Lookup column.

7. Click Finish.

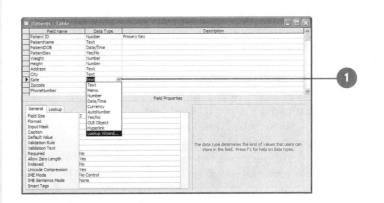

12

Planning Table Relationships

When you place data into separate tables, you need some way of merging this data together for forms and reports. You can do this by establishing table relationships that indicate how data in one table relates to data in another.

Specifying Common Fields

Data from several different tables is related through the use of common fields. A common field is a field existing in two or more tables, allowing you to match records from one table with records in the other tables. For example, the Patients table and the Encounters table might both contain a Patient ID field, which functions as a primary key that identifies a specific patient. Using Patient ID as a common field allows you to generate reports containing information on both the patient and the encounters you had with the patient. When you use a primary key as a common field, it is called a **foreign** key in the second table.

Building Table Relationships

A table containing patient names and a second table containing patient addresses exist in a one-to-one relationship if each patient is limited to only one address. Similarly, a one-to-many relationship exists between the Patients table and the Encounters table because a single patient could have several encounters. In a one-to-many relationship like this, the "one" table is called the **primary table**, and the "many" table is called the **related table**.

Finally, if you allow several patients to be recorded on a single encounter (as in the case of group therapy sessions in psychiatry), a many-to-many relationship exists between the Patients and Encounters tables.

Table Relationships	
Wizard Choice	**Description**
One-to-one	Each record in one table is matched to only one record in a second table, and visa versa.
One-to-many	Each record in one table is matched to one or more records in a second table, but each record in the second table is matched to only one record in the first table.
Many-to-many	Each record in one table is matched to multiple records in a second table, and visa versa.

Finally, if you allow several customers to be recorded on a single order (as in the case of group purchases), a many-to-many relationship exists between the Customers and Orders tables.

Maintaining Referential Integrity

Table relationships must obey standards of **referential integrity**, a set of rules that control how you can delete or modify data between related tables. Referential integrity protects you from erroneously changing data in a primary table required by a related table. You can apply referential integrity when:

- The common field is the primary table's primary key.

- The related fields have the same format.

- Both tables belong to the same database.

Referential integrity places some limitations on you.

- Before adding a record to a related table, a matching record must already exist in the primary table.

- The value of the primary key in the primary table cannot be changed if matching records exist in a related table.

- A record in the primary table cannot be deleted if matching records exist in a related table.

Access can enforce these rules by cascading any changes across the related tables. For example, Access can automatically copy any changes to the common field across the related tables. Similarly, if a record is deleted in the primary table, Access can automatically delete related records in all other tables.

As you work through these issues of tables, fields, and table relationships, you will create a structure for your database that will be easier to manage and less prone to data-entry error.

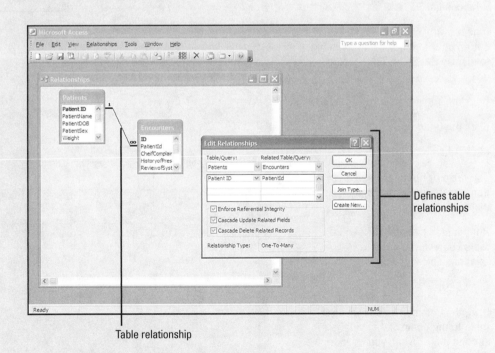

Table relationship

Defines table relationships

12

Defining Table Relationships

You can define table relationships in several ways. When you first create tables in your database using the Table Wizard, the wizard gives you an opportunity to define table relationships. You can also define relationships in the Database window or in Design view. This method gives you more control over your table relationships and also gives you a quick snapshot of all the relationships in your database. After you define a relationship, you can double-click the connection line to modify or add to the relationship.

Define Table Relationships

1. In the Database window, click the Relationships button on the Database toolbar.

   If relationships are already established in your database, they appear in the Relationships window. In this window you can create additional table relationships.

2. If necessary, click the Show Table button on the Relationship toolbar to display the Show Table dialog box.

3. Click the Tables tab.

4. Click the table you want.

5. Click Add.

   The table or query you selected appears in the Relationships window.

   Repeat steps 4 and 5 for each table you want to use in a relationship.

6. Click Close.

7. Drag the common field in the first table to the common field in the second table. When you release the mouse button, a line appears between the two tables, signifying that they are related. Also, the Edit Relationships dialog box opens, in which you can confirm or modify the relationship.

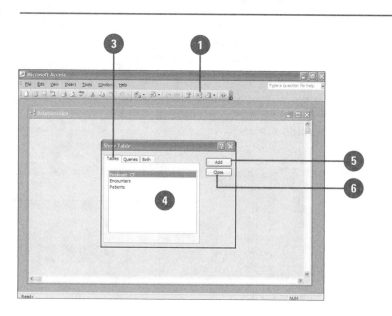

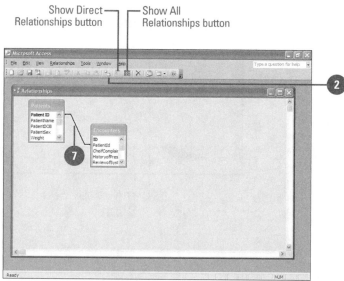

Show Direct Relationships button | Show All Relationships button

8 Click the Join Type button if you want to specify the join type. Click OK to return to the Edit Relationships dialog box.

9 Click Create to create the relationship.

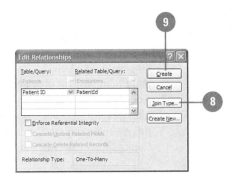

Did You Know?

You can view the relationships you want to see. Click the Show Direct Relationships button on the Relationship toolbar to see tables that are directly related to each other. Click the Show All Relationships button on the Relationship toolbar to see all the relationships between all the tables and queries in your database.

You can print the Relationships window. Open the Relationships window you want to print, click the File menu, click Print Relationships, select the print settings you want, and then click OK.

You can delete a table relationship. In the Relationships window, select the line that joins the tables that you no longer want related to one another. Click the Edit menu, and then click Delete. In the message box, click Yes to confirm that you want to permanently delete this relationship. You will not be able to undo this change.

Join Types

Join Types	Description
Include rows only where the joined fields from both tables are equal	Choose this option if you want to see one record in the second table for every record that appears in the first table. The number of records you see in the two tables will be the same.
Include ALL records from "xxx" (the first table) and only those records from "yyy" (the second table) where the joined fields are equal	Choose this option if you want to see all the records in the first table (even if there is no corresponding record in the second table) as well as the records from the second table in which the joined fields are the same in both tables. The number of records you see in the first table might be greater than the number of records in the second table.
Include ALL records from "yyy" (the second table) and only those records from the "xxx" (the first table) where the joined fields are equal	Choose this option if you want to see all the records in the second table (even if there is no corresponding record in the first table) as well as the records from the first table in which the joined fields are the same in both tables. The number of records you see in the second table might be greater than the number of records in the first table.

12

Ensuring Referential Integrity

Referential integrity in table relationships keeps users from accidentally deleting or changing related data. If a primary table contains a list of employees and related tables contain additional information about those employees, and an employee quits, his record is removed from the primary table. His records should also be removed in all related tables. Access allows you to change or delete related data, but only if these changes are cascaded through the series of related tables. You can do this by selecting the Cascade Update Related Fields and Cascade Delete Related Records check boxes in the Edit Relationships dialog box.

Ensure Referential Integrity

1. In the Database window, click the Relationships button on the Database toolbar.

2. Double-click the join line for the relationship you want to work with.

3. Click to select the Enforce Referential Integrity check box to ensure that referential integrity always exists between related tables in the database.

4. If you want changes to the primary field of the primary table automatically copied to the related field of the related table, click to select the Cascade Update Related Fields check box.

5. If you want Access to delete records in the related tables whenever records in the primary table are deleted, click to select the Cascade Delete Related Records check box.

6. Click OK.

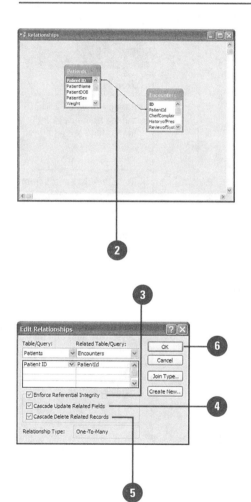

Locating and Managing Data with Access

13

Introduction

Once you've created a database, you'll want to be able to manage the records and information within that database. Microsoft Office Access 2003 gives you numerous ways to manage the records and information stored within the database.

Some of the techniques you might utilize to manage your databases could include sorting records in either ascending or descending order based on the contents of a specific field and filtering certain records out of a database for a special mailing to certain patients.

Other techniques include creating queries to help you retrieve specific information about particular patients. A **query** is a description of the records you want to retrieve from a database. As the name implies, a query helps answer specific questions about the information in your database, for example, "Which patients have had encounters in the last six months?" or "Who did we prescribe Prozac to in the last two years?" The description of the records you want to retrieve identifies the names of the fields and the values they should contain; this description is called the selection criteria. With a query you can do the following:

- ◆ Focus on only the information you need by displaying only a few fields from a large table.

- ◆ Apply functions and other expressions to fields to arrive at calculated results.

- ◆ Summarize and group values from one table and display the result in another table.

- ◆ Retrieve information stored in multiple tables, even if the tables are not open.

Sorting Records

You can change the order in which records appear in a table, query results, forms, or reports by sorting the records. You can select a field and then sort the records by the values in that field in either ascending or descending order. Ascending order means that records appear in alphabetical order (for text fields), from most recent to later, (for date fields), or from smallest to largest (for numeric fields). In Descending order, the order is reversed. You might also want to sort records by more than one field; this is referred to as a **secondary sort**. For example, in a table containing information about patients, you might need to sort the records first by patient gender, and then, in records with the same patient gender, sort records by age or by preexisting conditions.

Sort Records

1 In the Datasheet view, display the table, query results, form, or report in which you want to sort records.

2 To sort multiple columns, rearrange them to be adjacent.

3 Click the column selector of the column you want to sort. To select another column, press and hold Shift, and then click the column selector.

4 Click the Sort Ascending button on the Table Datasheet toolbar (A to Z), or click the Sort Descending button on the Table Datasheet toolbar (Z to A).

Sorted results

Filtering Out Records

Instead of displaying all the records in a table, you can use a **filter** to display only those records that you want to see. You can display records based on a specific value in one field or on multiple values in multiple fields. You can filter by selecting the field value on which to base the filter in Datasheet view or by using Filter By Form to help you create more complex filters involving multiple field values. After you apply a filter, Access displays only those records that match your specifications. You can remove a filter to return the datasheet to its original display.

Filter a Table by Selection

1. Display the table in Datasheet view.

2. Right-click the field value on which you want to base the filter.

3. Click Filter By Selection. Notice that the bottom of the Table window tells you the number of records matching your filter criteria. Also, the notation FLTR in the status bar indicates that a filter is currently in effect.

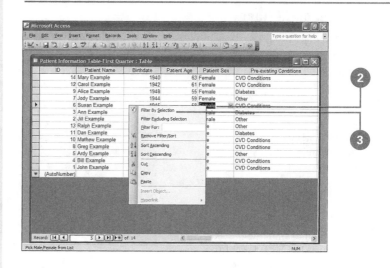

Clear a Filter from a Table

1. Display the table with the filter in Datasheet view.

2. Click the filtered table, and then click the Remove Filter button on the Table Database toolbar.

Did You Know?

You can save a filter as a query.
Display the filtered table in Datasheet view, click the Records menu, point to Filter, and then click Advanced Filter/Sort. Click the Save As Query button on the Filter/Sort toolbar, type a name, and then click OK.

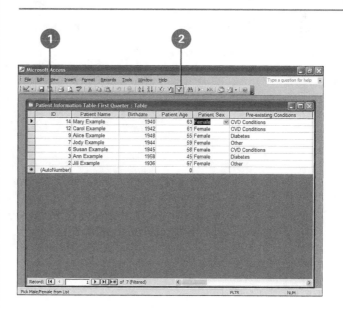

Creating Complex Filters Using Forms

The Filter By Form feature allows you to create a more complex filter. Adding criteria on a particular tab in the form restricts the filter so that records must match all the criteria on the form for the records to be displayed; this is called an AND filter. To expand the filter to include more records, you can create an OR filter by specifying criteria on the subsequent Or tab in the Filter By Form grid. To be displayed, a record needs to match only the criteria specified on the Look For tab or the criteria specified on any one of the Or tabs.

Create an AND or OR Filter

① In Datasheet view, click the Filter By Form button on the Table Datasheet toolbar.

② Click in the empty text box below the field you want to filter.

③ Click the list arrow, and then click the field value by which you want to filter the records.

④ For each field by which you want to filter, click the list arrow, and select the entry for your filter. Each new field in which you make a selection adds additional criteria that a record must match to be included.

⑤ If you want to establish Or criteria, click the Or tab at the bottom of the form to specify the additional criteria for the filter. If not, proceed to step 6.

⑥ Click the Apply Filter button on the Filter/Sort toolbar.

> **Did You Know?**
>
> **You can clear previous filters.** If necessary, click the Clear Grid button on the Filter/Sort toolbar to clear the previous filter.

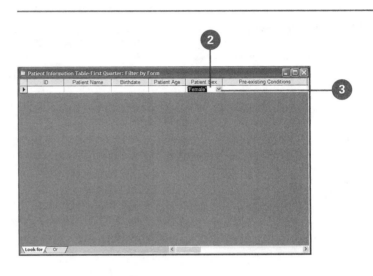

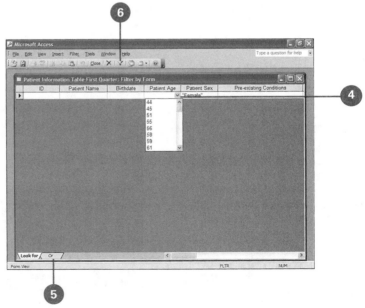

Understanding the Different Types of Queries

Access offers several types of queries that help you retrieve the information you need—select queries, crosstab queries, action queries, and parameter queries.

- A **select query** retrieves and displays records in the Table window in Datasheet view.

- A **crosstab query** displays summarized values (sums, counts, and averages) from one field in a table, and groups them by one set of fields listed down the left side of the datasheet and byanother set of fields listed across the top of the datasheet.

- An **action query** performs operations on the records that match your criteria. There are four kinds of action queries that you can perform on one or more tables: **delete queries** delete matching records; **update queries** make changes to matching records; **append queries** add new records to the end of a table; and **make-table queries** create new tables based on matching records.

- A **parameter query** allows you to prompt for a single piece of information to use as selection criteria in the query. For example, instead of creating separate queries to retrieve patient information for each patient with diabetes, you could create a parameter query that prompts the user to enter a disease, and then continues to retrieve those specific patient records with that disease.

Creating Queries in Access

As with most database objects you create in Access, there are several ways to create a query. You can create a query from scratch or use a wizard to guide you through the process of creating a query.

With the Query Wizard, Access helps you create a simple query to retrieve the records you want. All queries you create and save are listed on the Queries tab in the Database window. You can then double-click a query to run it and display the results. When you run a select query, the query results show only the selected fields for each record in the table that matches your selection criteria. Of course, once you have completed a query, you can further customize it in Design view. As always, you can begin creating your query in Design view without using the wizard at all. Queries are not limited to a single table. Your queries can encompass multiple tables as long as the database includes a field or fields that relate the tables to each other.

Creating a Query Using a Wizard

A query is a simple question you ask a database to help you locate specific information within the database. When you create a query with the **Query Wizard**, you can specify the kind of query you want to create and type of records from a table or existing query you want to retrieve. The Query Wizard guides you through each step; all you do is answer a series of questions, and Access creates a query based on your responses. All queries you create are listed on the Queries tab in the Database window.

Create a Simple Query Using the Query Wizard

1. In the Database window, click Queries on the Objects bar, and then double-click the Create Query By Using Wizard icon.

2. Select a table or existing query.

3. Click to select the fields that you want included in the query.

4. Click Next to continue.

5. If you selected numeric or date fields in step 3, indicate whether you want to see detail or summary information.

6. If you choose Summary, click Summary Options to specify the calculation for each field, and then click OK.

7. Click Next to continue.

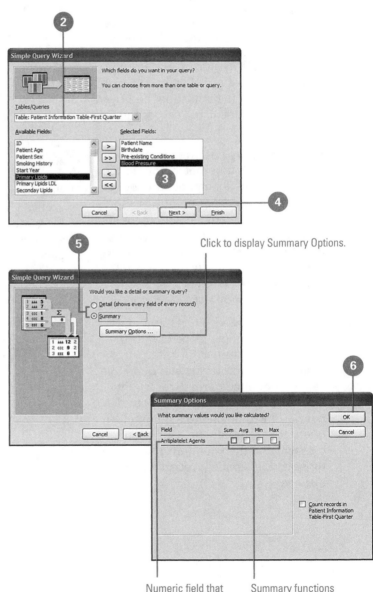

Click to display Summary Options.

Numeric field that you can summarize.

Summary functions

8 In the final wizard dialog box, type the name of the query.

9 Choose whether you want to view the results of the query or modify the query design in Design view.

10 For more help on queries, select the Display Help On Working With The Query? check box.

11 Click Finish.

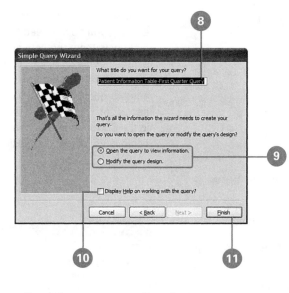

Did You Know?

You can include fields from another source. Click the Tables/Queries list arrow if you want to include a field from another source.

Name of query   Type of query

Patient Name	Seconday Lipids	Primary Lipids LDL	Physical Acitivity Frequency	Diabetes Glucos	Diabet
John Example	144	150	1	70	4.0
Jill Example	139	144	0	85	5.5
Ann Example	137	123	2	99	3.6
Bill Example	115	117	1	105	4.1
Ardy Example	143	149	4	102	6.0
Susan Example	140	155	0	76	4.2
Jody Example	150	160	2	69	3.9
Greg Example	129	122	4	111	5.4
Alice Example	138	132	1	100	6.0
Mathew Example	145	145	0	73	4.1
Dan Example	151	110	0	81	4.3
Carol Example	123	135	3	96	5.2
Ralph Example	117	118	2	81	5.7
Mary Example	40	141	2	94	3.7

Records retrieved by the query

Creating a Query in Design View

Although a wizard can be a big help when you are first learning to create a query, you do not need to use a wizard. If you prefer, you can create a query without the help of a wizard. Instead of answering questions in a series of dialog boxes, you can start working in Design view right away. As you create a query, you can include more than one table or even another query in Design view. You can use comparison operators, such as >, <, or =, to compare field values to constants and other field values in the Criteria box. You can also use logical operators to create criteria combining several expressions, such as >1 AND <5.

Create a Query in Design View

1. In the Database window, click Queries on the Objects bar.

2. Click New, click Design View, and then click OK.

3. Select the table or query you want to use.

4. Click Add.

5. Repeat steps 3 and 4 for additional tables or queries, and then click Close.

6. Double-click each field you want to include in the query from the field list.

7. In the design grid, enter any desired search criteria in the Criteria box.

8. Click the list arrow in the Sort box, and then specify a sort order.

9. Click the Save button, type a name for the query, and then click OK.

See Also

See "Performing Calculations in Queries" on page 315 for information on using the expression builder to add search criteria.

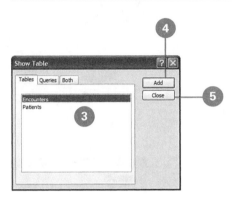

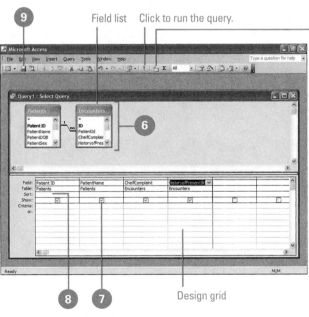

Field list   Click to run the query.

Click to add more tables to the query.

Design grid

Getting Information with a Query

Open and Run a Query

1. In the Database window, click Queries on the Objects bar.

2. Click the query you want to run.

3. Click the Open button.

   The query opens in a table called a dynaset. The dynaset displays the records that meet the specifications set forth in the query.

Access saves and lists the queries you create on the Queries tab in the Database window. You can double-click a query to run it and display the results. When you run a query, the query results show only the selected fields for each record in the table that matches your selection criteria.

13

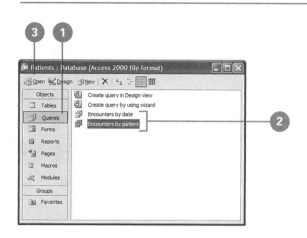

Dynaset

Modifying a Query in Design View

Once you have completed a query, you can further customize it in Design view. However, you can also create a query in Design view without using the wizard. Queries are not limited to a single table. Your queries can encompass multiple tables as long as the database includes a field or fields that relate the tables to each other. You can create a query using specific criteria and sort the results. If you no longer want to include a table or field, you can remove it from the query. In some cases you might want to hide a field from the query results while keeping it part of the query design for selection design purposes.

Modify a Query in Design View

1. In the Database window, click Queries on the Objects bar.

2. Click the query you want to modify, and then click the Design button.

3. Double-click or drag each field you want to include in the query from the field list.

4. In the design grid, enter any search criteria in the Criteria box.

5. Click the list arrow in the Sort box, and then specify a sort order.

6. To hide a field, clear the Show check box.

7. To delete a field, select the field, and then press Delete.

8. Click the Save button on the Query Design toolbar.

Did You Know?

You can sort the retrieved records. Display the query in Datasheet view, select the field in which you want to sort, and then click the Sort Ascending or Sort Descending button on the Table Datasheet toolbar.

You can remove a table. In the query, right-click the table, and then click Remove Table.

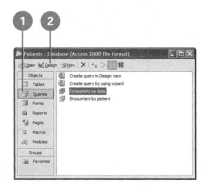

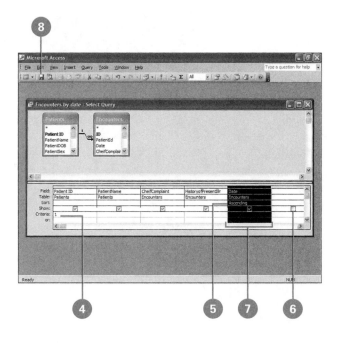

Performing Calculations in Queries

In addition to the built-in functions you can use to compare values in a query, you can use the **Expression Builder** to create your own calculations using arithmetic operators. By clicking the operator buttons you want to use and entering constant values as needed, you can use the Expression Builder to include expressions in a query. For example, to determine fees based on a contracted amount with a health plan, you can create an arithmetic expression in your query to compute the results. When you run the query, Access performs the required calculations and displays the results. You can also insert functions, such as AVG and Count, to perform other operations. When you insert a function, <<expr>> appears in parentheses, which represents an expression. Select <<expr>> and replace it with a field name, which you can select in Expression Builder.

Create a Calculated Field

1. Within Query Design view, position the insertion point in the Field row of a blank column in the design grid.

2. Click the Build button on the Query Design toolbar.

3. Double-click the field (or fields) you want to use in the calculation.

4. Build an expression using the operator buttons and elements area.

   ◆ Click the button corresponding to the calculation you want.

   ◆ Click the Operators folder, click the Arithmetic folder, and then click the operator you want to use.

   ◆ Click the Functions folder, click Built-In Functions, and then click the function you want to use.

5. Type any other values (constants) you want to include in the expression.

6. Click OK.

7. Click the Run button on the Query Design toolbar.

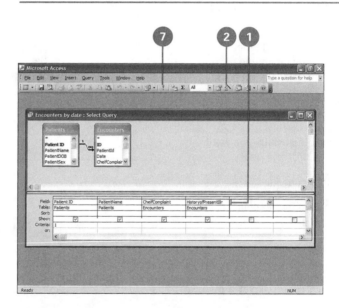

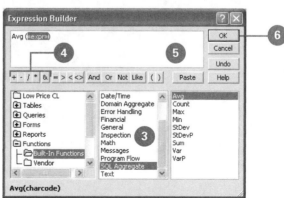

Summarizing Values with a Crosstab Query

A **crosstab query** allows you to summarize the contents of fields that contain numeric values, such as Date fields or Number fields. In this type of query, the results of the summary calculations are shown at the intersection of rows and columns. For example, you can use a crosstab query to calculate the total number of patient encounters you had, broken down by chief complaint. Crosstab queries can also involve other functions such as the average, sum, maximum, minimum, and count. You cannot update crosstab queries. The value in a crosstab query cannot be changed in order to change the source data.

Create a Crosstab Query

1. In the Database window, click Queries on the Objects bar, click New, click Crosstab Query Wizard, and then click OK.

2. From the list at the top of the dialog box, select the table or query that contains the records you want to retrieve.

3. Click Next to continue.

4. Double-click the field(s) you want to use in the crosstab query.

5. Click Next to continue.

6. Select the field for the columns in the crosstab query.

7. Click Next to continue.

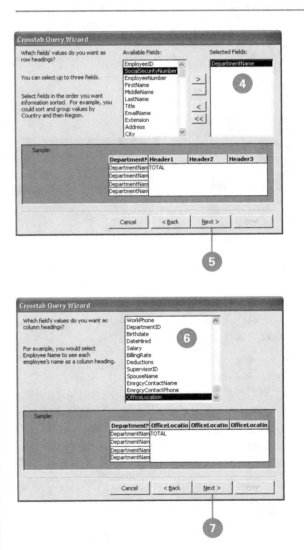

8 Click the field whose values you want to be calculated and displayed for each row and column intersection.

9 Click the function you want for the calculation to be performed.

10 Select the Yes, Include Row Sums check box if you want to see a total for each row, or clear the check box if you do not want to see a total for each row.

11 Click Next to continue.

12 Enter a name for your query.

13 Indicate whether you want to immediately view the query or modify the design.

14 Click Finish.

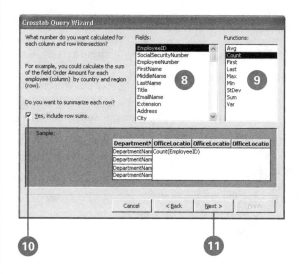

Did You Know?

You can use a PivotTable instead of a crosstab query. Display crosstab data without creating a separate query in your database either by using the PivotTable Wizard in a form, or by creating a PivotTable list in a data access page.

You can change column headings in a crosstab query. If you want to change the column headings, open the query in Design view, and then open the Properties dialog box for the query. Enter the column headings you want to display in the Column Headings property box, separated by commas.

Overall total

Total broken down by employee location

Creating a
Parameter Query

When you need to change the criterion value for a query, you either must edit the old query or create a new one. However, if the change involves simply altering a value, you might consider using a parameter query. A **parameter query** prompts the user for the value of a particular query field, rather than having the value built into the query itself. For example, if you want to display all the encounter records for a particular patient, a parameter query can prompt you for the patient name, saving you from creating a separate query for each patient.

Create a Parameter Query

1. In Query Design view, click the Criteria box.

2. Enter the text of the prompt surrounded by square brackets.

3. Click the Run button on the Query Design toolbar.

4. Enter a criteria value in response to the prompt.

5. Click OK.

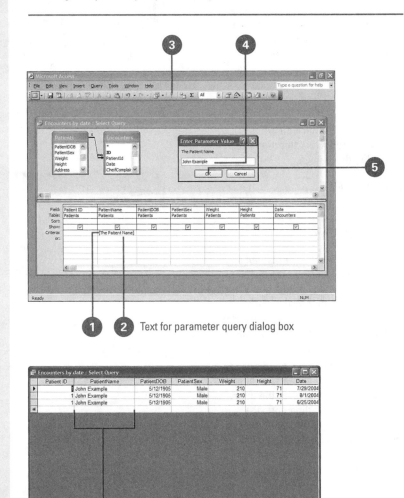

Text for parameter query dialog box

Access retrieves records with the John Example patient.

> ## Did You Know?
>
> *You can rename a field.* Access assigns a name to a calculated field. If you want a different name, click the field in the design grid, and then click the Properties button on the Query Design toolbar. Enter a new name in the Caption box, and then click OK.

Finding Duplicate Fields

In some tables, you need to find records that have duplicate values in particular fields. For example, in a table of patient encounters, you might want to discover which patients have multiple encounters. You can create a query that retrieves all the records from the Encounters table that have duplicate values for the Patient Name field. Access provides the Find Duplicate Query Wizard to guide you through each step to help you create the query.

Find Duplicate Records

1. In the Database window, click Queries on the Objects bar, click New, and then double-click Find Duplicates Query Wizard.

2. Choose the table or query that you want to search for duplicate records.

3. Click Next to continue.

4. Select the field or fields that might contain duplicate information.

5. Click Next to continue.

6. Select any other fields that you want displayed in the query.

7. Click Next to continue.

8. Enter a name for the new query.

9. Specify whether you want to view the query results or further modify the query design.

10. Click Finish.

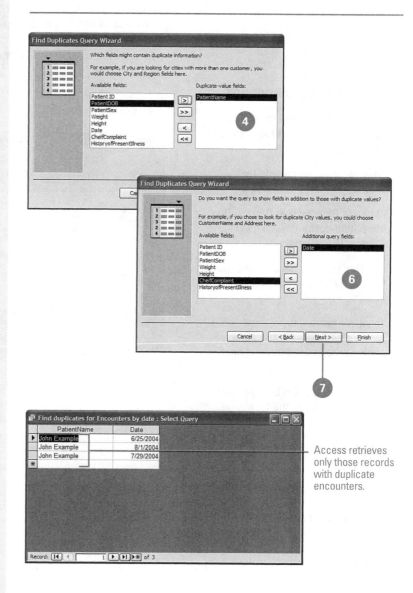

Access retrieves only those records with duplicate encounters.

Identifying Object Dependencies

As you develop a database, you create a relationship between objects to share data and provide the information in forms and reports. When you make changes to one object, it might affect another object. For example, if you no longer need a field in a table, instead of deleting it right away and possibly creating problems, you can check object dependencies to make sure that the field you want to delete is not used in another table. Checking for object dependencies helps you save time and avoid mistakes. Access generates dependency information by searching name maps maintained by the Name AutoCorrect feature. If Track Name AutoCorrect Info is turned off on the General tab in the Options dialog box, you cannot view dependency information.

View Dependency Information

1. In the Database window, click the object in which you want to view dependencies.

2. Click the View menu, and then click Object Dependencies.

3. Click the Objects That Depend On Me option or the Objects That I Depend On option.

   The Dependency pane shows the list of objects that use the selected object.

4. To view dependency information for an object listed in the pane, click on the Expand icon (+) next to it.

5. To open an object in Design view, click the object on the task pane.

6. When you're done, click the Close button on the task pane.

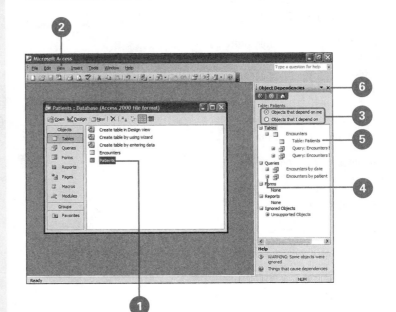

Did You Know?

You can view a list of database objects. Click the File menu, click Database Properties, and then click the Contents tab. When you're done, click OK.

Backing Up a Database

It is vital that you make back up copies of your database on a regular basis so you don't lose valuable data if your computer encounters problems. Access makes it easy to create a back up copy of a database with the Back Up Database command, which works like the Save As command. When you make a back up copy of your database, save the file to a removable disk or network drive to make sure the file is safe if your computer encounters problems. If you need the back up copy of the database, you can use the Open button to restore and view your data.

Back Up an Access Database

1. Save and close all objects in a database.

2. Click the File menu, and then click Back Up Database.

3. Click the Save-In list arrow to select a location for the back up copy.

4. Specify a different backup name.

5. Click Save.

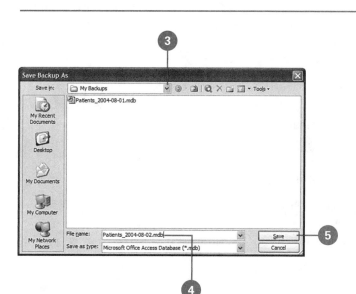

Compacting and Repairing a Database

What do you do when your database starts acting erratically, or when even the simplest tasks cause Access to crash? Problems of this type can occur when a database gets corrupted or when the database file becomes too large. A database can become corrupted when, for example, Access suffers a system crash. Access can repair many of the problems associated with a corrupted database. The size of the database file may also be the trouble. When you delete objects such as forms and reports, Access does not reclaim the space they occupied. To use this space, you have to **compact** the database, allowing Access to rearrange the data, filling in the space left behind by the deleted objects.

Compact and Repair a Database

① Make sure all users close the database.

② Open the database with administrative privileges.

③ Click the Tools menu, and then point to Database Utilities.

④ Click Compact And Repair Database.

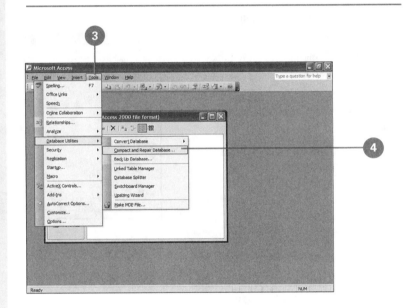

Presenting Data with Access

14

Introduction

Microsoft Office Access 2003 makes it easy to use your data in a form to enter data, in a report to print for review, or on the Web using a data access page, which allows you to create dynamic Web pages.

Forms allow a database designer to create a user-friendly method of data entry. Instead of entering records in the grid of rows and columns in Datasheet view, you can use a form that can represent a paper form. Such a form can minimize data-entry errors and the training time for users because it closely resembles the paper-based form containing the information you want to enter in your table. In an industry such as healthcare, where more than 25 billion pieces of paper were used in the U.S. in 2002, this feature is particularly important. A form can include fields from multiple tables, so you don't have to switch from one table to another when entering data. You can add borders and graphics to the form to enhance its appearance.

To print a simple list of the records in your table, you can click the Print button. But if you want to include calculations, graphics, or a customized header or footer, you can create a report. A report is a summary of information in one or more tables. Reports allow you to include enhancements that a simple printout of records in a table does not provide. In many cases a report answers important questions about the contents of your database.

What You'll Do

Create a Form Using a Wizard

Work with a Form in Design View

Enter and Edit Data in a Form

Modify a Form in Design View

Create a Report Using a Wizard

Modify a Report in Design View

Perform Calculations in Reports

Format a Form or Report

Align and Group Controls

Create a Data Access Page Using a Wizard

Work with a Data Access Page in Design View

Format a Datasheet

Change the Page Setup

Preview and Print Information

Create Mailing Labels

Creating a Form Using a Wizard

To create a simple form in Access, you can use one of the AutoForm wizards. These wizards quickly arrange the fields from the selected table or query into an attractive form. In a form created with the AutoForm: Columnar Wizard, you see each record's data displayed vertically, and with the AutoForm: Tabular Wizard, you see each record's data horizontally. With the AutoForm: Datasheet Wizard, the form displays the records in Datasheet view. After you create a form, you can save and name it so that you can use it again. If you need a more custom form, you can use the Form wizard to select the information you want to include from a variety of places.

Create a Custom Form Using the Form Wizard

① In the Database window, click Forms on the Objects bar, and then double-click the Create Form By Using Wizard icon.

② Click the list arrow for choosing a table or query on which to base the form, and then click the name of the table or query you want.

③ Specify the fields that you want included in the form by double-clicking the fields.

④ Click Next to continue.

⑤ Determine the arrangement and position of the information on the form (Columnar, Tabular, Datasheet, or Justified). Click Next to continue.

⑥ Specify the style of the form, which affects its formatting and final appearance. In the preview area of the dialog box, you can see a preview of the selected style.

⑦ Click Next to continue.

⑧ Enter a name for your form.

⑨ Indicate whether you want to open the form or display it in Design view.

⑩ Click Finish.

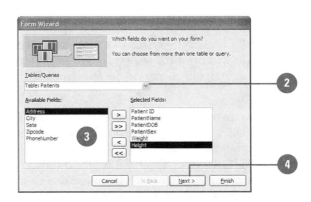

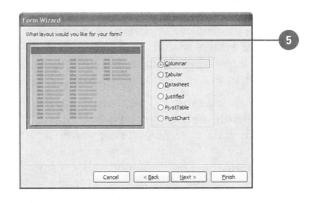

Custom form

Create a Form Using the AutoForm Wizard

1. In the Database window, click Forms on the Objects bar, and then click the New button.

2. Click AutoForm: Columnar (to display records in a column), AutoForm: Tabular (to display records in rows), or AutoForm: Datasheet (to display records in Datasheet view).

3. Click the list arrow, and then click the name of a table or query on which to base the form.

4. Click OK.

   After a moment, Access creates a form and displays it in Form view.

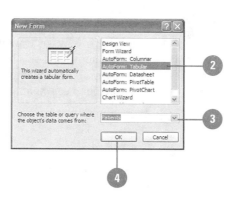

Field values   Field names

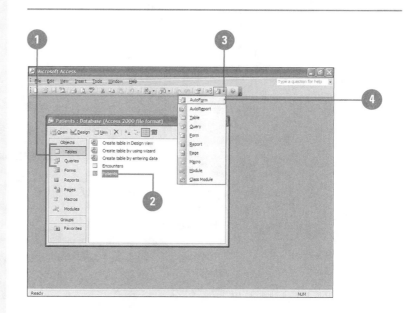

Create a AutoForm

1. In the Database window, click Tables or Queries on the Objects bar.

2. Click the table in which you want to create an AutoForm.

3. Click the New Object button list arrow on the Database toolbar.

4. Click AutoForm.

> **Did You Know?**
>
> *You can save a new form.* While the new form is displayed, click the Save button on the Form View toolbar. Type the name of your form in the Save As dialog box, and then click OK.

Working with a Form in Design View

Although a wizard can be a big help when you are first learning to create a form, you can create a form without the help of a wizard if you have a good idea of how you want the form to look. Instead of answering questions in a series of dialog boxes, you can start working in Design view right away. You can create, modify, move, and format controls to create the exact form you want.

Create or Modify a Form in Design View

1. In the Database window, click Forms on the Objects bar, and then click the New button, or click a form and click the Design button.

   If you're modifying a form, skip step 2.

2. In the New Form dialog box, click Design View, select the table or query with the data you want to use, and then click OK.

3. If necessary, click the Field List button on the Form Design toolbar to add a bound control.

4. Select the field you want to add to the form.

5. Drag the field to the location in the form where you want the field to appear, and then release the mouse button to position the field.

6. Create new controls as needed.

7. Format the text in the form, as needed.

8. Click the Save button on the Form Design toolbar to name the form, and then save it in the database.

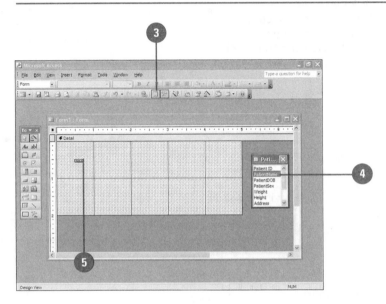

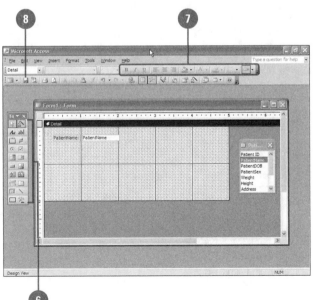

Entering and Editing Data in a Form

Database designers often display data in forms that mimic the paper forms used to record data. Forms facilitate data entry and record viewing. They can also contain buttons that allow you to perform other actions, such as running macros, printing reports, or creating labels. The options that appear on a form depend on what features the database designer included. A form directs you to enter the correct information and can automatically check your entries for errors. Access places the data you've entered in the form into the proper table. You can open a form in Form view or Design view. Form view allows you to view all the information associated with a record; Design view allows you to modify the form's design.

Enter a New Record in a Form

1. In the Database window, click Forms on the Objects bar.

2. Click the form you want to use.

3. Click the Open button.

4. Click the New Record button.

5. Enter the data for the first field.

6. Press Tab to move to the next field or Shift+Tab to move to the previous field.

When you have finished entering the data, you can close the form, click the New Record button to enter another record, or view a different record.

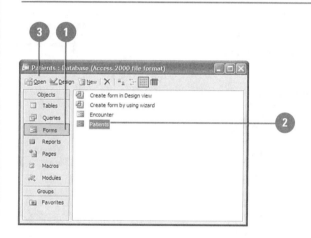

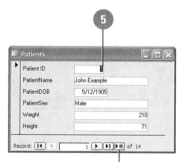

Did You Know?

You can delete a record from a form. In Forms view, display the record you want to delete, click the Delete Record button on the Form View toolbar, and then click Yes.

Modifying a Form in Design View

Controls can make a form easier to use and improve its appearance. Controls also allow you to display additional information on your forms. To create a control on a form, you click the appropriate control button on the Toolbox. The Toolbox appears by default in Design view; however, if the Toolbox was closed for some reason, you need to redisplay it when you want to create new controls on a form. With the control pointer, drag in the form where you want the control to appear. You can also edit controls to change text and delete controls that you no longer want.

Add Controls to a Form

1. Open the form in which you want to add controls in Design view.

2. Click the button on the Toolbox for the type of control you want to create.

3. In the Form window, drag the pointer to draw a box in the location where you want the control to appear.

4. Select the field you want to add to the form.

5. Drag the field to the location in the form where you want the field to appear, and then release the mouse button to position the field.

6. If a smart tag appears indicating an error, click the Smart Tag Options button, and then click an option.

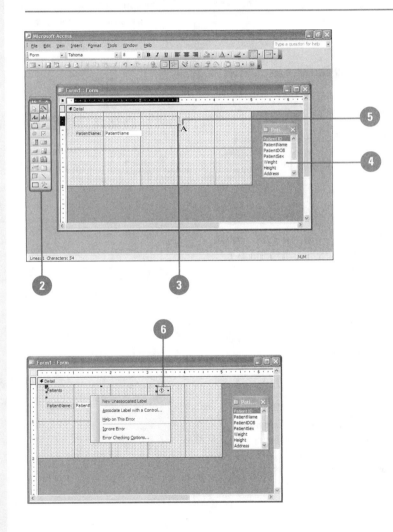

> ## Did You Know?
>
> **You can create list boxes or combo boxes with a Control Wizard.** In Design view, click the Combo Box or List Box button on the Toolbox, and then drag a rectangle. When you release the mouse, the Control Wizard starts. Follow the step-by-step instructions.

Edit Controls in a Form

1. Open the form in which you want to edit controls in Design view.

2. Click the Select Object button on the Toolbox.

3. Click the control you want to edit.

   Small black boxes, called handles, appear around the control to indicate it is selected. You can use them to resize the control.

4. To remove the control, press Delete.

5. To edit the control, click the control to place the insertion point, and then use the Backspace or Delete key to remove text or type to insert text.

Modify Control Properties

1. Open the form or report in which you want to modify controls in Design view.

2. Double-click the object (control, section, or form) to open the object's property sheet.

   TROUBLE? *If the property sheet doesn't open, double-click the edge of the object.*

3. Enter the property information you want to add or change.

4. Click the Close button.

See Also

See "Modifying a Report in Design View" on page 332 for information on the different types of controls.

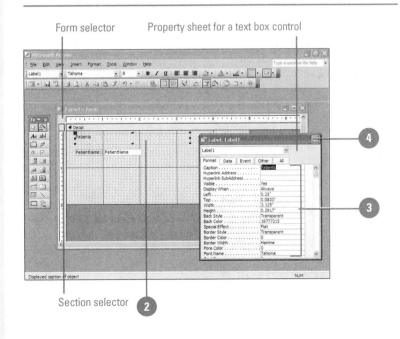

Form selector   Property sheet for a text box control

Section selector

14

Creating a Report Using a Wizard

One of the features you can use to create a simple report in Access is the **AutoReport Wizard**, which arranges data in a selected table or query as a formatted report. The AutoReport: Columnar Wizard displays each record's data vertically, while the AutoReport: Tabular Wizard displays the data for each record horizontally. You can also create a report using the **Report Wizard**, which allows you to select the fields and information you want presented and to choose from available formatting options that determine how the report will look.

Create and Save a Report Using the AutoReport Wizard

1. In the Database window, click Reports on the Objects bar, and then click New.

2. Click AutoReport: Columnar (to display records in a column), or click AutoReport: Tabular (to display records in rows).

3. Click the list arrow, and then click a table or query on which to base the report.

4. Click OK.

   Access displays the form in Print Preview, but you can switch to Design view, save, print, or close the report.

5. Click the Save button, type a name for your report, and then click OK.

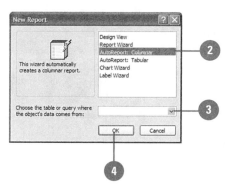

Did You Know?

You can create an instant report with the AutoReport command. In the Database window, select the table or query that contains the data you want formatted as a report. Click the Insert menu, and then click AutoReport. After a moment, Access generates a simple columnar report without headers or footers.

Create and Save a Report Using the Report Wizard

1. In the Database window, click Report on the Objects bar, and then double-click the Create Report By Using Wizard icon.

2. Click the list arrow for choosing a table or query on which to base the form, and then click the name of the table or query you want.

3. Select the fields you want to include, indicating the source of any fields you want to include from other tables or queries. Click Next to continue.

4. If necessary, specify any groupings of the records, choosing any or all of the selected fields (up to ten). Click Next to continue.

5. Specify the order of records within each group, sorting by up to four fields at a time, and then specify ascending or descending order. Click Next to continue.

6. Determine the layout and orientation of your report. Click Next to continue.

7. Specify the style of the report, which affects its formatting and final appearance. Click Next to continue.

8. In the final wizard dialog box, name your report, and then indicate whether you want to preview the report or display it in Design view. Click Finish.

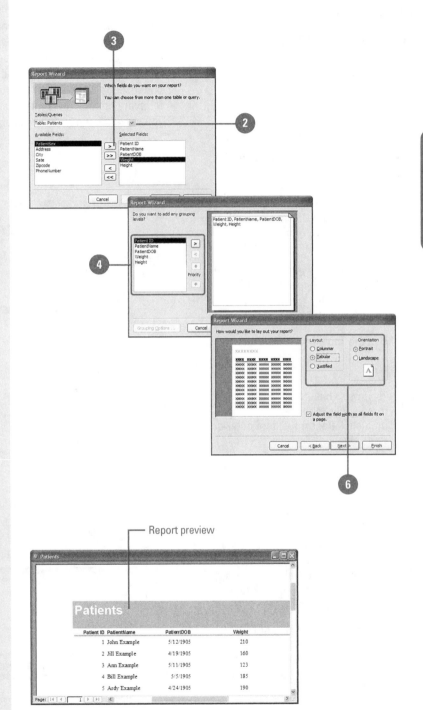

Report preview

14

Modifying a Report in Design View

When you create a report from scratch in Design view, three sections appear: Page Header, Detail, and Page Footer. Once you create the report, you need to populate it with data. You can add **bound controls**—fields of data from a table or query—directly from the Field List, or you can add other types of **unbound controls**—text boxes, labels, pictures, buttons, and so on—from the Toolbox. In Design view, you see two parts for every control: the control itself and its corresponding label. When you move a control, its corresponding label moves with it.

Create or Modify a Report in Design View

1. In the Database window, click Reports on the Objects bar, and then click New, or click a report, and then click Design; skip step 2.

2. In the New Report dialog box, click Design View, select the table or query on which to base the report, and then click OK.

3. Use the Toolbox and Field List to create or modify a report in Design view.

4. To view or hide headers and footers, click the View menu, and then click Report Header/Footer or Page Header/Footer.

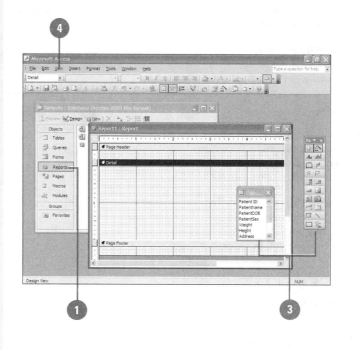

Add a Bound Control

1. Display the report in Design view, select the fields you want to include from the Field List; press Shift or Ctrl while you click to select multiple fields.

2. Drag the selected field or fields to the section in which you want the field to appear. Two boxes appear for each field: one containing the label and one for the field values.

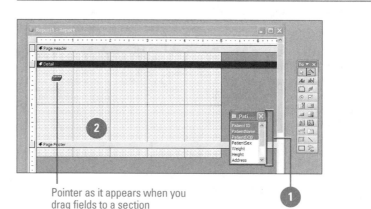

Pointer as it appears when you drag fields to a section

Add an Unbound Control

1. Display the report in Design view, and then click the Toolbox button to the control you want to add, such as a text box, a horizontal line, or a shape.

2. Drag to draw a box in the location where you want the control to appear.

Adjust Page or Section Spacing

1. Display the report or form in Design view whose page or section size you want to change.

2. Position the mouse pointer over the edge of the page or section.

3. Drag the resize pointer to a new location.

The ruler shows size of control as you drag.

The grid provides dots that help you align controls.

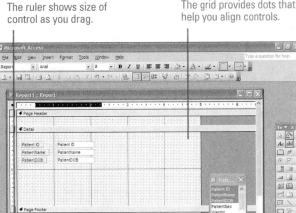

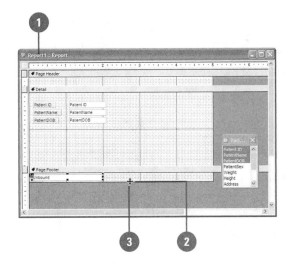

Performing Calculations in Reports

When you create a report, you might want to include summary information or other calculations. The wizards often include built-in functions, but you can use the **Expression Builder** to create your own by clicking buttons for the arithmetic operators you want to use and including constant values as needed. For example, if you want to determine staff bonuses based on a percentage of overtime hours worked, you can create an arithmetic expression to compute the results. When you generate the report, Access will perform the required calculations and display the results in the report. To display the calculations in the appropriate format, you can also use the Properties feature to specify formats for dates, currency, and other numeric data.

Choose Fields to Use in a Calculation

1. In Design view, create a text box control and position it where you want the calculated field to appear, or select an existing unbound control.

2. Click the Properties button on the Report Design toolbar.

3. Click the Control Source property box, which specifies what data appears in a control, and then click the Expression Builder button.

4. Click the equal sign (=) button.

5. Enter the values and operators you want to use.

   ◆ Click operator buttons to supply the most common operations.

   ◆ Double-click folders in the left pane to open lists of objects you can use in your expression, including existing fields, constants, operators, and common expressions.

   ◆ Manually type an expression.

6. Click OK to insert the calculation.

7. Click the Close button.

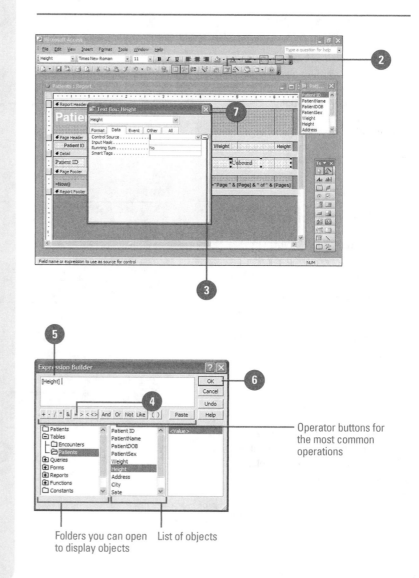

Operator buttons for the most common operations

Folders you can open to display objects

List of objects

Format Values in a Report

1. In Design view, position the insertion point in the field whose format you want to change, and then click the Properties button on the Report Design toolbar.

2. On either the All tab or the Format tab of the property sheet, click the Format property box, click the list arrow that appears, and then click the format you want to use.

   The names of the formats appear on the left side of the drop-down list, and examples of the corresponding formats appear on the right side.

3. If you are formatting a number (rather than a date), and you do not want to accept the default, "Auto," click the Decimal Places property box, click the list arrow, and then click the number of decimal places you want.

4. Click Close.

Did You Know?

You can use a builder. Access makes it easy to change many types of settings by providing builders, or tools that simplify tasks. The Expression Builder is just one of many builders in Access. You know a builder is available for a task when you click a property box and a Build button appears.

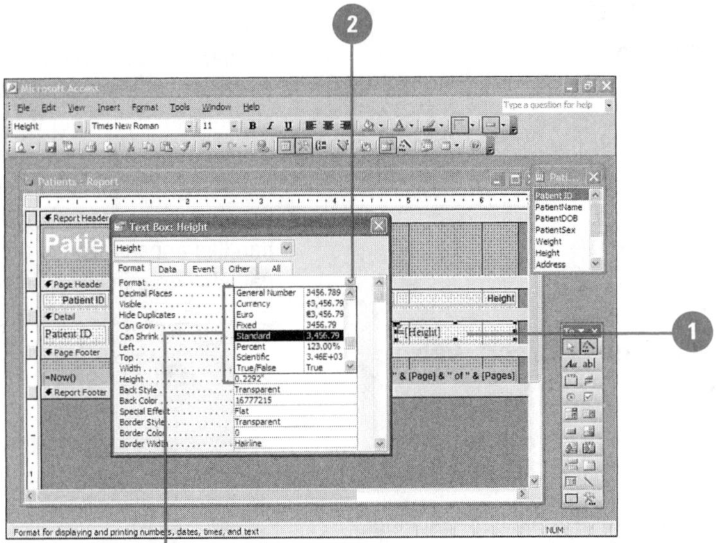

List of available number formats

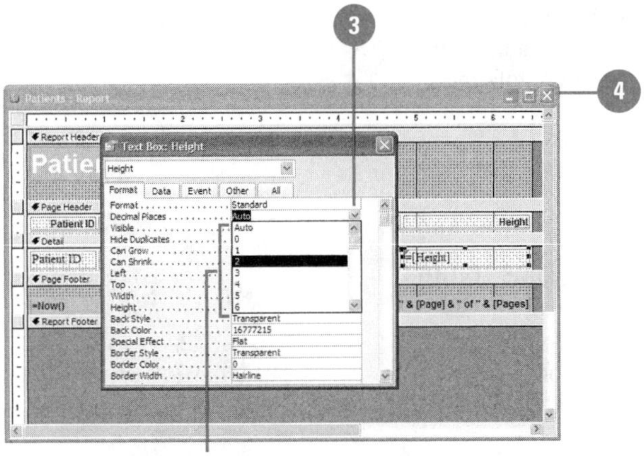

Possible number of decimal places for Currency format

14

Formatting a Form or Report

A fast way to format a form or report is with the **AutoFormat** button, available in Design view. When you click this button on the Form Design toolbar, you can select and preview a variety of layouts and styles. After you make your selections, Access formats the entire report or form consistently for you. After using AutoFormat, you can always make additional changes to the formatting using buttons on the Formatting (Form/Report) toolbar. If you don't see the header and footer sections, you can display them to add controls. When you select a control, sizing handles appear around the control, which you can drag to size it. You can also drag inside a selected control to move it to a new location.

Format a Form or Report with AutoFormat

1. Display the report or form you want to format in Design view.

2. Click the AutoFormat button on the Report Or Form Design toolbar.

3. Click the style option you want.

4. To apply attributes (Font, Color, or Border), click Options, and then select or clear the options you want to apply with AutoFormat.

5. Click OK.

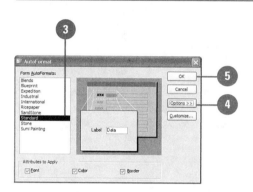

Format a Form or Report Using Formatting Tools

1. Display the report or form you want to format in Design view.

2. Select the item you want to format.

3. Use formatting buttons on the Formatting (Form/Report) toolbar to apply the following:

   ◆ Text style, color, and alignment.

   ◆ Box fill and line/border color, line/border width, and special effects, such as shadowed, etched, and raised.

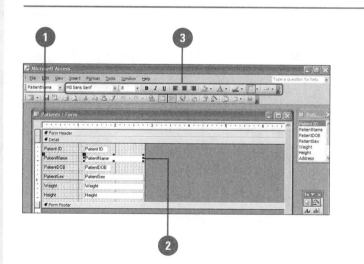

Show and Hide Headers and Footers

1. Display the form in Design view, and then display the Toolbox.

2. Click the View menu.

3. Click the Header/Footer you want to show or hide:

   ◆ Page Header/Footer displays a header and footer for each page.

   ◆ Form Header/Footer displays a header and footer for the form.

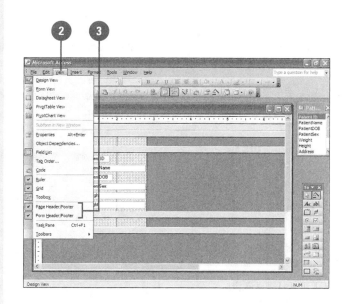

Resize or Move a Control

1. Display the form in Design view, and then display the Toolbox.

2. Select the control you want to format.

3. To resize a control, position the pointer over a sizing handle, and then drag to a new location.

4. To move a control, position the pointer over an edge of a control until the pointer changes to a black hand, and then drag to a new location.

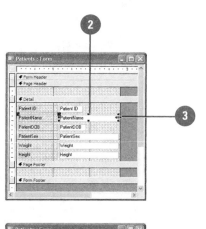

Did You Know?

Access inherits the theme from Windows XP. If the operating system is Windows XP SP1 or later, and you have chosen a theme other than Windows Classic, Access inherits the theme (color scheme, fonts, lines, etc.). Most of the views, controls, and dialog boxes will match the Windows theme.

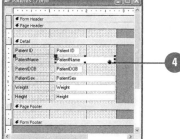

14

Aligning and Grouping Controls

Often when you work with multiple controls and objects, they look best when aligned with each other. For example, you can align three controls with the left-most control in the selection so that the left sides of all three controls align along an invisible line. You can also change the horizontal and vertical spacing between controls and objects. Access also lets you resize controls and objects relative to each other and group them together.

Align Objects and Controls to Each Other

1. Display the form or report in Design view, or, for a field border, in Form or Report view.

2. Select the controls and objects you want to align.

3. Click the Format menu, point to Align, and then click the alignment option you want.

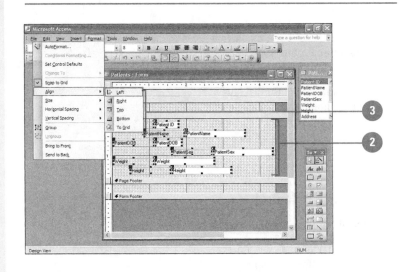

Change Horizontal or Vertical Spacing

1. Display the form or report in Design view, or, for a field border, in Form or Report view.

2. Select the controls and objects whose spacing you want to change.

3. Click the Format menu, point to Horizontal Spacing or Vertical Spacing, and then click the spacing option you want.

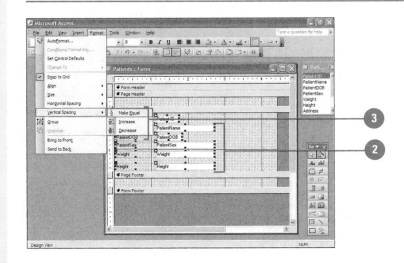

Change the Size of Controls and Objects

1. Display the form or report in Design view, or, for a field border, in Form or Report view.

2. Select the controls and objects you want to resize.

3. Click the Format menu, point to Size, and then click the sizing option that you want—To Fit, To Grid, To Tallest, To Shortest, To Widest, or To Narrowest.

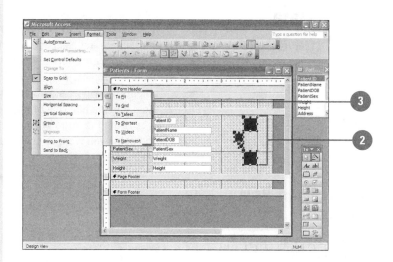

Group or Ungroup Controls and Objects

1. Display the form or report in Design view, or, for a field border, in Form or Report view.

2. Select the controls and objects you want to group or the object you want to ungroup.

3. Click the Format menu, and then click Group or Ungroup.

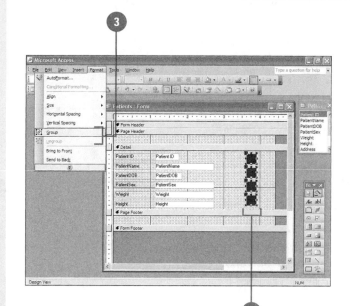

Did You Know?

You can turn off the Snap To Grid to align controls and lines the way you want. In Design view, the controls and other objects you create align themselves along an invisible grid as you move them. To gain greater control over the exact placement of lines and controls, you can turn off the Snap To Grid option. Click the Format menu, and then clear the Snap To Grid check box. Select this command to turn it on.

14

Creating a Data Access Page Using a Wizard

Data access pages allow you to create dynamic Web pages without the need of a Web server, unlike an Active Server Page (ASP) file. You can format data access pages, using many of the same tools you use when creating Access forms. Access organizes the data access pages in a separate object group in the Database window. Unlike other data objects, however, a data access page is stored in a file separate from the database file. One of the easiest ways to create a data access page is by using the Page Wizard. The wizard asks you to select the tables and fields you want to use, and how you want to group the fields on the Web page.

Create a Data Access Page Using a Wizard

1. In the Database window, click Pages on the Objects bar.

2. Double-click the Create Data Access Page By Using Wizard icon.

3. Select the table and fields that you want to appear in the data access page. Click Next to continue.

4. If you want, select any fields you want to act as group levels in the Web page. Click Next to continue.

5. Select the fields to sort the records in the page. Click Next to continue.

6. Enter a title for the data access page.

7. Indicate whether you want to open the page in Access or to modify its design in Design view.

8. Click Finish.

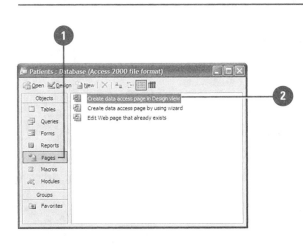

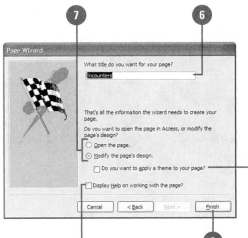

Click to choose a predefined theme when the page opens in the Design view.

Click to display Help on data access pages.

> ### Did You Know?
>
> **You can export to Web formats.** Click the File menu, click Export, click the Save As Type list arrow, click a format, and then click Export.

Working with a Data Access Page in Design View

If you want to create a data access page without the Page Wizard, you can create it in Design view. Design view allows you to choose the tables, fields, and other objects that you want to appear on the Web page. You can format the appearance of the page using the same techniques you apply when you create Access forms. You can use tools on the Toolbox to insert hyperlinks and Office data, such as PivotTables, Excel Charts, and Excel Spreadsheets. A **PivotTable** is an interactive table linked to a database that summarizes the data in a table or query in tabular format. Similarly, **PivotChart** is an interactive chart that is linked to a database.

Create or Modify a Data Access Page in Design View

1. In the Database window, click Pages on the Objects bar.

2. Double-click the Create Data Access Page In Design View icon, or click the page you want to modify, and then click the Design button.

3. If necessary, click the Field List button to display the list of tables and queries in the database.

4. Double-click the Tables or Queries folder, and then locate the table or query on which you want to base your page.

5. Drag a table or query icon from the field list to the Unbound section of the data access page.

6. Click a layout option, and then click OK.

7. Use the tools on the Toolbox to insert hyperlinks and other Office data, such as PivotTables, Charts, and Spreadsheets.

8. Click the Close button, click Yes if prompted to save your work, and then enter a file name for the resulting Web page.

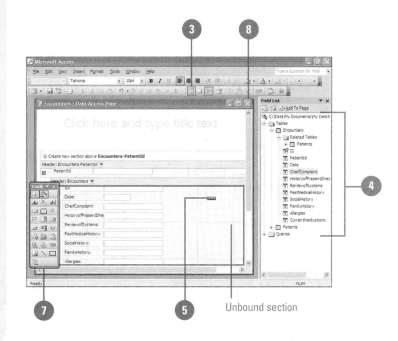

Unbound section

14

Formatting a Datasheet

If you want to print a datasheet, you can use formatting tools to make it look better than the standard display. You can apply special effects to cells, change the background and gridline color, and modify border and line styles. If you don't want to show the gridlines, you can hide either the horizontal or vertical gridlines, or both. The default display for a datasheet is to display the columns from left to right. If you prefer, you can change the column display to appear from right to left.

Format a Datasheet

1. Open the datasheet you want to format.

2. Click the Format menu, and then click Datasheet.

3. Click a cell effect option.

4. Select or clear the Horizontal or Vertical check box to show or hide gridlines.

5. Click the Background Color or Gridline Color list arrow, and then select a color.

6. Click the Border And Line Styles list arrow, and then select the styles you want.

7. Click a display direction option.

8. Click OK.

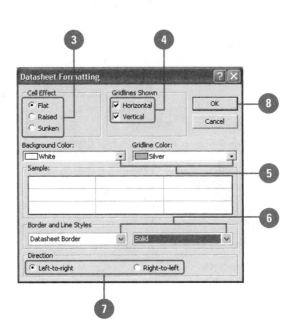

Did You Know?

You can change the font and font style in a datasheet. Open the datasheet you want to format, click the Format menu, click Font, select the font and style settings you want, and then click OK.

Changing the Page Setup

Once you have created a report or form, you can change the page setup, which includes the margin, paper size and orientation, and grid and column settings. Margins are the blank space between the edge of a page and the text. You can also select the page orientation (portrait or landscape) that best fits the entire document or any section. Portrait orients the page vertically (taller than it is wide), and landscape orients the page horizontally (wider than it is tall). When you shift between the two, the margin settings automatically change.

Change Page Setup Options

1. In the Database window, click the report, form, table, query, or any data you want to preview.

2. Click the File menu, and then click Page Setup.

3. To change margin settings, click the Margins tab, and then change the top, bottom, left, or right margins you want.

4. To change paper settings, click the Page tab, and then select the orientation (portrait or landscape), paper size and source, and printer for vendor labels you want.

5. To change column settings, click the Columns tab, and then change or select the column and row grid settings, column size, and column layout (Down, Then Across or Across, Then Down) you want.

6. Click OK.

Previewing and Printing Information

Before printing, you should verify that the data you want to print looks the way you want. You save time, money, and paper by avoiding duplicate printing. Print Preview shows you exactly how your data will look on each printed page. The Print Preview toolbar provides the tools you need to display the look of each page. You can print a report, a table, a query, or any data in a single step using the Print button, in which case Access prints a single copy of all pages in the report. If you want to print only selected pages or if you want to specify other printing options, use the Print command on the File menu.

Preview Data

1. In the Database window, click the report, form, table, query, or any data you want to preview.

2. Click the Print Preview button on the Database toolbar.

3. Use the One Page, Two Page, or Multiple Page buttons on the Print Preview toolbar to view the data.

4. Use the record navigation buttons (First, Previous, Record Selection box, Next, and Last) to display pages.

5. To print from the Print Preview window, click the Print button on the Print Preview toolbar.

6. When you're done, click the Close button on the Print Preview toolbar.

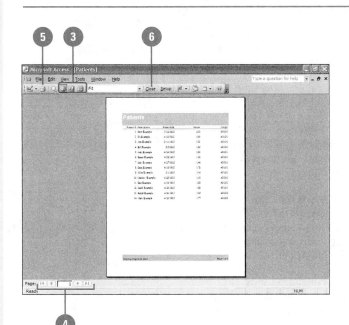

Did You Know?

You can create a report snapshot.
In the Database window, click the report you want to use, click the File menu, click Export, click the Save As Type list arrow, select Snapshot Format, enter a file name, and then click Save.

Print Data

1. Display the report, form, table, query, or any data you want to format in Design View.

2. Click the File menu, and then click Print.

3. If necessary, click the Name list arrow, and then select the printer you want to use.

4. Select the print range you want.

   ◆ To print all pages, click the All option.

   ◆ To print selected pages, click the Pages option, and then type the first page in the From box and the ending page in the To box.

   ◆ To print selected record, click the Selected Record(s) option.

5. Click OK.

Did You Know?

You can check spelling in tables. Before you print, its a good idea to check spelling. Display the table in Datasheet view, select the rows or columns you want to check, click the Spelling button on the Table Datasheet toolbar, and then use the Ignore and Change buttons to correct spelling mistakes. You can also use the Add button to add words to the dictionary.

Print

Printer	
Name:	HP LaserJet 4000 Series
Status:	Ready
Type:	HP LaserJet 4000 Series PS
Where:	Office
Comment:	Postscript Driver for HP 4000;

☐ Print to File

Print Range
- ○ All
- ◉ Pages From: ____ To: ____
- ○ Selected Record(s)

Copies

Number of Copies: 1

☑ Collate

Setup...   OK   Cancel

14

Creating Mailing Labels

Access provides a **Label Wizard** to help you create mailing labels quickly. The wizard supports a large variety of label brands and sizes. You can also create customized labels for brands and sizes not listed by the wizard, provided you know the dimensions of your labels and label sheets. You can create labels by drawing data from any of your tables or queries. In addition to data values, labels can also include customized text that you specify.

Create Mailing Labels

1. In the Database window, click Reports on the Objects bar, and then click the New button.

2. Click Label Wizard, select the table or query to be used in the mailing labels, and then click OK.

3. Select the type of mailing label you're using. Click Next to continue.

4. Specify the font style and color for the label text. Click Next to continue.

5. Double-click the field names in the Available Fields list to place them on your mailing labels. Type any text that you want to accompany the field values. Click Next to continue.

6. If necessary, select a field to sort your labels by. Click Next to continue.

7. Enter a name for your mailing labels report, and then choose whether to preview the printout or modify the label design.

8. Click Finish.

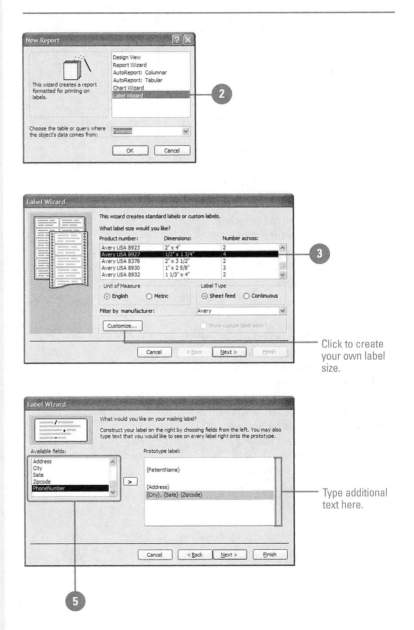

Click to create your own label size.

Type additional text here.

Communicating with Outlook

15

Introduction

Microsoft Office Outlook 2003 takes managing and organizing your daily routine to a new level. Its updated look gives you a larger viewing area and easier access to the tools that you want to use. You can customize its features so that they are seamlessly interwoven as you move from your electronic mail to your calendar to your notes to your journal.

Managing your personal communications and information has become an intricate and important aspect of everyday life at the workplace and at home. With Outlook, you can store, track, and manage all your information and communications in one place. You can track your appointments, meetings, and tasks on your Calendar and store information, including phone numbers, addresses, e-mail addresses, about all your patients, colleagues, business associates, family, and friends in your Contacts list. Use Notes to write reminders to yourself and Tasks to record your daily or weekly to-do list, checking them off as you complete them. Of course, one of the most important parts of your day is communicating, and Outlook provides the tools that help you address all your electronic communications needs.

Preparing for Outlook

Outlook is Microsoft's personal information manager and electronic mail (e-mail) software for handling incoming and outgoing e-mail messages.

To use Outlook as your personal information management (PIM) and e-mail tool, you need to be connected to the Internet or a network. Through this connection, you can take full advantage of the e-mail, scheduling, and contact capabilities of Outlook. Before you start Outlook for the first time, you need to know about the different types of connections and e-mail servers you can use with Outlook.

You can use Outlook on a standalone computer or one that is part of a network of computers, also called a **local area network (LAN)**. When you connect your standalone or networked computer to the Internet so you can communicate electronically, your computer becomes part of a worldwide network. You need two things to establish a connection to the Internet: a physical connection and an **Internet service provider (ISP)**.

Options for physical connections include a modem via a phone line (also called a dial-up network connection), a cable broadband modem, or a **digital subscriber line (DSL)** connected directly to your computer or through a LAN. Your options for an ISP, however, are numerous and vary greatly, both in cost and features, and depend upon the type of physical connection you choose. ISPs can include your local telephone or cable company, or a company, such as MSN or AOL (American Online), that provides only Internet access service.

The ISP provides the names of your incoming and outgoing **e-mail servers**, which collect and store your e-mail until you are ready to retrieve or send it. If you are using a modem, your ISP provides the phone number and modem settings needed to establish an Internet connection.

If you are working on a LAN that uses its own mail server, such as Microsoft Exchange Server, to send and receive e-mail, your network administrator provides all the information that you need for establishing a connection. However, you still need to set up your Outlook Profile with the Exchange mail connector. You will need the Exchange Server name from your system administrator.

Once you establish your connection, you can send and receive e-mail, or you can communicate using instant messaging, participating in a chat room, or subscribing to a newsgroup.

There are several different types of e-mail accounts that you can use with Outlook: POP3, IMAP, and HTTP:

- **Post Office Protocol 3 (POP3)** is a common e-mail account type provided by ISPs. Messages are downloaded from the e-mail server and stored on your local computer.

- **Internet Message Access Protocol (IMAP)** is similar to POP3 except that messages are stored on the e-mail server.

- **Hypertext Transfer Protocol (HTTP)** is a common type of Web e-mail account. Messages are stored, retrieved, and displayed as individual Web pages. Hotmail is an example of an HTTP e-mail account.

Using Outlook for the First Time

When you start Outlook for the first time, what you see depends on whether you installed Outlook as a new program or as an upgrade. In either case, a setup wizard appears to step you through the process of setting up a profile and an e-mail service. A **service** is a connection to an e-mail server where you store and receive e-mail messages. Outlook can be used with more than one e-mail account on the most common servers. Before you use Outlook, you are usually asked to create a profile. A **profile** is a collection of all the data necessary to access one or more e-mail accounts and address books. You need to specify information about your e-mail account, including your account name, your password, and the names of the incoming and outgoing e-mail servers, which you need to get from your ISP. If you installed Outlook as an upgrade, Outlook 2003 uses the existing profile settings.

Use Outlook for the First Time

1. Click the Start button on the taskbar, point to All Programs, point to Microsoft Office, and then click Microsoft Office Outlook 2003.

2. Type a name for your profile, and then click OK.

3. Click the Add A New E-Mail Account option, and then click Next.

4. Select the type of your e-mail account, and then click Next.

5. Read the Account Settings information, enter the required information, and then click Finish.

Did You Know?

You can have more than one e-mail account. Click the Tools menu, click E-Mail Accounts, click the View Or Change Existing E-Mail Accounts option, click Next, click Add to add a new e-mail account (or click Change to modify an existing account), read and follow the setup wizard instructions, and then click Finish.

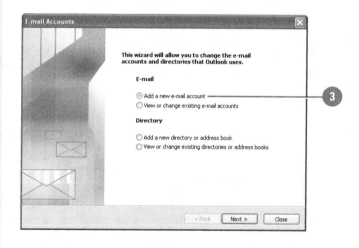

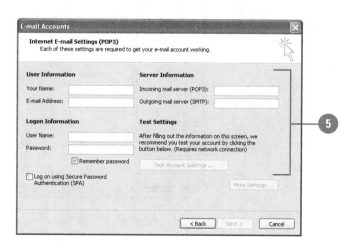

15

Viewing the Outlook Window

Title bar. The title bar displays the name of the current folder, in this case the Inbox folder, followed by the name of the Outlook program.

Menu bar. The menu bar provides the menus of commands you use to accomplish your tasks in Outlook.

Standard toolbar. The Standard toolbar provides buttons you click to quickly execute commands. The buttons on this toolbar change depending on the current view. You can also display the Advanced toolbar for access to additional commands.

Navigation pane. The Navigation pane is your central station for moving around in Outlook. The Folder list is located in the upper portion of the Navigation pane, and the Outlook view bars occupy the lower portion.

Folder list. The Folder list displays the contents of the folder you select. In Outlook you store in information in folders and the folder you use depends on the Outlook item you are using. Some of the default folders in Outlook include Inbox, Calendar, Contacts, Tasks, Notes, Journal, Deleted Items folder, and so on.

Outlook view bars. Click one of the four major Outlook view bars—Mail, Calendar, Contacts, or Tasks—to work in that view. You can use the other Outlook views—Notes, Folder List, or Shortcuts—by clicking one of the icons located below the view bars.

Folder pane. In Mail view, the middle pane of the Outlook windows displays the contents of the folder you select. You can control how the contents are displayed (e.g., by date, order of importance, sender, and so on).

Reading pane. The Reading pane gives you a greater area for reading your e-mail messages without having to scroll to view them.

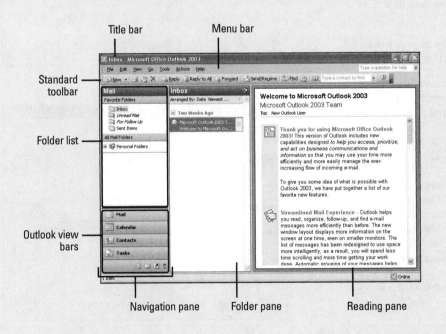

Using Outlook Today

You can start your day with a preview of your meetings, appointments, and tasks, and a list of new e-mail messages awaiting you. Outlook Today can display your Calendar, Tasks, and Inbox so you can see what you have in store for the day. You can customize the look of Outlook Today by specifying which folders you want to display, the number of days displayed in your calendar, the number of tasks, and the layout of the Outlook Today pane. You can also set Outlook Today to open each time you start Outlook, making it your "start" or "home" page.

View Outlook Today

1. Click the Outlook Today button on the Advanced toolbar to display the Outlook Today page.

Did You Know?

You can display or hide the Advanced toolbar. Click the View menu, point to Toolbars, and then click Advanced to clear or select the option. If a check mark appears before Advanced, the toolbar is already displayed.

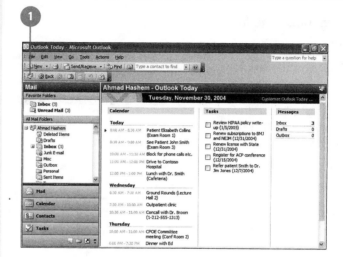

Customize Outlook Today

1. Click the Outlook Today button on the Advanced toolbar.

2. Click the Customize Outlook Today button on the Outlook Today page.

3. Set the options you want.

   ◆ Display the Outlook Today page at startup

   ◆ Display message folders.

   ◆ Set the number of days in the Calendar.

   ◆ Display and sort tasks.

   ◆ Choose the page style.

4. Click the Save Changes button.

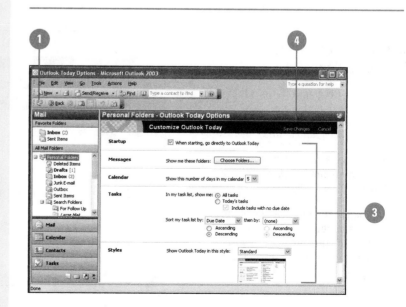

Using the Navigation Pane

The Navigation pane is designed to display more of what you need to see in a simple and straightforward layout. When you click an Outlook view bar in the Navigation pane, the entire Outlook window transforms to provide a clear, uncluttered view of your Mail, Calendar, Contacts, and Tasks. The Notes, Folder list, and Shortcuts views do not appear by default, but you can access each view by clicking its icon at the bottom of the Navigation pane. You can customize the look of the Navigation pane so it better suits the way you work. For example, you can reorder the view bars and determine whether a view appears as a view bar or an icon.

Use the Navigation Pane to Move Around

1. Click a button on the Navigation pane.

    TIMESAVER *Press Ctrl+1 to open the Mail view. Press Ctrl+4 to open the Task view.*

Did You Know?

You can use the Go menu to navigate Outlook. Click the Go menu, and then move to any location or display any folder in Outlook.

Change the Look of the Navigation Pane

1. Click the Configure Buttons button on the Navigation pane.

2. Point to Navigation Pane Options.

3. To remove a view from the Navigation pane, clear the check box for the view button.

4. To change the order in which the buttons appear on the Navigation pane, click the name of the view button in the list, and then click the Move Up or Move Down button.

5. Click OK.

Click to change the timeline display.

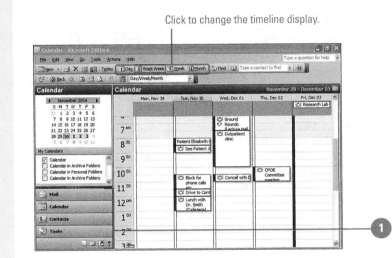

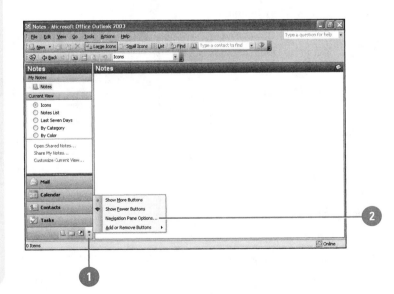

Viewing Items and Folders

When you use Outlook, you work with views. The main views in Outlook are Mail, Calendar, Tasks, Contacts, Notes, and Shortcuts. Within those views, Outlook stores related items in folders. For each of these views, you can choose how to display the items and folders in which you stored the items.

View an Item

1. Click a view bar or icon on the Navigation pane to switch to that Outlook view.

2. Click the Current View list arrow to display the available options.

3. Click the view you want to apply.

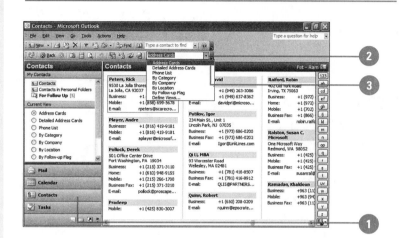

View a Folder

1. Click the Folder List icon on the Navigation pane.

2. Click a folder in the Folder list.

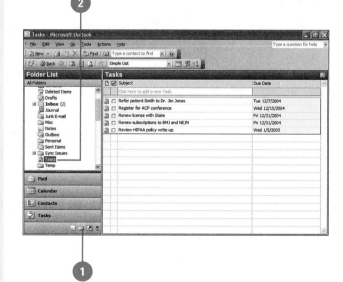

Did You Know?

You can customize a view. Click the Current View list arrow, and then click Define Views. Use the dialog box to create a new view or modify existing view options to better suit your working environment or needs.

You can display views. Click the View menu, point to Arrange By, and then click Show Views In Navigation Pane to list views in the Navigation pane (as well as in the Current View list box).

Creating a Contact

A **contact** is a person or company with whom you want to communicate, such as a patient or a fellow healthcare professional. One contact can have several mailing addresses, various phone and fax numbers, e-mail addresses, and Web sites. You can store all this data in the Contacts folder along with more detailed information, such as job titles, birthdays, and anniversaries. When you double-click a contact, you open a dialog box in which you can edit the detailed contact information. You can also directly edit the contact information from within the Contacts folder. If you send the same e-mail message to more than one person, you can group contacts together into a distribution list.

Create a Contact

1. Click the Contacts button, and then click the New button on the Outlook toolbar.

2. Type the contact's first and last name in the Full Name box.

3. Type as much information as you know about the contact in the appropriate boxes on the General tab.

4. Click the Details tab, and then type as much information as you know in the appropriate boxes.

5. Click the Save And Close button.

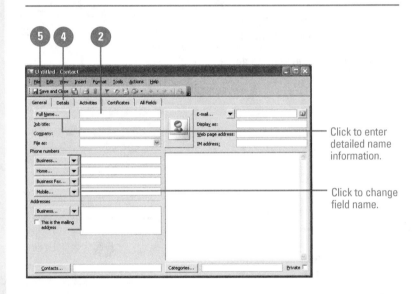

Click to enter detailed name information.

Click to change field name.

Insertion point

Open and Update an Existing Contact

1. Click the Contacts button on the Navigation pane.

2. Double-click the contact you want to update.

3. Use the normal editing commands to update the information.

4. Click the Save And Close button.

Change Contacts Views

① Click the Contacts button on the Navigation pane.

② Click a view option button.

- ◆ Address Cards
- ◆ Detailed Address Cards
- ◆ Phone List
- ◆ By Category
- ◆ By Company
- ◆ By Location
- ◆ By Follow-Up Flag

③ To customize the current view, click Customize Current View.

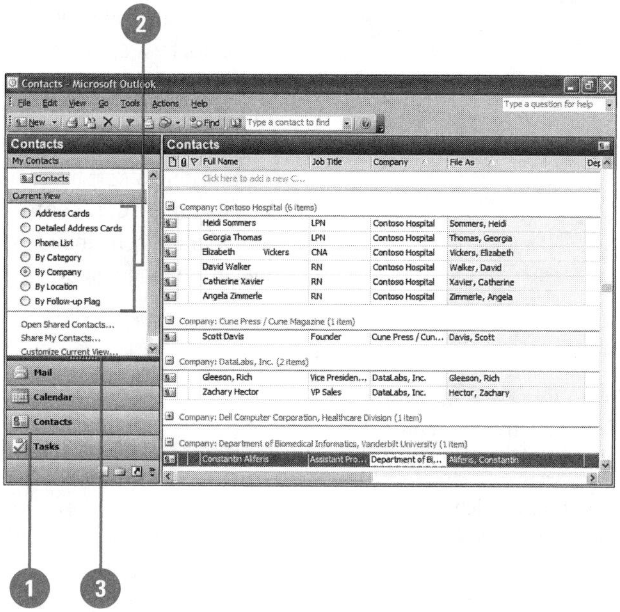

Did You Know?

You can find a contact quickly. Click Contacts on the Navigation pane, and then start typing the name of the contact you want to find. The contact that best matches the text is displayed.

You can delete a contact. Click Contacts on the Navigation pane, click the contact you want to delete, and then click the Delete button on the Standard toolbar. Any journal entries that refer to that contact remain intact.

15

Sorting Contacts

Outlook allows you to sort contacts in any view and by any field, either in ascending order (A to Z) or descending order (Z to A). You can sort contacts by a specific field or by a column header appearing at the top of the view's table (Company, Job Title, Personal Home Page, and so on). When sorted in a view, the contacts maintain the same view, but their order has changed. It's also possible to generate multi-layered sorts within a sort by adding more fields to the sort. For example, you might want to sort contacts by their company names first and then alphabetically by their last names. The second field fine tunes the search by introducing a second criterion.

Sort Contacts

1 Click the Customize Current View link in the Navigation pane, and then click the Sort button.

2 Click the Sort Items By list arrow, and then click the desired sort field.

3 Click the Ascending or Descending option.

TIMESAVER *Click a column head in a table format view to sort in ascending order by that column; click the column head again to re-sort in descending order.*

You can add a second sort field.

4 Click the first Then By list arrow, select the desired sort field, and then click the Ascending or Descending option.

5 Click OK.

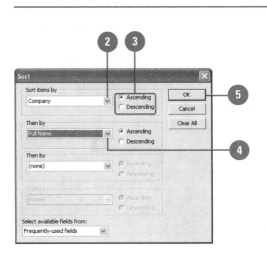

Indicates contacts sorted by company name in ascending order

Did You Know?

You can change the name format of contacts. Change the name format of contacts in the Contact dialog box. Edit the entry in the Full Name box, and then select a different choice in the File As list, or edit the entry in the Display As box.

Creating a Distribution List

A **distribution list** is a collection of contacts usually grouped together because of a specific task or association and then identified by one name. You can use a distribution list in your e-mail messages, task requests, and other distribution lists. When you address an e-mail message using a distribution list, you are sending the message to everyone whose address is included in the list. Because a distribution list often contains many names, it provides a faster, more efficient way to address an e-mail message to multiple recipients.

Create a Distribution List

1. Click the Contacts button on the Navigation pane.

2. Click the Actions menu, and then click New Distribution List.

3. Type the name for the distribution list.

4. Click Select Members to select names from your Contacts folder.

5. If necessary, click Add New, and then enter the display name and e-mail address for the person you want to add to the list. If you want to add this person to your Contacts folder, click the Add To Contacts check box. Click OK.

6. Click Categories, check the category or categories you want to apply to this distribution list, and then click OK.

7. Click the Save And Close button.

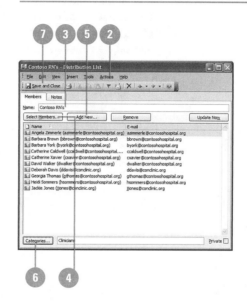

Did You Know?

You can sort a distribution list by category. If you associate a distribution list with a category, you can then sort and view the names in the list.

Creating and Addressing an E-Mail Message

When you create an e-mail message, the Untitled Message window opens with all the tools you need to communicate electronically. Your first step is addressing the message. You must identify who will receive the message or a copy of the message. For each recipient, you enter an e-mail address. You can enter the address manually by typing it in the To or Cc box, or you can select an address from your list of contacts. If you enter multiple addresses, you must separate the addresses with a semicolon (;). You can type a semicolon after each recipient's e-mail address, or you can just press Enter after a recipient's address. Addressing a new message also means indicating the purpose of the message by entering a subject. Try to indicate the intent of the message as briefly and clearly as possible.

Create and Address an E-Mail Message

1. Click the Mail button on the Navigation pane to display the Inbox folder.

   TIMESAVER *Press Ctrl+N to create a new mail message.*

2. Click the New button on the Standard toolbar.

3. Enter the e-mail address of each recipient, or click the To button.

4. Enter the e-mail addresses for those recipients who should receive a copy of the message, or click the Cc button.

5. Type a subject that indicates the purpose of the message.

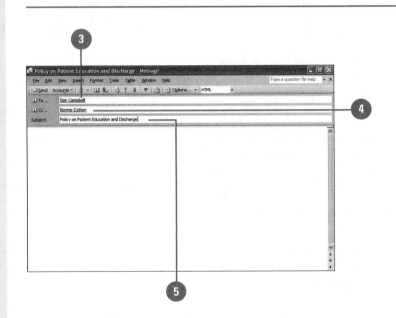

Did You Know?

You can save time with AutoComplete Addressing. If you begin to enter the e-mail address of a recipient to which you have previously sent a message, Outlook recognizes the address and completes it using AutoComplete Addressing.

Write a Message

1. In the message window, click in the message area.

2. Type the content of your message.

3. Right-click any word that appears with a green or red wavy underline to display a list of suggested corrections, and then correct the error, if necessary.

4. Click a suggested word to replace the error, or click one of the other options.

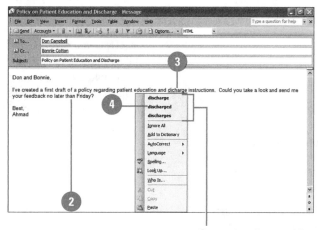

Suggestions for correcting the misspelled word

Select Addresses for an E-Mail Message

1. In the message window, click the To or Cc button.

2. If necessary, click the Show Names From The list arrow, and then click the Address Book that contains the addresses you need.

3. Click the name of a recipient.

4. Click the To button or the Cc button. To select multiple recipients in the list, click the first name, and then press and hold Shift (to select adjacent names) or Ctrl (to select nonadjacent names) as you click the other recipient names.

5. To send a blind copy (address not included in recipients' list) of your message, select the recipient, and then click Bcc.

6. Click OK.

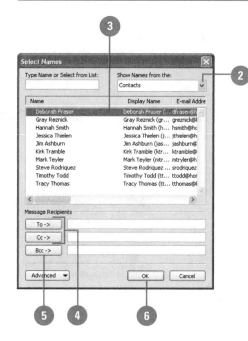

Formatting Message Text

You can specify a file format for message text. The Plain Text format is one that all e-mail programs recognize, but it doesn't support text formatting. The Rich Text and HTML formats allow text formatting, but are not always supported. However, most programs that don't recognize Rich Text or HTML, convert the message to plain text. When you use Rich Text or HTML, you can use tools, such as bold, italicize, and underline text, on the Formatting toolbar to help draw the reader's attention to key words and emphasize the meaning of your message. With Word as the Outlook e-mail editor, you can take advantage of Word's formatting features when you write the text of your e-mail messages.

Format the Message Text

1. Open the message you want to format.

2. Click the Message Format list arrow, and then select Rich Text, HTML, or Plain Text.

3. Select the text you want to format.

4. If you selected Rich Text or HTML, use the tools on the Formatting toolbar to format the message text.

   ◆ The Font list arrow.

   ◆ The Font Size list arrow.

   ◆ The Bold, Italics, or Underline buttons.

   ◆ The Font Color list arrow.

   ◆ The Align Left, Center, or Align Right buttons.

   ◆ The Numbering or Bullets button.

Did You Know?

You can specify the file format for all messages. Click the Tools menu, click Options, click the Mail Format tab, click the Compose Text In This Format list arrow, and then select HTML, Rich Text, or Plain Text.

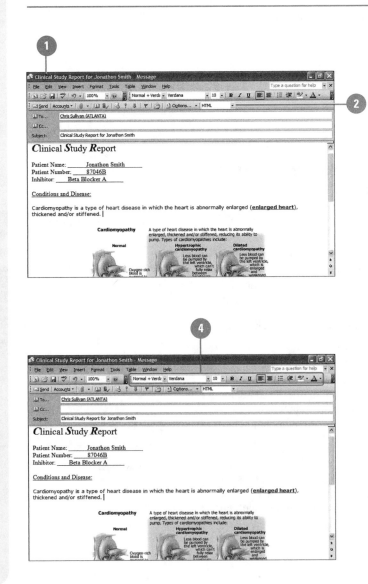

Attaching a File or Item to a Message

You can also add an attachment to your e-mail messages. An attachment can be a file, such as a document or a picture. The attachment can also be an Outlook item, such as a contact, task, or note. When you add an attachment to a message, an attachment icon appears under the Subject box, identifying the name and size of the attachment. Although you can add multiple attachments to a message, you should limit the number and size of the attachments. The size of the attachment affects the time it takes to send the message. The larger the attached file, the longer it takes to send. If an attached file is too large, the message might not be sent. After you send the message with the attachment, which appears with a paper clip icon, message recipients can double-click the attachment icon to open and view the file or item.

Attach a File to a Message

1. Compose a new message, or open an existing message.

2. Click the Insert File button on the Standard toolbar.

3. Navigate to the folder that contains the file.

4. Click the file you want to attach.

5. Click Insert.

File name and size of attachment appear here.

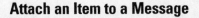

Attach an Item to a Message

1. Compose a new message, or open an existing message.

2. Click the Insert File list arrow on the Standard toolbar.

3. Click Item.

4. Navigate to the folder that contains the item.

5. Click the item you want to attach.

6. Click OK.

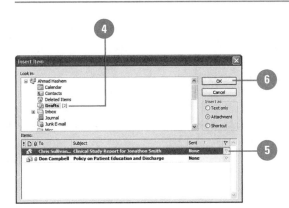

15

Using Stationery

Your e-mail messages can be as expressive as you are or want to be. Outlook provides stationery that you can apply to your e-mail messages to give them a personalized look. The stationery in Outlook comes in a wide variety of patterns, colors, and designs.

Apply Stationery to a Message

1. Click the Mail button on the Navigation pane.

2. Click the Actions menu.

3. Point to New Mail Message Using.

4. Click More Stationery.

5. Click the stationery you want to use.

6. Click OK.

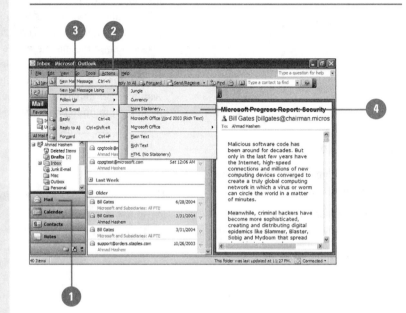

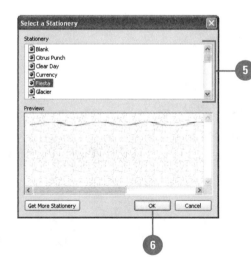

Did You Know?

You can download additional stationery from Microsoft.com. Click the Get More Stationery button in the Select A Stationery dialog box, and then download new stationery.

You can create your own stationery. Click the Tools menu, click Options, click the Mail Format tab, click Stationery Picker, and then click New. Complete the Create New Stationery dialog box.

Stationery applies only to HTML formatted messages. You can use stationery only if you use HTML as your message format. If you are using the Plain Text or Rich Text format message setting, you can't apply stationery to your message.

Creating a Signature

If you type the same information at the end of each e-mail message that you create, then you can automate that task by creating a signature. A signature can consist of both text and pictures. You can customize your signature with a variety of formatting styles, such as font type, size, and color. For example, for your personal correspondence you can create a signature that includes a closing, such as Best Regards and your name; for business correspondence, you can create a signature that includes your name, address, job title, and phone and fax numbers. You can even include a logo image.

Create a Signature

1. Click the Tools menu, click Options, and then click the Mail Format tab.

2. Click Signatures.

3. Click New.

4. Type a name for the new signature, and then click Next.

5. Type your signature text, and then select the signature.

6. Click the Font and Paragraph buttons to customize the text.

7. Click Finish.

8. Select a signature for the message you create, and for your replies and forwarded messages.

9. Click OK.

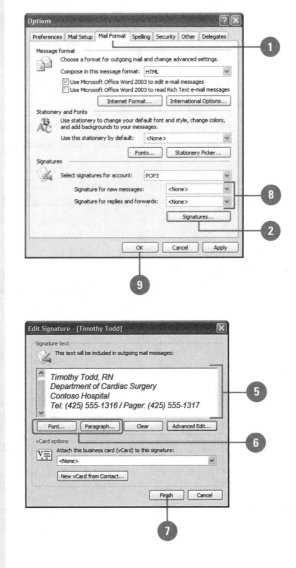

Did You Know?

You can switch between signatures. To switch between two signatures, right-click the default signature that appears automatically in your new message, click E-mail Signature, and then click the signature you want to use in the current message.

Working with a Signature

You can create as many signatures as you want, and you can create them using Outlook or Word as your editor. If you create your signatures using Outlook, you are limited to using the two file formats available with the Outlook editor: you can create simple signatures for messages sent in Plain Text format and complex signatures with a logo for messages sent in HTML or Outlook Rich Text format. You can quickly switch from one signature to another. After you create a signature, you can modify it at any time. Because you can have multiple e-mail accounts, you can have different signatures for your different accounts.

Edit a Signature

1 Click the Tools menu, click Options, and then click the Mail Format tab.

2 Click Signatures, select the signature you want to change, and then click Edit.

3 Make your changes.

4 Use the Font and Paragraph buttons to format the signature.

5 Click OK, and then click OK twice.

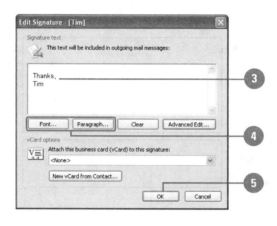

Select a Different Signature for a Different Account

1 Click the Tools menu, click Options, and then click the Mail Format tab.

2 Click the Select Signatures For Account list arrow, and then select the account you want to use.

3 Click the Signature For New Messages list arrow, and then select the signature you want.

4 Click the Signatures For Replies And Forwards list arrow, and then select the signature you want.

5 Click OK.

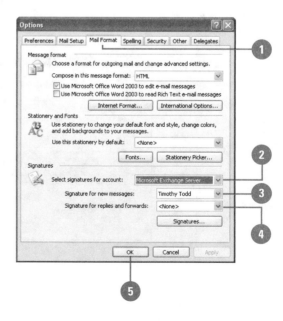

Sending Messages

When you click the Send button, Outlook connects to the e-mail server, and moves the message to the Outbox folder, which sends your message to its recipient and checks the server for incoming mail. You can also send and check for messages whenever you want by clicking the Send/Receive button on the Standard toolbar. When you send a message, you can specify the level of importance and the level of sensitivity. Levels are set as Normal by default. You can also set delivery options to indicate that you want messages delivered on specific dates or replies to messages sent to another address.

Send a Message

1. Create a new message, or open an existing message saved in the Drafts folder.

2. Click the Send button.

> ### Did You Know?
>
> *You can resend a message.* Click the Mail view button, click Sent Items, open the message you want to resend, click the Actions menu, click Resend This Message, and then click Send.

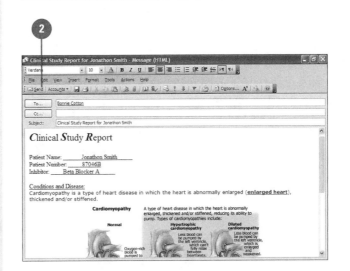

Set Message Delivery Options

1. In the message window, click the Options button on the toolbar.

2. Specify the level of Importance and the level of Sensitivity.

3. Select the check boxes with the delivery options you want, and then specify additional settings:

   ◆ Have Replies Sent To

   ◆ Save Sent Message To

   ◆ Do Not Deliver Before

   ◆ Expires After

4. Click Close.

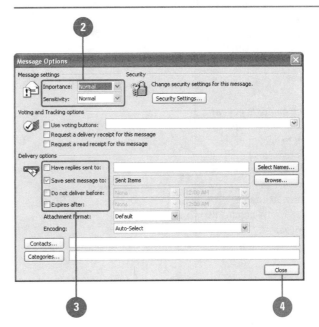

Receiving and Reading Messages

Messages that have been sent to you are stored on your e-mail server until Outlook retrieves them. By default, Outlook retrieves your mail at regular intervals. You can also retrieve your messages between scheduled retrieval times by clicking the Send/Receive button. When a message is retrieved, its message header appears in the Outlook Inbox. Click the message header to display the contents of the message in the Reading pane, which increases the area for reading your e-mail. If you receive e-mail messages in plain-text format with extra blank lines that make reading the message difficult, Outlook uses Text AutoCleanup to remove the extra lines when you view the message in the Reading pane, open the message, or print the message. To restore the extra blank lines, click the yellow banner in the Reading pane or message window.

Receive and Read Messages

1. Click the Send/Receive button on the Standard toolbar. The content of the first message in the Inbox appears in the Reading pane.

2. To display another message in the Inbox, click the message header.

3. Read the contents of the message in the Reading pane.

Did You Know?

You can close the Reading pane. Click the Reading Pane button on the Advanced toolbar. Closing the Reading pane gives you more room to scroll through the list of messages you have, without having to display message content.

You can preview the contents of your messages. If you have lots of messages that you want to scan quickly, you can set Outlook to display the first three lines of the e-mail message directly below the message header by enabling AutoPreview. To enable AutoPreview, click the View menu, and then click AutoPreview.

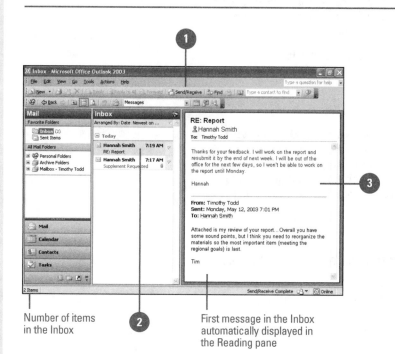

Number of items in the Inbox

First message in the Inbox automatically displayed in the Reading pane

Flagging Messages

As you look through the list of messages that you have received, you might find messages that require your attention, though you don't have the time to respond when you are reading the message. To make sure you don't overlook an important message, you can click the flag icon next to the message to mark it with a Quick Flag. The Quick Flag icon will help jog your memory so you can respond promptly to the message. The For Follow Up folder provides an up-to-date list of all the messages marked with Quick Flags for every folder in your mailbox.

Flag a Message

1. Click the Mail button on the Navigation pane.

2. Click the Inbox folder.

3. Scan your messages to see if any require follow up.

4. Click the Quick Flag icon located on the right side of the message header that you want to flag. Your Quick Flag icon changes color, and a copy of the message moves to your For Follow Up folder.

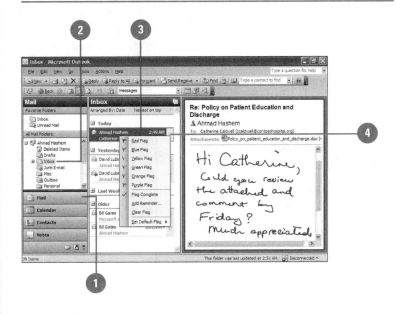

Follow Up a Message

1. Click the Mail button on the Navigation pane.

2. Click the For Follow Up folder in the Folder list to display messages marked for follow up.

3. To remove follow-up items, click the Quick Flag icon on a message.

Message marked for follow up

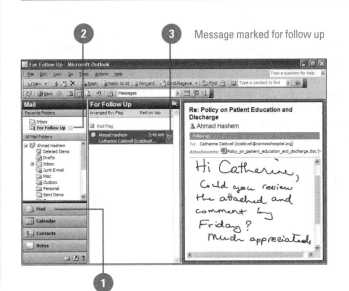

> ### Did You Know?
>
> **You can sort messages according to flag color.** To sort messages by flag color, click the View menu, point to Arrange By, and then click Flag.

15

Replying to and Forwarding a Message

You can respond to messages in your Inbox in two ways: you can reply to the person who sent you the message, or you can forward the message to others. Replying to a message sends a copy of the original message and new text that you type to the sender, or to both the sender and all the other original recipients. You can reply by returning a message to only the sender or to the sender and all other original recipients. The reply message recipient sees RE: and the original subject in the message header. Forwarding a message sends a message to someone who was not on the original recipient list. You can also type additional information at the start of the forwarded message before sending the message. To forward a message, you click the Forward button. The recipient sees FW: and the original subject in the message header.

Reply to a Message

1. Select the message to which you want to reply.

2. Click the Reply button to reply to the sender only, or click the Reply To All button to send a message to the sender and all the recipients of the original message.

3. Type any new message text.

4. Click the Send button.

Did You Know?

Outlook sends a copy of the attachment in a forwarded message. When you forward a message, Outlook includes a copy of any attachments received with the original message.

You can customize reply and forwarded messages. Click the Tools menu, click Options, click the Preference tab, click E-Mail Options, and then select an option to specify how Outlook should handle the text of messages that you reply to or forward.

Subject automatically inserted with RE: added to indicate you are replying to a message

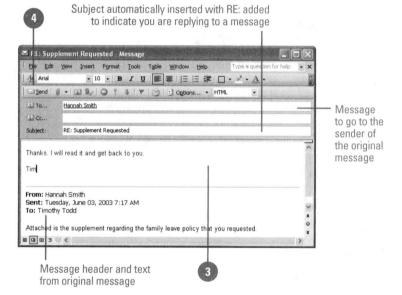

Message to go to the sender of the original message

Message header and text from original message

Forward a Message

1. Select the message that you want to forward.

2. Click the Forward button on the toolbar.

3. Enter the name(s) of the recipient(s) in the To and Cc boxes.

4. Type any new message text.

5. Click the Send button.

Did You Know?

You can change the format options for replies and forwards. Click the Tools menu, click Options, click the Preferences tab, click E-Mail Options, select the reply to and forward a message option you want, click OK, and then click OK again.

Outlook does not resend the attachment in the reply message. When you reply to a message, Outlook doesn't include a copy of the attachment; however, it does lists the file name(s).

Add an e-mail address to your contact list. Open the e-mail message, right-click the e-mail address you want, click Add To Contacts on the shortcut menu, enter any additional information, and then click the Save And Close button.

See Also

See "Creating and Addressing an E-Mail Message" on page 358 for more information on addressing an e-mail message.

Subject automatically inserted with FW: added to indicate this is a forwarded message

15

Finding and Filtering Messages

By using the Find pane in your Inbox, you can easily and quickly locate one particular piece of e-mail among what may be hundreds of stored messages. If you know that the message contains a specific word or phrase in its title, contents, or properties, you can conduct a search using that word or phrase as the criteria. If you assign categories to your messages, you can locate them searching by category. You can use a filter to view only the items that meet the conditions you have defined. For example, you can filter your messages so the only ones that appear are those that you flagged as high priority or have categorized as business items.

Find a Message

1. Click the Find button on the toolbar. The Find pane appears above the Inbox.

2. In the Look For box, type a word or phrase that is contained in the message you want to locate.

3. Click the Search In list arrow, and then select one of the options to narrow or broaden the scope of the search.

4. Click Find Now.

5. To redisplay all your messages, click Clear.

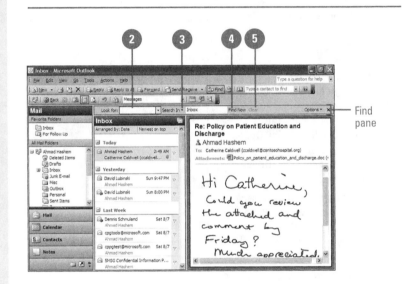

Find pane

Did You Know?

You can use Outlook's Advanced Find feature. If you cannot locate the message you want using Find, click Options in the Find pane, click Advanced Find, specify the conditions for the advanced find, and then click Find Now.

Filter Your Messages Based on Content

1️⃣ In Mail view, display the folder you want to customize.

2️⃣ Click the View menu, point to Arrange By, point to Current View, and then click Customize Current View.

3️⃣ Click Filter.

4️⃣ Click the Messages tab.

5️⃣ To filter your messages that include a specific word or phrase, enter the word or phrase in the Search For The Word(s) list box, and then select one of the options provided in the In list box.

6️⃣ To filter your messages using preset conditions, click the Search For The Word(s) list arrow, and then select the option that you want to use as a filter.

7️⃣ Click OK.

8️⃣ Click OK.

Did You Know?

You can filter your messages by sender or recipient. In the Filter dialog box, click From (sender) or Sent To (recipient), and then select the name of the contact whose messages you want to display.

You can filter messages sent to you. In the Filter dialog box, click the Where I Am check box (to insert a check mark), click the Where I Am list arrow, and then select an option. For example, you can display only those messages where you are included on the To line with other people.

15

Organizing Messages in Folders

To help you organize your messages using folders, you can use Outlook 2003's new Ways To Organize pane. Although Outlook provides the Inbox folder, this folder will become cluttered with messages unless you decide how you want to handle the messages that you have read. Some messages will be deleted immediately; others you will reply to or forward. With the exception of the deleted messages, all messages will remain in the Inbox until you move them elsewhere. To organize the messages you want to keep, you can create folders and move messages between the folders.

Create a New Folder

1. Click the Inbox folder in Mail view.

2. Click the Tools menu, and then click Organize.

3. Click New Folder.

4. Type a new name for the folder.

5. Click the Folder Contents list arrow, and then click Mail And Post Items.

6. Select where you want to store the new folder.

7. Click OK.

8. When you're done, click the Close button in the Ways To Organize pane.

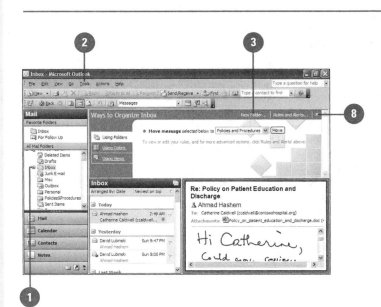

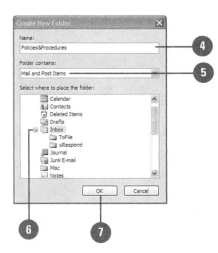

Did You Know?

You can save a mail message as a file. Click the mail message you want to save, click the File menu, click Save As, click the Save As Type list arrow, click a file type, type a new file name, and then click Save.

Sort items within a folder. If available, click a column button to sort items in the folder by that column in either ascending or descending order.

Delete a Folder

1. Display the folder you want to delete.

2. Right-click the message you want to delete, and then click Delete "foldername."

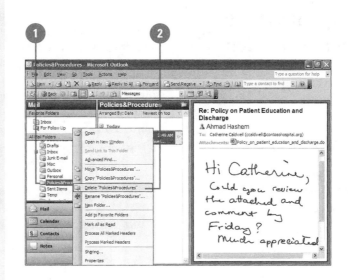

Move a Message to a Folder

1. Display the folder that contains the message you want to move.

2. Click the Tools menu, and then click Organize.

3. Click the Using Folders tab.

4. Select the message you want to move.

5. Click the Move Message list arrow, and then select the folder.

6. Click Move.

7. When you're done, click the Close button.

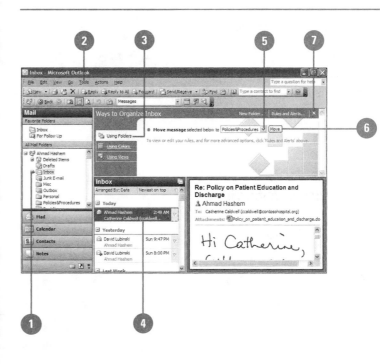

15

Managing Messages with Color and Rules

You can color-code the messages that you send to or receive from particular contacts for quick and easy recognition. Use the Ways To Organize pane to specify how you want to apply color to your messages. You can also display folders using specific views. Outlook provides a way to organize each of your folders using specific criteria, known as **rules**, that you set. For example, you can set your Inbox to store incoming messages from a particular patient in an existing folder.

Color-Code Your Messages

1. Open the folder that contains the messages you want to color-code.

2. Click the Tools menu, and then click Organize.

3. Click the Using Colors tab.

4. Specify whether you want to color-code messages sent to or received from a specific contact.

5. Select the color you want Outlook to use to code the messages.

6. Click Apply Color.

7. When you're done, click the Close button in the Ways To Organize pane.

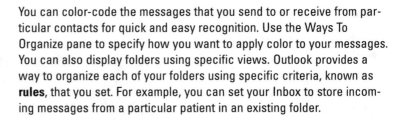

Right-click a Quick Flag icon to select a colored flag for a message.

Manage Messages Using Views

1. Open the folder that you want to specify a specific view.

2. Click the Tools menu, and then click Organize.

3. Click the Using Views tab.

4. Click a view.

5. When you're done, click the Close button in the Ways To Organize pane.

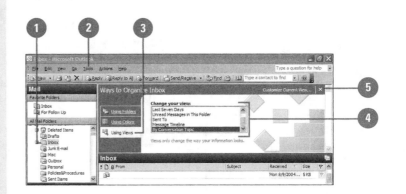

Manage Messages Using Rules

1. Click the Tools menu, and then click Rules And Alerts.

2. Click the E-Mail Rules tab, and then click New Rule.

3. Click a start option.

4. Select the criteria you want, and then follow the wizard instructions.

5. Click Next to continue each step of the wizard.

6. When you're done with the wizard, click Finish.

7. Click OK.

E-mail rule

E-mail rule description

Did You Know?

You can color-code your folders and messages. In the Ways To Organize pane, click the Using Colors tab, select the folder or message that you want color-coded, and then apply the colored Quick Flag that will help you quickly identify the contents of the item.

You can move a message automatically by creating a rule. Click the Using Folders tab, and then click the Rules and Alerts button to enter the specifications for the rule.

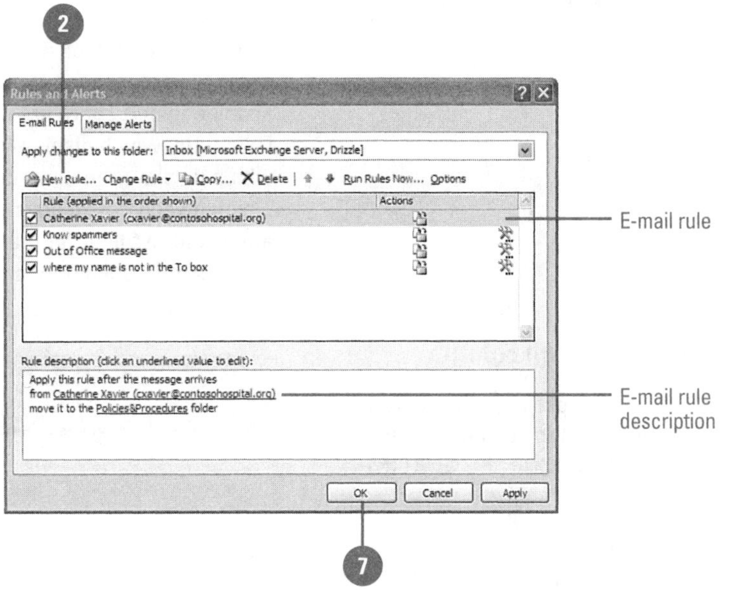

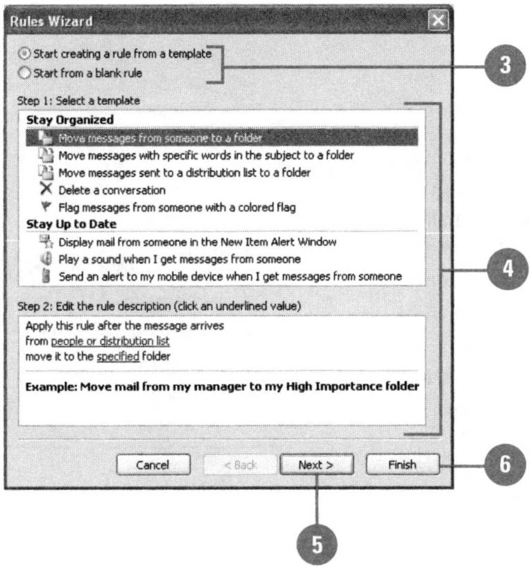

Using Search Folders

Outlook's search folders are another way that Outlook makes managing mail easier. Search folders are not like the folders that you create or even like the Outlook default folders. Search folders store information about your messages, without having to move the messages to a specific folder. There are several search folders already created: For Follow Up, which displays the message you flag; Unread Messages, which displays the unread mail you have accumulated; Large Messages, which displays messages by size (largest to smallest). You can also create a search folder for the messages that meet your specific criteria, such as messages from a particular patient or about a specific subject.

Customize a Search Folder

1. In Mail view, right-click the search folder you want to customize, and then click Customize This Search Folder.

2. Click Criteria.

3. Select the options you want.

4. Click OK.

5. Click OK.

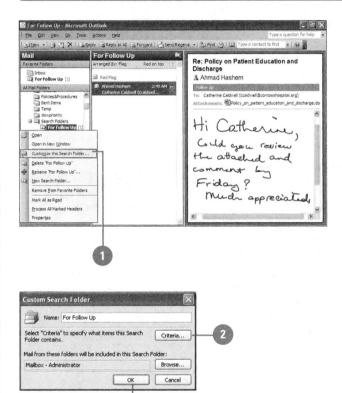

Did You Know?

You can send e-mail with tracking and delivery options. Create a new mail message, click the Options button on the Standard toolbar, select the delivery options or the tracking options you want, and then click Close.

You can change the e-mail format to a Web page format. Click the Format menu, and then click HTML. The Format menu changes to provide Web page formatting commands.

Create a Search Folder

1. In Mail view, click the File menu, point to New, and then click Search Folder.

2. Scroll down the list, and then click Create A Custom Search Folder.

3. Click Choose.

4. Type the name of the folder.

5. Click Criteria.

6. Specify the criteria for the messages for this search folder.

7. Click OK.

8. Click Browse, select the folders you want searched, and then click OK.

9. Click OK.

10. Click OK.

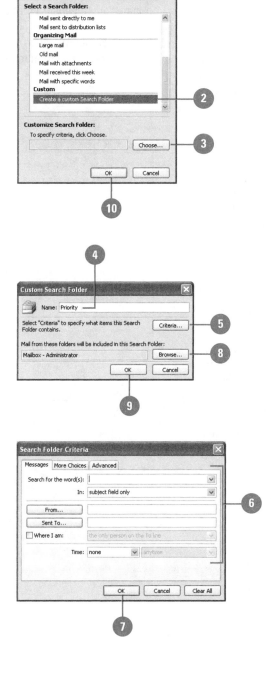

Did You Know?

You can retrieve mail messages from the Deleted Items folder. Items remain in the Deleted Items folder until you empty it. To retrieve mail messages from the Deleted Items folder, click the Folder List button on the Navigation pane, and then click Deleted Items. Drag an item to the Inbox or to any other folder icon in the Folder list.

You can empty the Deleted Items folder. To empty the Deleted Items folder and permanently delete its contents, right-click Deleted Items in the Folders list, click Empty "Deleted Items" Folder, and then click Yes to confirm the deletion.

15

Reducing Junk E-Mail and Spam

You can have Outlook handle junk e-mail for you. You can specify what should be considered junk e-mail and how Outlook should handle that e-mail. You can ensure that e-mail from certain addresses or domains, which might seem to be junk e-mail, but is actually from a person or site that you are interested in gets to you. You can also make sure that the mail you send isn't treated as junk e-mail.

Reduce Junk E-Mail and Spam

1. Display your Inbox.

2. Click the Tools menu, and then click Options.

3. On the Preferences tab, click the Junk E-Mail button.

4. On the Options tab, select the options that you want to enable.

5. Click the Safe Senders tab, and then specify the messages from the addresses or domains that should never be treated as junk e-mail.

6. Click the Safe Recipients tab, and then specify the messages sent to the e-mail addresses or domains that should never be treated as junk mail.

7. Click the Blocked Senders tab, and then specify the messages from addresses or domains that should always be treated as junk e-mail.

8. Click OK, and then click OK again.

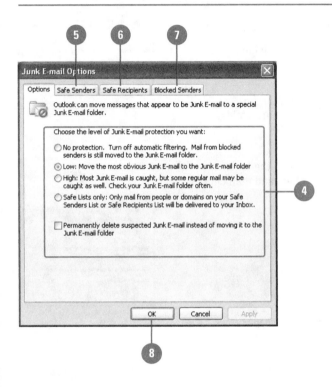

Did You Know?

You can deal with junk mail as it arrives. If you receive a message that is junk mail, click the Actions menu, point to Junk E-Mail, and then select the option for dealing with the message.

Archiving Messages

Archiving compresses messages into files that are stored on your hard drive. You can archive messages manually or automatically using AutoArchive. This Outlook tool automates the task of archiving your messages (as well as files and folders) based on a period of time you set. For example, you could archive all the messages you sent in the last six months. Archived items are saved in the personal store (.pst) file format. This format compresses the message so it takes up less space. It also stores the file on your computer and not on the e-mail server.

Set Archive Options for Your Inbox

1 In Mail view, click Inbox.

2 Click the Tools menu, and then click Options.

3 Click the Other tab, and then click the AutoArchive button.

4 Specify the options you want for your Inbox.

5 Click OK, and then click OK again.

Did You Know?

You can retrieve an archived file. Click the File menu, and then click Import And Export to start the Import And Export Wizard. Select the Import From Another Program Or File option, click Next, scroll down and click Personal Folder File (.pst), click Next, click Browse, navigate to the folder where the archive is stored, double-click the archive, click Next, and then click Finish. The file is restored to the Inbox.

15

Setting Up Instant Messaging

Before you can send and receive instant messages, you need to get a passport. Not the kind you need to travel the world, but the kind that you need to travel the Internet—a Microsoft .NET Passport. Microsoft .NET Passport is an online service that makes it possible for you to use your e-mail address and a single password to securely sign in to any participating .NET Passport Web site or service around the world. You need a .NET Passport to use MSN-related software, such as Windows Messenger. You can use a wizard to set up your Windows XP user account to register for a new .NET Passport. If you already have a .NET Passport, you only need to associate your e-mail address with the Passport.

Get a .NET Passport

1. Click the Start button on the taskbar, and then click Control Panel.

2. Double-click User Accounts.

3. Click an account, and then click Set Up My Account To Use A .NET Passport.

4. Click Next.

5. Make sure the Yes option is selected if you have an e-mail address, and then click Next; otherwise, click the No option, and then follow the instructions.

6. Click the No option to register for a new .NET Passport, and then click Next twice to open the .NET registration Web site.

   If you have an existing .NET Passport, click the Yes. I Want To Sign In With My Passport option, click Next, type your e-mail address and .NET Passport password, click Next, and then click Finish.

7. Click Yes to acknowledge any security warnings that might appear, and then follow the instructions for registering.

8. Click Finish.

Click if you do not have an e-mail account

Starting Windows Messenger

Windows Messenger is an instant messaging program that allows you to exchange instant messages with a designated list of contacts over the Internet. An **instant message** is an online typewritten conversation in real time between two or more contacts. Instant messages require both parties to be online, and the communication is instantaneous. You and your contacts don't have to be MSN members to use Windows Messenger, but you both need a .NET Passport. After you start Windows Messenger, you sign in to let others online know you are connected. When you're done, you sign out.

Start Windows Messenger and Sign In and Out

1. Click the Start button on the taskbar, point to All Programs, and then click Windows Messenger.

   TIMESAVER *Double-click the Windows Messenger icon in the notification area on the taskbar.*

2. If you're not already signed in, click the Click Here To Sign In link, and then enter your user name and password.

3. To sign out, click the File menu, and then click Sign Out.

Did You Know?

You can change your online status anytime. Click the File menu, point to My Status, and then click the status you want: Online, Busy, Be Right Back, Away, On The Phone, Out To Lunch, or Appear Offline.

You can close Windows Messenger while you are signed in. Click the Close button. Windows Messenger continues to run in the background as long as you are signed in.

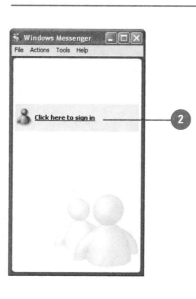

List of contacts online and offline

I Want To list of commands

15

Adding Contacts

After you start Windows Messenger and sign in, you can send instant messages to anyone who has either MSN Messenger or Windows Messenger installed on their computer, has a .NET Passport or corporate instant messaging account, and is currently online. If you often exchange instant messages with certain friends, family members, or colleagues, you can add them as contacts.

Add a Contact

1. In the Windows Messenger window, click Add A Contact.

2. Click the By E-Mail Address Or Sign In Name option, and then click Next.

3. Type the e-mail address of the contact, and then click Next.

4. Click Finish.

Did You Know?

You can search for an e-mail address. Click the Search For Contact option, and then enter as much information about the contact as you have. Select to search the Address Book on your computer or to search the Hotmail Member Directory.

Add a Contact

Windows®
Messenger .net

How do you want to add a contact?

○ By e-mail address or sign-in name ⎯⎯⎯⎯⎯⎯ 2

○ Search for a contact

If we can't add the contact to your list, this wizard will help you invite that person to start using this service.

< Back   Next >   Finish   Cancel

Add a Contact

Windows®
Messenger .net

Please type your contact's complete e-mail address

hsmith@homesense-inc.com ⎯⎯⎯⎯⎯⎯ 3

Example: name_123@hotmail.com
myname@msn.com
example@passport.com

< Back   Next >   Finish   Cancel

Enabling Instant Messaging

Outlook uses smart tags to identify contacts in an e-mail message who also use Windows Messenger. When you display an e-mail message in the Reading pane, or open a message in Outlook, the Person Names Smart Tag appears next to the sender's name. When you click the Person Names Smart Tag, Outlook displays a menu with options to send an instant message and check online status. Before you can display the Person Names Smart Tag and start Windows Messenger, you need to enable smart tag and instant messaging options in Outlook.

Enable Instant Messaging in Outlook

1. In Outlook, click the Tools menu, and then click Options.

2. Click the Other tab.

3. Select the Enable The Person Names Smart Tag check box.

4. Select the Display Messenger Status In The From Field check box.

5. Click OK.

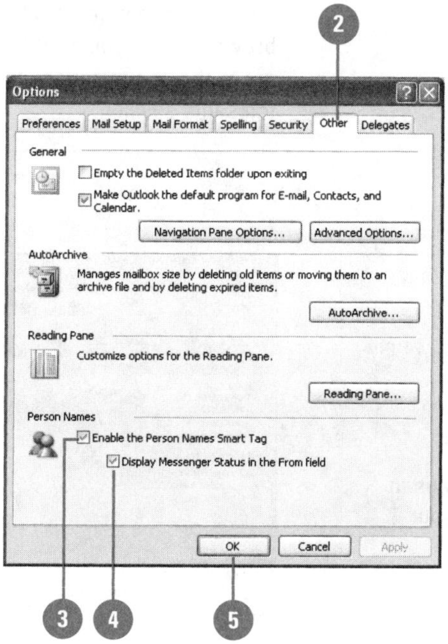

Did You Know?

Get new e-mail quickly. The moment you receive new e-mail messages, the New Mail icon appears next to the clock on the taskbar. You can double-click the icon to switch to your Inbox. Depending on your e-mail service, you might have to log on to a network or dial in to an Internet service provider (ISP) to receive your new e-mail messages.

15

Sending and Receiving Instant Messages

When you display a message in the Reading pane, or open a message in Outlook, the Person Names Smart Tag appears next to the sender's name. You can click the Person Names Smart Tag to display a menu with options to send an instant message and check online status. When you select Send Instant Message from the smart tag menu in Outlook, a Conversation window from Windows Messenger opens, where you can type your message and send and receive instant messages. While you are communicating in Windows Messenger, you can click a link to view your Inbox or send an e-mail message to a Windows Messenger contact. Outlook needs to be your default e-mail program, and your e-mail address cannot be from MSN or Hotmail, which opens Web mail in your browser. After you start a conversation with someone, you can add others to the conversation, so that up to five people are communicating in the same session.

Start an Instant Message from Outlook

1. Open a message from a contact signed in to Instant Messenger.

2. Click the Person Names Smart Tag.

3. Click Send Instant Message.

   A Conversation window opens to begin a conversation with your contact.

Did You Know?

You can open an instant message using the Alert icon. If you are signed in to Windows Messenger, yet the window is not open, an alert appears when you receive an instant message. Click the alert in the notification area on the taskbar to start a conversation.

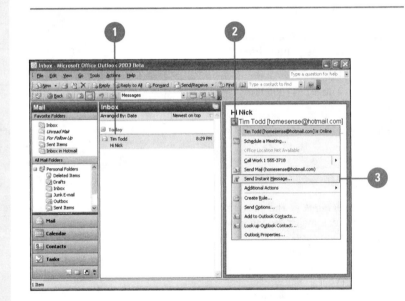

Send and Receive Instant Messages

1. If necessary, double-click the contact to whom you want to send an instant message in Windows Messenger.

2. In the Conversation window, type the message.

   The text wraps to another line to fit in the window; however, if you want to start a new line of text, press Shift+Enter.

3. To add another person to the conversation, click Invite Someone To This Conversation, and then double-click a contact.

4. Click Send or press Enter.

5. Wait for a reply.

Select text and then click to change the font type.

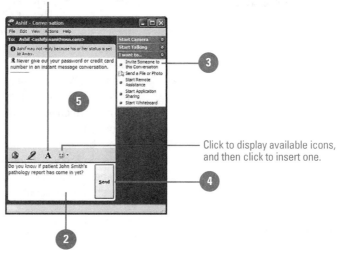

Click to display available icons, and then click to insert one.

Send an E-Mail from Windows Messenger

1. In Windows Messenger, right-click the contact to whom you want to send an e-mail message.

2. Click Send E-Mail.

3. Type your message, and then click Send.

Did You Know?

You can quickly switch back to Outlook. In Windows Messenger, click the Go To My Inbox link. Outlook needs to be your default e-mail program, and your e-mail address cannot be from MSN or Hotmail, which opens your browser.

15

Sending a File During an Instant Message

Just as you can send a file attached to an e-mail message, you can send a file during an instant message conversation. You can send many types of files, including referral letters, documents, pictures, and scanned images. When you send a file, a request to transfer the file is sent to your contact. You are notified when your contact accepts or declines your request. When someone sends you a file during an instant message, the Conversation window displays the sender's name, the name of the file, and its size. You can then accept or decline the transfer of the file. Before you receive files over the Internet, be sure you have virus protection software on your computer. When you receive a file, a message dialog box related to viruses might open. If your computer is located on a network behind a firewall, you might not be able to send files to those outside the firewall. If you want to send files to those behind the firewall, you need to manually open the connection; check with your network administrator for details.

Send a File in an Instant Message

1. Start a conversation with the contact to whom you want to send the file.

2. Click Send A File Or Photo.

3. Navigate to the drive and folder that contains the file you want to send, and then click it.

4. Change the file name if necessary, and then click Open.

5. Wait for the recipient to accept or decline the file.

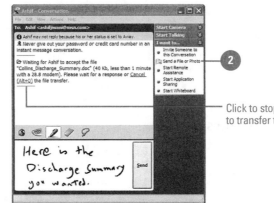

Click to stop the request to transfer the file.

Did You Know?

You can accept and open a file. When an invitation to transfer a file appears in the Conversation window, click the Accept link, click OK, and then click the link to open the file.

Managing Information with Outlook

Introduction

Healthcare professionals are bombarded each day with information in the form of e-mails, voice mails, faxes, reports, memos, and so on. Microsoft Office Outlook 2003 provides an easy and efficient way to track and organize most of the information that comes your way. As a busy healthcare professional, you can use Outlook tools for your personal information management needs. With Outlook, you can organize and manage your day-to-day information, from e-mail and calendars to contacts and tasks. It's easy to share information with others and organize and view your schedule and communications in one place.

Using the Calendar feature, you can manage your time by scheduling all the meetings and patient appointments you have. Among its many features, the Outlook Calendar lets you schedule **Appointments** (dates that are noted with data referring to that day's activity) and **Events** (an appointment that lasts 24 hours or more). Outlook also allows you to share your calendar with others. In Outlook, you view the schedules of your coworkers before you schedule meetings or patient appointments so that you can determine when the needed individuals in your group are available.

You can use Outlook to create a to-do list and assign the items on the list to others as need from Tasks. Rather then cluttering your desk or obscuring your computer with sticky pad notes, use Notes to jot down your immediate thoughts, ideas, and other observations. With everything related to your work in one place, you can always locate what you need—files, notes about a new medication, or even the time of a phone call with a certain patient. Just check the Journal timeline to find it. To help organize and locate information, Outlook allows you to group, sort, and filter items.

What You'll Do

View and Customize the Calendar

Schedule an Appointment and Event

Schedule Meetings and Resources

Respond to Meeting Requests

Update and Cancel Meeting Requests

Schedule Online Meetings

Create and Update Tasks

Organize Tasks

Assign and Monitor Tasks

Manage Tasks

Track Activities with Contacts

Record Items in the Journal

Open and Modify Journal Entries

Organize Items by Categories

Customize How You View Items

Create and Modify Notes

Preview and Print Items from Outlook

Viewing the Calendar

The **Calendar** is an electronic version of the familiar paper daily planner. You can schedule time for patient visits, completing specific tasks, meetings, vacations, holidays, or for any other activity with the Calendar. When you open the Calendar for the first time, it opens in Day view, which displays your activities for the day. You can change the Calendar to show activities for the Work Week (five business days), Week (all seven days), or Month. These four views are referred to collectively as Day/Week/Month view. In Day/Week/Month view, the Calendar is split into two sections: the Appointment area and the Date Navigator. The Appointment area serves as a daily planner where you can schedule activities by the day, work week, full week, or month. Appointments are scheduled activities such as a patient's visit, and occupy a block of time in the Appointment area. Events are activities that last 24 hours or longer, such as a conference, and do not occupy blocks of time in your calendar. Instead, they appear in a banner at the beginning of a day.

Open and Change the Calendar View

1. Click the Calendar button on the Navigation pane.

2. You can change the Calendar view in several ways.

   ◆ Click the View menu, point to Current View, and then click the view option you want.

   ◆ Click one of the Calendar view buttons on the Standard toolbar.

   ◆ Click the left arrow or right arrow on the Date Navigator to change the current month.

   ◆ Click a date on the Date Navigator to view that day's schedule. The date highlighted in red is today's date.

Date Navigator   Calendar view buttons

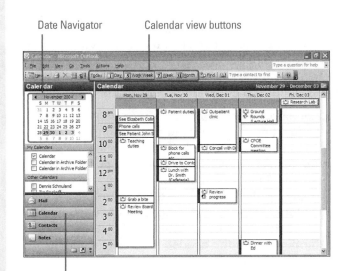

Customizing the Calendar

As with other folders in Outlook, you can customize Calendar to suit your needs. For example, you can change the background color or the text font if you like. You can also set Calendar to display week numbers (from 1 to 52) to the left of each week in the Date Navigator. If you change the background color of the Calendar, it only applies to Day and Work Week views. The Week and Month views use system colors. Another way to customize the Outlook Calendar is to change the work week settings. For example, if you are a nurse and you work three twelve-hour shifts a week, Wednesday through Friday, you might want to change the work week in your Calendar to reflect this. You can change the days included in the work week, the start day of the work week, the start and end times of the work day, and the first week of the work year.

Customize the Calendar View

1. Click the Tools menu, and then click Options.

2. Click the Preferences tab, and then click Calendar Options.

3. Click the Calendar Work Week options you want to customize.

4. Select the Calendar Options check boxes you want.

5. Click the Background Color list arrow, and then select a color you want for your calendar.

6. Click the Time Zone, Free/Busy Options, or Resource Scheduling button to customize these options.

7. Click OK.

8. Click OK.

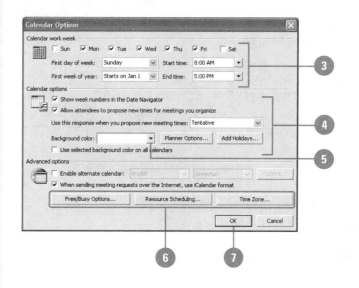

Did You Know?

You can save your Calendar as a Web page. Switch to Calendar view, click the File menu, click Save As Web Page, select the duration and publishing options you want, enter a title and file name, and then click Save. Once the Calendar is published, you can open the file in a Web browser.

16

Scheduling an Appointment and Event

In Outlook, an **appointment** is any activity you schedule that blocks a small portion of your time, such as a patient visit. An **event** is any appointment that lasts one or more full days (24-hour increments), such as a seminar, a conference, or a vacation. You can mark yourself available (free or tentative) or unavailable (busy or out of the office) to others during a scheduled appointment or an event. You enter appointment or event information in the same box; however, when you schedule an event, the All Day Event check box is selected; the check box is cleared when you schedule an appointment.

Schedule an Appointment

1. Click the Calendar button on the Navigation pane.

2. Click the start time of the appointment in the Appointment area.

3. Type a short description of the appointment, and then press Enter.

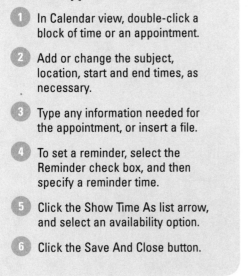

Include Appointment Details

1. In Calendar view, double-click a block of time or an appointment.

2. Add or change the subject, location, start and end times, as necessary.

3. Type any information needed for the appointment, or insert a file.

4. To set a reminder, select the Reminder check box, and then specify a reminder time.

5. Click the Show Time As list arrow, and select an availability option.

6. Click the Save And Close button.

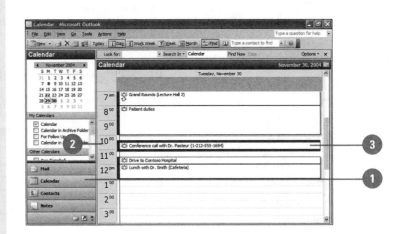

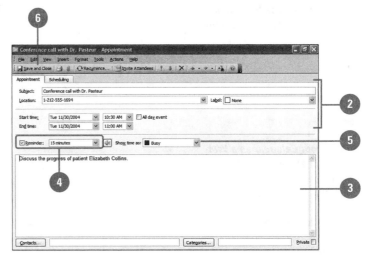

Schedule an Event and Include Details

1. Click the Calendar button on the Navigation pane.

2. Click the top of the day in the Appointment area.

3. Type a description of the event, and then press Enter.

4. Double-click the event.

5. Add or change the subject, location, start and end times, as necessary.

6. Type any information needed for the event, or insert a file.

7. To set a reminder, select the Reminder check box, and then specify a reminder time.

8. Click the Show Time As list arrow, and then select an availability option.

9. Click the Save And Close button.

Did You Know?

You can schedule a recurring appointment. In Calendar view, select a block of time, click the Actions menu, click New Recurring Appointment, fill in the appointment times and recurrence information, click OK, and then click the Save And Close button.

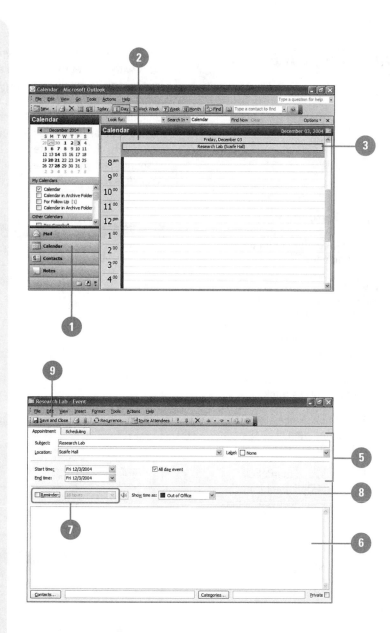

16

Scheduling Meetings ▶

Scheduling a meeting often involves more than just asking people you work with to meet to discuss a subject. Scheduling a meeting can mean inviting people outside your organization, locating a place to have the meeting, making sure you have the right equipment for the meeting. Outlook can help you do all this. When you schedule a meeting using Outlook you are sending a special kind of e-mail message—a meeting request. Each invited attendee and the person responsible for the resource that you may have requested receive a meeting request message. It is to this message that the invitee must respond.

Schedule a New Meeting

① Click the Calendar button on the Navigation pane.

② Scroll the Date Navigator to display the date you want to schedule the meeting.

③ Click the Actions menu, and then click Plan A Meeting.

④ Click Add Others, and then click Add From Address Book.

⑤ Click the Show Names From The list arrow, and then click Contacts or Global Address Book.

⑥ Click a name, and then click Required and Optional for each person you want to invite to the meeting.

⑦ Click OK.

⑧ Click Make Meeting.

⑨ Enter meeting related information, and then click the Send button.

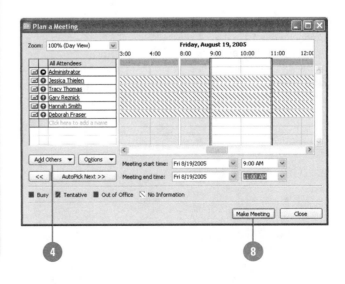

Scheduling Meeting Resources

If you work on a network that uses Microsoft Exchange Server, you can reserve resources, such as a conference room or overhead projector, for your meetings. You reserve a resource by "inviting" it to your meeting. Resources are added to the Global Address List by the system administrator, who also designates a person to manage the schedule for the resource. When you schedule a resource, a meeting request is sent to the person assigned to the resource, and that person accepts or declines the invitation based on the availability of the resource.

Schedule Resources for a New Meeting

1. Click the Calendar button on the Navigation pane.

2. Scroll the Date Navigator to display the date you want to schedule the meeting.

3. Click the Actions menu, and then click Plan A Meeting.

4. Click Add Others, click Add From Address Book, and then display the names you want.

5. Select the required and optional attendees.

6. Select the resource you need, and then click Resources.

7. Click OK.

8. Click Make Meeting.

9. Enter meeting related information, and then click the Send button.

> ### Did You Know?
>
> **You can schedule a resource for an existing meeting.** In Calendar view, double-click the scheduled meeting, click the Scheduling tab, click Add Others, click Add From Address Book, display the resources you want, click Resources, click OK, and then click Send Update.

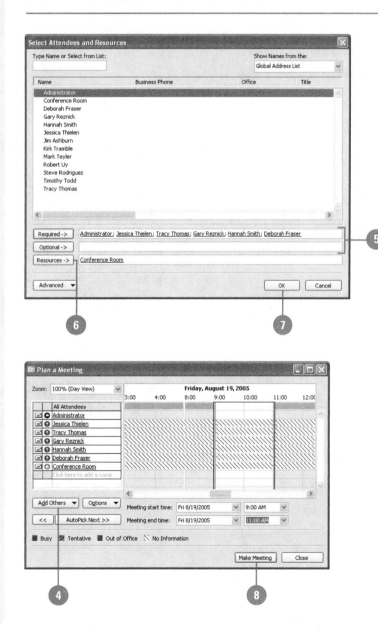

16

Responding to Meeting Requests

When you receive a meeting request it appears in your Inbox such as any message would. The difference is when you view the message you can also view your calendar to see where the meeting is scheduled. Once you are sure whether or not you can attend a meeting, then you use the Accept button or the Decline button at the top of the meeting request e-mail. If you want to propose a different time, you can use the Propose Time button. A message is sent to the sender of the meeting request with your response. If you need to view your calendar while viewing the meeting request e-mail, you can use the Calendar button.

Accept a Meeting Request

1. Display your Inbox, and then click the e-mail with the meeting request.

2. To view the meeting in your Calendar, click the Calendar button on the toolbar, review, and then close the Calendar.

3. Click Accept.

4. Click the Send The Response Now option.

5. Click OK.

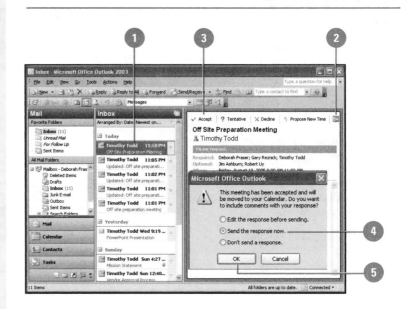

Propose a New Meeting Time

1. Display your Inbox, and then click the e-mail with the meeting request.

2. Click Propose New Time.

3. Specify a new meeting time.

4. Click Propose Time.

5. Enter information in the e-mail regarding the meeting, and then click the Send button.

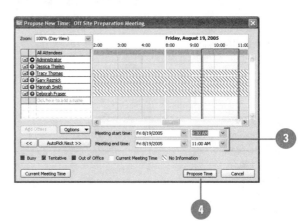

Decline a Meeting Request

1. Display your Inbox, and then click the e-mail with the meeting request.

2. To view the meeting in your Calendar, click the Calendar button on the toolbar, and then close the Calendar.

3. Click Decline.

4. Click the Edit The Response Before Sending option.

5. Click OK.

6. Type a message that explains why you are unable to attend the meeting.

7. Click the Send button.

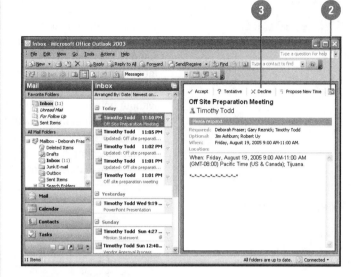

Did You Know?

You can automate and track meeting resources. If you are responsible for resources made available for meetings, click the Tools menu, click Options, click Calendar Options on the Preference tab, click Resource Scheduling, and then select the options for dealing with requests for resources, and then click OK.

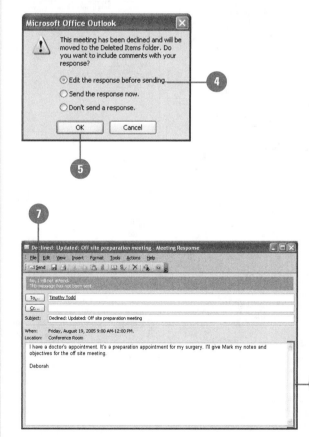

16

Updating and Canceling Meeting Requests

Planning meetings can be a difficult task when you have to coordinate multiple schedules, schedules that often change with little or no notice. You can spend endless hours on the phone trying to keep all the meeting attendees up-to-date. However, there is an easier way. You can use the Outlook Calendar to reschedule or cancel meetings. You can send a meeting update request, or cancel the meeting, if necessary via e-mail to let everyone who should be at the meeting know about the change without having to spend hours on the phone. When you send attendees an updated meeting request, the attendee receives an e-mail message, the original meeting is deleted, and the new meeting time is added to his/her Calendar. If you send a cancellation notice about the meeting, the meeting is deleted from the attendees' Calendars.

Update a Meeting Request

1. Display your Calendar, and then double-click the scheduled meeting.

2. Click the Scheduling tab, and then scroll to a new day, if necessary.

3. Click a new slot, and then drag the length of the meeting.

4. If necessary, click Add Others to invite others or add more resources, and then click OK.

5. Click the Send Update button.

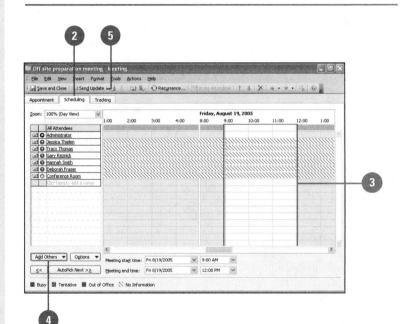

Cancel a Meeting Request

1. Display your Calendar, and then double-click the scheduled meeting.

2. Click the Actions menu, and then click Cancel Meeting.

3. Click the Send Cancellation And Delete Meeting option, click OK, and then click the Send button.

Scheduling Online Meetings

Using NetMeeting, you can conduct two-way communications between participants, using sound and video, such as consulting with a colleague on a patient case. However, you must have a sound card, speakers, a microphone, and preferrably a video camera installed on all the computers that are to connect to each other. If you don't have these items, you can still communicate by using typed messages in a chat window. A chat window is a window that you use to exchange typed messages instantaneously. In NetMeeting, you can also use a whiteboard, which is a blank screen that simulates the marker boards used in conference rooms. In addition to the Whiteboard, you can also share files and applications. Before you can begin using NetMeeting for online meetings, you must set the program up on your computers.

Schedule an Online Meeting

1. In Calendar view, select the date and time you want for the meeting.

2. Click the Actions menu, click Plan A Meeting, and then click Make Meeting.

3. Invite the required and optional attendees.

4. Enter the subject of the meeting.

5. Select the This Is An Online Meeting Using check box.

6. Specify the times for the meeting.

7. Type the Directory Server provided by your network administrator.

8. Complete the meeting request form as needed.

9. Click the Send button.

Did You Know?

You can use Internet Explorer to install NetMeeting. Start Internet Explorer, click the File menu, select New, click Internet Call, and then the follow the steps in the wizard.

16

Managing Information with Outlook

Creating and Updating Tasks

To create a task, you click the New Task button on the Standard toolbar. A New Task dialog box opens. Type the Subject, which is the text of the task. This text appears in the Subject column in the Tasks folder. You can also set a Due Date (the date by which the task must be completed), Start Date, the Priority (Low, Normal, or High), and you can check the Reminder check box to have a reminder window open the morning of the due date. To keep track of the task, you can set the Status (Not Started, In Progress, Completed, Waiting On Someone Else, or Deferred) and the Percentage Complete (0 to 100%). You can type additional information about the task in the Notes area at the bottom of the dialog box.

Create or Update a Task

1. In the Tasks folder, click the New Task button on the Standard toolbar or double-click the task.

2. Type a short description of the task in the Subject box.

3. Click the Due Date list arrow, and then click the due date.

4. Click the Start Date list arrow, and then select the start date.

5. Click the Status list arrow, and then click an option.

6. Select the percentage in the % Complete box, and then type a new percentage.

7. Click in the Notes area, and then type additional information about the task.

8. Click the Save And Close button.

Did You Know?

You can use tasks to track hospitalized patients. Create a task per patient. The task's start date is the patient admission date, and the task's due date is the patient's expected discharge date.

Organizing Tasks

You can display tasks in a variety of views. The default Simple List view displays the task's description, the due date, and a check box to indicate that the task is completed. To see more information about each task, you can switch to Detailed List view, which includes columns for the task's priority, whether a file is attached, the status of the task, the percentage complete, and the category of each task. Detailed List view does not include the column with the check box to indicate that a task is completed (although in both views, completed tasks are indicated with strikethrough text). To show all your tasks in order by due date, you can switch to Task Timeline view to see a horizontal timeline with tasks noted on their due dates.

Change Tasks Views

1. Click the Tasks button on the Navigation pane.

2. You can change the Tasks view in several ways.

   ◆ Click the View menu, point to Arrange By, point to Current View, and then click By Category.

   ◆ Click the Detailed List option in the Navigation pane.

   ◆ Click the Next Seven Days option in the Navigation pane.

   ◆ Click the Task Timeline option in the Navigation pane.

   ◆ Click the Simple List option in the Navigation pane.

Did You Know?

You can hide tasks in a grouped view. Hide tasks in grouped views (By Category and By Person Responsible) by clicking the minus sign to the left of the group name. When you do this, the tasks collapse under the group header and the minus sign changes to a plus sign. To display the tasks in that group again, click the plus sign to the left of the group name.

Task Timeline

16

Assigning Tasks to Others

Because most projects involve the efforts and input of several people, it will often be necessary to delegate responsibilities for a task to other members on your team of contacts. In Outlook, you can assign and send a task assignment to a co-worker. To assign a task, you open the Task dialog box, click the Assign Task button, and then assign the task to someone in your Contacts list. If a task is assigned to you, you will receive an e-mail that contains the task request. You can accept or decline the task, and send your reply back to the sender.

Assign a Task

1. Double-click the task or create a task.

2. Click the Assign Task button on the Standard toolbar.

3. Click the To button, select a recipient, click the To button, and then click OK.

4. Click the Send button.

Assign Task button toggles to Cancel Assignment

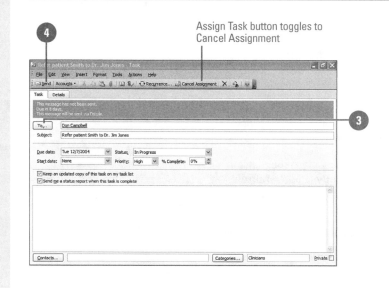

Accept or Decline a Task

1. Open the task request.

2. Click the Accept button or the Decline button.

3. To reply to the sender with a comment, click Edit The Response Before Sending, click OK, type a comment, and then click the Send button.

4. To send the response without comment, click the Send The Response Now button.

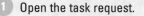

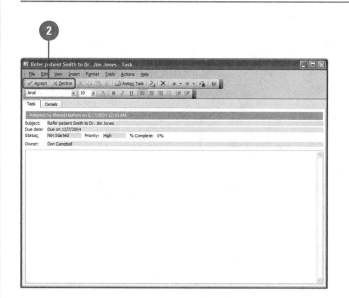

Monitoring Task Progress

After you've passed along ownership of a task, you will want to keep track of it. Whenever it's edited, you'll want to check the changes, just as you will need to know any supplemental information about the task and stay up to date on its status. Outlook enables you to automatically keep track of assigned tasks and receive regular updates on their progress. When you create a task, you are designated as the owner of that task. As its owner, you are the only person who can edit the task, unless you assign it to someone else and they accept the assignment. In that case, however, you can still opt to maintain an updated copy in your Tasks folder and obtain status updates whenever the task is edited or completed.

Receive Updates for an Assigned Task

1. Double-click the task.

2. Click the To button, select a recipient, click To, and then click OK.

3. If it is not already selected, select the Keep An Updated Copy Of This Task On My Task List check box.

4. If it is not already selected, select the Send Me A Status Report When This Task Is Complete check box.

5. Click the Send button.

6. Click the Assignment option on the Navigation pane.

Did You Know?

You can cancel a task assignment. In Task view, double-click the task, and then click the Cancel Assignment button on the Standard toolbar.

You can arrange the tasks to view all the tasks you have assigned. In Task view, click the View menu, point to Arrange By, point to Current View, and then click Assignment.

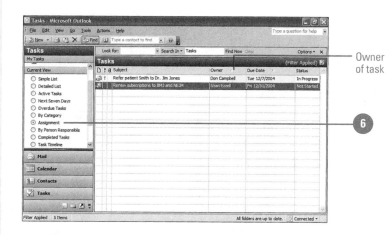

Owner of task

16

Managing Tasks

As you work with tasks, you'll want to keep your Tasks folder updated to reflect the status of each task. One obvious tactic is to mark each task as completed once you've finished the task. To do this, you open the Task dialog box and then change the Status box to Completed or the % Complete box to 100%. Once you've marked a task as complete, it appears in the Tasks folder with a line through it. Some tasks are jobs that you need to complete on a regular basis. In this case, you can make a task recurring. Recurring tasks have a small icon with two circling arrows in the Tasks folder.

Mark a Task as Completed

1. Double-click the task.

2. Click the Status list arrow, and then click Completed.

   TIMESAVER *In views with a Status column, click the Status column for the task, click the list arrow, and then click Completed.*

3. Click the Save And Close button.

   TIMESAVER *In Simple List view, click the Complete check box.*

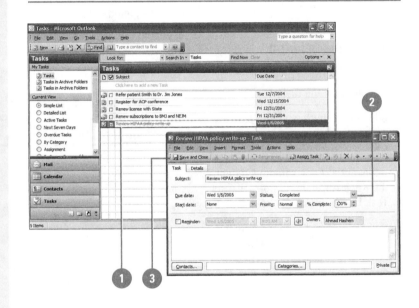

Change a Task to Recurring

1. Double-click the task.

2. Click the Recurrence button on the Standard toolbar.

3. Click the recurrence pattern option you want.

4. Select the check boxes with the recurrence pattern you want.

5. Click the end date option you want.

6. Click OK.

7. Click the Save And Close button.

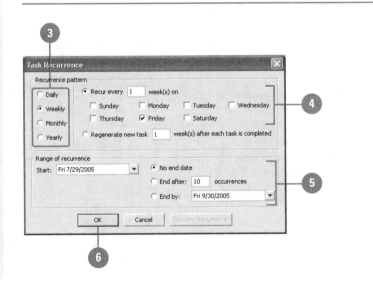

Tracking Activities with Contacts

A powerful feature in Outlook is the ability to track your activities associated with each contact. You can create a journal entry to track the length of time you spend dealing with a contact such as a patient, and you can take notes during this entry. You can also schedule meetings with a contact and assign tasks to a contact. All journal entries, meetings, and tasks associated with a contact appear on the Activities tab in the Contact dialog box. Journal entries are handy for tracking the amount of time you spend dealing with a contact, and for taking notes about that contact. To associate a journal entry with a contact, you select the contact, and then click New Journal Entry For Contact from the Actions menu.

Create a Journal Entry for a Contact

1. In the Contacts folder, click a contact to select it.

2. Click the Actions menu, and then click New Journal Entry For Contact.

   TIMESAVER *Right-click the contact, and then click New Journal Entry For Contact on the shortcut menu.*

3. Click Start Timer to start the timer.

4. Click in the message box, and then type notes about the contact.

5. Click Pause Timer to stop the timer.

6. Click the Save And Close button.

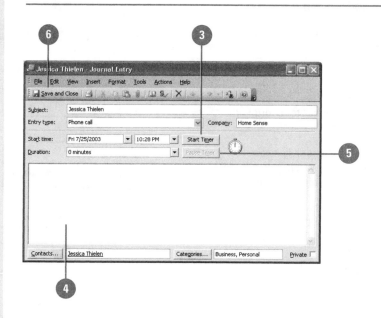

Recording Items in the Journal

The Outlook **Journal** is a diary of all the activities and interactions from your day. With everything organized on a timeline, you can see an overview of what you accomplished and when and how long certain activities took. The Journal also provides an alternate way to locate a particular item or a file. You can have the Journal automatically record entries of your phone calls, e-mail messages, meeting requests and responses, tasks, faxes, and documents on which you've worked. You must record tasks, appointments, personal conversations, and existing documents manually.

Automatically Record New Items and Documents

1 Click the Tools menu, and then click Options.

2 Click Journal Options.

3 Select the check boxes for the items you want to record in the Journal automatically.

4 Select the check boxes of the contacts for whom you want to record the selected items.

5 Select the check boxes of the programs that you want recorded.

6 Click OK.

7 Click OK.

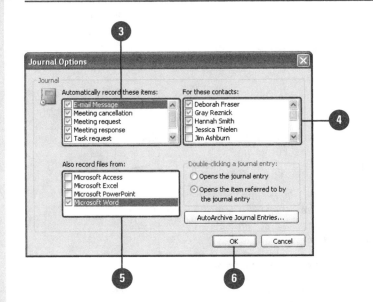

Record a Journal Entry Manually

1. Click the Folder List icon on the Navigation pane, and then click Journal.

2. Click the New button on the Standard toolbar.

   TIMESAVER *Press Ctrl+N in Journal view to create a new journal entry.*

3. Enter text in the Subject box that describes the journal entry.

4. Click the Entry Type list arrow, and then select the type of activity you want to record.

5. Specify the date, time, and duration of the activity.

6. Type a description of the activity.

7. Assign an entry to a contact, if necessary.

8. Assign a category, if necessary.

9. Click the Save And Close button.

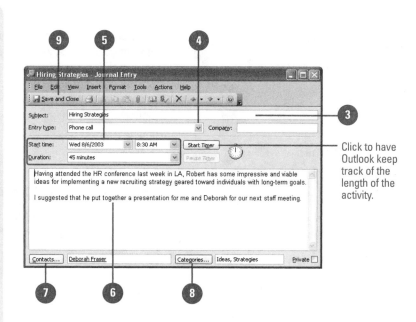

Click to have Outlook keep track of the length of the activity.

Did You Know?

You can time how long an activity takes. Open the Journal, click New, enter a subject, select the type of entry, and then click the Start Timer to begin timing how long the activity takes. Take notes as you continue the activity. Click Pause Timer if necessary, and then click Start Timer to resume. Click Pause Timer when you have completed the activity.

You can display the Journal icon on the Navigation pane. Click the Configure Buttons button, point to Add Or Remove Buttons, and then click Journal.

Opening and Modifying Journal Entries

Journal entries and their related items, documents, and contacts are easy to open, move, and even delete. When you modify a journal entry, its associated item, document, or contact is not affected. Likewise, when you modify an item, document, or contact, any existing related journal entries remain unchanged. If you no longer need a journal entry, you can select the entry and press Delete or click the Delete button to remove it.

Open the Journal

1 Click the Folder List icon on the Navigation pane.

2 Click Journal in the list of folders.

TIMESAVER *Press Ctrl+8 to open the Journal.*

3 Click the Current View list arrow, and then select the view in which you want to display your journal entries.

◆ Select the view that displays the journal entry in a way that best meets your needs.

Click to change timeline

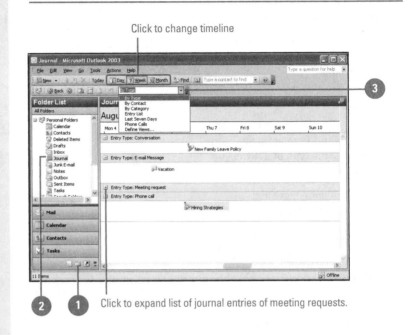

Click to expand list of journal entries of meeting requests.

Modify a Journal Entry

1 Open the Journal.

2 Double-click the journal entry to open it in its own window.

3 Modify the journal entry by selecting the options you want to change.

4 Click the Save And Close button.

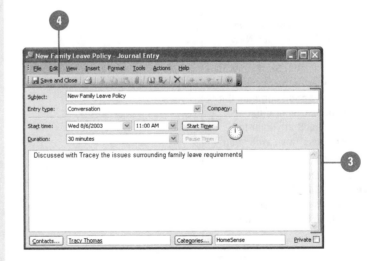

Organizing Items by Categories

A **category** is one or more keywords or phrases you assign to items so you can later find, group, sort, or filter them. Categories provide additional flexibility in how you organize and store items and files. By using categories you can store related items in different folders or unrelated items in the same folder, and still compile a complete list of items related to a specific category. Outlook starts you off with a **Master Category List** of some common categories, but you can add or remove them to fit your purposes.

Assign and Remove Categories to and from an Outlook Item

1. Click any Outlook item to select it.

2. Click the Edit menu, and then click Categories.

3. Select or clear check boxes to assign or remove categories.

4. Click OK.

Categories currently assigned to the selected item

Add or Remove a Master Category

1. Click any item to select it.

2. Click the Edit menu, and then click Categories.

3. Click Master Category List.

4. To add a category, type a new category name, and then click Add.

5. To remove a category, click the category you want to remove, and then click Delete.

6. Click OK.

7. Click OK.

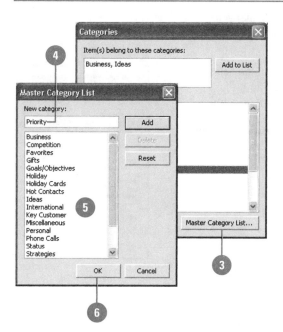

Customizing How You View Items

You can look at items, such as messages, in a variety of ways, or views. By default, the messages in your Inbox are listed by the date you received them. You can quickly reorder your messages by clicking one of the column headings so your messages appear in alphabetical order by the name of the sender. To control what and how much information you see, you can choose a default view or customize a view in Outlook so your items always appear in an order or format that works best for you. Outlook allows you to group, sort, and filter items. Group organizes items based on a particular field (an element for storing a particular type of information). Sort arranges items in ascending or descending order according to a specified field. Filter shows items that match specific criteria, such as "High Priority."

Customize the View of Your Messages

1 In Mail view, display the folder you want to customize.

2 Click the View menu, point to Arrange By, point to Current View, and then click Customize Current View.

3 Click Fields.

4 Double-click the fields that you want to appear in the Folder view.

5 Double-click the fields that you don't want to appear in the Folder view.

6 To change the order of the fields, click the field in the Show These Fields In This Order list box, and then click the Move Up or Move Down button until the field is in the position you want

7 Click OK.

8 Click OK.

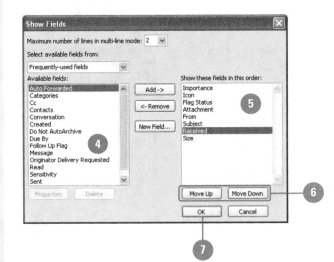

Settings you can customize

Set a Filter to Show Certain Items and Files

1. Click the View menu, point to Arrange By, point to Current View, and then click Customize Current View.

2. Click Filter.

3. Type a word to search for.

4. Click the In list arrow, and then click a field.

5. Enter the sender, recipient, and time frame as necessary.

6. Click OK.

7. Click OK.

Remove a Filter

1. Click the View menu, point to Arrange By, point to Current View, and then click Customize Current View.

2. Click Filter.

3. Click Clear All.

4. Click OK.

5. Click OK.

Creating and Modifying Notes

Notes in Outlook are electronic versions of paper sticky notes. Notes replace the random scraps of paper on which you might jot down reminders, questions, thoughts, ideas, or directions. Like the popular sticky notes, you can move an Outlook note anywhere on your screen and leave it displayed as you work. Any edits you make to a note are saved automatically. The ability to color-code, size, categorize, sort, or filter notes makes these notes even handier than their paper counterparts. When you open a new Note window in Outlook, you simply type text to create a note. The first paragraph becomes the note name in the Notes folder. Outlook inserts the date and time that you created the note for your reference.

Create a Note

1. Click the Notes button on the Navigation pane, and then click the New button on the Standard toolbar.

    TIMESAVER *Press Ctrl+N in Notes view, or press Ctrl+Shift+N in any another view to create a note.*

2. Type your note.

3. Click the Close button.

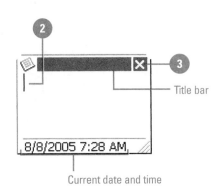

8/8/2005 7:28 AM

Title bar

Current date and time

Modify a Note

1. Click the Notes button on the Navigation pane, and then double-click a note icon.

2. Type new text or edit the existing text.

3. Click the Close button.

> ### Did You Know?
>
> **You can delete a note.** Select the note or notes you want to delete, and then click the Delete button on the Standard toolbar.

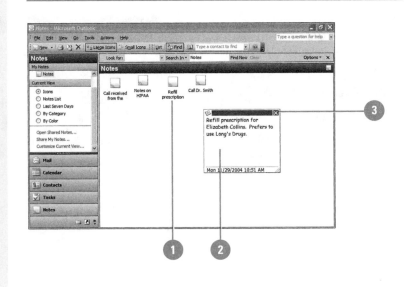

Previewing Items from Outlook

Just as you might preview a document in Word before printing it, you can preview items, such as a message, task list or calendar, in Outlook. In Print Preview, you can change the page set up for the current printing style. For example, the calendar print styles include the Daily Style, Weekly Style, Monthly Style, Tri-Fold Style, Calendar Style, and Memo Style. The default or preset printing style is different for each view depending on what type of information you are printing. Note that Print Preview is not available for HTML formatted messages.

Preview an Item or View

1. Click the item you want to print.

2. Click the File menu, point to Page Setup, and then click a print style (styles differ depending on the item you choose).

3. Click the File menu, and then click Print Preview.

4. Use the Page Up and Page Down buttons to display pages.

5. Use the One Page and Multiple Pages buttons on the Print Preview toolbar to view pages.

6. To change page setup format (layout and fonts), paper, and header/footer options, click Page Setup.

7. To print from the Print Preview window, click the Print button on the Print Preview toolbar.

8. When you're done, click the Close button on the Print Preview toolbar.

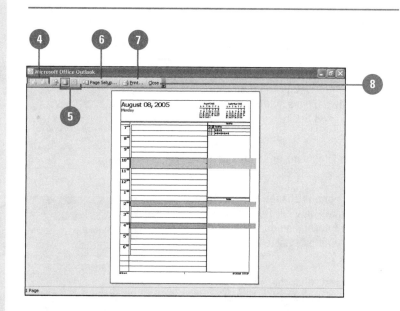

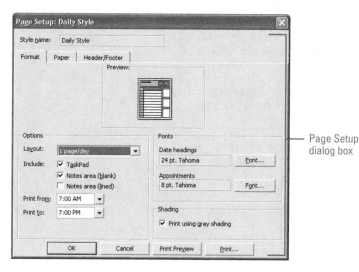

Page Setup dialog box

16

Printing Items from Outlook

You can print any item in Outlook. You can click the Print button on the Standard toolbar to print the selected item using the default print settings. The default or preset printing style is different for each view depending on what type of information you are printing. Printing options change depending on the item and view. There are different printing options available in table, calendar, and card views. To choose a printing option, use the Print command on the File menu. You cannot print from a timeline or an icon view.

Print an Item or View

1. Click the item you want to print.

2. If necessary, click the File menu, point to Page Setup, and then click a print style (styles differ depending on the item you choose).

3. Click the File menu, and then click Print.

   Printing options change depending on the item and view. Refer to the table for information on the printing options available for different views.

4. If necessary, click the Name list arrow, and then select a printer.

5. Select a print style.

   If you want, click Define Styles to specify the print style settings you want.

6. Click the Number Of Pages list arrow, and then select All, Odd, or Even.

7. Specify print options or a print range. Options vary depending on the item you selected.

8. Click OK.

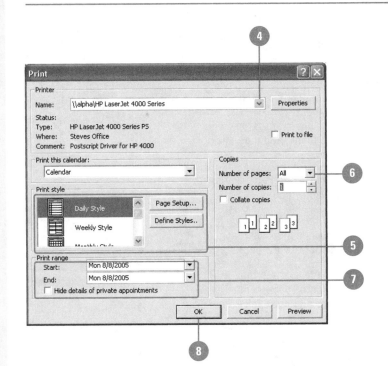

Creating a Publication with Publisher

17

Introduction

When you need to create a great looking publication about your department or practice, such as a business card, letterhead, patient newsletter, Web page, or brochure, use Microsoft Office Publisher 2003 to get the job done quickly and easily.

Publisher is a **desktop publishing program**—software you can use to combine text, graphics, and original drawings with sophisticated formatting, all in one easy-to-use package. With Publisher you can use creative layout and design techniques that were once in the exclusive realm of high-priced publishers or graphic designers.

Publisher combines the fundamental power of a word processor and the creativity of a graphics package into a program that is flexible and easy to use. This combination lets you create unique and exciting documents that you could not easily create in any other single application.

After you create a publication, you can enter and edit text. Text objects are enclosed in a frame, which serves as a container to hold a block of text. If you created a publication with a task pane, you see placeholder text, which you replace with your own text in the frame. You can add more text by adding new text frames or by inserting text into an existing text frame. For example, to add a new heading (or some other text) to a patient newsletter, you create a text frame. You create new frames using the corresponding frame tool located on the toolbar at the left side of the window.

Once you have created the publication you want, you can print it on your own printer, package it (electronically) to submit it to a commercial printer, or even publish it on the World Wide Web. In fact, you can do all of these things to the same publication.

Viewing the Publisher Window

Title bar
The title bar contains the name of the active publication. *Unsaved Publication* is a temporary name Publisher uses until you assign a new one.

Menu bar
The ten menus give you access to all Publisher commands.

Objects toolbar
The toolbar contains buttons to create and select objects, such as text or picture frames.

Standard and Formatting toolbars
These toolbars contain buttons that give you quick access to a variety of frequently used publisher commands.

Publication
Enter text and graphics here.

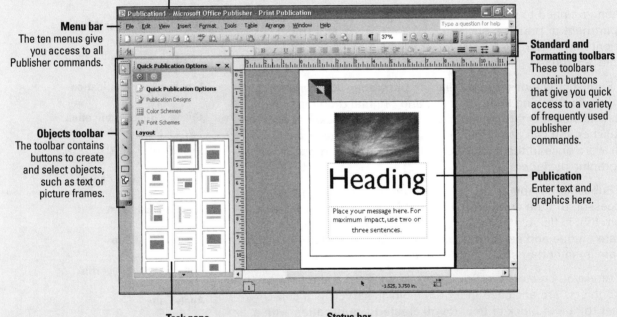

Task pane
The task pane provides easy access to publication options.

Status bar
The status bar tells you the location of the insertion point in a publication and provides icons that allow you to switch pages.

Creating a Quick Publication

Occasionally you'll want to create a one-page publication that does not fit into any of the categories listed in the Publisher's Catalog—for example, a title page for a scientific report. When you want to create a page quickly, use Quick Publications. After Publisher creates a page based on your selection, you can modify the layout and select options, such as Color Schemes and Font Schemes, on the Quick Publications Options task pane to help you customize the page.

Create a New Quick Publication

1. Start Publisher.

   If you have already started Publisher, click the File menu, and then click New.

2. Click the Publications For Print to expand the list.

3. Click Quick Publications.

4. Click the thumbnail that displays the design for the publication you want to create.

5. Click a layout.

6. Click Color Schemes or Font Schemes to customize the layout.

7. Click a text box placeholder, and then replace it with your text.

8. To replace a picture, click the picture, click the Insert menu, point to Picture, and then click From File or Clip Art.

9. Click the Save button on the Standard toolbar, select a location, name the file, and then click Save.

Did You Know?

You don't have to display the New Publication task pane at startup. Click the Tools menu, click Options, click the General tab, clear the Use New Publication Task Pane At Start Up check box, and then click OK.

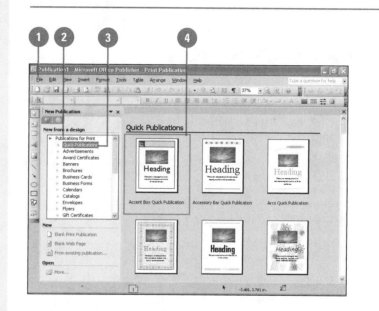

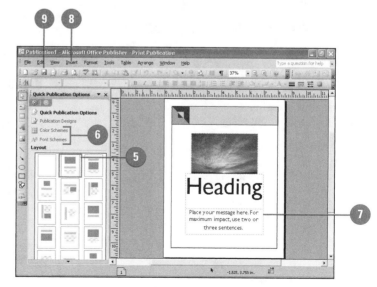

17

Creating a New Publication

When you first start Publisher, you see the New Publication task pane which you can use to create a new publication or open an existing publication. You have several options for creating a new publication. You can choose a publication design for newsletters, calendars, resumes, labels, and business forms, or you can start from a blank publication. You can create a publication based on the job you want to get done, or on design sets for special events, personal stationery, or fundraisers for your hospital, to name a few. You can also create publications for print, Web site, or e-mail.

Create a New Print Publication

1. Start Publisher.

   If you have already started Publisher, click the File menu, and then click New.

2. Click the Publications For Print or Design Sets to expand the list.

3. Click the type or category of publication you want.

   Click a category identified with an arrow to see its subcategories.

4. Click the thumbnail that displays the design for the publication you want to create.

5. Click the options on the task pane you want.

6. Click Color Schemes or Font Schemes to customize the layout.

7. Click a text box placeholder, and then replace it with your text.

8. Click the Save button on the Standard toolbar, select a location, name the file, and then click Save.

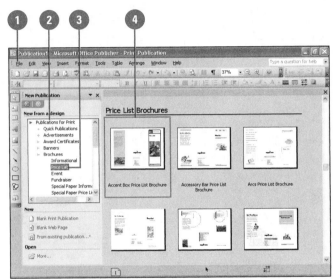

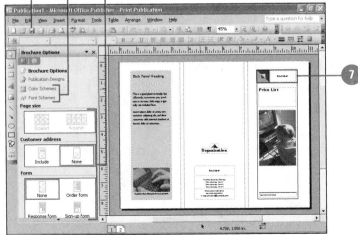

Creating a Blank Publication

Publisher's preset designs can be a big help in getting you started when you create a new publication. Every so often, however, you want to create a unique publication, and none of the preset designs will do the job. In that case, you can start a blank publication. If you know how to create and use frames, you can create a publication from scratch. Nevertheless, you can still display the task pane to help you think of design elements and options, including orientation and layout. If none of the sample blank publications meet your needs, you can also create a custom page.

Create a Blank Publication

1. Start Publisher.

   If you have already started Publisher, click the File menu, and then click New.

2. Click the Blank Publications.

3. Click a blank design type.

4. Click the thumbnail that displays the design for the publication you want to create. If necessary, click Yes to insert pages.

5. Click the design option on the task pane you want.

6. Click Color Schemes or Font Schemes to customize the layout.

7. Click a text box placeholder, and then replace it with your text.

8. Click the Save button on the Standard toolbar, select a location, name the file, and then click Save.

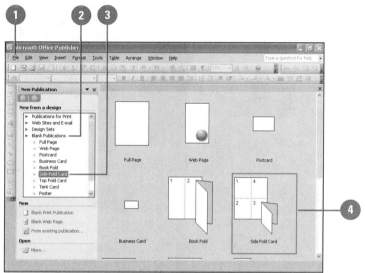

> ### Did You Know?
>
> **You can open an existing publication.** Click the Open button on the Standard toolbar, select the publication you want to open, and then click Open.

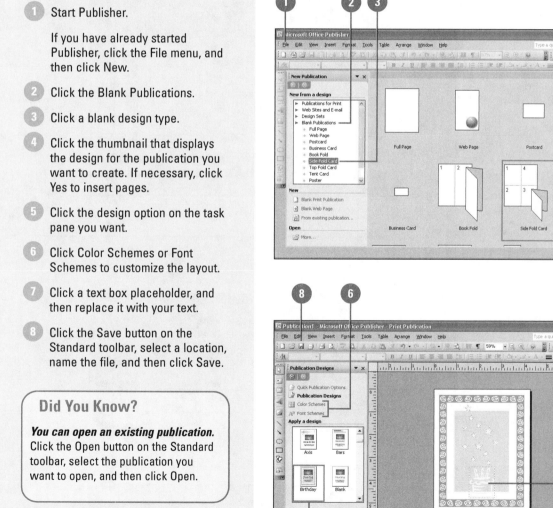

17

Changing Your View

You can view the pages in your publication in a one-page or a two-page spread. A two-page spread mimics the layout of a book or magazine that is lying open in front of you, where two pages face each other. You can also switch among various magnification levels. Viewing the page at a reduced size allows you to see an overview of your design. Zooming in on the pages makes type legible and provides a higher degree of accuracy when creating or positioning frames.

View a Publication in One or Two-Page View

1. Click the View menu, and then click Two-Page Spread.

   A check mark next to Two-Page Spread indicates two-page view. No check mark indicates one-page view based on your responses to the wizard.

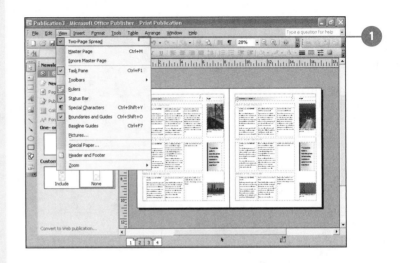

Change the View Size of a Page

1. Click the Zoom list arrow on the Standard toolbar.

2. Select the view percentage you want.

Did You Know?

You can switch between two different view sizes. Press the F9 key to toggle back and forth between actual size (100%) and the current view size.

You can zoom and scroll using Microsoft IntelliMouse. Roll the wheel to scroll, or press and hold Ctrl and roll the wheel to zoom.

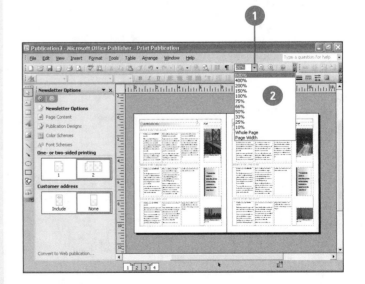

Inserting and Deleting Pages ▶

As you layout your publication, you may find it necessary to add a page or two in order to include more information or graphics. You can do this anytime during the design process. After viewing your publication, you may need to delete a page. If so, you can only delete one page or one spread at a time. You can see information on the other pages of a publication by clicking the page thumbnail in the status bar at the bottom of the window. Each thumbnail corresponds to a page on your publication.

Insert One or More Pages

1️⃣ Display the page before or after the one you want to insert.

2️⃣ Click the Insert menu, and then click Page.

3️⃣ If necessary, select the type of left-hand and right-hand page you want to insert, and then click More.

4️⃣ Type the number of pages you want to add.

5️⃣ Click the option to indicate the location of the new pages.

6️⃣ Click OK.

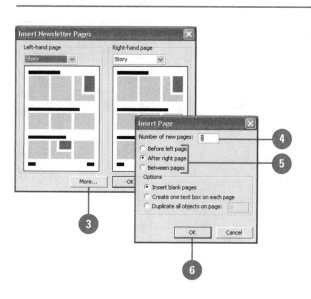

Delete a Page

1️⃣ Move to the page you want to delete.

2️⃣ Click the Edit menu, and then click Delete Page.

In one-page view, Publisher deletes the page.

3️⃣ In two-page view, click the option to indicate the pages you want to delete.

4️⃣ Click OK.

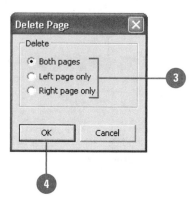

17

Inserting and Editing Text

When you create a publication, Publisher places generic text in a text frame, which is called a **text object**. The frame serves as a container in which you can easily format, move, and resize an area of text. The generic text acts as a placeholder. Replace the placeholder text with your own text. The insertion point indicates where text appears when you type. You can insert and update information, such as your practice name and address. If you change the information, Publisher updates it throughout the publication.

Insert and Edit Text in a Frame

1. Click the text in a frame if it isn't already selected.

   The small boxes on the frame indicate that it is selected.

2. Click to place the insertion point where you want to enter or edit text.

3. To delete text, press Delete or Backspace.

4. Type the text you want to enter.

5. Click outside the text frame to deselect it.

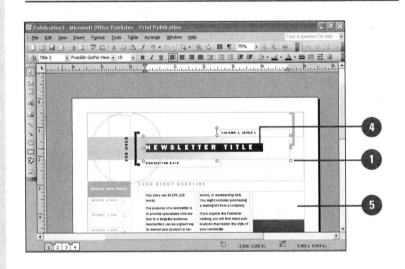

Change Edit Options

1. Click the Tools menu, and then click Options.

2. Click the Edit tab.

3. Select the editing check boxes you want, including:

   ◆ Drag-and-drop text editing

   ◆ Automatic selecting or formatting entire word

   ◆ Automatic hyphenating in new text frame

4. Click OK.

Enter or Update Personal Information

1. Click the Edit menu, and then click Personal Information.

2. Select the Personal Information Set you want to edit.

3. Enter the personal information for that set.

4. Click Update.

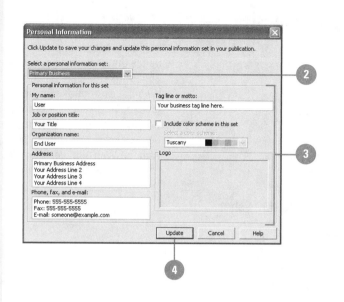

Insert Personal Information

1. Click the Insert menu, and then point to Personal Information.

2. Click the personal information set you want.

A new text frame is created. Each personal information component must remain in its own separate text frame.

Did You Know?

Insert page numbers. Click in the text or table frame where you want to insert a page number, click the Insert menu, and then click Page Numbers.

You can check spelling in a publication. Click the Spelling button on the Standard toolbar, click Ignore, or click the correct spelling, and then click Change. When you're done, click OK.

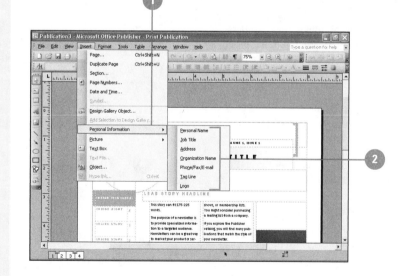

17

Creating a Web Site

The World Wide Web is your path to communicating with the greatest number of people without incurring printing and mailing costs. Use Publisher to create publications for your Web site. You can create Web pages that include text, calendars, practice specialty, driving directions, and forms. You can use the Web Site Options task pane to add general Web pages or ones with special functionality to tell patients how to contact you or display the credentials of your medical staff, to name a few. When you have completed your Web site, you can preview the Web pages as they will appear on the World Wide Web. Once you are satisfied with the Web site, you can also use the Save As Web Page feature to save the publication for the Web.

Create a Web Site in Publisher

1. Start Publisher.

   If you have already started Publisher, click the File menu, and then click New.

2. Click Web Sites And E-Mail, and then click Web Site.

3. Click a design type.

4. Click the thumbnail that displays the design for the publication you want to create.

5. Click a layout from the Navigation bar.

6. Click a text box placeholder, and then replace it with your text.

7. Click the page icons at the bottom of the window to switch between pages.

8. Click the Save button on the Standard toolbar, select a location, name the file, and then click Save.

Did You Know?

You can preview the Web site in your browser. Open the Web publication, click the File menu, and then click Web Page Preview.

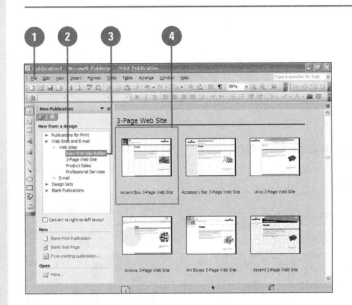

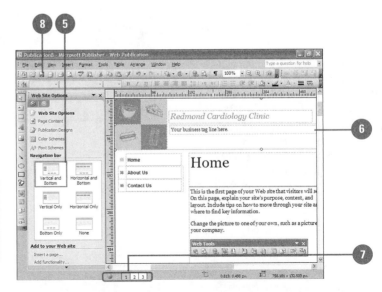

Add Functionality Pages

1. Open the Web page in which you want to add functionality, and then display the Web Site Options task pane.

2. Click Add Functionality (scroll down the task pane if necessary).

3. Select the check boxes for the enhanced functionality options you want to add.

4. Click OK.

    Publisher adds pages to the Web site with the added functionality.

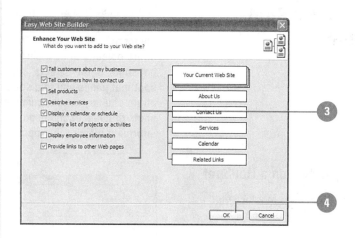

Insert Web Pages

1. Open the Web page in which you want to add functionality, and then display the Web Site Options task pane.

2. Click Insert A Page (scroll down the task pane if necessary).

3. Select the page type you want to add.

4. To select the number of pages and the location where you want to insert the pages, click More.

5. Click OK.

    Publisher adds pages to the Web site with the added functionality.

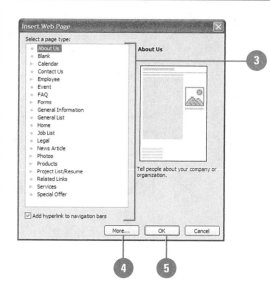

Did You Know?

You can publish the Web site. Open the Web publication, click the Publish To The Web button on the Web Tools toolbar, select a location on a Web server, specify a name, and then click Save.

Adding a Hot Spot Hyperlink

You can use text and objects in your Web site to create hyperlinks to other Web pages. You can specify a specific part of a publication or an object to be a hyperlink. This type of hyperlink is called a **hot spot**. An entire object can be a single hot spot or an object can contain multiple hot spots. Some objects, such as navigation buttons, contain a single hot spot that jumps you to a specific address. For other objects, such as a photo of a large multi-building medical center, you can have several hot spots that link each hospital building in the photo to a page that provides information about that particular hospital.

Create a Hyperlink on a Hot Spot

1. Open the Web page in which you want to add a hyperlink on a hot spot.

2. Click the Hot Spot Tool button on the Web Tools toolbar.

3. Drag to create a rectangle around the area you want a hot spot.

4. Enter the Internet address.

5. Click OK.

See Also

See "Inserting Hyperlinks" on page 454 for information on creating text hyperlinks to other pages.

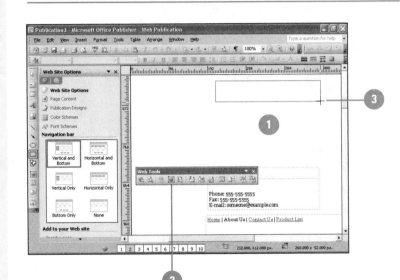

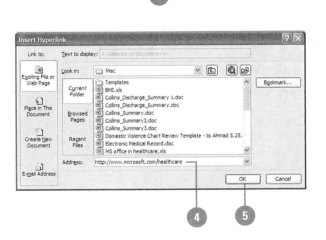

Applying Color

You can change the look of your publication by selecting a **color scheme**—a predesigned layout containing a variety of colors for bullets, backgrounds, color, and lines to create specific moods. You can use the default color scheme or apply a custom one that you develop. Apply color schemes at any time—not just when you create the pages. You can also modify any color in a color scheme, and you can create and save your own custom color schemes.

Apply Background Colors

1. Click the Format menu, and then click Background.

2. Click a background color or click More Colors, select another one, and then click OK.

3. Point to the gradient or pattern you want to use.

4. Click the list arrow, and then click Apply To The Page or Apply To All Pages.

5. When you're done, click the Close button on the task pane.

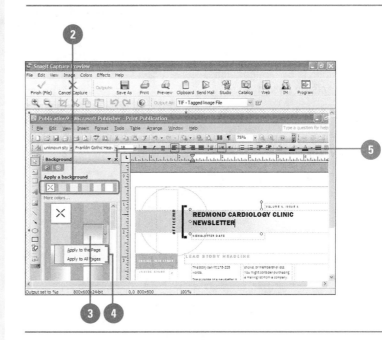

Create a Custom Color Scheme

1. Click the Format menu, and then click Color Scheme.

2. Click Custom Color Scheme.

3. Click any New list arrow(s), and then select the colors you want.

4. Click Save Scheme, type a name for your scheme, and then click OK.

5. Click OK.

6. When you're done, click the Close button on the task pane.

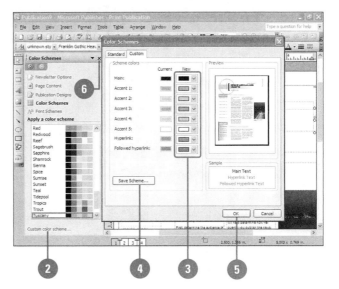

17

Adding Design Gallery Elements

The **Design Gallery** contains a variety of objects, such as buttons, reply forms, logos, calendars, and borders, you can insert into your publications. The Design Gallery organizes elements by category or design. You can also add your elements to the Design Gallery. The Design Gallery Object button on the Objects toolbar makes it easy and convenient to add Design Gallery objects to your publication.

Add Design Gallery Elements

1. Click the Design Gallery button on the Objects toolbar.

2. Click the Objects By Category tab or the Objects By Design tab.

3. Click the Design Gallery element you want to add.

4. Click Insert Object.

5. To move the object, drag it to an new location.

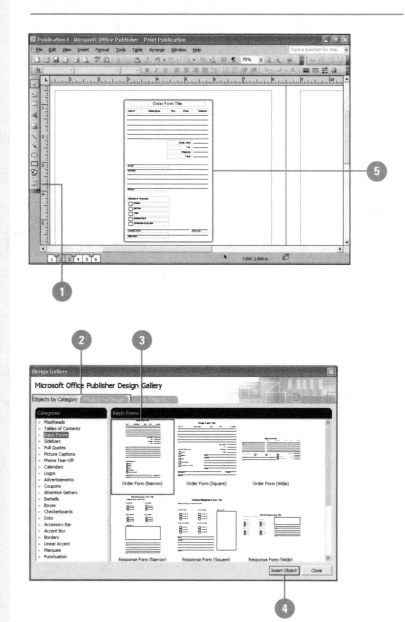

Checking Your Design

You can check the design of your publication for errors. The **Design Checker** looks over your publication for problems, such as empty frames, text in overflow areas off the page, covered objects, objects in nonprinting regions, disproportional pictures, and poor spacing between sentences. Once the Design Checker identifies problems, it suggests solutions, which you can accept or ignore. You determine Design Checker's settings in its Options box.

Check Your Design

1. Click the Tools menu, and then click Design Checker.

2. Point to the design suggestions in the Design Checker task pane.

3. Click the list arrow, and then click an option to view, fix, or ignore the item.

4. When you're done, click the Close button on the task pane.

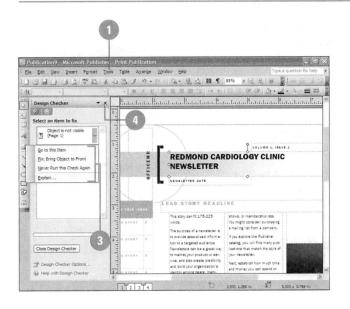

Change Design Checker Options

1. Click the Tools menu, and then click Design Checker.

2. Click Design Checker Options.

3. Click the Checks tab.

4. Select the check boxes for the types of errors you want to find.

5. Click OK.

6. When you're done, click the Close button on the task pane.

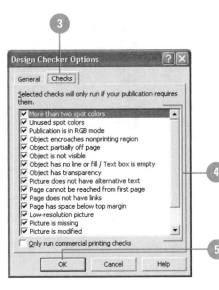

17

Setting Up the Page

When you set up a publication, you can determine how you want it to print. Page layout determines the general size and orientation of your publication and affects how the pages will be arranged when you print. Paper size refers to the physical dimensions of the paper in your printer. Publisher's page size refers to the dimensions of your publication, which can be the same, smaller, or larger than the paper size.

Set Up the Page and Printer

1. Click the File menu, and then click Page Setup.

2. Click the Layout tab.

3. Click the publication layout type you want.

4. Specify the orientation options you want for the publication layout.

5. Click the Printer And Paper tab.

6. To set printer options, click Properties.

7. Specify the paper options you want.

8. Click OK.

Did You Know?

You can automatically display the Print Troubleshooter. Click the Tools menu, click Options, click the General tab, select the Automatically Display Print Troubleshooter check box, and then click OK.

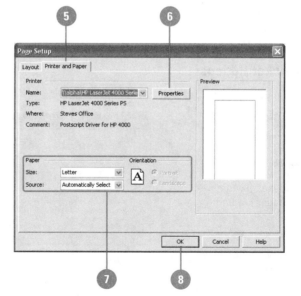

Using Commercial Printing Tools

Publisher provides full support for commercial printing, including automatic conversion to spot or process color with automatic color separation. In addition, advanced tools such as **trapping** (overlapping the edges of different colors), graphic link management, and font lists provide commercial printers with the features they need to print high-quality publications. Check with your commercial printer for the specific settings and options you need to complete your print job.

Change Color Print Settings

1. Click the Tools menu, point to Commercial Printing Tools, and then click Color Printing.

2. Click the color define option you want.

3. Specify the inks or colors you want.

4. Click OK.

Change Trapping Preferences

1. Click the Tools menu, point to Commercial Printing Tools, point to Registration Settings, and then click Publication.

2. Select the trapping and overprinting check boxes you want.

3. If necessary, click Reset All to restore settings.

4. Click OK.

> **Did You Know?**
>
> **You can get an embedded font list.** Embed a font when the printer doesn't have it. Click the Tools menu, point to Commercial Printing Tools, and then click Fonts.

17

Printing Publications

The whole point of creating publications is to publish them, which—except for Web pages—means printing the publications you've created. If you have a printer connected to your computer you can print publications right away. If you have special printing needs, however, you might want to use a commercial printer who can deliver high-quality color documents. **The Pack And Go Wizard** compacts all the information a printer needs across multiple disks, embedded fonts, includes linked graphics, and prints composite and separation proofs. If needed, you can double-click the Unpack.exe file to unpack and open the Pack And Go file.

Print a Publication on Your Printer

1. Click the File menu, and then click Print.

2. Specify the pages that you want to print.

3. If necessary, click Advanced Print Settings to select separation or composite options, resolution, printer's marks, bleeds, font substitution, and special print output.

4. Click OK.

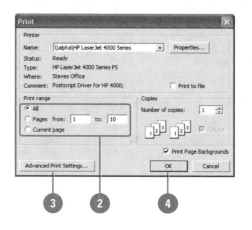

Create a File for Commercial Printing

1. Click the File menu, point to Pack And Go, and then click Take To A Commercial Printing Service.

2. Click Next to begin creating the file.

3. Specify the drive and directory where you want to save the file. Click Next to continue.

4. Click the graphics and font information you want to include. Click Next to continue.

5. Click Finish.

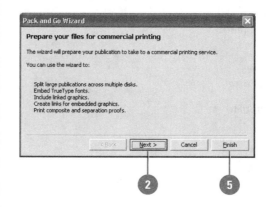

Designing a Publication with Publisher

Introduction

After you create a publication in Microsoft Office Publisher 2003, you can modify any design element you see. Each element in a publication is enclosed in a **frame**. The frame serves as a container to hold objects, such as a block of text, a picture, or a graphic element you've created yourself. If you created a publication using the task pane, you see placeholder text, which you replace with your own text in the frame. You can add more elements by adding new frames. For example, to add a new heading (or some other text) to a brochure, you create a text frame. To add a graphic, you create a picture frame and then insert a graphic. You create new frames using the corresponding frame tool located on the toolbar at the left side of the window. After you create a frame, you can move it or change its size to allow for more text (in the case of a text frame) or a larger or smaller image (as in a picture frame). You can rotate frames or change their order when you want to place different pictures or text on top of, or behind each other. And with the Design Gallery you can add ready-made elements such as banners, business cards, calendars, newsletters, and signs.

If you already know how to use Microsoft Word's text and picture frames, you'll be on familiar ground with Microsoft Publisher's frames. If using frames is new to you, you will find working with frames a snap to learn.

What You'll Do

Set Up Layout Guides

Create a Frame

Work with Text

Connect Text Frames

Create a Consistent Look

Create Tables

Work with Pictures and Shapes

Wrap Text Around an Object

Layer Objects

Group Objects Together

Align with Precision

Rotate and Flip Objects

Setting Up Layout Guides

Each page of a publication—like any business letter—should have uniform margins. This gives your publication a consistent, professional look. Since a publication is composed of many elements (which may have their own margins), each page is controlled using layout guides. Since they are automatically included in each page of a publication, layout guides are located on background pages. In publications with mirrored pages, any adjustment made to one page is automatically reflected on its companion page.

Set Up Layout Guides

1. Click the Arrange menu, and then click Layout Guides.

2. Click the Margin Guides tab.

3. Specify the measurement for each of the margin guides you want to adjust.

   - The Left margin guide is the white space at the left of a non-mirrored page.

   - The Right margin guide is the white space at the right of a non-mirrored page.

   - The Top margin guide is the white space at the top of the page.

   - The Bottom margin guide is the white space at the bottom of the page.

4. Click the Grid Guides tab, and then select the value for the column and row guides you want to adjust.

5. Click the Baseline Guides tab, and then select the value for the horizontal guides you want to adjust.

6. Click OK.

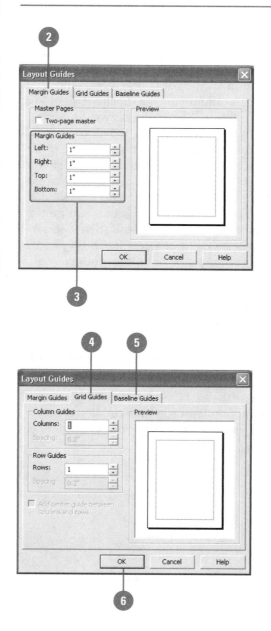

Creating a Frame

Before you can type text, insert a table, import a picture, design WordArt, or insert an OLE object, you must draw the appropriate frame for that type of object. The frame serves as a container to hold objects, such as a block of text, a picture, or a graphic element you've created yourself.

Create a Frame

1. Click the corresponding frame toolbar button to create the type of object you want.

   Refer to the table for information on the different tools.

2. Position the pointer on the page where you want the frame.

3. Press and hold the mouse button, while you drag diagonally.

   The frame boundary will appear.

4. Release the mouse button when you have created a frame the size you want.

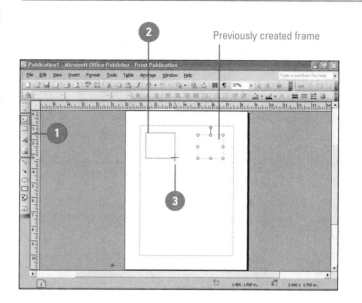

Previously created frame

Did You Know?

You can show or hide frame boundaries and guides. To show boundaries, click the View menu, and then click Boundaries And Guides. To hide boundaries, click the View menu, and then click Boundaries And Guides again.

Frame Toolbar Buttons

Icon	Button Name	Purpose
	Text Box Tool	Create a frame for text
	Insert Table Tool	Create a frame for a table
	Insert WordArt Tool	Create a frame for stylized text
	Picture Frame Tool	Create a frame for a picture or clip art

18

Working with Text

When you want to add new text to your publication, you need to create a text frame. Using the Text Frame tool, you drag a rectangle that will contain your text. When you release the mouse, the insertion point blinks inside the frame, indicating that you can start typing. After entering text, you can resize and move the text box, or format the text to change its font, size, and color. Similarly, you can also change the color of the background of the frame (behind the text) and add interesting borders to the frame.

Create a Text Frame

1. Click the Text Box button on the Objects toolbar.

2. Position the mouse pointer where you want the frame to start.

3. Click and Drag to create a rectangle the size you want.

4. Type the text you want in the frame.

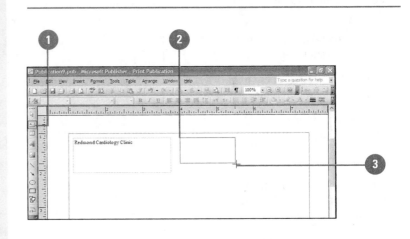

Resize or Move a Text Frame

1. Click the text frame to select it.

2. To resize a text frame, drag a handle.

3. To move a text frame, position the pointer over the dotted edge of the frame, and then drag the text frame to a new location.

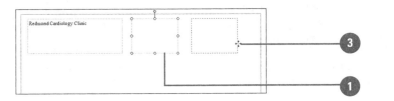

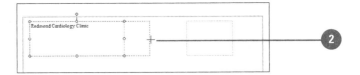

Format Text in a Frame

① Select the text that you want to format.

② Right-click the selected text.

③ Point to Change Text.

④ Click a command to change a specific characteristic of the text in the selected frame.

⑤ Select the format options you want.

⑥ Click OK.

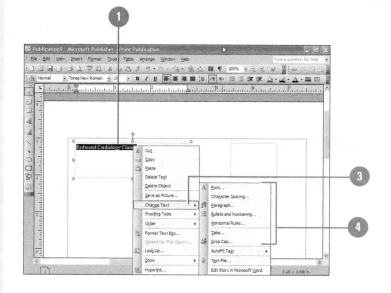

Format a Text Frame

① Select the text frame you want to format.

② Use the Fill Color, Line Color, Font Style, Line/Border Style, Dash Style, Arrow Style, and Shadow Style buttons on the Formatting toolbar.

Did You Know?

You can improve the appearance of large fonts by changing character spacing. Characters formatted in very large fonts often look too far apart. To adjust the space between characters, click the Format menu, and then click Character Spacing.

You can change line spacing. Adjust the amount of space between lines of text with the Paragraph command on the Format menu.

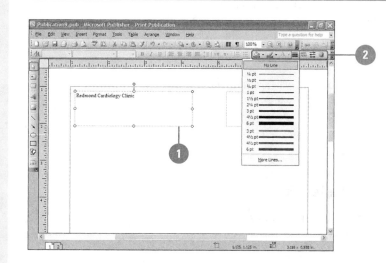

18

Connecting Text Frames

You can control the way the text flows in your publications. You can link and unlink frames that are adjacent to each other on the same page or different pages. Special text frame buttons appear when text is in the overflow area or when two or more text frames are linked in a chain. You can insert continued notices to help readers follow text from page to page. In addition, you can use **AutoFit Text** to resize text to fit the size of the text frame. When you insert a text file, you can have Publisher use AutoFlow to insert the text in frames and connect them together.

Connect Text Frames

1. Select the first text frame you want to connect.

   This frame can be empty or it can contain text.

2. Click the Connect Text Frames button on the Connect Frames toolbar.

3. Position the pitcher pointer over the empty text frame you want to connect.

4. Click the empty text frame to connect the two frames.

   Any overflow text will flow into the newly connected text frame.

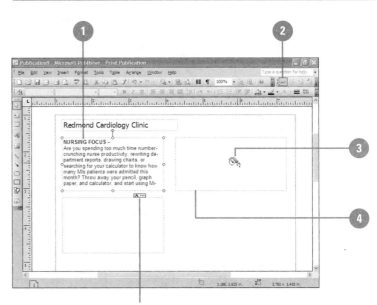

Indicates there is overflow text

Disconnect a Text Frame

1. Select the text frame you want to disconnect.

2. Click the Disconnect Text Frames button on the Connect Frames toolbar.

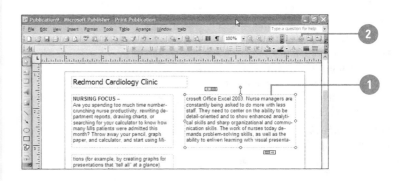

Insert a Continued Notice

1. Select the text frame in which you want to add a notice.

2. Click the Format menu, and then click Text Box.

3. Click the Text Box tab.

4. Select one or both of the Include Continued On Page and Include Continued From Page check boxes.

5. Click OK.

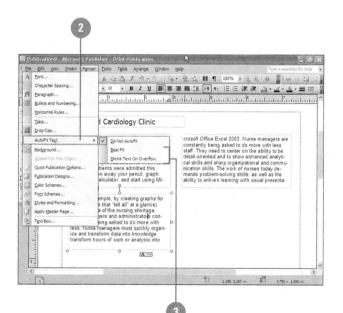

AutoFit Text

1. Select the text frame you want to format.

2. Click the Format menu, and then point to AutoFit Text.

3. Click Best Fit or Shrink Text On Overflow.

   To turn off AutoFit Text, click Do Not AutoFit.

> **Did You Know?**
>
> *You can delete a text frame from a chain.* Select the text frame you want to delete, click the Edit menu, and then click Delete Object.

18

Creating a Consistent Look

When you create a collection of related publications, such as those for a specific event or organization, make sure that all the publications look similar. By using consistent choices of colors, design elements, and text formatting, your readers will instantly recognize that all your publications are related to the same effort or organization. Publisher's Catalog and color schemes can help you achieve consistent designs and colors. Use **text styles**, which store text formatting settings, to ensure your text formatting is consistent in all your publications. After creating a text style in a publication, you can import the style to other publications.

Create a New Style by Example

1. Select the text with the style you want.

2. Click the Format menu, and then click Styles And Formatting.

3. Click Create New Style.

4. Enter a name for the new style.

5. Click each of the formatting options, and then change the formatting settings for the new style.

6. Click OK.

Apply a Style

1. Select the text or text frame to which you want to apply a style.

2. Click the Style list arrow on the Formatting toolbar.

3. Select a style.

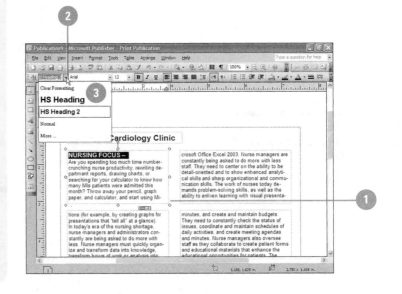

Delete a Style

1. Click the Format menu, and then click Styles And Formatting.

2. Point to the style you want to remove, and then click the list arrow next to it.

3. Click Delete.

4. Click Yes to confirm that you want to delete the style.

5. Click the Close button on the task pane.

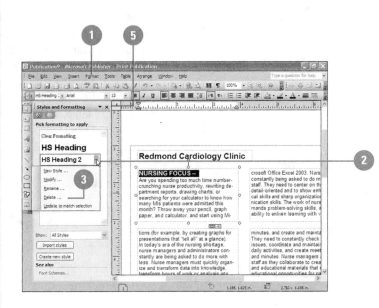

Import a Style

1. Click the Format menu, and then click Styles and Formatting.

2. Click Import Styles.

3. Double-click the publication that contains the styles you want to import.

4. Click the Close button on the task pane.

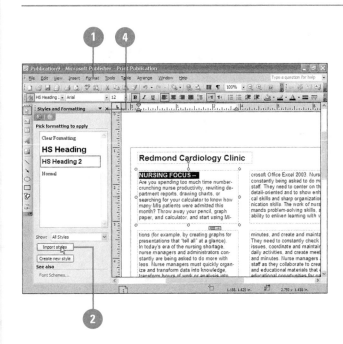

Did You Know?

You can pick up and apply a style. Select the word or text object whose format you want to use. Click the Format Painter button on the Standard toolbar, and then select the text to which you want to apply the format.

You can change a style. Click the Format menu, click Styles And Formatting, click the list arrow for the style you want to change, click Modify, change the style, and then click OK.

18

Creating Tables

A **table** is an arrangement of text in a grid of rows and columns. Within a table, the intersection of a row and a column is a called a **cell**. You can use tables to align text. Tables are a convenient way to create dosage schedules, calendars, and forms. You create a table with the Table Object Tool button on the Objects toolbar. After you create a table, you can format the color, line and border style, or shadow of individual cells or the entire table. You can also use the Table AutoFormat feature to apply sets of lines and borders to rows and columns, or individual cells.

Create a Table Frame

1. Click the Insert Table button on the Objects toolbar.

2. Position the mouse pointer where you want the frame to start.

3. Drag to create a rectangle the size you want.

4. Enter the number of rows and columns you want the table to have.

5. Click the formatting you want.

6. Click OK.

   Click in a cell to begin entering text in the table.

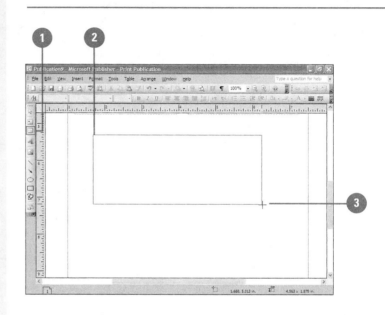

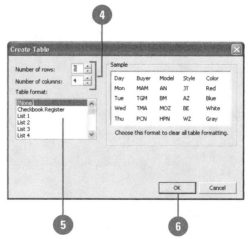

> ### Did You Know?
>
> ***You can format a cell like any other text.*** Select the text in the cell and use the tools on the Formatting toolbar.

Format a Table

1. Select the rows, columns, or cells you want to format, and then right-click the selection.

2. Click the Format menu, and then click Table.

3. Select the line color and line weight you want.

4. Click the border buttons to add the frames around the selection.

5. Click OK.

Did You Know?

You can format a table quickly. Select the table, click the Table menu, click Table AutoFormat, click the format you want, and then click OK. If you want, click Options to specify what parts of the table you want to format.

You can select a table, column, or row. Click the column or row, click the Table menu, point to Select, and then click Table, Column, or Row.

You can insert a table column or row. Select the column to the left or the row above where you want to insert a column or row, click the Table menu, point to Insert, and then click Columns To The Left or Columns To The Right.

You can delete a table column or row. Select the column or row you want to delete, click the Table menu, point to Delete, and then click Columns or Rows.

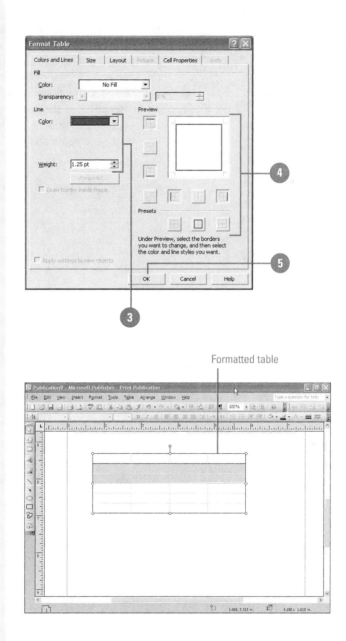

Formatted table

Working with Pictures and Shapes

When you want to insert a picture from a file or a clip art picture from the Clip Gallery, you need to create a picture frame. Using the Picture Frame Tool button, you can create a frame and insert a picture or clip art. Then you can modify the picture. You can also create your own original drawing. Using the drawing tools on the Objects toolbar, you can create lines and basic shapes, as well as custom shapes that include stars, cartoon balloons, arrows, and many more elements that are sure to add interest to your publication.

Create a Picture Frame

1. Click the Picture Frame button on the Objects toolbar, and then click Picture From File.

2. Position the mouse pointer where you want the picture frame to start.

3. Drag to create a rectangle the size you want.

4. Double-click the file you want to insert.

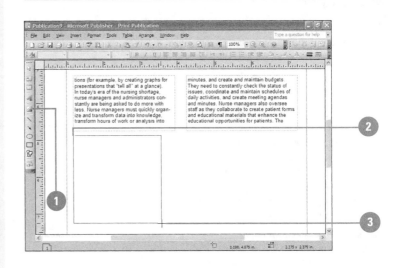

Change the Picture

1. Select the picture you want to change.

2. Use the buttons on the Picture toolbar to change the picture.

3. Click a blank area to deselect the picture and hide the Picture toolbar.

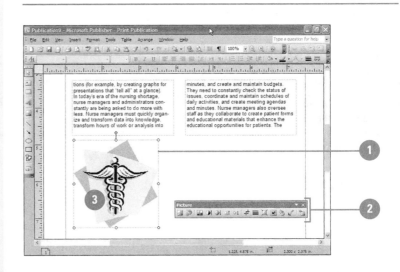

Create a Line, Arrow, Oval, or Rectangle

1 Click the Line, Arrow, Oval, or Rectangle button on the Objects toolbar.

2 Position the mouse pointer where you want the object to start.

3 Click and drag to create an object the size you want.

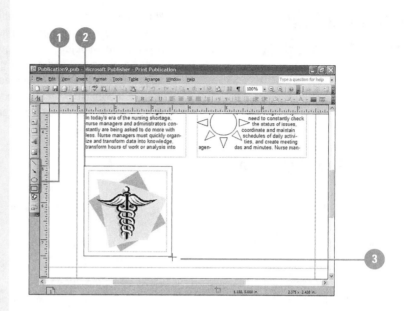

Create a Custom Shape

1 Click the Custom Shapes button on the Objects toolbar.

2 Point to a category, and then click the shape you want to create.

3 Position the mouse pointer where you want the shape to start.

4 Drag to create a shape the size you want.

Did You Know?

You can change shape properties.
Right-click the shape, point to Change Shape, point to or click the formatting command you want, and then click the format option you want.

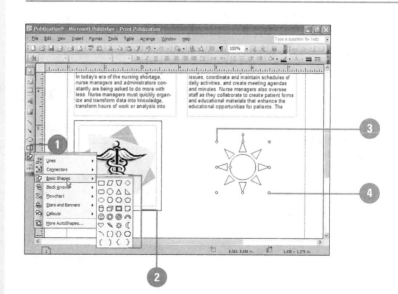

18

Wrapping Text Around an Object

You can wrap text around an object, such as a graphic, to attractively integrate text and objects in a publication. By default, Publisher flows text around an object's rectangular frame. So that there are no unsightly gaps between text and nearby graphics, you can wrap the text to flow tightly around irregularly shaped or round objects. Use the Text Wrap feature in Publisher to have text follow the outlines of the object itself. Brochures and newsletters often use this technique to combine text and graphics.

Wrap Text Around an Object

1. Select the text frame that you want to wrap.

2. Click the Format menu, and then click Text Box.

3. Click the Layout tab.

4. Click a Wrapping Style option.

5. Click OK.

6. Drag the object to overlap the text frame.

   The text object must be under the graphic object.

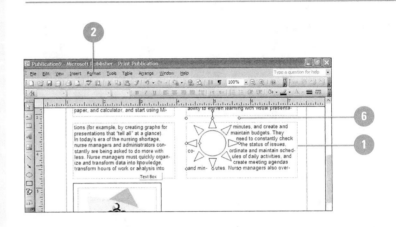

Did You Know?

Drawn objects must be filled to wrap text around them. If you want text to wrap around a shape you've drawn, fill the shape with a color. Publisher won't flow text around a transparent shape. By default, Publisher wraps tightly around drawn shapes.

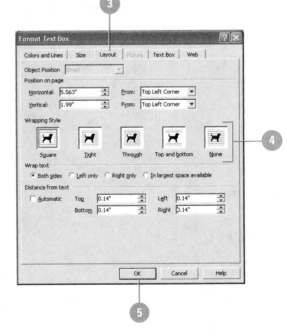

Fine-tune Text Flow Around an Object

1. Click the object which you want the text to flow around.

2. Click the Text Wrapping button on the Picture toolbar, and then click Edit Wrap Points.

3. Position the pointer over an adjust handle until you see the adjust pointer, and then drag the handle to change the shape of the boundary.

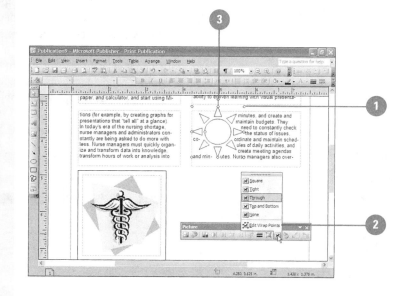

Add an Adjust Handle

1. Click the object which you want the text to flow around.

2. Click the Text Wrapping button on the Picture toolbar, and then click Edit Wrap Points.

3. Press and hold Ctrl as you click the dotted-line boundary.

Did You Know?

You can precisely control the shape of an object's boundary. Adjust handles appear at corners or other significant changes in direction of the shape. The more complex the shape, the more adjust handles you see. You can delete extra adjust handles.

You can create a simpler boundary around a picture by removing an adjust handle. Click the object, point to the adjust handle, and then press Ctrl as you click it.

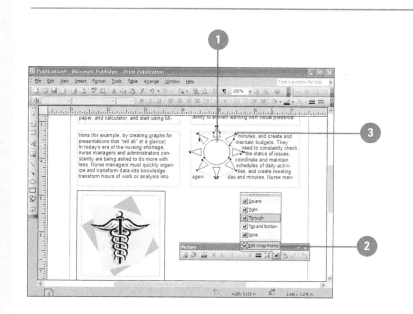

18

Layering Objects

Like pieces of paper arranged on your work surface, you can arrange objects in a publication on top of each other. The object you created or edited last appears on top of the stack of other objects. Layering objects allows you to achieve effects like shadows and complex designs that include many shapes. You can rearrange the order of the objects in the stack by sending individual objects behind one another, or to the back of the stack, or by bringing other objects in front of one another, or to the front of the stack.

Change Object Stacking Order

1. Select the object you want to change.

2. Click the Arrange menu, point to Order, and then click Bring to Front or Send to Back.

   ◆ Bring To Front

   ◆ Send To Back

   ◆ Bring Forward

   ◆ Send Backward

Did You Know?

You need to ungroup objects before changing the order. If you see no change in the order of the objects in the stack, click the Ungroup Object button, and then select the object you want to move. Be sure to regroup the objects after you are satisfied with the layers.

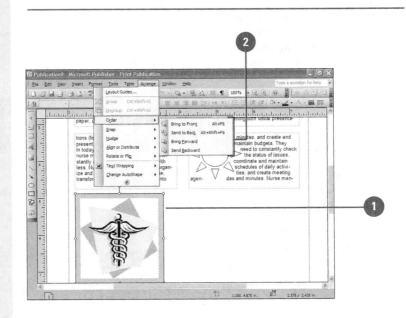

Grouping Objects Together

Often you want Publisher to treat several objects as a single one. That way, if you decide to move one object, you can also move other objects. In Publisher, you can accomplish this with the **grouping** feature. Group objects when you want to move, resize, or format a set of objects as a single object. If you decide that you want to work with each object independently, you can ungroup them.

Group Objects

1. Select the first object you want to group.

2. Press and hold Shift while you click the other objects that you want to group together.

3. Click the Group Objects button.

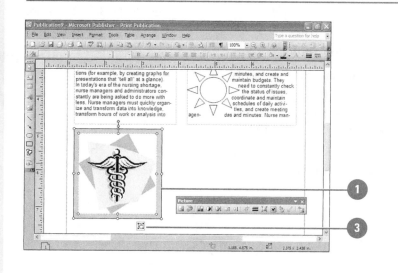

Ungroup Objects

1. Select the object you want to ungroup.

2. Click the Ungroup Objects button.

Did You Know?

Sizing handles help identify grouped objects. When you click an object and you see multiple highlighted frames but only one set of sizing handles, it means that the object is part of a group.

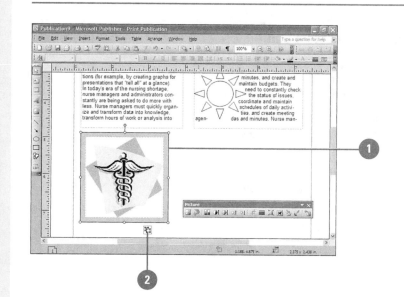

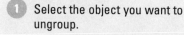

18

Aligning with Precision

Not only can you align objects with each other, you can create controls within a publication that help you align objects. You can create an unlimited number of **ruler guides**—green vertical and horizontal lines you place on a page—to help you line up any objects you choose. Ruler guides can be moved and deleted as you see fit, can be placed on foreground and background pages, and can vary from page to page. Once in place, an object appears to have a magnetic attraction to a ruler guide due to the Snap To feature.

Create a Ruler Guide

1. Point to the vertical or horizontal ruler.

2. Drag from the ruler to create a vertical or horizontal guide.

3. Release the mouse button when the guide is in position.

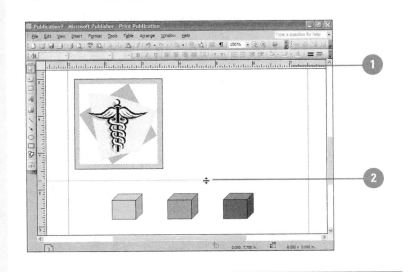

Snap an Object to a Guide

1. If necessary, click the Arrange menu, point to Snap, and then click To Guides to turn the feature on.

2. Drag the object you want to snap to a ruler guide.

3. Release the mouse button once the object snaps to the guide.

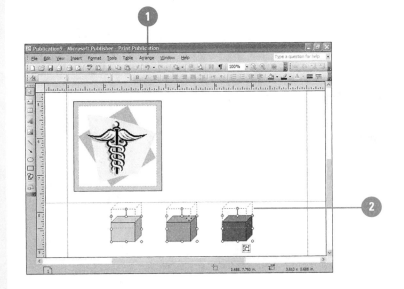

Align Objects

1. Press and hold Shift while clicking each object you want to align.

2. Click the Arrange menu, and then point to Align Or Distribute.

3. Click the align or distribute option you want.

See Also

See "Setting Up Layout Guides" on page 432 for information on aligning objects to the layout guides.

Did You Know?

You can clear all ruler guides quickly. Click the Arrange menu, point to Ruler Guides, and then click Clear All Ruler Guides.

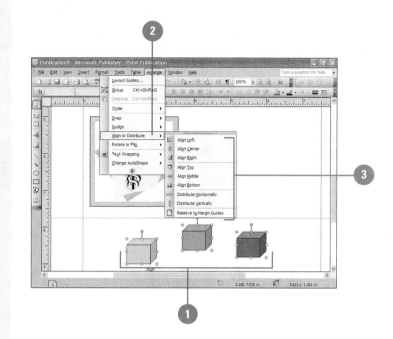

Rotating and Flipping Objects

To fit objects together in a specific way or to achieve a dramatic effect, consider rotating an object. Flipping objects, either vertically or horizontally, is a fast way to change their position. You can flip an object horizontally or vertically to create a mirror image of it along its vertical or horizontal axis.

Rotate an Object

1. Select the object you want to rotate.

2. Position the pointer over the rotate handle (green handle that points up from the object).

3. Drag to free rotate the object.

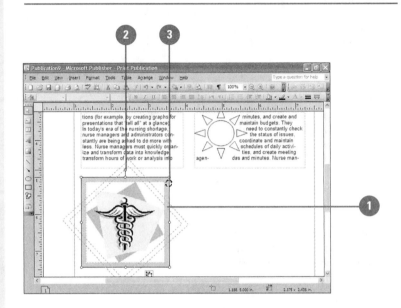

Flip an Object Horizontally or Vertically

1. Select the object you want to flip.

   You can flip all Publisher objects, except for text objects.

2. Click the Rotate/Flip button on the Standard toolbar, and then click Flip Horizontal or Flip Vertical.

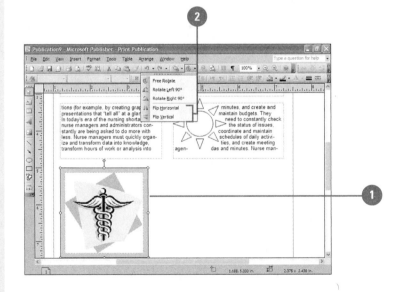

Creating Web Pages with Office Programs

19

Introduction

World Wide Web technology is now available for all your Microsoft Office 2003 programs. You can add **hyperlinks** (graphic objects or text you click to jump to other Office documents and intranet or Internet pages) to your Office documents. Office makes it easy to create a Web page without learning HTML, the coding system used to format Web pages. In addition, you can save any document as a Web page to your hard drive just as you would save an Office document. You can also preview how your document will look as a Web page in your Office program or in your browser. Without ever leaving an Office program, you can turn a document into a Web page. Office allows you to work with people around the world as if they were around a conference table.

What You'll Do

Design Web Pages

Open Web Pages

Insert Hyperlinks

Use and Remove Hyperlinks

Enhance Web Pages

Preview Web Pages

Save Documents as Web Pages

Save Documents as Single File Web Pages

Save Slides as Web Graphics

Publish Web Pages

Hold an Online Meeting

Send Documents by E-Mail

Get Documents from the Web

Designing Web Pages

Web pages are multimedia documents that provide information and contain **links** to other documents on the Internet, an intranet, a local network, or a hard disk. These links—also called **hyperlinks**, **hypertext**, or **hypermedia**—are highlighted text or graphics that you click to follow a pathway from one Web page to another. Linked Web pages, often called a **Web site**, are generally related by topic.

Web pages are based on **Hypertext Markup Language** (HTML)—a simple coding system used to format Web pages. A browser program, such as Microsoft Internet Explorer, interprets these special codes to determine how a certain Web page should be displayed. Different codes mark the size, color, style, and placement of text and graphics as well as which words and graphics should be marked as hyperlinks and to what files they link.

As the World Wide Web becomes a household word and many organizations, including medical associations, publishers, healthcare providers, and pharmaceutical companies create intranet and Internet Web sites—both of which use HTML documents—the ability to create, read, open, and save HTML documents directly from Office becomes an important time saver.

HTML and Office 2003

Office 2003 uses HTML as a companion file format. That means that Word, Excel, Access, PowerPoint, and Publisher all can save and read HTML documents without any compatibility problems. Additionally, Office recognizes the .html filename extension as accurately as it does those for its own programs (.doc, .xls, .mdb, .ppt, and .pub). In other words, you can use the familiar Office tools and features you use to create printed documents to create and share Web documents. Anyone with a browser can view your Office Web documents.

Converting Documents to Web Pages

In addition to creating Web pages from scratch in Office programs, you can also save any existing document as a Web page to your hard disk, intranet, or Web server. These HTML documents preserve such features as styles, revision marks, PivotTables, linked and embedded objects, and so forth. When the layout or an item in your document can't be converted to HTML in exactly the same way, a dialog box explains what items will be changed and how.

Each Office file saved as HTML creates a handful of individual files. For example, each graphic, worksheet, or slide in an Office document becomes its own file. To make it easy to manage these multiple files, Office creates a folder with the same name, and in the same location, as the original HTML file for the document. Any Office document saved as a Web page consists of an HTML file and a folder that stores supporting files, such as a file for each graphic, worksheet, slide, and so on.

Opening Web Pages

After saving an Office document as a Web page, you can open the Web page, an HTML file, in Office. This allows you to quickly and easily switch from HTML to the standard program format and back again without losing any formatting or functionality. For example, if you create a formatted chart in a PowerPoint presentation, save the presentation file as a Web page, and then reopen the Web page in PowerPoint, the chart will look the same as the original chart in PowerPoint. Office preserves the original formatting and functionality of the file.

Open an Office Web Page

1. Click the Open button on the Standard toolbar.

2. Click the Files Of Type list arrow, and then click All Web Pages.

3. Click one of the icons on the Places bar for access to often used folders.

4. If necessary, click the Look In list arrow, and then select the folder where the file is located.

5. Click the name of the file.

6. Click Open.

   To open an Office Web page in your default Web browser, click the Open button list arrow, and then click Open In Browser.

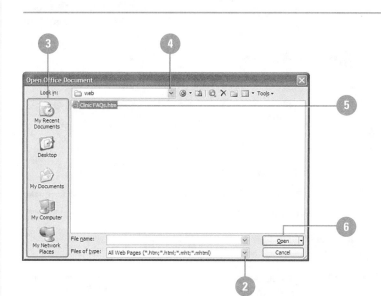

Did You Know?

You can create a blank Web page in Word. In Web Layout view, the New Blank Document button on the Standard toolbar changes to the New Web Page button. Click it to open a new HTML document quickly. Enter text, graphics, and frames as needed.

Inserting Hyperlinks

When you reference information included earlier in a document, you had to duplicate material or add a footnote. Now you can create a **hyperlink**—a graphic object or colored, underlined text that you click to move (or **jump**) to a new location (or **destination**). The destination can be in the same document, another file on your computer or network, or a Web page on your intranet or the Internet. Office inserts an absolute link—a hyperlink that jumps to a fixed location—to an Internet destination. Office inserts a relative link—a hyperlink that changes when the hyperlink and destination paths change—between documents. You must move the hyperlink and destination together to keep the link intact.

Insert a Hyperlink Within a Document

1. Click where you want to insert the hyperlink, or select the text or object you want to use as the hyperlink.

2. Click the Insert Hyperlink button on the Standard toolbar.

3. Click Place In This Document.

4. Click a destination in the document.

   The destination can be a Word heading or bookmark; an Excel cell reference or range name; a PowerPoint slide, slide title, or custom show; or an Access object.

5. Type the text you want to appear as the hyperlink.

6. Click ScreenTip.

7. Type the text you want to appear when someone points to the hyperlink.

8. Click OK.

9. Click OK.

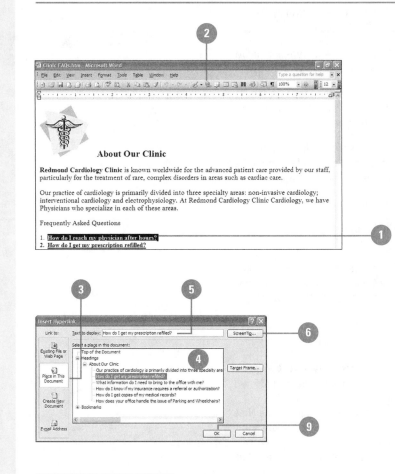

Insert a Hyperlink Between Documents

1. Click where you want to insert the hyperlink, or select the text or object you want to use as the hyperlink.

2. Click the Insert Hyperlink button on the Standard toolbar.

3. Click Existing File Or Web Page.

4. Enter the name and path of the destination file or Web page.

   ◆ Or click the File, Web Page, or Bookmark button; select the file, Web page, or bookmark; and then click OK.

5. Type the text you want to appear as the hyperlink.

6. Click ScreenTip.

7. Type the text you want to appear when someone points to the hyperlink.

8. Click OK.

9. Click OK.

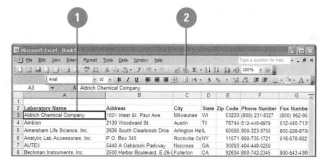

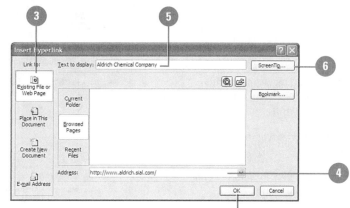

Did You Know?

You can create a hyperlink to send e-mail messages. Click where you want to insert the hyperlink, click the Insert Hyperlink button on the Standard toolbar, click E-Mail Address, enter the recipient's e-mail address, enter a subject, enter the hyperlink display text, and then click OK.

Hyperlinks in Access appear as labels. In Access, a hyperlink appears as a form or report label and uses the Caption property as the display text for the hyperlink.

Using and Removing Hyperlinks

Hyperlinks connect you to information in other documents. Rather than duplicating the important information stored in other documents, you can create hyperlinks to the relevant material. When you click a hyperlink for the first time (during a session), the color of the hyperlink changes, indicating that you have accessed the hyperlink. If a link becomes outdated or unnecessary, you can easily revise or remove it. Office repairs broken links. Whenever you save a document with hyperlinks, Office checks the links and repairs any that aren't working. For example, if a file was moved, Office updates the location.

Use a Hyperlink

1. Position the mouse pointer (which changes to a hand pointer) over any hyperlink.

2. Click the hyperlink or press and hold Ctrl, and then click the hyperlink (in Word).

   Depending on the type of hyperlink, the screen

   ◆ Jumps to a new location within the same document.

   ◆ Jumps to a location on an intranet or Internet Web site.

   ◆ Opens a new file and the program in which it was created.

   ◆ Opens Outlook and displays a new e-mail message.

3. Navigate between open hyperlinked documents with the Web toolbar.

   ◆ Click the Back or Forward button to move between documents.

   ◆ Click the Start Page button to go to your home page.

   ◆ Click the Search The Web button to go to a search page.

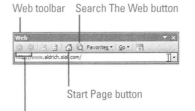

Web toolbar   Search The Web button

Start Page button

Back and Forward buttons

Edit a Hyperlink

① Right-click the hyperlink you want to edit, and then click Edit Hyperlink.

② If you want, change the display text.

③ If you want, click ScreenTip, edit the custom text, and then click OK.

④ If necessary, change the destination.

⑤ Click OK.

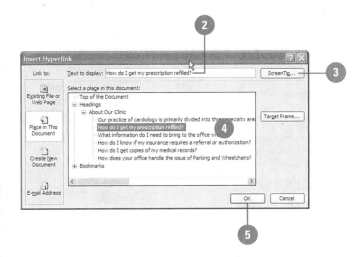

Remove a Hyperlink

① Right-click the hyperlink you want to remove.

② Click Remove Hyperlink.

TIMESAVER *Drag the I-beam pointer across the hyperlink to select it, and then press Ctrl+Shift+F9 to delete a hyperlink.*

③ If necessary, delete the text or object.

Did You Know?

Display the Web toolbar. Click the View menu, point to Toolbars, and then click Web.

Format a hyperlink. You can change the look of a hyperlink just as you do other text—select it and apply attributes. Right-click the hyperlink, click Select Hyperlink, and then use the Bold, Italic, Underline, Font, and Font Size buttons on the Formatting toolbar.

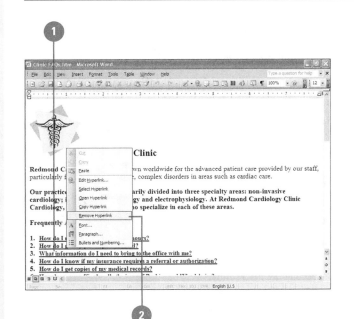

Enhancing Web Pages

A basic Web page usually includes text, graphics, and hyperlinks. You can change the look of your Web site by selecting a **theme**—a pre-designed visual layout that changes text formatting (such as font type, size, format, and color), as well as bullets, backgrounds, colors, and horizontal lines to create a specific mood. Each theme has two color variations: default and vivid. Some themes include animations. You can make your Web site easier to navigate by adding **frames**—separate panes that contain unique content and scroll independently. For example, you might place navigation links in one frame and a home page link in another frame.

Use Themes to Add a Color Scheme in Word or Access

1. Open the Word document or Data Access page in Design view to which you want to add a theme.

2. Click the Format menu, and then click Theme.

3. Click a theme to view a sample.

4. Select the Vivid Colors check box to view a theme color variation.

5. Click OK.

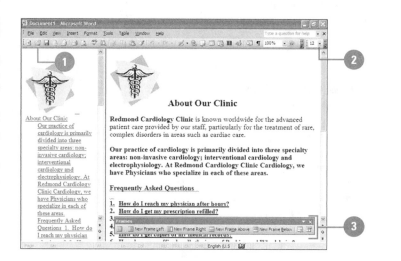

Add or Remove Frames in Word

1. Open the Word document to which you want to add or remove a frame.

2. Right-click any toolbar, and then click Frames to display the Frames toolbar.

3. Click the appropriate button to add or remove a frame.

Previewing Web Pages

After you create or enhance a Web page, you should preview it in a Web browser, such as Microsoft Internet Explorer, or in the Office program to make sure others see your Web page the same way you do. **Web Page Preview** displays the open file in your default browser even if you haven't saved it yet. **Web Layout view** shows you how a document will be displayed on the Web. If the document includes formatting or layouts that cannot be achieved in HTML, Word switches to an HTML layout that closely matches the original look.

Preview a Web Page in a Browser

1. In an Office program, open the Web page you want to preview.

2. Click the File menu, and then click Web Page Preview.

3. Scroll to view the entire page, click hyperlinks to test them, and so forth.

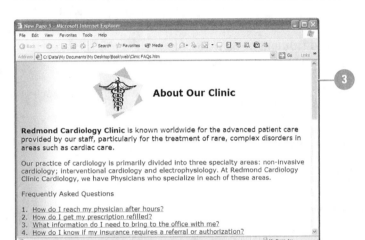

Preview a Web Page in Word

1. Open the Word document you want to preview.

2. Click the Web Layout View button.

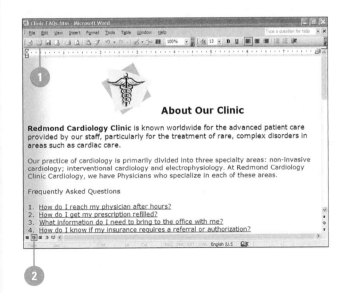

Did You Know?

Office takes advantage of Web technologies. Office takes advantage of Internet Explorer support for HTML and Cascading Style Sheets to bring the familiar Office look and feel to HTML documents. For example, underlining and tables in HTML format appear nearly identical to the Office document format.

Saving Documents as Web Pages

No matter what Office program you are working in, you can save your document as a Web page. Then others can use a browser to view and even edit your document over the Internet or an intranet. You can continue to open and work with the file from its original Office program. Web pages use **Hypertext Markup Language** (HTML)—a simple coding system that specifies the formats a browser uses to display the document. Any Office document saved as a Web page consists of an HTML file and a folder that stores supporting files, such as a file for each graphic, worksheet, slide, and so on. Office selects the appropriate graphic format for you based on the image's content.

Save an Office Document as a Web Page

1. Open the Office document you want to save as a Web page.

2. Click the File menu, and then click Save As Web Page.

3. Select the drive and folder in which to store the file.

4. Type a name for the file.

5. Click Save.

   The Web page is saved in the selected folder, and the supporting graphics and related files are saved in another folder with the name of the Web page.

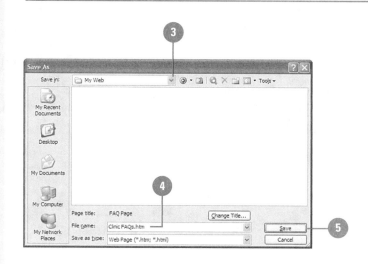

Did You Know?

You can save your Calendar in Outlook as a Web page. Switch to the Calendar view you want to save, click the File menu, click Save As Web Page, select the duration and publishing options you want, enter a title and file name, and then click Save.

Save an Excel Worksheet as an Interactive Web Page

1. Open the Excel workbook you want to save as a Web page.

2. Click the File menu, and then click Save As Web Page.

3. Select the drive and folder in which to store the file.

4. Select an option to save the entire workbook or the selection.

5. Select the Add Interactivity check box if you want others to be able to edit the file.

6. Type a name for the file.

7. Click Save.

   The Web page is saved in the selected folder, and the supporting graphics and related files are saved in another folder with the name of the Web page.

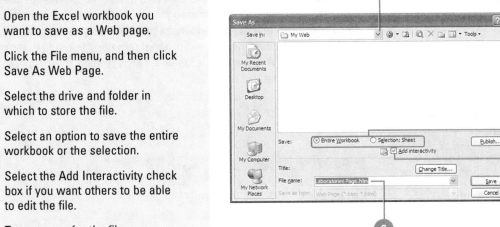

See Also

See "Creating a Data Access Page Using a Wizard" on page 340 for information on creating Web pages in Access.

Saving Documents as Single File Web Pages

A single file Web page saves all the elements of a Web site, including text and graphics, into a single file. When you save a document as a single file Web page, all the Web site elements are stored together in one file in the MHTML format, which is supported by Internet Explorer 4.0 or later. A single file makes it easy to manage the Web site. When you move the Web site, you don't need to worry about forgetting linked files stored in another folder. A single file also makes it easy to send an entire Web site as an e-mail attachment.

Save an Office Document as a Single File Web Page

1. Open the Office document you want to save as a Web page.

2. Click the File menu, and then click Save As Web Page.

3. Click the Save As Type list arrow, and then click Single File Web Page.

4. Select the drive and folder in which to store the file.

5. Type a name for the file.

6. Click Save.

   The Web page is saved as a single file.

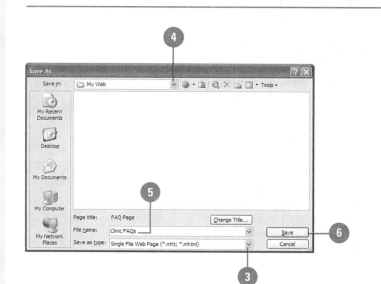

> **Did You Know?**
>
> **You can reduce Web page size by filtering HTML in Word.** You can save Web pages in filtered HTML to reduce the file size. In Word, click the File menu, click Save As Web Page, click the Save As File Type list arrow, click Web Page, Filtered, and then click Save.

Saving Slides as Web Graphics

As you develop a Web site, you can incorprate slides from any of your PowerPoint presentations. You can save any slide in a presentation in the GIF or JPEG Web graphic format. **Graphics Interchange Format (GIF)** is a form of compression for line drawings or other artwork. Office converts to GIF such images as logos, graphs, line drawings, and specific colored objects. **Joint Photographic Experts Group (JPEG)** is a high-quality form of compression for continuous tone images, such as photographs. Office converts to JPEG such images as photographs or other images that have many shades of colors.

Save a PowerPoint Slide as a Web Graphic

1. Open the PowerPoint presentation with the slide you want to save as a Web graphic, and then display the slide.

2. Click the File menu, and then click Save As Web Page.

3. Click the Save As Type list arrow, and then click GIF Graphics Interchange Format or JPEG File Interchange Format.

4. Select the drive and folder in which to store the file.

5. Type a name for the file.

6. Click Save.

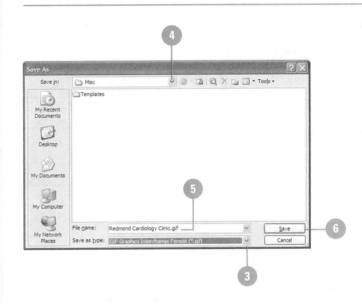

See Also

See "Saving a File with Different Formats" on page 12 for information on saving files with different file formats.

Publishing Web Pages

At times, you'll want to publish a copy of your current Office document in HTML format directly to a **Web server** (a computer on the Internet or intranet that stores Web pages) so others can view and manipulate your data. Publishing to a Web server is as simple as saving a file. With the **Office Web Components**, you can elect to let anyone using Internet Explorer 4.01 or later interact with your data from Excel or Access. Any data published to a Web page can be returned to its Office program for additional analysis and tracking.

Publish PowerPoint Slides as a Web Page

1 Open the presentation with the item you want to publish.

2 Click the File menu, and then click Save As Web Page.

3 Click Publish.

4 Select the options you want to include in the Web page.

5 Select the browsers that you want others to be able to use to view your Web page.

6 Click Change, type a title for the Web page, and then click OK.

7 Type the folder and file name for the published Web page.

8 If you want, select the Open Published Web Page In Browser check box to preview the page in a browser.

9 Click Publish.

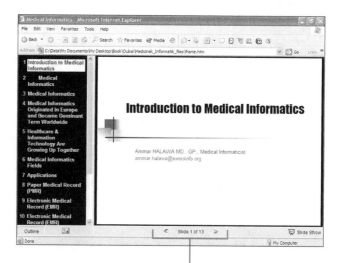

Click the buttons on the navigation bar to move from slide to slide.

> **Did You Know?**
>
> *You can manage your Web files.* With access privileges, you can add, move, or delete files stored on a Web server from the Windows Explorer just as you would with a file server.

Publish Excel Worksheet Items as a Web Page

1. Open the workbook with the item you want to publish.

2. Click the File menu, and then click Save As Web Page.

3. Click Publish.

4. Select the items you want to publish in the Web page.

5. Click Change, type a title for the Web page, and then click OK.

   Click Yes or No to apply the rule to the current contents of the folder.

6. Type the folder and file name for the published Web page.

7. If you want, select the Open Published Web Page In Browser check box to preview the page in a browser.

8. Click Publish.

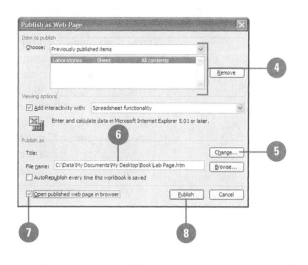

19

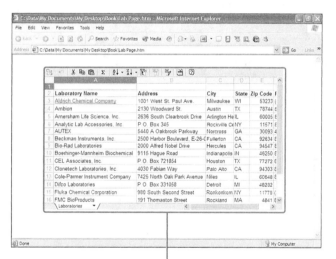

Published worksheet

Did You Know?

Office Web components provide interactivity. The Spreadsheet component provides basic spreadsheet functionality so users can enter data, create formulas, recalculate, sort, filter, and add basic formatting. The Chart component provides automatic updates to charts as the underlying data changes. The PivotTable component is created either in Excel or on a Data Access page and provides efficient analysis of data by enabling users to browse, sort, filter, group, and total report data.

Holding an Online Meeting

What's the most convenient way to meet with fellow clinicians from around the world? **NetMeeting**—a conferencing program for meeting and collaborating over the Internet or a corporate intranet. Participants share and exchange information as if they were in one room. The **host** starts the meeting and controls access to the document. When the host allows editing, participants can work on the document one at a time. Otherwise, they cannot make changes, but they can see any changes the host makes. All participants can talk to each other, video conference, share programs, collaborate on documents, send files, exchange messages in Chat, transfer files, and draw in the Whiteboard.

Schedule a Meeting

1. Click the Tools menu, point to Online Collaboration, and then click Schedule Meeting.

2. Enter participants' names or e-mail addresses, a subject, and the meeting location.

3. Click Browse, and then double-click a document you want to send.

4. Select a start and end date and time.

5. Type a message.

6. Click the Send button.

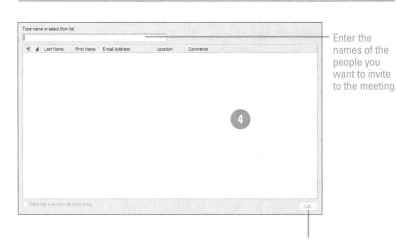

Hold a Meeting

1. Open the document you want to share.

2. Click the Tools menu, point to Online Collaboration, and then click Meet Now.

3. If this is your first meeting, enter your personal information, select a server, and then click OK.

4. Select the participants for the meeting, and then click Call.

Enter the names of the people you want to invite to the meeting.

Click to start NetMeeting running in the background.

Collaborate in an Online Meeting

1 As the host, click the Allow Others To Edit button on the Online Meeting toolbar.

2 When collaboration is turned on, click anywhere in the document to gain control. If you are a participant, double-click anywhere in the document to gain control.

3 Click the Allow Others To Edit button again to turn off the collaboration, or press Esc if you don't have control of the document.

Participate in an Online Meeting

◆ Use the buttons on the Online Meeting toolbar to participate in an online meeting.

Did You Know?

You can join an online meeting. If you receive an online meeting call, click Accept in the Join Meeting dialog box. If you receive an Outlook reminder for the meeting, click Start This NetMeeting (host), or Join This NetMeeting (participant). To receive an Outlook reminder to join a meeting, you need to have accepted the meeting from an e-mail message.

Online Meeting Toolbar

Button	Description
	Allows the host to invite additional participants to the online meeting
	Allows the host to remove a participant from the online meeting
	Allows participants to edit and control the presentation during the online meeting
	Allows participants to send messages in a Chat session during the online meeting
	Allows participants to draw or type on the Whiteboard during the online meeting
	Allows either the host to end the online meeting for the group or a participant to disconnect

Sending Documents by E-Mail

The quickest way to send a copy of a document is to send an electronic copy by e-mail. Without having to open your e-mail program and attach the file, you can send any Office document to others from within that program. The E-Mail button in your Office document opens a new message in your e-mail program and inserts a standard message header at the top of the open file so you can send it as an e-mail message. When you send a document in an e-mail message, the recipient can only review the document. With an attachment, the recipient can open, modify, and save changes to the document.

Send a Document in an E-Mail Message

1. Open the worksheet you want to send.

2. Click the File menu, point to Send To, and then click Mail Recipient.

3. Click the To or Cc button.

4. Select the contacts to whom you want the message sent.

5. Click OK.

6. Type introduction text.

7. Click the Send This Sheet button.

Send a Document as an E-Mail Attachment

1. Open the workbook you want to send.

2. Click the File menu, point to Send To, and then click Mail Recipient (As Attachment). Your default e-mail program opens, displaying a new e-mail message window.

3. Click the To or Cc button, select the contacts to whom you want the message sent, and then click OK.

4. If you want, type a related message.

5. Click the Send button.

Did You Know?

You can close an e-mail message without sending it. If you decide not to send the message, just click the E-Mail button on the Standard toolbar to hide the message header.

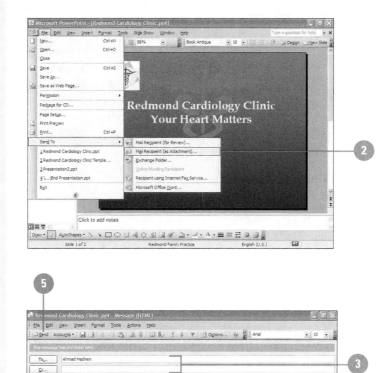

Getting Documents from the Web

File Transfer Protocol (FTP) is an inexpensive and efficient way to transfer files between your computer and others on the Internet. You can download or receive from another computer any kind of file, including text, graphics, sound, and video files. To download a file, you need an ID and password to identify who you are. Anonymous FTP sites are open to anyone; they usually use anonymous as an ID and your full e-mail address as a password. You can also save the FTP site address to revisit the site later.

Add or Modify FTP Locations

① Click the Open button on the Standard toolbar.

② Click the Look In list arrow, and then click Add/Modify FTP Locations.

③ Type the complete address for an FTP site.

④ Type your e-mail address as the password.

⑤ Click Add.

⑥ Click OK.

Access an FTP Site

① Click the Open button on the Standard toolbar.

② Click the Look In list arrow, and then click the FTP site you want to log in to.

③ Select a Log On As option.

④ Enter a password (your E-mail address or personal password).

⑤ Click OK.

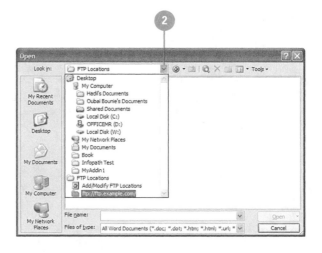

Working Together on Office Documents

Introduction

Healthcare professionals don't work in isolation—they form care teams. They share information, communicate, and collaborate. Microsoft SharePoint technology, known as SharePoint Team Services, is a collection of products and services which provide the ability for people to engage in communication, document and file sharing, calendar events, sending alerts, tasks planning, and collaborative discussions in a single community solution. SharePoint enables organizations to develop an intelligent application which connects their personnel, teams, and information so that users can be part of a Knowledge Community.

Before you can use SharePoint Team Services, SharePoint needs to be set up and configured on a Windows 2003 Server by your network administrator or Internet service provider.

SharePoint is integrated into Office 2003 and enables you to share data and documents using the Shared Workspace task pane directly from Office Word 2003, Office Excel 2003, or Office PowerPoint 2003. The Shared Workspace task pane allows you to see the list of team members collaborating on the current project, find out who is online, send an instant message, and review tasks and other resources. You can use the Shared Workspace task pane to create one or more document workspaces where you can collect, organize, modify, share, and discuss Office documents. The Shared Workspace task pane displays information related to the document workspaces stored on SharePoint Team Services. In addition, you can also use SharePoint to send a document as a "live" attachment (which is saved as a document workspace in SharePoint) to an Outlook e-mail message. When a recipient receives a "live" attachment, he or she can connect to the document workspace.

Viewing SharePoint Team Services

Microsoft SharePoint displays the contents of its home page so you can work efficiently with your site. The available pages are: The Home Page, Manage Content Page, Manage Users Page, Changing your Portal Site Navigation, Changing Settings, and Site Settings. You can navigate within the site by clicking on each of the links within the home page. Certain Administrative Access rights are needed in order to view these pages.

Home Page view is the first page your users see when they access the URL for Microsoft SharePoint Server. If you are within a Windows 2003 Active Domain and have a Domain Account, you will not be prompted to type in your user credentials and password. If you do not have an account you will be asked to type in your credentials to have the page display your SharePoint Site. Please contact your Systems Administrator if you do not have access to the SharePoint Server.

Documents and Lists Page view allows you to manage content to your SharePoint Site. You can create Portal sites, a Document Library, Upload Graphic Images in an Image Library Site, Create Calender Events, Create an Address Book of Contacts, Setup Project Events, Create a Web Discussion site, and setup Surveys. Within your Document and Lists page you will be able to administer your content to provide users with content management capabilities.

Manage Users Page view allows you to add users to your SharePoint Site. If their email address is located within their Domain Account on Windows 2003, then SharePoint will email the users you created and invite them to join in to the SharePoint Server. From the Manage Users Page you can add, delete, and change the permissions of a user for your site.

Home Page

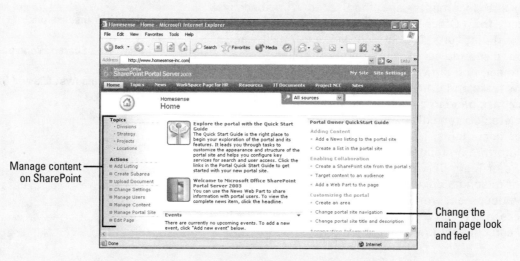

Manage content on SharePoint

Change the main page look and feel

Documents and Lists Page

Adds a new portal site

Adds documents to the site

Adds graphics to the site

Manage Users

Adds new users

List of users

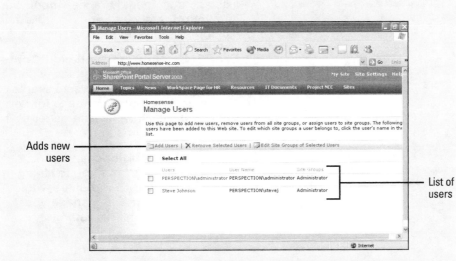

Administering SharePoint Team Services

Administering Microsoft SharePoint is easy within the site settings. The available pages are: The Home Page, Manage Content Page, Manage Users Page, Changing your Portal Site Navigation, Changing Settings, and Site Settings. You can navigate within the site by clicking on each of the links within the home page. Certain Administrative Access rights are needed in order to view these pages.

Changing your Portal Site Navigation Page gives you a hierarchy structure to make changes to other portal sites within SharePoint. If you want to move your site to the top-level within SharePoint or Modify your sub-level pages, you can do so with SharePoint Portal Site Navigation Page.

Quick Launch bar

Location of the site logs

Name of the SharePoint server

Changing Settings Page allows you to swiftly customize the look and feel of your portal site. You can change the title, description, and logo for the site. You can change the URL for creating sites based on the published templates for your site. You can also add a change management process by having the site approved by a manager before being published, and allowing you to change your contact information for your site.

Site Settings Page has four different categories: General Settings, Portal Site Content, Search Settings and Indexed Content, and User Profile, Audiences, and Personal Sites.

- ◆ **General Settings** offers additional security features, which allows you to manage the alerts settings, change your default SMTP e-mail server, change the location of your SharePoint Site, and modify the Regional Language Settings to your site.

- ◆ **Portal Site Content** allows you to manage the site structure, view your site lists and document libraries, import data into your SharePoint Server, and add link listings to your site.

- ◆ **Search Settings and Indexed Content** allows you to create Meta tags within your SharePoint Server, create search crawler to investigate your site for new key words which will create better search results within your site.

- ◆ **User Profile, Audiences, and Personal Sites** allows you to change and manage your user profiles within your site. You can also manage your audiences and personal settings.

Changing Settings

Change publishing
settings

Change home
page settings

Change template
settings

Change Search and
Index results

Change site
navigation

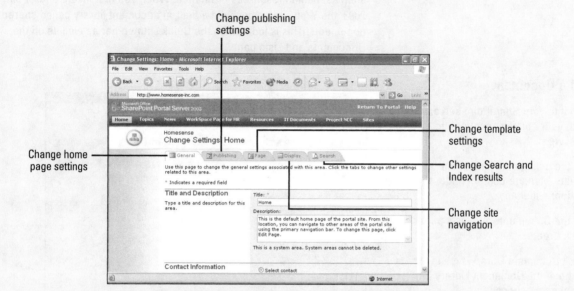

Site Settings

Administer the
SharePoint site

Administer portal
site content

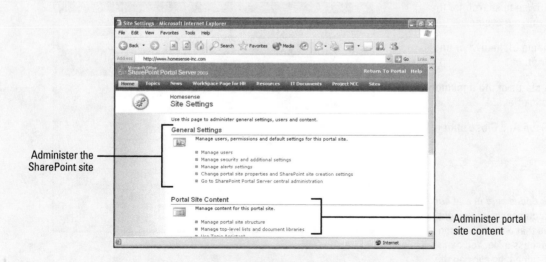

Storing Documents in the Library

A SharePoint **Document Library** is a central depository of files you can share with other employees, team members and permissible members with access. Within the Document Library you can create a list of common documents, such as policies and procedures, drug references, practice guidelines, and organization-wide documents for departments such as, human resources or finance. When you first install SharePoint 2003, the Web site comes with a built-in document library called shared documents. This is located on the Quick Launch bar as well as on the Documents and Lists page.

Upload a Document

1. Log into your SharePoint server with your domain account and password.

2. On the main home page, click Create Manage Content under the Actions Sidebar.

3. On the Documents and Lists page, click Create.

4. Click Document Library, type in the name of the Document Library for creating a new page.

5. Click Upload Document.

6. Type the location of the document, or click Browse to search for the document on your system.

7. Type the name of the owner and a brief description.

8. Select the status of the document, and then click Save.

9. Click the Save And Close button.

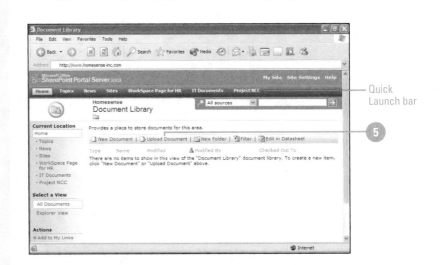

Quick Launch bar

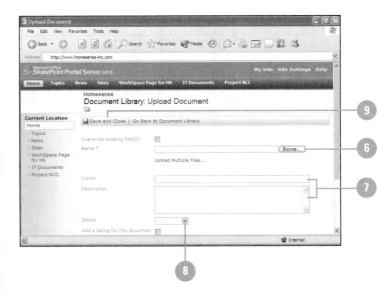

> ### Did You Know?
>
> **You can check documents in and out.**
> SharePoint's document management system ensures that only one person at a time can access a file. You can check out a document by clicking the Content Menu in the document library and then clicking Check Out.

Viewing Team Members

After you have setup a portal page, you need to specify a user access list to the site. Specifying a user access list controls who can access the site as well as as who has administrative privileges. With integration to Microsoft Active Directory, users can be managed with the same groups as your domain. The access will allow your users to perform specific action in your site by assigning them to the appropriate groups.

Add New Members to the Site

1. Log into your SharePoint server with your domain account and password.

2. On the main home page, click Give User Access To The Portal.

3. On the Manager Users page, click Add Users.

4. Type the name of their domain account, and then click Next.

5. Click the type of permissions you want to give this user:

   ◆ **Reader.** Gives the user read only access to the portal site.

   ◆ **Contributor.** Gives the user write access to the document libraries and lists.

   ◆ **Web Designer.** Gives the user the ability to create lists and document libraries and customize the overall look and feel of the site.

   ◆ **Administrator.** Gives the user full access of the portal site.

   ◆ **Content Manager.** Gives the user the ability to manage lists, libraries, sites and moderate the discussions.

   ◆ **Member.** Gives the user the ability to personalize the portal site content and create lists.

6. Click Next, fill out any additional information, and then click Finish.

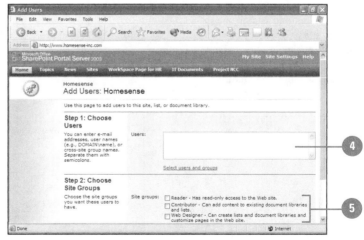

Setting Up Alerts

An Alert notifies you when there is new information which has been changed on the portal site. You can customize your areas of interests and define when you want to be notified after the site has been updated. You can define an alert to track new matches to a search query, changes to the site page, or a new site addition.

Create Your E-Mail Alert

1 Log into your SharePoint server with your domain account and password.

2 In a Portal Site, click Alert Me.

3 Define your delivery options, and then click Next.

4 Click Advanced Options, if you want to set up filters.

5 Click OK.

Did You Know?

You can use the following filter categories to be alerted with: search queries, document and listings, areas, new listings, sites added to the site directory, sharepoint lists and libraries, list items, portal site users, and backward compatible document library folders.

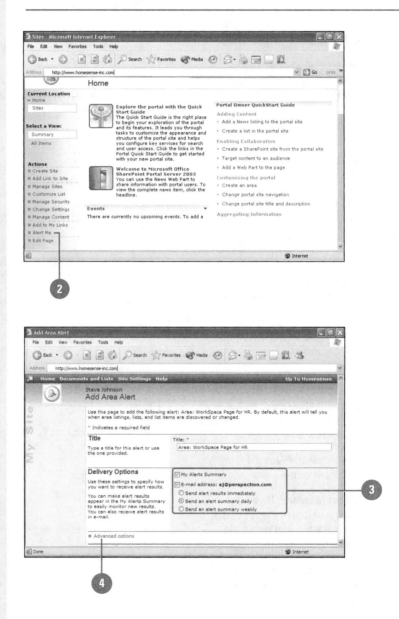

Assigning Tasks

Assigning a task is another way you can use SharePoint to collaborate on the site. By creating a task, you can manage your team with status updates and a central way for you to manage the effectiveness of your team's work. Since this is a Web based system, everyone can access this with a simple Web browser.

Add a Task Item to your Site

1. Log into your SharePoint server with your domain account and password.

2. On the main home page, click Create Manage Content under the Actions Sidebar.

3. Click Create, and then click Tasks.

4. Type the name of the task, add in an optional description, click Yes if you want to add the task to the menu bar, and then click Create.

5. Click New Item.

6. Type the title, set the priority, status and completion percentage, assign your resource, add a description, and then set your due date.

7. Click the Save And Close button.

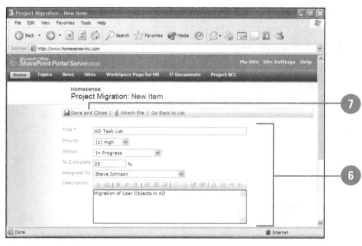

> ### Did You Know?
>
> **You can use the upload button to add an attachment.** A general rule of thumb would be to keep your attachments under 1 MB, however, unless your administrator has set rights on your site, you are free to upload as much as you want.

Creating an Event

Creating an event allows you to send out notices on upcoming meetings, deadlines, and other important events. This is helpful if you need to send out information to a wide range of people or in a project you are working on. If you are looking to set up a meeting to a large group of people you may want to set up an event which is seen by everyone who logs in.

Set Up New Events

1. Log into your SharePoint server with your domain account and password.

2. On the main home page, click Create Manage Content under the Actions Sidebar.

3. Click Create, and then click Events.

4. Type the name of the event, add in an optional description, click Yes if you want to add the event to the menu bar, and then click Create.

5. Click New Item.

6. Type the event title, select a begin and end event time, a description, the location, and then select a reoccurrence option.

7. Click the Save And Close button.

> ### Did You Know?
>
> ***You can use a new collaboration feature in Outlook 2003 called meeting Workspace.*** Meeting Workspace allows you to gather information and organize everyone when you create a schedule meeting event. To create a Meeting Workspace in Outlook 2003, prepare a calender event and setup your attendees for the event. Then click on Meeting Workspace to link this to your SharePoint Server. You may need to type in the URL of your SharePoint server. Please get this from your System Administrator.

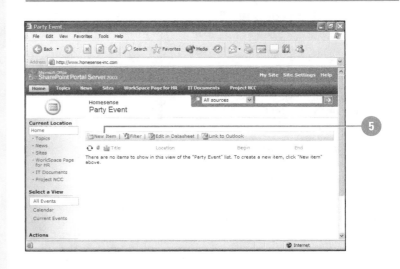

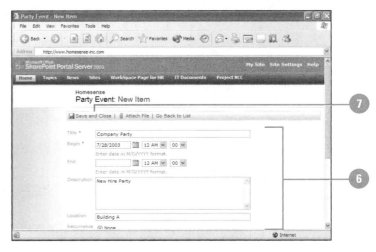

Link to Events in Outlook

1. On the Events Page, click Link To Outlook.

2. If a security dialog box appears asking for your approval prior to add a folder, click Yes.

   You will be prompted to type in your credentials of your user account.

3. Type in your Domain User credentials and password, and then, click OK.

4. Click Other Calendars to view your SharePoint calendar.

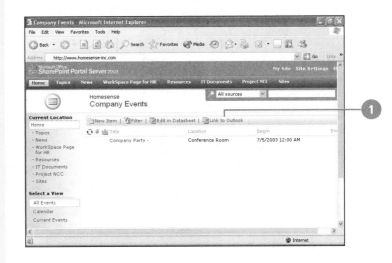

Did You Know?

You will not be able to change the events in your SharePoint calendar folder within Outlook 2003. You will only have read access rights within Outlook 2003. To change the SharePoint calendar information, return to your SharePoint Site and modify the information under your Events Site.

20

Creating Contacts

Do your team members ever need to find each other's cell phone number or the phone number of a referring physician? You can create a contact list when you want to have a central database of your team information. You will have the ability to manage information about contacts, vendors, and employees that your team has involvement with.

Create a Contact List

① Log into your SharePoint server with your domain account and password.

② On the main home page, click Create Manage Content under the Actions Sidebar.

③ Click Create, and then click Contacts.

④ Type the name of the contact, add in an optional description, click Yes if you want to add the contacts list to the menu bar, and then click Create.

⑤ Click New Item.

⑥ Type the contact name, and then add in all appropriate information on your contact.

⑦ Click the Save And Close button.

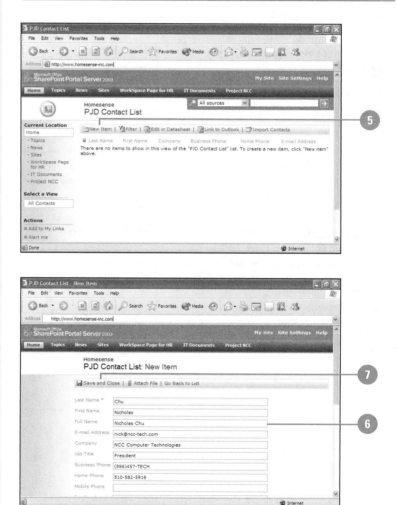

Link to Contacts in Outlook

1. On the Contacts Page, click Link To Outlook.

2. If a security dialog box appears asking for your approval prior to add a folder, click Yes.

   You will be prompted to type in your credentials of your user account.

3. Type your Domain User credentials and password, and then, click OK.

4. Click Other Contacts to view your SharePoint contacts.

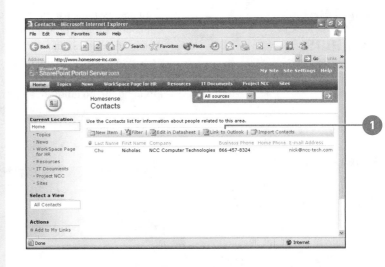

Did You Know?

You will not be able to change the contact information in your SharePoint contacts folder within Outlook 2003. You will only have read access rights within Outlook 2003. To change the SharePoint contacts information, return to your SharePoint Site and modify the information under your Contacts Site.

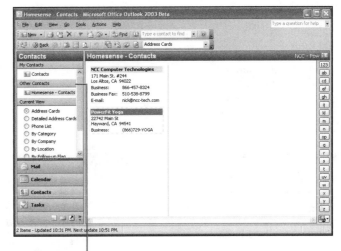

Holding Web Discussions

Web discussions are threaded discussions which allows users to collaborate together in a Web environment. Users can add and view discussions items, add in documents during the discussions and carry on conversations. Since the discussions are entered into a different area from the shared document, users can modify the document without effecting the collaborative discussion. Users can add changes to read only documents and allows multiple users to create and edit discussions items simultaneously.

Hold a Web Discussion

1. Log into your SharePoint server with your domain account and password.

2. On the main home page, click Create Manage Content under the Actions Sidebar.

3. Click Create, and the click Discussion Boards.

4. Type the name of the Discussion Board, add in an optional description, click Yes if you want to add this to the menu bar, and then click Create.

5. Click New Discussion.

6. Type the subject name, and then add in all appropriate information on your discussion.

7. Click the Save And Close button.

Working with Shared Workspace

Using Shared Workspace icons allow you to connect to your SharePoint Server in a Office 2003 program. Each icon displays different information on your document. Users can view the status of a document, see the availability of a document, display properties of a document, and list additional resources, folders, and access rights of a document. You can also show the current tasks which are assigned for your document, display the online team members of your group, and display the workspace information.

Use Shared Workspace in an Office 2003 Program

1. Log into your SharePoint server with your domain account and password.

2. In a Office 2003 program, click on the Tools menu, and then click Shared Workspace.

   If you open Shared Workspace for the first time you may be prompted to create a new workspace area.

3. Use the Shared Workspace Navigation bar tools.

   - **Status.** Displays the current checked-in/checked-out status of your current document.

   - **Members.** Shows you who is online from your Team Members Group.

   - **Tasks.** Shows you the current tasks assigned for this current document and the completion status.

   - **Documents.** Displays the name and workspace of the selected document.

   - **Links.** Displays additional resources, folders, and lists the access of files.

   - **Document Info.** Displays the author of the document and the properties of the document.

Documents

Status   Tasks   Links

Document Information

Members

20

Installing Windows 2003 and SharePoint Server 2003

In order for you to install the new version of SharePoint, you must Install Windows 2003 Server. Windows 2003 Server uses the new .NET Architecture Internet Information Server (IIS) 6.0, Microsoft SMTP (Simple Mail Transport Protocol) Service and Microsoft SQL Server 2000 Desktop Engine (MSDE 2000) or Microsoft SQL Server 2000 Enterprise or Standard Edition (64-bit), with Microsoft SQL Server 2000 SP3 or later.

Install SharePoint server

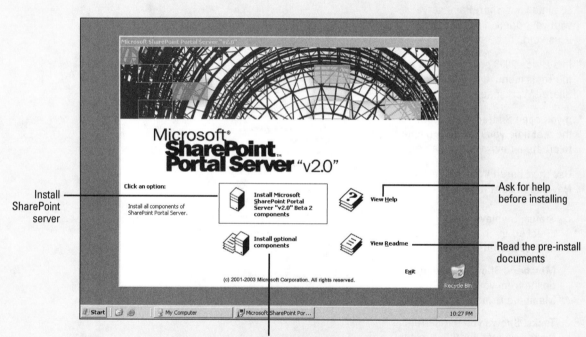

Ask for help before installing

Read the pre-install documents

Install database and additional components

Organizing Notes with OneNote

21

Introduction

Microsoft Office OneNote 2003 might seem at first glance like little more than a digital notepad—a place to scribble notes and draw pictures. That's not entirely incorrect. OneNote can function just like a yellow legal pad. You can take notes, draw pictures, highlight, and scratch out text. However, OneNote is much more. OneNote enables you to flag important items within your notes and search for them later. You can create detailed multilevel outlines, gather and paste research information from a variety of sources, insert images, move notes around between pages and sections, and create Outlook tasks directly from your notes. You can integrate handwriting, drawing, audio, and video, all in one place for easy search and access.

Think of your OneNote notebook as the electronic equivalent to a paper notebook. You can set up your OneNote notebook in any way that you like. Notes on OneNote are entered on **pages**. A page can store any piece or pieces of information, such as a patient encounter, a portion of an article, or lecture notes. Pages are organized into **sections**. Sections help you organize notes on a particular subject and quickly access them by clicking a section tab near the top of the current page. Use **folders** to group sections together, such as to gather prior year notes or notes about a separate clinic at which you practice. The **Notebook** is where all your folders, sections, and note pages are stored.

Viewing the OneNote Window

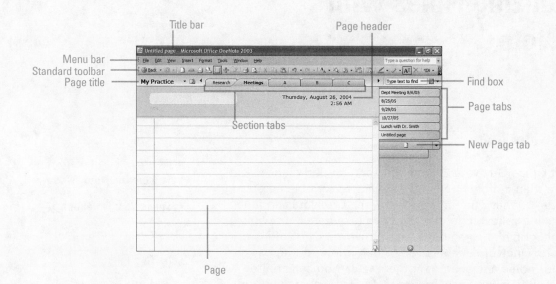

Title bar: The title bar displays the title of the current page.

Menu bar: The menu bar provides the menus or commands you use to accomplish your tasks in OneNote.

Standard toolbar: The Standard toolbar provides buttons you click to quickly execute commands. You can customize the toolbars.

Find box: The Find box is where you enter text and search on notes containing this text.

Section tabs: Section tabs represent different sections in your OneNote notebook, and are convenient for keeping pages about the same topic together. Each section is actually a separate .one file.

Page tabs: Page tabs represent the pages in a section. The tab displays the title of the page. If you do not create a title for the page, the page tab is labeled with the first typed or handwritten note that you enter on the page, by default.

Page: The page is the large white surface that provides a free-form note-taking space. You can take notes by clicking and typing anywhere on the page or, if you are using a Tablet PC, by placing your pen on any spot on the page and writing. As you take notes, the page expands horizontally and vertically to accommodate your notes.

New Page tab: Clicking on the new page tab enables you to quickly add a new page at the end of the current section.

Page header: The page header is the colored section above the page. The page header contains the title area and the automatic date and time stamp. The page header always remains visible at the top of the page, no matter how much your page expands.

Page title: The page title is part of the page header and is displayed in the page tab.

Expanding Your Notebook

OneNote is very flexible in allowing you to capture and organize your notes any way you prefer. You take notes in the pages in each section of your OneNote notebook. Each page is made up of a page header and the main note-taking area of the page. Pages can contain subpages, which are additional pages with smaller tabs than the primary pages. By adding several subpages to a page, you can create groups of pages, enabling you to further organize your notes.

Add a Page of Notes

1. Click the Insert menu.

2. Click New Page.

   A new page is inserted at the end of the current section.

3. Click the page title area and type a title for your page.

4. Notice the automatic date and time stamp, and click it to change it if needed.

5. Click anywhere on the page and start typing (or handwriting) notes.

6. Click on another area of the page to enter another note. You can use formatting as well.

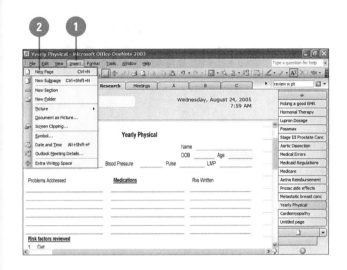

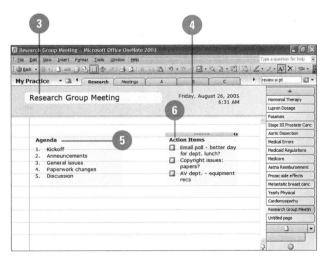

21

Add a Subpage

1. Display the page for which you want to create a subpage.

2. Click the Insert menu, and then click New Subpage.

   A new subpage is created with the same header as the page and a smaller page tab.

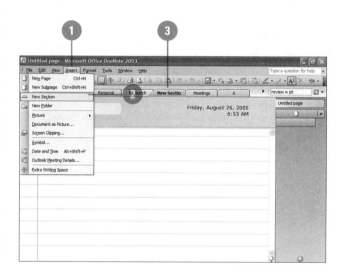

Add a Section or a Folder

1. Click the Insert menu.

2. Click New Section or New Folder.

   A new section or folder is created after the current section.

3. Right-click on the new section or folder to rename it.

Rearranging Notes

You will notice that if you close and open OneNote, it preserves the order of pages, sections, and folders. You can easily rearrange those, however, to group notes about a particular topic together, for example. OneNote will keep the new order of your notes.

Change the Order of Pages

1. Point to the tab of the page that you want to move.

2. Hold the mouse button down, and drag to the right.

3. Notice the small arrow to the right of the page tab, which serves as an indicator of where the page will appear when you release the mouse button.

4. Drag the mouse pointer to the location where you want to move the page, keeping an eye on the small arrow. Release the mouse pointer when you reach the new location.

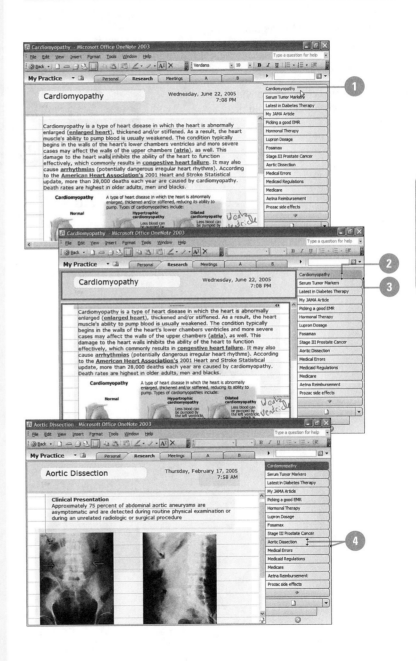

Change the Order of Sections or Folders

1. Right-click a section or folder tab.

2. Click Move on the shortcut menu.

3. Select a location for the section or folder.

4. Click Move.

5. You can also click Create New Folder to create a new folder.

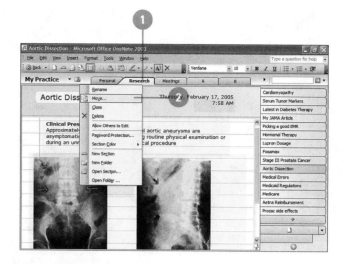

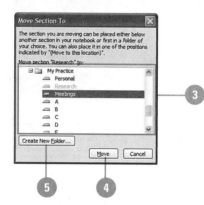

Flipping Through Pages

Much like you can flip through the pages in a paper notebook, you can also flip through the pages in a OneNote section to quickly review their contents.

Flip Through Pages

1. Click a page tab, and hold down the mouse button. You will see the content of the current page.

2. Hold down the mouse button, and move the pointer over to another page tab to display its contents.

3. Repeat as needed. Release the mouse button only after you are finished flipping through your notes.

Inserting Pictures and Documents

You can easily import pictures, documents, and files into OneNote. This enables you to annotate them as part of your notes. For example, if you have a file with an X-ray image, you can incorporate it into your notes and annotate it as you prepare for a presentation or lecture. Note that if you insert a document, such as a Word or Excel document, OneNote creates an image of that document and inserts it as a graphic. OneNote will not be able to retrieve such a graphic by searching on its textual content. However, you can add your own text description to the graphic to help you search for and find it later.

Insert a Picture

1. Click the Insert menu.

2. Point to Picture.

3. Click From File.

4. Open the folder with the picture you want to insert.

5. Click the picture you want to use.

6. Click Insert.

7. You can optionally annotate the picture after inserting it.

> ### Did You Know?
>
> **You can insert pictures directly from a scanner or a digital camera.** Follow the same steps above but in step 3, click From Scanner or Camera. This is particularly useful for taking pictures of patients or scanning documents received by mail and adding them to OneNote.

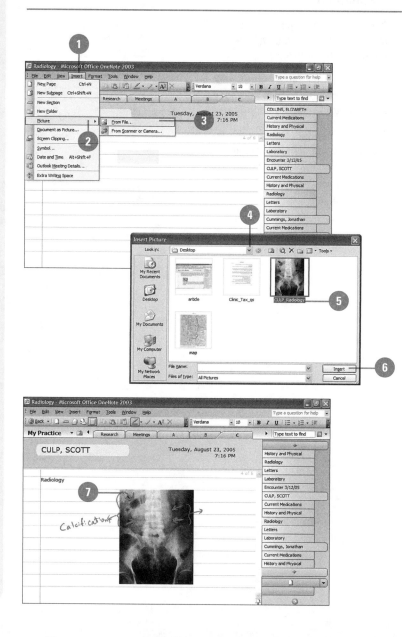

Insert a Document As a Picture

1. Click the Insert menu.

2. Click Document as Picture.

3. Open the folder with the document you want to insert.

4. Click the document you want to use.

5. Click Insert.

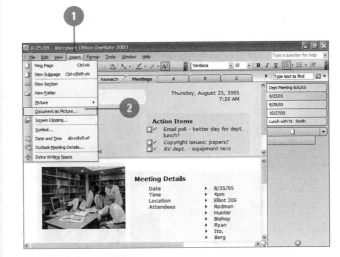

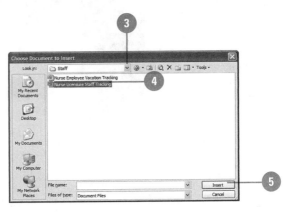

Creating Screen Clippings

Using screen clippings is a great way to collect snippets of text and graphics from anywhere on your screen and insert them into your notes. For example, you can capture a portion of a document or Web site, insert it into your notes, and highlight or annotate important sections of the clipping for later reference. Note that if the snippet contains text, it is still stored as a graphic, so OneNote will not be able to retrieve it by searching on its text content. However, you can add your own text description to the clipping to help you search for and find it later.

Create Screen Clippings

1. Display the screen from which you plan to create the clipping.

2. Switch to OneNote and position the cursor at the point where you would like the clip to be inserted.

3. Click the Insert menu, and then click Screen Clipping.

4. Drag a rectangle with the mouse or pen over the region of the screen to include in the clip.

   The clip will be inserted into your note and copied to the Clipboard.

Did You Know?

Create screen clippings quickly, even if OneNote is not open. Simply right-click the OneNote program icon in the notification area, at the far right of the taskbar, and then click Create Screen Clipping on the shortcut menu.

Did You Know?

You can paste the clipping directly into other programs. When OneNote makes a screen clipping, it automatically stores a copy in the Clipboard, so you can press Ctrl+V to paste it directly into other programs, such as Outlook.

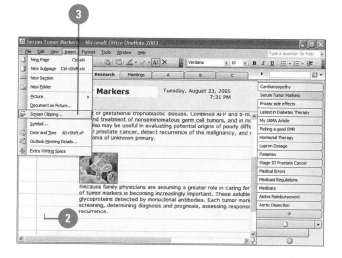

Tracking Notes with Flags

Using flags is a great way to track important items and mark them for follow-up. You can flag notes as Important, Remember for Later, and Definitions, and even customize your own note flags. Later, you can use OneNote's Note Flags Summary task pane to display all your flagged items. This task pane makes it easy for you to find all the notes you flagged over a variety of pages. For example, you can view all notes that are flagged with the To Do note flag, and then save the results as a To Do List page in your notebook.

Flag a Note

① Place the mouse or pen pointer next to the note you want to flag.

② Click the Format menu, and then point to Note Flags.

③ Click on the flag you want to use, such as To Do.

View Flagged Notes

① Click the View menu, and then click Note Flags Summary.

The Note Flags Summary task pane appears.

② Click a note flag to display the note.

③ Optionally, click the arrow in the Search area to change the scope of your search.

④ You can also click the Create Summary Page button to create a page with your note flag summary and add it to the current section.

Searching Your Notes

One of the key advantages to keeping your notes in OneNote is that you can search the pages and sections in your notebook and find the notes that contain keywords, names, or phrases. You can even search the notes you handwrite on a Tablet PC.

Search Your Notes

1. Type the text you're looking for in the Find box.

2. Click the green arrow to begin the search.

3. Click the left or right arrow to flip through the notes that match your search criteria.

4. Click View List to view a list of all pages that match your search criteria.

5. Optionally, click the arrow at the bottom of the task pane to change the scope of your search, such as searching only a portion of your notes.

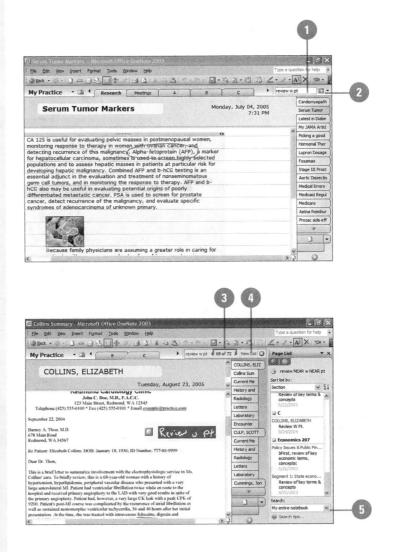

Integrating with Outlook

OneNote is integrated with Outlook in two ways. First, you can import information from your Outlook calendar into your notes. If you are preparing to take notes in a meeting that was set up using Outlook 2003, you can insert the details of the meeting from your Outlook calendar into OneNote. Second, you can create Outlook items, such as contacts, appointments, and tasks, from OneNote directly. For example, if you are taking notes about a patient and need to create an Outlook appointment to review the patient progress, you can do so without leaving OneNote.

Insert Outlook Meeting Details into OneNote

① Click where you want to insert the Outlook meeting details.

② Click the Insert menu.

③ Click Outlook Meeting Details.

OneNote displays a window with meeting information coming from Outlook.

④ If needed, click the calendar or the date buttons to change the date.

⑤ Click the meeting you want to use.

⑥ Click Insert Details.

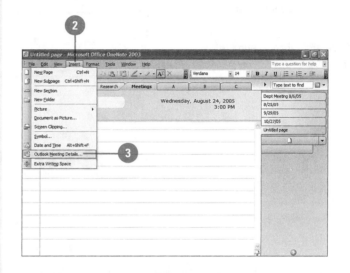

Create an Outlook Item from OneNote

1. Click the Tools menu.

2. Point to Create Outlook Item.

3. Click the type of item you want to create—appointment, contact, or task.

4. Fill in the details about the Outlook item.

5. Click Save and Close to add the item to Outlook.

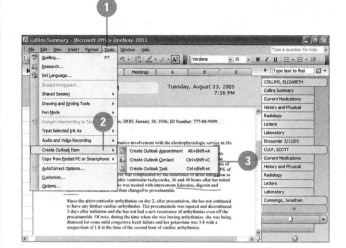

E-mail a OneNote Page

① Click the File menu, and then point to Send To.

② Click Mail Recipient.

③ Enter the email address of the recipient or recipients in the To field.

④ Type an introduction to your note for the recipient to see.

⑤ Click Send a Copy.

Did You Know?

You can e-mail pages to non-OneNote users. They will still be able to see the pages.

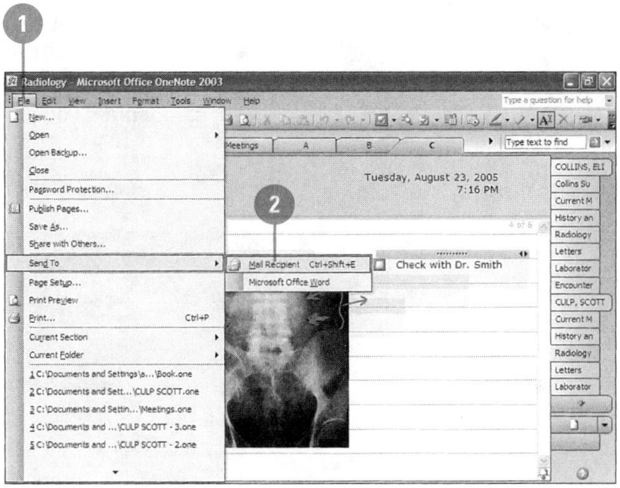

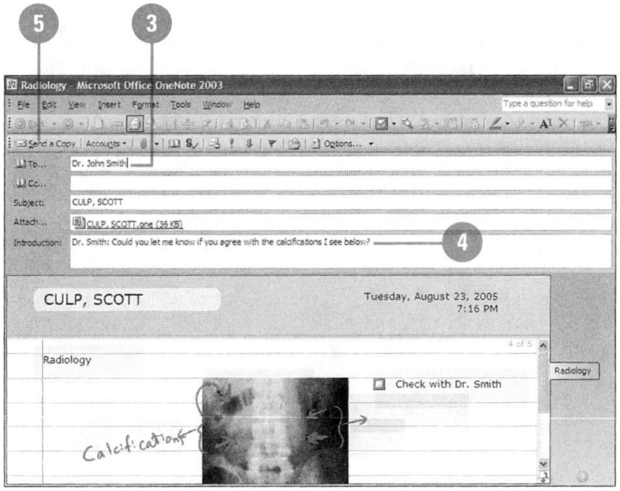

Working with Stationery

Stationery provides a template for your pages, such as a meeting stationery that already has places for the agenda, the attendees, and action items, or a patient encounter stationery following the SOAP format. OneNote offers a set of stationeries you can choose from, and you can easily add your own.

Create a New Page Using Stationery

1. Click the Format menu.

2. Click Stationery.

3. Click on the plus sign next to a category of stationery to expand the list.

4. Click on a stationery to use.

A new page will be created at the end of the current section based on the stationery you chose.

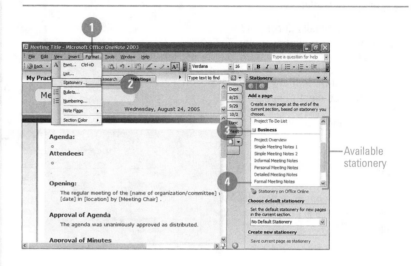

Available stationery

Create Your Own Stationery

1. Create the page that you want to use as stationery.

2. Click the Format menu.

3. Click Stationery.

4. Click Save Current Page as Stationery.

5. Enter a name for your stationery.

6. Optionally, you can click to set the stationery as default for all new pages in the current section.

7. Click Save.

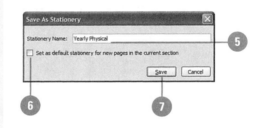

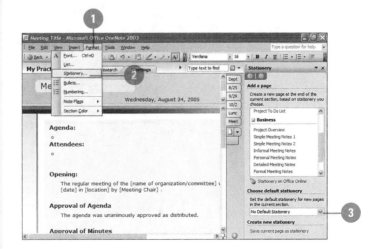

Set Default Stationery

1. Click the Format menu.

2. Click Stationery.

3. Click the arrow next to the stationery list and select a stationery to use as the default for new pages in the current section.

Using Advanced OneNote Features

OneNote offers a rich set of functionality that goes beyond the basics we covered so far. Some of the advanced features are covered here, including protecting the privacy of notes in a section using a password. This is especially important for healthcare professionals. You can also record audio and video notes within OneNote, and OneNote will keep track of what you were typing or writing as you recorded. You also can publish your OneNote pages to other files or to your organization's intranet to share them with others.

Protect Your Notes with a Password

1. Click the File menu.

2. Click Password Protection.

3. Click the Set Password button to password protect the current section.

4. Enter the password you want to use.

5. Click OK.

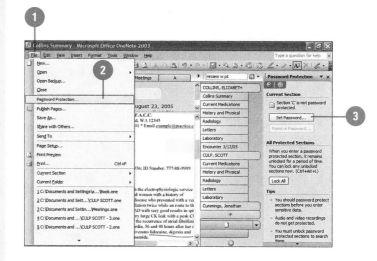

Record Audio and Video Notes

① Click the View menu, and then point to Toolbars.

② Click Audio and Video Recording.

③ Click the Record button to start recording.

You can take written notes as the recording is going on. OneNote keeps track of what you are typing or writing at the time the notes are recorded.

④ Click the Stop button to stop the recording.

⑤ Click the Play button to play back the recording. OneNote highlights the text you were typing or writing at the time the recording was made.

21

Publish Your Notes

1. Select the pages you want to publish.

2. Click the File menu.

3. Click Publish Pages.

4. Select a location for the published file.

5. Enter a name for the published file.

6. Choose a type for the published file.

7. Click the Publish button.

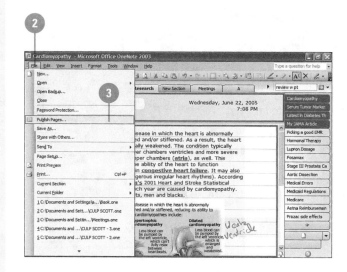

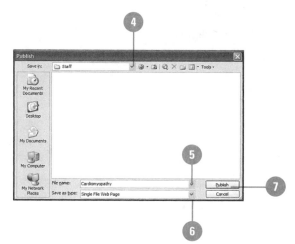

Natural Input with the Tablet PC

Introduction

Tablet PCs are gradually making their way into the mainstream of healthcare. They offer everything a notebook computer does, but they also offer more mobility and more natural input using handwriting recognition, digital ink, and speech recognition. With a Tablet PC and the right software, a clinician can pull up medical records from a central server, annotate an X-ray image, dictate notes, prescribe medications that are transmitted wirelessly to the pharmacist, and use the device to show the patient an educational video of a procedure.

Tablet PCs are the natural complement to Office 2003 for healthcare professionals. Using the Tablet PC with Office 2003, you can insert hand drawings in Word, annotate an Excel spreadsheet, write down audience comments in PowerPoint during a presentation, and speak to your computer instead of typing.

Because it's beyond the scope of this book to teach everything about Tablet PCs, we will show you the basics of Tablet PCs and how they work with Office 2003 applications. In general, the Tablet PC enables three new "natural input" methods:

- ◆ **Handwriting recognition:** You write with the Tablet PC pen and your writing is converted into typed text. Handwriting recognition can be used with any application that accepts input, and is entered using the Tablet PC Input Panel.

- ◆ **Digital ink:** You use the pen to write, draw, or annotate without needing to convert it into typed text.

- ◆ **Speech recognition:** The voice equivalent to handwriting recognition. Speech recognition is often used with Word 2003, although it can be used anywhere in Office 2003, such as dictating an e-mail to Outlook.

Choosing the Right Tablet PC

If you decide to purchase a Tablet PC, the following are some of the basic things to look out for:

Design: There are two basic designs: a slate or a convertible. The slate has a slimmer profile and is lighter weight, and the keyboard is a separate but attachable piece. This design is generally preferred by professionals working in a clinical environment who spend a lot of time on the move and who usually use the mouse and pen more than the keyboard. The convertible has a built-in keyboard and is generally preferred by professionals who spend more time in the office than in the clinic.

Processor: Most Tablet PCs provide clock speeds approaching or surpassing 1 GHz (gigahertz), which is adequate to handle most of the applications you'll be using in healthcare.

Memory: Our experience is that Tablet PCs for healthcare applications require at least 1GB (gigabyte) of RAM. Less RAM than that tends to result in slower performance.

Hard drive: Hard drives tend to range from 20GB to 80GB, providing plenty of room for the operating system, medical practice applications, medical dictionaries, and other references. It's good to purchase toward the higher end on hard drives, simply because they usually don't cost that much more, and it's better to have too much storage space than not enough.

Battery life: Be sure you ask about this or check the specifications sheet. You will probably need a device that can last long on a single battery charge. Most vendors today offer Tablet PCs that last about three hours on a single battery charge, but some offer more. You might want to consider getting one or two spare batteries, as well.

Additional accessories: Tablet PCs can use other popular accessories you might want to consider. A **docking station** is important if you need to quickly connect and disconnect your Tablet PC to external devices in your office, such as a large monitor, speakers, and keyboard. A **headset** is a must if you plan to use speech recognition. Choose a noise-canceling headset to eliminate surrounding noise. Extra **pens** come in handy. Some come with eraser tips on the back end (just like a pencil), and some come with switches on the barrel for right-tapping or assigning other functions.

Note: Bill Crowns, M.D., contributed to this section.

Using the Input Panel

With the Input Panel, you can use handwriting in any application. The purpose of the Input Panel is to receive your input and feed it to your application as typed text. There are two ways to open the Input Panel. You can tap the Input Panel button on the taskbar, or you can tap the Input Panel icon that appears automatically when Tablet PC detects the pen near the insertion point in any compatible program.

You can use one of three methods to enter text using the Input Panel. You can switch among the three methods by clicking on the corresponding button on the left side of the Input Panel.

- ◆ The first time you open the Input Panel, it displays the **writing pad**. Using the solid line as a guide, you can enter your handwriting, just as if writing on a piece of lined paper.

- ◆ The **character pad** is great for entering text one letter at a time. This can be useful when you want to enter items such as medical abbreviations, drug names, e-mail or Web site addresses, or filenames.

- ◆ The onscreen **keyboard** lets you enter text just like you would on a standard keyboard by tapping an individual key at a time.

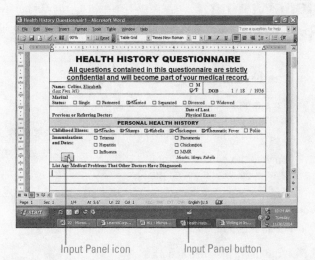

Input Panel icon   Input Panel button

Writing pad

Character pad

Onscreen keyboard

22

Using and Improving Handwriting Recognition

Handwriting recognition works amazingly well in the Tablet PC. The Input Panel is where you make your handwriting. You can also improve the accuracy of handwriting recognition by adding words to the dictionary. This is particularly useful for medical terms or abbreviations that are not already known to the Tablet PC.

Use Handwriting Recognition

1. Place the pen close to any insertion point in an Office program such as Word 2003.

2. Tap with the pen on the Input Panel icon, which automatically appears.

3. Tap the Writing Pad button if it's not already tapped.

4. Write using the solid line as a guide.

5. The Tablet PC's interpretation of your handwriting appears right below what you write. You can tap on this to make corrections if needed.

6. Tap Insert.

Improve Handwriting Recognition

1. Open the Input Panel and write a medical term.

2. If the term is not recognized properly, click on the box that appears under your writing to correct it.

3. Make the correction, and then click Add to Dictionary to add the term to your personal dictionary. Recognition for this term will improve the next time you write it.

Did You Know?

You can buy a "healthcare-friendly" Tablet PC. Some Tablet PC vendors, such as Motion Computing, are offering Tablet PCs that can recognize up to 212,000 additional medical terms. Contact the vendor directly for more information.

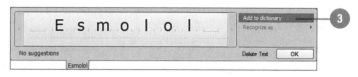

22

Using Digital Ink

Digital ink is a powerful communication tool that allows you to write, draw, or annotate just like you do using regular pen and paper, except that with digital ink, you can save your notes on your Tablet PC, search through them, e-mail them, and publish them on a Web site. A clinician viewing X-ray images on a Tablet PC could annotate the image and send it to a colleague for review, for example.

Almost every member of the Office 2003 suite has the capability to add ink. And where you can add ink, you can erase it. In general, you can add ink to any part of a document, and in Word you can even add ink comments. The following are the main differences between the different inking styles:

◆ Ink annotations can be hidden, and do not require a special box. This is available in Word, Excel, and PowerPoint.

◆ Ink drawing and writing fits only within a special ink box you create for it, and is not hidden when the Hide Annotations button is clicked. Word, PowerPoint, Excel, and Access can use ink drawing and writing.

◆ Ink comments are available only in Word 2003, and are just like comments used during collaborative writing—the comments appear in the margin and can be hidden.

In addition, when Outlook 2003 is configured to use Word 2003 to edit email messages, it inherits many of the inking capabilities built into Word 2003; specifically, ink drawing and writing and ink comments.

Set Up Outlook 2003 for Ink

1 Tap the Tools menu in Outlook 2003.

2 Select Options.

3 Tap the Mail Format tab.

4 Check the box to Use Microsoft Office Word 2003 to edit e-mail messages.

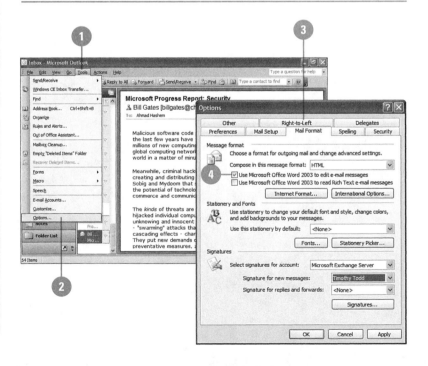

Use Ink Annotations

1 Display the Ink Annotations toolbar if it's not already displayed.

2 Pick the pen or highlighter you prefer from the Annotation Pen button.

3 Pick the color from the Line Color button.

4 Annotate using the pen or highlighter.

5 If necessary, use the eraser to remove portions of your annotation.

6 You can hide your annotations or redisplay them by tapping the Show/Hide Markup button.

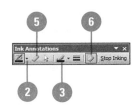

22

Use Ink Annotations in PowerPoint Presentation Mode

① During your presentation, hover with the Tablet PC pen on the screen to display the control icons on the lower-left side. Tap the pen icon.

② Select the pen or highlighter you would like to use.

③ Annotate your slide.

④ When you are finished with the presentation, you will be given the option to save your annotations or discard them.

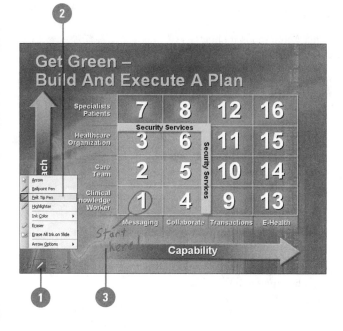

Use Ink Drawing and Writing

① Display the Ink Drawing and Writing toolbar if it's not already displayed.

② Pick the pen or highlighter you prefer from the Drawing and Writing Pen button.

③ Pick the color from the Line Color button.

④ Draw or write using the pen or highlighter.

⑤ If necessary, use the eraser to remove portions of your drawing or writing.

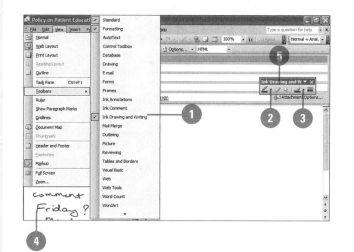

Use Ink Comments

1 In Word, or in Outlook using Word as your e-mail editor, highlight with the pen the text on which you would like to comment.

2 Tap the Insert menu and choose Ink Comment.

3 Use the pen to write your comment. You can draw within the comment box as well.

Did You Know?

You can use ink comments in Outlook 2003. To do this, you need to configure Outlook to use Word to edit e-mail messages. Follow the steps described earlier in this chapter.

22

Setting Up Speech Recognition

You're probably wondering whether speech recognition is really ready for prime time. It is. Speech recognition enables you to speak into a microphone and have the computer convert your spoken words into text. Some training is required, but it's not as cumbersome or time consuming as it was just a few years ago. Speech input also enables you to control your Tablet PC through the use of your voice. Using the Command feature of speech input, you can control applications by saying the names of the menus and commands on which you want the computer to act.

We recommend using the speech recognition feature with a good noise-canceling headset in a quiet environment. You must enable and train the speech tools before you can use speech recognition. Do this by turning on speech recognition in the Tablet PC Input Panel. Use the What Can I Say dialog box to discover the commands that you can use in Dictation and Command modes. The included voice tools are very good at what they do, but they're not perfect. Expect some time in editing, as well as some frustration at the start. Your accuracy and your skill with the tools will improve over time.

Set Up Speech Recognition

1. Open the Input Panel and tap the Tools and Options button.

2. Tap the Speech tool.

3. Click Next and follow the instructions.

4. When done, the speech buttons appear on the Tablet PC Input Panel.

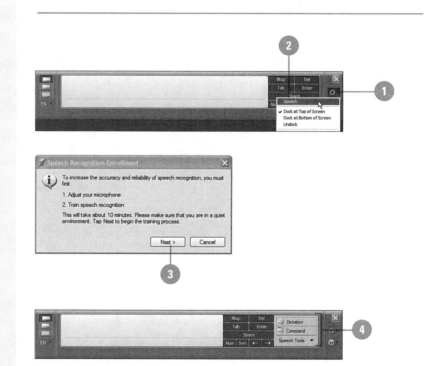

Using Speech Recognition

There are two basic modes of speech recognition on the Tablet PC. First, there is Dictation mode, where you can enter text into most Windows XP–compatible programs just by speaking into the microphone. The second mode, called Voice Command, enables you to do many things with your voice that you normally do with your tablet pen, keyboard, or mouse, such as open documents, start new documents, and save or print files.

Use the Dictation Mode

You can begin using speech recognition after completing at least one of the voice training programs. If there is a program open into which you want to enter text, all you have to do is tap the Dictation button on the Tablet PC Input Panel and begin speaking. Each time you pause, the words you just spoke are converted into text and entered into the program just as if you had typed them with a keyboard or used the Input panel.

You must voice all punctuation within the sentence while using dictation mode, such as saying "comma," "quotation mark," or "period." If you use a word that's not in the Tablet PC dictionary or a speech recognition error occurs, you always have the option of spelling the word out letter by letter. All you have to do is say "spell it," and then spell the word. Also, when correcting dictated text, be sure to check for words that sound the same, such as "they're," "there," and "their."

Use the Command Mode

To activate Voice Command mode, you can tap the Input Panel Voice Command button with your tablet pen, or you can simply say "Voice Command" while in Dictation mode. Many of the voice commands are context-specific; that is, how the command is carried out often depends on what program you're using and what you are doing. Voice commands let you do things such as open and close programs, scroll up or down inside a window, and switch between programs. If you're unsure of what commands you can give, just say, "What can I say" while in voice command mode and a window will open with a list of all the available voice commands.

Control Speech Recognition

The first commands you need to know are about how to control the speech-recognition system. After you turn on speech recognition by tapping Dictation or Command, you will be able to switch to either Dictation or Voice Command mode by saying either "dictation" or "voice command." You can also say "microphone" to turn off the microphone. But because the microphone will then be turned off, you must tap on either Dictation or Command to turn speech recognition back on.

You can also switch between modes easily so that you can accomplish almost anything just by using your voice. For example, you can begin dictating into Microsoft Word, then switch to Voice Command mode to use the menus to take actions on the text you just spoke. This enables you to have a virtually hands-off experience with your application.

Common Commands

Understanding the commands that you can use in each mode is important so that you can be as effective as possible using speech

22

recognition. Table 22.1 shows some of the most common commands available in Dictation mode, and Table 22.2 covers handling common symbols and punctuation in Dictation mode.

Whereas Tables 22.1 and 22.2 deal with voice commands in Dictation mode, Table 22.3 deals with voice commands in Command mode. It shows some of the most useful commands you'll use when commanding your computer.

Table 22.1   Common Voice Commands in Dictation Mode

Voice Command	Action	Example
Dictate into Foreground Application		
"Force num <number>"	Speak numbers instead of words	Force num 2
"New line"	Insert a single carriage return	New line
"New paragraph"	Insert two carriage returns	New paragraph
"Spell it <spelling>"	Spell a word exactly	Spell it <procainamide>
"Spell that"	Spell a word in all caps	Spell that <PROCAINAMIDE>
Controlling Speech		
"Microphone"	Turns off microphone	Microphone
"Voice command"	Switches to Command mode	Voice command

Table 22.2	Common Symbols and Punctuation in Dictation Mode		
Symbol	**Voice Command**	**Symbol**	**Voice Command**
&	"Ampersand"	+	"Plus sign"
*	"Asterisk"	#	"Pound sign"
@	"At sign"	?	"Question mark"
\	"Backslash"	;	"Semicolon"
^	"Carat"	/	"Slash"
:	"Colon"	~	"Tilde"
,	"Comma"	_	"Underscore"
--	"Dash"	"	"Quote"
$	"Dollar sign"	"	"End quote"
•	"Dot"	(	"Open paren"
=	"Equals"	)	"Close paren"/"end paren"
!	"Exclamation"	<	"Less than"
-	"Hyphen"	>	"Greater than"
¼	"One quarter"	[	"Bracket"
½	"One half"	]	"Close bracket"/"end bracket"
%	"Percent sign"	'	"Single quote"
.	"Period"		

Table 22.3   Commonly Used Voice Commands in Command Mode

Voice Command	Action	Example
Starting and Switching to Applications		
"Launch <application name>"	Starts the application you specify. You can also use "Open" and "Start" to do the same thing.	"Launch Microsoft Word"
"Switch to <application name>"	Switches to the open application you specify.	"Switch to Microsoft Excel"
Selection and Correction		
"Correct <phrase>"	Selects the phrase and gives you choices for correction.	"Correct <your application>"
"Correct that"	Provides correction options for the selected text.	"Correct that"
"Delete <phrase>"	Deletes the specified phrase.	"Delete <your application>"
"Delete <phrase> through <phrase>"	Deletes a large section of text.	"Delete <your application> through <voice commands>"
"Scratch that"	Undoes the last word or phrase dictated.	"Scratch that"
"Select line"	Selects the entire current line, from left margin to right margin.	"Select line"
"Select <phrase>"	Selects the specified phrase.	"Select <your application>"
"Select <phrase> through <phrase>"	Selects a large section of text.	"Select <your application> through <voice commands>"

Table 22.3 Continued

Voice Command	Action	Example
Selection and Correction		
"Select next phrase"	Selects the next phrase.	"Select next phrase"
"Select paragraph"	Selects the entire current paragraph.	"Select paragraph"
"Select sentence"	Selects the current sentence.	"Select sentence"
"Select word"	Selects the word that the cursor is currently on.	"Select word"
"Unselect that"	Unselects the selection.	"Unselect that"
Navigation		
"Go to beginning of line"	Moves the cursor to the beginning of the current line.	"Go to beginning of line"
"Go to bottom"	Moves the cursor to the bottom of the current page.	"Go to bottom"
"Go to end of line"	Moves the cursor to the end of the current line.	"Go to end of line"
"Go to top"	Moves the cursor to the top of the page.	"Go to top"
Uppercase and Lowercase		
"All caps that"	Capitalizes all letters of the selection.	"All caps that"
"Cap that"	Capitalizes the word or phrase selected.	"Cap that"

22

Table 22.3 Continued

Voice Command	Action	Example
Uppercase and Lowercase		
"Capitalize"	Capitalizes the word or phrase selected.	"Capitalize"
"No caps that"	Uncapitalizes the word or phrase selected.	"No caps that"
"Uncapitalize"	Uncapitalizes the word or phrase selected.	"Uncapitalize"
Editing Operations		
"Copy that"	Copies the selection to the Clipboard.	"Copy that"
"Cut that"	Cuts the selection from the document and adds it to the Clipboard.	"Cut that"
"Paste that"	Pastes the contents of the Clipboard into the document.	"Paste that"
"Undo that"	Undoes the last action.	"Undo that"
Keyboard Simulation		
"Backspace"	Deletes the character to the left of the cursor.	"Backspace"
"Delete"	Deletes the selection or character to the right of the cursor.	"Delete"
"Enter"	Inserts a carriage return.	"Enter"

Table 22.3 Continued		
Voice Command Simulation	**Action**	**ExampleKeyboard**
Keyboard Simulation		
"Move down"	Moves the cursor down one line or cell in the document.	"Move down"
"Move left"	Moves the cursor one character or cell to the left.	"Move left"
"Move right"	Moves the cursor one character or cell to the right.	"Move right"
"Move up"	Moves the cursor one character or cell up.	"Move up"
"Next cell"	Moves the cursor to the next cell in the selection, or the next cell to the right.	"Next cell"
"Page down"	Moves the document down one page.	"Page down"
"Page up"	Moves the document up one page.	"Page up"
"Space"	Inserts a character space.	"Space"
"Tab"	Inserts or executes a tab.	"Tab"
Controlling Speech		
"Dictation"	Switches to Dictation mode.	"Dictation"
"Microphone"	Turns off the microphone.	"Microphone"

22

Healthcare Products to Enrich Your Office Experience

Introduction

Microsoft Office 2003 is certainly useful to healthcare professionals as is, but you can purchase additional products from third-party companies and add them to Microsoft Office 2003 to make your experience even more compelling as a healthcare professional. These additional products offer functionality such as access to medical journals, medical spellchecking, and drug reference information. You learn some of these products in this chapter.

Medical Journals from Ovid Technologies

Whether you are writing a patient note and would like to check treatment guidelines, or researching a topic for a scientific paper you are writing, Journals@Ovid provides access to a database of more than 1,000 peer-reviewed medical journals in more than 100 medical specialties. This Web service is accessible from any Office product, including Word, Outlook, PowerPoint, Excel, and Publisher. You can right-click on a specific medical term within a document and look up information on that term within the Ovid Technologies journal database. Ovid titles include the New England Journal of Medicine, JAMA, British Medical Journal, and more. Once you conduct the search, you can select an article and view the entire full text if your institution is a subscriber to Ovid, or you can access the article through the PayPerView feature.

Install Journals@Ovid

1. Click Research on the Tools menu.

2. Click Research Options.

3. Click Add Services.

4. Type the following address in the address box: http://msrp.ovid.com/MSOffice/MSOffice.

5. Click Add.

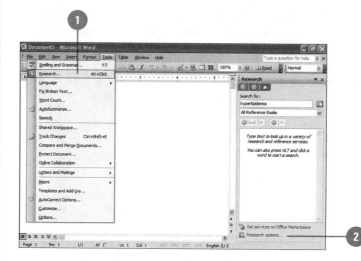

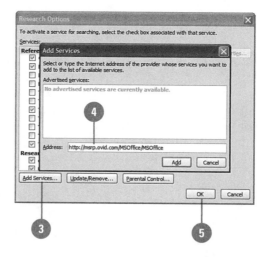

Look Up Articles in Journals@Ovid

① Select the text for which you would like to search.

② Right-click, and select Look Up.

③ Select Journals@Ovid in the Research pane.

④ Click the arrow to start the search.

⑤ Click View Article to view the article content (requires purchase for a fee).

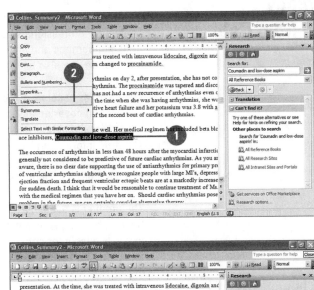

How to Get Journals@Ovid

You can either purchase the PayPerView service or your group can purchase an institutional subscription. Contact Ovid directly for more information:

Ovid Technologies
100 River Ridge Drive
Norwood, MA 02062 USA

Internet: www.ovid.com

Phone: (800) 343-0064 or (781) 769-2599

E-mail: ovidinfo@ovid.com

23

Pharmacology Reference from Gold Standard

Do you find it difficult to remember all the dosage information or medication interactions? Clinical Pharmacology OfficePak from Gold Standard allows healthcare professionals using Office 2003 to easily access thousands of drug monographs and important medication management information. The information can also be instantly incorporated into Office 2003 documents.

Clinical Pharmacology OfficePak features a comprehensive array of drug information covering all U.S. prescription drugs, over-the-counter medications, herbal and nutritional products, and new and investigational drugs. The drug information includes a description of the drug, indications, contraindications, dosage, interactions, adverse reactions, cost information, and even product photos.

The product is available in two formats. An Internet format works within the Research pane just like the Journals@Ovid product, and a Smart Tag format is available for access without Internet connectivity. We describe the Smart Tag format here.

Look Up Drug Information

1. Contact the maker of Clinical Pharmacology OfficePak to purchase and install the product.

2. Move the mouse over the medication name to display the Smart Tag icon.

3. Click on the Smart Tag icon to bring up menu options.

4. Click on a menu option, such as Product Photographs, to display its content.

5. The contents appear in a separate window.

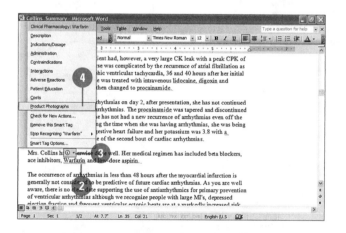

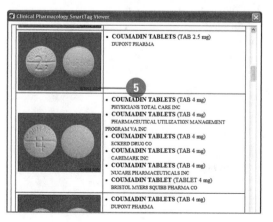

How to Get Clinical Pharmacology OfficePak

Clinical Pharmacology subscription is $459.00 per year per individual. Volume licensing options are available for organizations. Contact the vendor directly for more information:

Gold Standard
320 W. Kennedy Blvd., Suite 400
Tampa, Florida 33606 USA

Internet: http://cp.gsm.com

Phone: (800) 375-0943

E-mail: info@gsm.com

23

Stedman's Medical/ Pharmaceutical Spellchecker

A medical spellchecker is a must for healthcare professionals using Office 2003. Without it, medical terms in Office 2003 documents will be flagged automatically as if they were typos, and actual typos in medical terms will not be caught. Stedman's medical spellchecker works in the background and spellchecks nearly half a million total medical, drug, and bioscience terms from more than 60 major medical specialties.

How to Get Stedman's Medical/Pharmaceutical Spellchecker

The Standard Edition of Stedman's is $99.95. Contact the vendor directly for more information:

Lippincott Williams & Wilkins
P.O. Box 1600
Hagerstown, MD 21741-1600 USA

Internet: http://www.stedmans.com/

Phone: (800) 638-3030

E-mail stedmans@LWW.com

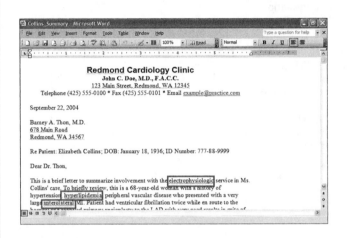

Medical terms in Office 2003 documents are flagged as typos without a medical spellchecker.

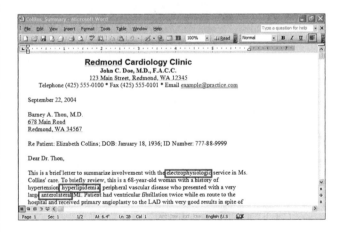

Medical terms in Office 2003 documents are properly recognized when a medical spellchecker is installed.

Motion Computing Medical Pak

The Motion Medical Pak is a suite of Tablet PC–optimized applications designed to provide healthcare professionals with everyday tools from a drug reference guide to customizable forms. The Motion Medical Pak requires Microsoft Office 2003 and OneNote 2003, and includes

- ◆ Gold Standard Multimedia Clinical Pharmacology OfficePak
- ◆ Elsevier Dorland Medical Dictionary and Spell Checker
- ◆ Standard Register's physician office forms

How to Get Motion Computing Medical Pak

The Medical Pak sells for $99.99 with the purchase of a Motion Computing Tablet PC. Contact the vendor directly for more information:

Motion Computing, Inc.
8601 RR 2222
Building II
Austin, TX 78730 USA

Internet:
http://www.motioncomputing.com

Phone: 1-866-MTABLET

E-mail: sales@motioncomputing.com

Motion Medical Pak includes a set of commonly used healthcare forms. It also includes a drug reference and a medical spellchecker.

EMR Assistant from ScanSoft

The EMR Assistant is a patient records management system using Microsoft Office 2003 with ScanSoft's PaperPort and Dragon NaturallySpeaking. The product provides premade healthcare form templates using Microsoft Word 2003 that can be completed via a keyboard or by speaking on a Tablet PC or a desktop computer. You can easily create additional form templates using Microsoft Word 2003.

How to Get ScanSoft EMR Assistant

The ScanSoft EMR Assistant is priced at $1,500 per seat, with quantity discounts. Contact the vendor directly for more information:

ScanSoft, Inc.
9 Centennial Drive
Peabody, MA 01960 USA

Internet:
http://www.scansoft.com/emr

Phone: (978) 977-2000

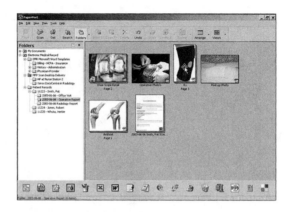

ScanSoft EMR Assistant uses Microsoft Office 2003 with ScanSoft's PaperPort and Dragon NaturallySpeaking.

Troubleshooting

t

Access

Publisher

Objects

Preparing for printing

Word

Borders and numbered lists

Envelopes

Mail merge

Page formatting

Printing

Protecting a document

Saving file versions

Sharing data with other programs

Text editing

Index

How can we make this index more useful? Email us at indexes@quepublishing.com

How can we make this index more useful? Email us at indexes@quepublishing.com

Index   545

How can we make this index more useful? Email us at indexes@quepublishing.com

How can we make this index more useful? Email us at indexes@quepublishing.com

How can we make this index more useful? Email us at indexes@quepublishing.com

How can we make this index more useful? Email us at indexes@quepublishing.com

F

How can we make this index more useful? Email us at indexes@quepublishing.com

How can we make this index more useful? Email us at indexes@quepublishing.com

How can we make this index more useful? Email us at indexes@quepublishing.com

How can we make this index more useful? Email us at indexes@quepublishing.com

How can we make this index more useful? Email us at indexes@quepublishing.com

How can we make this index more useful? Email us at indexes@quepublishing.com

How can we make this index more useful? Email us at indexes@quepublishing.com

Index **567**

How can we make this index more useful? Email us at indexes@quepublishing.com

How can we make this index more useful? Email us at indexes@quepublishing.com

How can we make this index more useful? Email us at indexes@quepublishing.com

How can we make this index more useful? Email us at indexes@quepublishing.com

How can we make this index more useful? Email us at indexes@quepublishing.com

U - V

How can we make this index more useful? Email us at indexes@quepublishing.com

How can we make this index more useful? Email us at indexes@quepublishing.com

How can we make this index more useful? Email us at indexes@quepublishing.com

X - Y - Z